THE SOCIAL PSYCHOLOGY OF MUSIC

THE SOCIAL PSYCHOLOGY OF MUSIC/SECOND EDITION

Paul R. Farnsworth

THE IOWA STATE UNIVERSITY PRESS

PAUL R. FARNSWORTH is Professor Emeritus in the Psychology Department at Stanford University. He earned all three of his degrees at Ohio State University—B.A. in 1921, M.A. in 1923, and Ph.D. in 1925—but did some graduate work at the University of Missouri. Dr. Farnsworth is a member of honorary fraternities in the fields of education, mathematics, psychology, and sociology as well as of Phi Beta Kappa. He has authored several books and many articles in the areas of social psychology and the psychology of music, and served as editor of *Annual Review of Psychology* from 1956 to 1968.

© 1969 The Iowa State University Press, Ames, Iowa 50010. All rights reserved. Composed and printed by The Iowa State University Press. Second edition, 1969. Standard Book Number: 8138-1547-9. Library of Congress Catalog Card Number: 74-84944.

First edition © 1958 by Holt, Rinehart, and Winston, Inc.

To MAX FREDERICK MEYER, *pioneer in experimental aesthetics*

CONTENTS

PREFACE, xi

INTRODUCTION, xiii

Chapter One. THE PSYCHOLOGICAL APPROACH TO MUSIC, 3. Frequent Invalidity of Common Sense, 4. History Lag, 5. Search for Alternative Hypotheses, 6. Limitations of Psychomusical Investigations, 8. Possibilities of Research in Experimental Aesthetics, 9. Absence of Absolutes, 13. Preview of Later Chapters, 14.

Chapter Two. MUSICAL SCALES, 17. Pythagorean Scale of Ancient Greece, 19. Scales of Just Intonation, 20. Mean-Tone Temperaments, 22. Equal Temperament in World Music, 23. Detectability of Scale and Note Differences, 24. Other Possible Scales, 27. Summary, 29.

Chapter Three. THE INTERVAL, 33. Distinctive Quality, 33. Vibrato and Trill, 34. Apparent Pitch of Intervals, 35. Major-Minor Effect in Intervals—A Fiction, 36. Finality Effects, 37. Interval Resolutions, 39. Tonality, 40. Consonance and Dissonance, 42. Summary, 44.

Chapter Four. MELODY, 47. Principles of Attention and Learning, 49. Melody and Pitch Level, 50. Melody and Loudness, 53. Melody and Timbre, 56. Melody and Sonance, 58. Melody and Noise, 59. Melody and Tempo, 60. Melody and Rhythm, 61. Harmony, 65. Summary, 67.

Chapter Five. LANGUAGE ASPECTS OF MUSIC, 69. Desire for Communication, 69. Embodied Meaning (Grammar or Syntax), 70. Designative Meaning, 71. Alleged

Mode and Key Effects, 72. Major and Minor Modes, 73. Color-Tone Linkage, 76. "Language of the Emotions," 78. Adjective Lists for Classifying Music, 80. Variables Which Give Meaning to Music, 83. Expression of Tensions, 87. Music as a Universal Language, 90. Psychoanalytic Symbolism, 91. Summary, 94.

Chapter Six. NATURE OF MUSICAL TASTE, 97. Eminence, 100. Enjoyment, 110. Knowledge of Composers, 112. Programs, 113. Number of Recordings, 117. Space Allocations, 117. Individual and Group Differences, 119. Criteria and Conditioners of Taste, 122. Summary, 133.

Chapter Seven. THE MEASURES OF MUSICAL TASTE, 135. Variety of Measures, 135. Auditory Tests, 135. Paper-and-Pencil Tests, 141. Polling, 143. Orchestral Programs, 143. Broadcasts of Recordings, 144. Record Listings, 145. Scholarly Texts, 146. Boredom, 148. Summary, 149.

Chapter Eight. THE NATURE OF MUSICAL ABILITIES, 151. Ability—Appropriate Descriptive Term, 151. Generality of Ability, 152. Are Abilities in Music Related to Other Art Abilities? 154. Academic Intelligence and Musical Abilities, 155. Heritability of Musical Abilities, 156. Musical Abilities and Physical and Mental Structure, 159. Adlerian Views on Ability, 162. Jungian Views on Ability, 163. Freudian Views on Ability, 164. Imagery as a Source of Abilities, 165. Developing Abilities, 166. Training Methods: General Problems, 168. Training Methods: Special Problems, 172. Creativity, 175. Summary, 181.

Chapter Nine. THE MEASUREMENT OF MUSICAL ABILITIES, 185. Tests of Verbal Knowledge, 185. Tests Which Stress Nonverbal Musical Skills, 189. Unstandardized Aptitude Tests, 191. Original Seashore Battery, 194. Tilson-Gretsch Test for Musical Aptitude, 195. 1939 Revision of Seashore Measures of Musical Talents, 196. Kwalwasser-Dykema Music Tests, 198. Kwalwasser Music Talent Test, 200. Storey Tests, 200. 1932 and 1954 Drake Tests, 201. Wheeler Battery, 202. Whistler-Thorpe Musical Aptitude Test, 202. Lundin Tests, 203. Gaston Test of Musicality, 204. Wing Standardized Tests of Musical Intelligence, 204. Gordon Mu-

sical Aptitude Profile, 205. Taylor Tests, 206. Bentley
Measures of Musical Abilities, 206. Strong Vocational
Interest Test, 207. Future of Music Aptitude Tests,
207.

Chapter Ten. APPLICATIONS OF MUSIC TO INDUSTRY AND
THERAPY, 209. Physiological Changes, 210. Music and
General Activity, 214. Effects of Music on Achieve-
ment, 215. Present Status of Music Therapy, 219.

EPILOGUE, 225

APPENDICES
A: The Musical Taste of an American Elite, 227
B: Glossary, 229

NOTES AND REFERENCES, 235

SUBJECT INDEX, 283

NAME INDEX, 291

PREFACE

So FAR there has been little agreement as to what the boundaries of the psychology of music are. One text may stress laboratory data and do a minimum of theorizing, another may present fewer "facts" but be far more philosophical in approach. One may treat of music and musicians as if the cultural milieu were of little importance, another may show more concern with the social determination of music activities.

Of course no book can include all knowledge that at one time or another has been said to be subsumed under the psychology of music. However, an author properly can be asked to present what he regards as a coherent picture of the phenomena of the field, its major problems, and the solutions he deems most plausible. This then is what the present book attempts to do.

This edition of *The Social Psychology of Music* closely follows the format and social science bias of the first edition. However, Chapter 2, "Music Scales," has been completely rewritten since in its earlier form it had proved rather difficult to comprehend. It is hoped that, as now written, its concepts and relevance will be clearer. Additional data and theories, combed from recent articles and books, appear in the other chapters. Although they largely concern topics treated in the first edition, there are exceptions. Attention should be called particularly to a relatively new research area, the matter of music grammar (embodied meaning) which in this past decade has increasingly interested psychologists and others. Much of the work on this problem comes under the heading of information theory. Although the treatment of music grammar in the text is brief, the accompanying chapter notes contain a fairly extensive bibliography.

Unfortunately a shortcoming of the first edition remains with the second—a heavy emphasis on the so-called serious music of the West, with attention paid only here and there to the several varieties of jazz, to chance music, to folk music, and to other sorts of music of the Orient and Occident. Over the years there has been a continuing breakdown of music's rules and traditions, and we now appear to be allowing any social group to label as music what it will. Perhaps then the author should not be censured too strongly when he rather arbitrarily sets limits for his endeavors, if he decides to devote most of his time and energy to the varieties of music he knows best.

To write for both psychological and musical audiences is a difficult task, yet this book attempts it. It is the author's belief that the reader will need no more psychological knowledge than that which any intelligent and reasonably well educated adult usually possesses. But unless the reader has some sustained interest in music he probably will not look beyond the title of this book. His musical knowledge, however, need not be extensive. To help him with the psychological and musical terms with which he may be unfamiliar, a glossary is provided on pages 229–33.

The author is indebted to many people and publishing houses. Since in general they know of his appreciation he will not name them here. An exception must be made, however, in the case of the Stanford University Press, which kindly allowed him to take over for the 1958 edition almost the entire manuscript of his earlier *Musical Taste*. This material now makes up much of Chapters 6 and 7.

P.R.F.

INTRODUCTION ❦

Since 1958, the year of this book's first edition, the pace of research in what might be called the more traditional areas of the psychology of music has certainly not quickened. A few more music tests are on the market, but, as before, most psychological researches seem to have been undertaken either to capture an academic degree or to provide avocational activities for those busy chiefly with other matters.

Two early American books have influenced music psychology research, although they are not formal texts in the psychology of music. One was Pratt's *The Meaning of Music* (1931) which was a series of essays rather than a textbook and hence made no attempt to cover the experimental literature. Showing a high degree of sophistication, Pratt's little book was written in large part as a defense of formalism.

The other work, printed in 1929, was given the rather frightening title *The Musician's Arithmetic*. Its author, Max Meyer, to whom the present book is dedicated, was one of the most brilliant theorists and experimenters in the field. Indeed it was the manuscript of Meyer's treatise which first stirred the interest of this author in the psychology of music. Meyer's book offered exciting neurological speculations as well as important research data, but it is admittedly difficult to read and therefore has had an extremely limited audience. Although over the years the present writer has become increasingly disappointed at the slow growth of scientific neurology and has occupied himself less and less with theorizing along the lines suggested by Meyer, he still appreciates Meyer's refreshing approach and feels that the serious student will find *The Musician's Arith-*

metic, Meyer's early articles, and his more recent *How We Hear* well worth careful attention.

AMERICAN WORKS

The psychology of music has been the subject of a number of American textbooks issued since the middle 1930's. The year 1937 saw the publication of Diserens and Fine's *A Psychology of Music* and Mursell's *The Psychology of Music.* The former book not only dealt with experimental literature but also devoted considerable space to the origin of music, animal auditors, mythology and folklore, and the relation of music to magic and sorcery and to religion, melancholy, and ecstasy. The Mursell book philosophized much more and interpreted research data rather narrowly in terms of Gestalt theory. Mursell's advice to music teachers was reserved for *Music and the Classroom Teacher* and other treatises.

C. E. Seashore's *Psychology of Music* was issued in 1938. With no interest in those aspects of music which are primarily sociopsychological, Seashore limited himself largely to a description of the excellent but apparatus-bound studies of his own laboratories. He attempted some years later to broaden his coverage of the field with *Why We Love Music* and *In Search of Beauty in Music.* Seashore prided himself on following no "school" of psychology. Yet he was one of the most ardent hereditarians psychology has produced, and his books quite clearly reflect this nativistic bias.

In 1940 one of Seashore's students, Max Schoen, published *The Psychology of Music.* Built on his earlier work, *The Beautiful in Music,* Schoen's book presented a well-rounded picture of the experimental findings through the 1930's. A later, more philosophical work of Schoen's appeared as *The Understanding of Music.*

No comprehensive texts appeared after 1940 until 1953, when Révész's well-known *Einführung in die Musikpsychologie* was translated into English and published in Great Britain in somewhat revised form. A year later it was issued in the United States under the title *Introduction to the Psychology of Music.* Révész's book contained a good survey of the European findings in music psychology but touched only lightly on American research. The tone of the Révész volume was absolutistic and hereditarian.

The first edition of Lundin's *An Objective Psychology of Music* was also published in 1953. As the only American text to appear in thirteen years, it had the important task of digesting the research materials of more than a decade. This book has a cultural and rela-tivistic flavor and an inter-behavioristic orientation.

Clyde Noble's *The Psychology of Cornet and Trumpet Playing,* which appeared in 1964, is a spendid example of the work of both an able psychologist and a professional musician. It was followed in 1967 by the second edition of Lundin's excellent *An Objective Psychology of Music.*

FOREIGN WORKS

Interest in the psychology of music seems to be awakening or expanding in Israel, Poland, USSR, and other countries overseas. Albert Wellek's interesting *Musikpsychologie und Musikasthetik* appeared in 1963, along with rumors of an English translation which unfortunately has not yet appeared. And if one can judge by the charts, tables, and bibliography, some of which are in English, the 1966 text *Ongaku Shinrigaku* (Music Psychology) by Professor Takao Umemoto of Kyoto University's School of Education could become, if translated into a western European language, a most use-ful source book of Japanese research in the area of musical aesthetics. C. W. Valentine's *The Experimental Psychology of Beauty* has three chapters which bear directly on research in music. Although this British book was published in 1962, it deals little with recent ex-perimental work. It offers, however, a valuable survey of Valentine's own earlier researches and of the other studies which appeared dur-ing the period when he was contributing most heavily to the aesthetics area.

RESEARCH OUTLETS AND AIDS

On the test and training side, the *Journal of Research in Music Education* has become the most important vehicle of publication. (The more recently founded *Missouri Journal of Research in Music Education* appears to have somewhat similar publication aims.) The music therapists, who have increased both in numbers and in status, have dropped the annually published *Proceedings* (after eleven years of life) for the new *Journal of Music Therapy.* The *Review of Psychology in Music,* which it was hoped would become a truly international research journal, had its birth and death in the first half of the 1960's. The new *Council for Research in Music Education,* published jointly by the University of Illinois and the

Office of the Superintendent of Public Instruction of Illinois, seems to be both valuable and viable. In 1966 these two sponsors issued another new periodical, *The Journal of Aesthetic Education,* which occasionally may be of interest to the experimentalist in music psychology.

Attention should also be called to the founding in 1967 of the Ohio State University Center for Experimental Research in the Arts Information Storage and Retrieval Project (Room 131, Lord Hall, 124 West 17th Ave., Columbus, Ohio 43210). Its second publication is a *Thesaurus of Coordinate Index Terms for Literature Related to Experimental Research in the Arts* (Jan. 1968). At least of tangential interest to the area of the psychology of music is the new Translations Center for Musicological Studies and Documents established in the Department of Music in Brooklyn College (Brooklyn, N.Y. 11210) as a joint project of the American Musicological Society and the Music Library Association. Other possible aids are the *RILM Abstracts* (International RILM Center, Queens College, Flushing, N.Y. 11367) which cover "Psychology and Hearing" as their Section #82.

The reader who wishes to keep abreast of the work being done in psychological aesthetics should consult the *Journal of Aesthetics and Art Criticism,* which once a year carries a list of articles most of which have appeared during the previous calendar year. After noting the articles which interest him and before reading the articles themselves, the reader would be advised to examine *Psychological Abstracts.* For a more comprehensive coverage of the older articles than is offered by this book, the reader is referred to *A Bibliography of Periodical Literature in Musicology and Allied Fields and a Record of Graduate Theses Accepted* (published as volumes 1 and 2 in 1940 and 1943 by the American Council of Learned Societies); to A. R. Chandler, "A Bibliography of Experimental Aesthetics, 1865–1932" (*Ohio State University Studies, 1* [1933]); to A. R. Chandler and E. N. Barnhart, *A Bibliography of Psychological and Experimental Aesthetics, 1864–1937* (Berkeley, University of California Press, 1938); and to W. A. Hammond, *A Bibliography of Aesthetics and of the Philosophy of the Fine Arts from 1900 to 1932* (New York, Longmans, Green, 1934).

THE SOCIAL PSYCHOLOGY OF MUSIC

CHAPTER ONE ⚓ *The Psychological Approach to Music*

IT IS OFTEN SAID that psychology was born from a union of philosophy and the natural sciences. With passage of time, however, the social sciences began to envelop psychology until at present many of the research problems and techniques of cultural anthropology, communication theory, sociology, and psychology are surprisingly alike. This growth of psychology—its retention of its older affiliations with the natural sciences (and even occasionally with philosophy) and the addition of its newer interests in the social science area—is reflected in the development of the psychology of music. Past workers in the field, notably members of the Carl Seashore group at the University of Iowa, rather limited themselves to experiments of the natural science sort. Others, particularly the researchers of the past few years, have tended to be at least equally interested in problems adapted to the techniques of the social sciences. It is natural that those who deal primarily with the biological aspects of music should feel that the more important antecedents of musical activity are to be found in the nature of the human organism, whereas those further removed from the natural science laboratory should look more to cultural forces for their explanations.

The more biologically oriented of the psychological aestheticians, at least in the time period between the World Wars, were hereditarians almost to a man. Like the intelligence testers of the same decades, they were convinced that it was possible to tap innate musical capacities regardless of the cultural setting or the musical history of the testee. They maintained that these capacities could not be improved by experience or by specific training. Naturally such a philosophy was most irritating to those musicians who had devoted their lives to the improvement of tonal perception and con-

3

trol and who knew that their labors had not been in vain. However, with time, the psychologists have come to agree with the musicians that the "musical ear" can indeed be improved and that there are no culture-free tests.

While the present treatise attempts to cover the major experiments of the psychology of music whatever the techniques employed, its orientation is admittedly a sociopsychological one. Believing as he does that the earlier workers tended to overstress the importance of the biological and physical bases of musical behavior almost to the point of ignoring its cultural determinants, the author has here tried to bring the picture a little more in balance. No doubt the result will seem to some to be an overbalance on the cultural side. But whatever the effect, the choice has been deliberate. Its justification will perhaps become clearer as the book is read.

FREQUENT INVALIDITY OF COMMON SENSE

The behavorial scientist tends to question the validity of much that he perceives. He is less likely than the layman to accept the obvious—what the dictionary terms "common sense"—for he has found that he and others "know" many things that are simply not true. Let us take as an illustration the very widespread belief that marijuana heightens the auditory capacities. Even many musician addicts are convinced that they are more sensitive to tonal stimuli when given this drug. Yet psychophysiological research gives no support to the idea.[1]* Alertness and the feeling of alertness are related but are by no means identical phenomena.

Or let us consider the almost universal belief that blacks are more sensitive to tone and rhythm than are whites. Large numbers of these two American subgroups have been tested in tonal memory and in the discrimination of differences in pitch, loudness, time, rhythm, and timbre. No striking black (or white) superiority has ever been demonstrated. In the several studies in this area the racial differences that do emerge are so slight that one group or another yields the higher average score because of factors local to the immediate testing situation (Chap. 8). If the superiority of either one of these subgroups were at all impressive, it would transcend these local conditions and make itself unmistakably apparent.[2]

Common sense teaches that some humans are born monotones. These unfortunates cannot carry tunes and are doomed

---

* The superscripts scattered throughout the pages of this book refer to the numbered notes and references to be found at the end of the book.

to go through life embarrassed by the fact that they cannot sing or perhaps even recognize our national anthem—a disability especially serious when in the presence of superpatriots. The follower of common sense typically accepts the fatalistic genetics of earlier decades and does nothing about the matter. To him the monotone quite clearly is the victim of an inherent anatomical defect. But luckily there are psychologists and music educators who check on common sense. They have shown that most if not all monotones have psychological rather than biological disabilities and can be helped to overcome their tune weakness. Monotones are most often males who have met with emotional difficulties in the early grades of school.[3] Possessed of more than average dislike of the schoolroom, or of the music teacher, or of both, and quite frequently holding to the attitude that singing is an activity for sissies, monotones may become uncooperative during that early period when music fundamentals are usually most easily learned. Later in life they will find that with great effort they can master the concept of pitch but that they must have considerable aid from psychologists or music educators to do so.

Although many other illustrations could be given of the occasional invalidity of common sense, let us content ourselves with just one more example. Capacities for handling two-four, three-four, four-four, six-four, and even eight-four beats per measure have generally been assumed to be "instinctive." American music students handle such rhythms without formal training but flounder when asked to beat out the five-four or the seven-four. Man simply lacks the "instinct" for these latter, says common sense. Yet if this were so, the lack should be general and not limited to a few culture areas. The psychologist Max Meyer should not have found natives of North Africa dancing and swaying to these unusual (to us) rhythms. But according to his observations, certain of the natives were almost as skillful with the five- and seven-four as we are with the two- and three-four. Later, on his return to his American laboratory, he found it quite easy to train his students to tap out the five- and seven-four with great accuracy.[4] These young Americans soon forgot that they had no "instinct" for such activities. In fact their present-day descendents are finding five-four (and twelve-four) time increasingly used in jazz music.

HISTORY LAG

Common sense then needs to be checked on before it can safely be accepted as valid information. But the "I saw it in print and so it must be true" attitude also causes grief to the scientist. He finds that, because of a sort of intellectual inertia or historical lag, the "facts" recorded in the textbooks and journal articles of one decade tend to remain in print even in the face of considerable and quite adequate refutation. Thus the notion was early written into textbooks that the great vocalists sang *pure, steady* tones. Happily this invalid observation appears in print now but rarely. In fact it is a wonder that anyone ever did hold to the purity idea, for one needs only to listen to a relatively pure tone, say that of a tuning fork, to realize that it is the *impure* and not the *pure* tone with which music deals. And there is a host of excellent psychological works on the vibrato which demonstrate beyond doubt the unsteadiness of the preferred vocal and violin tone.

Other almost totally incorrect sets of musical rules can be found in some of the older books on baton movements. Typical diagrams show a preponderance of straight-line motions and periods of relative rest at the beat-instants. Bartholomew checked these diagrams against the baton performances of conductors.[5] He attached a tiny lamp to the end of a baton which had been so wired that the light dimmed at the exact instant of the beat. By photographing the path of the light this experimenter found curvilinear rather than straight-line motions and points of rest closer to the "ands" after the respective beats. The fastest, not the slowest, speeds were often at the beat-instants!

On occasion, printed misinformation has been retained for practical reasons, the ethical aspects of which are not of a high order. As an illustration let us take one of the author's minor studies. Around 1930 considerable research was being undertaken with a certain make of player piano. Its manufacturer had long been advertising that it offered sixteen different intensities of hammer strokes, roughly twice the loudness possibilities of its two chief rivals. This statement was true enough from the standpoint of physics as there actually were twice as many intensity holes on the music roll being studied. But as the author clearly proved, only *one half* of its loudness differences were discriminable by the typical layman whereas *all* of its rivals' were. Musically and practically speaking, then, the competing instruments were equally good in their handling of loudness differences. Yet the advertising went on unchanged!

SEARCH FOR ALTERNATIVE HYPOTHESES

Another characteristic of the scientist is his willingness to consider more than one hypothesis. While the layman may be content with one apparently reasonable "cause" for some phenomenon, the scientist investigates a variety of possible antecedents. It looks reasonable, for example, to assume that the true beat in music[6] has a rate which is determined by some organic rhythm like the heartbeat, and for many years the assumption of an intimate connection between body function and music response was treated as a fact. But Lund put the matter to test in an attempt to see whether there might not be some other determinants.[7] Although he did not find what these latter were, he did show that true beat and heartbeat have little association. During 1939 this psychologist took meticulous measurements of many performances of the Roth Quartet and of several symphony orchestras and found the true beat to vary all the way from 40 to 100 pulsations—a far cry from the 70–75 beats the heart gives each minute.

The scientist is trained to check his hypotheses against whatever objective evidence can be collected, to discard his theories promptly if they are incompatible, and then to search for new (or modifications of the old) hypotheses which will better fit the objective evidence. His training differs from that of the layman who all too often accepts an oversimplified hypothesis and holds to it even when faced with extensive contradictory evidence. Thus the astrologers, laymen with antiscience biases, have rather generally accepted the hypothesis that the particular conjunction of heavenly bodies which occurs each year under the Sign of Libra (during late September and most of October) somehow causes persons born at this time of the year to be musical and artistic. While forced to admit that many eminent musicians have been born at other times of the year, the astrologers assert, without bothering to gather evidence, that far more musical geniuses have been born under Libra. They seem content to rest their case on the mention of a few eminent persons who were born at this allegedly propitious time of the year. Of course the scientist has rather different theories to account for the appearance of musical and artistic geniuses, but he is willing to test the validity of the astrological view. Starting perhaps with the hypothesis that the birthdates of eminent musicians should be found evenly distributed throughout the year, *not* bunched, he takes the birthdates of several thousand of the world's most eminent composers of the past and finds how many fall on each day of the year.

The scientist in question, the present writer, did just this[8] and was both surprised and horrified to learn that his hypothesis was invalid, that the birthdates were *not* evenly scattered throughout the year. His only consolation came from noting that the astrologers' favored sign of Libra had *even fewer* birthdates than it should have had were the distribution an even one. But he still had to explain why there was a piling up of birthdates in the late winter months— late January to the end of March. The author's next hypothesis held that the bunching had nothing to do with musicians as such but was a phenomenon occurring in Europe and America possibly associated with the many weddings of the late spring and early summer. If this hunch were valid, both the musicians and the nonmusicians (the entire populations) of cities like Vienna and New York should show the same birthdate trends. More butchers, bakers, and candlestick makers should also have been born during these late winter months. Following up this idea the author studied several tens of thousands of birthdates from these two cities and found exactly the same concentration peaks he had previously found for his composers. Thus his second hypothesis seems tenable since he has demonstrated that, regardless of what the astrologers' horoscopes pretend to show, no particular time of the year favors the birth of musicians over people in general. His data showed that the birthdates of a large sample of the citizens of Vienna and New York City, randomly selected over a certain time span, tended to fall more on the days of the late winter months than on other days. But the astrologers go merrily on with their Libra fantasies!

LIMITATIONS OF PSYCHOMUSICAL INVESTIGATIONS

The psychologist pieces together bits of information into an organized whole. But why does he choose to work on certain problems and not on others? His choice, it would seem, is to a great extent forced by the availability and cooperation of his subjects and by the degree to which the complex phenomena of music can be subjected to scientific analysis.

The first of these conditioners is common to almost all the research choices of the psychologist. Unless he is dealing with inanimate objects such as recordings, or working with subhuman animals which can be caged or with the semicaged school child or college sophomore who must cooperate willy-nilly, the psychologist often has great selection and motivation difficulties with his subjects. He commonly cannot get the cooperation of all those he might desire to test, and even those who do "cooperate" may answer his questions without sufficient care. His findings then are not always truly representative.

The second factor which limits psychomusical research operates throughout the social sciences and the humanities. Causal relations are rarely simple, and whenever analyses are to be made care must be taken that the dynamic interrelation of the phenomena in question is not disturbed. Otherwise the data resulting from the analyses will be devoid of musical meaning. The practical effect of this limitation is that many fascinating musical problems cannot be studied by the aid of any of the analytic techniques currently used by the psychologist or other scientist.

POSSIBILITIES OF RESEARCH IN EXPERIMENTAL AESTHETICS

Psychological research in aesthetics can often throw much light on what is taking place in a particular music area, i.e., it has a *descriptive* function. Research may sometimes yield in addition pertinent information on the *reasons* for some particular bit of music behavior. It can also be of considerable aid in *forecasting*. But no science offers criteria by which artistic responses can be rated as "eternally good," "proper for all time," "eternally bad," or "improper for all time." In other words the work of the psychological aesthetician leads to descriptions, explanations, and forecasts but does not reveal aesthetic absolutes.

Descriptive Function. To illustrate the first or descriptive function of psychological aesthetics we might well return to a consideration of vocal and violin vibrato.[9] Careful research in this area has demonstrated that the cultivated singing voice of the Occidental adult shows periodic changes in pitch in approximately 95 per cent of its tones. Regular changes in intensity and timbre have also been found to occur. For both violin and voice the tone pulsates a little less than 6.5 times a second. The extent of the pulsation of the violin tone (in the middle pitch range) is a trifle more than an eighth of a tone. For the vocal tone the vibrato extent is about a half-tone, although the listener can rarely believe this and interprets the range as somewhat smaller (a fifth of a tone). Both the musically trained and the relatively unmusical prefer the current vibrato rates to all others. Untrained individuals prefer a pitch range of approximately a quartertone, while the musically trained favor a pitch wobble of about a tenth of a whole tone.[10]

The typical vibratos of a number of virtuosos of the past have been carefully measured. Hence it is now possible for the aspiring young singer or violinist to compare his vibrato with that of his model by performing before some instrument which transmutes his own tonal efforts into visual stimuli. Usually the better trained singers have better control of their vibrato.[11]

VIBRATO OF SOME WELL-KNOWN SINGERS		
	Average Rate per Second	Average Extent in Whole Tones
Schumann-Heink	7.6	.38
Galli-Curci	7.3	.44
Caruso	7.1	.47
Rethberg	7.0	.49
Ponselle	6.9	.48
Chaliapin	6.8	.54
Jeritza	6.8	.53
Tetrazzini	6.8	.37
Talley	6.7	.54
Tibbett	6.6	.55
Gigli	6.5	.57
Hackett	5.9	.47
Homer	5.9	.51

Source: C. E. Seashore, *Psychology of Music*, New York, McGraw-Hill, 1938, p. 43 (with permission).

Little is known of the development of vibrato in the child. It would appear to be acquired, in part at least, through intentional and unintentional imitation, with the more rapidly maturing girls achieving adult-style vibrato earlier than boys. The boy soprano's voice is relatively free of vibrato, a fact that in years past made the voices of castrated males much desired for vocal ensembles and even for solo work. The countertenor (e.g. the contemporary singer Alfred Deller), whose voice ranges through the female alto, also has little vibrato. Some highly technical research done in England[12] has been interpreted as showing vibrato due in some degree to a biological control mechanism utilizing auditory feedback. In this study the experimenters interposed temporal delays between the singing and the singer's hearing of what he had sung.

Causal Function.[13] While the second or causal function of psychological aesthetics can be illustrated from any one of a large number of studies, let us limit ourselves to a consideration of only two, the first to be concerned with the determiners of tempo preferences and the second with the reasons for the high regard in which the old Cremona-made violins are held.

Tempo preferences have been found to vary considerably from person to person. This large range is no doubt due to a number of factors, but at least one of these factors has been isolated and found to be what might be termed "occupational tempo." Thus Foley found that women studying trades like dressmaking in which activity proceeds at a slow pace were prone to favor andante tempos; those working with power machines, a slow allegro. Typists, with their faster working speeds, tended to prefer a fast allegro bordering on presto. Their work speeds, it seems, so conditioned these women that they came to prefer these rates even outside the shop and office.[14]

And now for our second illustration of psychology's causal function. With the passage of time, the sales values of the violins built by the old masters of Cremona, Italy, have grown enormously. What makes a Stradivarius or some other old Cremona fiddle so magnificent? Is it its physical construction? Or may it not be, in part at least, a matter of attitude, of prestige long associated with this period of alleged violin-making supremacy?

A long-time investigator of the psychological and physical properties of violins is Saunders[15] who offers a number of interesting generalizations: (1) Neither the age of a violin nor its commercial value is related to its ease of playing. (2) The quickness of a violin's response is not a criterion of its worth. (3) Varnish[16] does little but lower the response curve a bit. (4) As for the effects of differing woods, Saunders asks us to await the conclusions of two Roman scientists, Pasqualini and Barducci, who are busily engaged in testing wood samples from four centuries ago to the present.

The suggestion that a particular instrument was made by a great master craftsman causes the listener to feel that its tone must surely be superior. It also stimulates him to pay more for this prestigeful old instrument than he would for even the "best" of the modern violins. All that is needed to prove that the suggestion hypothesis has some validity is to arrange a psychological experiment in which suggestive effects are eliminated by having Strads and their well-built modern imitations played behind a visual screen a number of times in random order. Saunders did just this when he presented his audiences the music of three unidentified violins— a new but well-built instrument, a "good" ten-year-old model, and a Stradivarius. The ten-year-old model received a small but definite majority of the preference votes. Saunders further reports that the Curtis String Quartet once gave eight concerts using both old masters and well-built new models but not disclosing which were which. A preponderance of the votes was cast for the second instrument used, whatever its type. The *Oxford Companion to Music*[17] reports that in London and several other places there have been similar failures to pick the older from the newer instruments. Indeed the results of a number of experiments prove that the person has yet to be found who can consistently pick the Strad. Yet if one is told which is the Cremona instrument, it will receive his vote almost every time. The old masters, it would seem, knew how to build marvelous fiddles. But along with the instruments they built reputations which are even more marvelous!

Forecasting Function. To illustrate the third or forecasting function of psychological aesthetics, let us look again to the psychology of suggestion and next to the forecasting of grades in conservatories of music. From what we know of the principles of suggestion we might forecast that musical preferences could be affected by an experimenter if he set himself the task of altering his subjects' likes and dislikes. That such effects can actually occur was shown by Rigg when he offered the same music to three groups of college students.[18] The members of one group were led to regard what they were hearing in a romantic light. No special psychological "atmosphere" was suggested to the members of the second group. The third group of students was successfully led to associate the music with Hitler and the Nazi movement. The proof that the three different "atmospheres" elicited three different degrees of acceptance was shown in the three mean preference scores. When thought of as Nazi music[19] the compositions were least appreciated. When the romantic atmosphere was suggested the acceptance was greatest. Thus when forecasting likes and dislikes, more than the object to be judged must be considered. As important or sometimes even more important is the constellation of attitudes associated with the object.

Knowing very well that to many laymen the word "classical" suggests high-brow, boring music, the arrangers of a Danish broadcast program of serious music changed the title of their series from "Classical Music" to "Popular Music" but kept unchanged the style of their musical offerings. The latter label, they felt, suggested pleasanter, easier-to-grasp music. That they had properly gauged the connotations of these terms was rather dramatically demonstrated in the fact that the number of listeners doubled after the changed titling.[20]

It can safely be predicted that certain compositions will be better liked if the listener is led to think they were composed by a man of great eminence. Thus if Bach's *Concerto in D Minor* is played to lay audiences who believe the composer to be the relatively unknown (to laymen) Buxtehude, the acceptance will be far less than if the listeners are told that the composer is their revered J. S. Bach.[21] Similar suggestive effects have been demonstrated in the area of jazz preferences and in the pictorial arts.

Now let us look at the forecasting of conservatory grades. Many colleges nowadays have established what they call "critical levels" of college aptitude, minimum scores which an applicant must reach in order to matriculate. These critical levels have been empirically determined from the scores of past failures. Thus they are of considerable value for forecasting, since persons making scores below these critical points will almost certainly fail before the time of graduation. Stanton, working at the Eastman School of Music, found a critical level of this type for entering music students.[22] She based her level on a test of tonal imagery, a case history, a college aptitude test, and a battery of music aptitude tests (Chap. 9). After years of experimentation, Stanton found she could foretell with considerable accuracy which of the applicants would be the failures.

ABSENCE OF ABSOLUTES

Because there are certain biological periodicities close to the 6 or 6.5 pulsations per second that is the vibrato rate the contemporary musician prefers above all other rates, one theorist has assumed this periodicity to be the "proper vibrato rate for all time." To him the fact that the musically elite currently prefer a rate identical with one of the periodicities of "nature" proves that they like what is biologically proper to like. This type of reasoning is not acceptable to the social scientist, for he knows that what is deemed proper in one period of time may not be so considered in the next.[23] The position taken in this book, the belief that scientific research does not yield absolutes and final answers, is well expressed by Tiffin in an article in which he describes some of his vibrato researches:

> This work is intended to present objective unequivocal information about the vibrato used by this generation of artists and students of voice. It is not contended that this type of vibrato is ultimately beautiful. No esthetic value judgment is included in the results. It may be argued that the vibrato in use by present day artists is a fad and that their voices would be improved if it were made less prominent or even entirely eliminated. This may quite possibly be true. Perhaps if this study is repeated fifty years hence, the average extent of the vibrato then in use will be found to be quite different from the one now employed. This will simply mean that standards

of artistry have changed, as all esthetic preferences change from time
to time. . . . No attempt is made to prophesy future artistic taste
nor to justify current preference in terms of ultimate esthetic principles.[24]

Absolutes are not revealed by psychological research for the
simple reason that there are no musical absolutes to be found. There
is for example no absolutely "good"[25] music, music whose goodness
transcends time and space. As the British psychologist Vernon
phrases it: "That music is 'good' which happens to appeal especially
to the subjective tastes of the musicians of the period, these tastes
being to a large extent determined irrationally by temperamental
and various environmental conditions, by suggestion, contra-sug-
gestion, conservatism and iconoclasticism."[26]

PREVIEW OF LATER CHAPTERS

Our first consideration will be the scale—the relative and
socially agreed upon placements of all the notes the musician attempts to play or sing. The interval, i.e. any two simultaneously or
successively played tones, and the melody, an interval succession felt
to possess unity, furnish the basic underpinnings of musical structure and are for this reason considered in Chapters 3 and 4.

Since the first (and often the only) question many laymen ask
about a piece of music is, "What story does the composition tell?" it
seemed appropriate to present in the fifth chapter material on music
as a possible medium of communication. As a person's attitude toward the meaning of a composition clearly forms an important part
of his taste, of his overall attitude toward that composition and its
composer, the language chapter is followed by two on musical taste—
Chapter 6 on the nature of taste and Chapter 7 on the several ways of
measuring it.

The discussion of the basic musical abilities and their measurement (Chaps. 8 and 9) might justifiably have appeared earlier in the
book, for in a very real sense all perception, affection, and attitude
presuppose abilities. There are other ways of viewing the problem,
however. A person's abilities will mature only if the social climate is
propitious. They can be expressed only in the context of a man's
own and his culture's taste, and this taste may prove stimulating or
inhibitory. In this limited sense then, ability may be thought to depend on taste and so deserve treatment, as it has in this book, after
taste has been considered.

The consideration of the applications to medicine and industry appears as the final chapter, for before one tries to apply any knowledge he should make certain that he has learned all he can about what he is to apply.

With this brief introduction to the social psychology of music, let us examine next the musical scale, the totality of those fixed (but relatively placed) pitch positions which the musician uses in his melodic and harmonic endeavors.

CHAPTER TWO 🎵 *Musical Scales*

A WORK OF ART can be defined as "an organization of information according to a set of rules, where the construction, tracing, or observation of this organization serves to alter a person's motivational state in a way sought by the individual."[1] In other words a man's actions can be termed artistic whenever he constructs, plays with, or observes artifacts which have some agreed-upon status and which elicit in him or in others the desire that the activities be continued and repeated. These artifacts, be they tonal or some other sort of configuration, need have no universal appeal. Music to a pygmy of Africa and to a graduate of a European conservatory of music may well have quite different connotations. Hence it is too much to hope that the boundaries of an art can ever be precisely delimited.

It goes almost without saying that music is composed of patterns of sound acceptable to the people of some subculture. Although avant-garde groups have become devoted now and then to soundless activities they insist are musical—note the fad of the 1960's of reading musical scores while producing hand and other gestures typically associated with music[2]—music refers traditionally to the elicitation of or the listening to auditory stimuli. Its sounds are either noisy with no perceptible pitch, or they are tonal and can be located on a high-low pitch continuum. The tones may differ not only in pitch but also in loudness, timbre, duration, volume, density, and perhaps in still other characteristics.[3] While all pitches are of potential musical use, only a few appear in any one composition. That is, convention limits the number and relative locations of the pitches. This chapter will consider the several attempts at pitch limitation, matters studied in music under the caption of scales.

Unlike the music of some other cultures in which the sounds

17

slide up or down without discrete steps and the patterns are rarely twice alike, the music of the West has been largely built around fixed tones as far back as there are records. These tones, the stepwise, ordered arrangement of which constitutes a scale, have been tied to a variety of pitch frequencies, with their exact pitch locations largely matters of local tradition or of convenience to the musical performer. Violin A for instance is most usually set at 435 cycles[4] in Austria and France and at 440 cycles in England and the United States. In the summer of 1963 the New York Philharmonic-Symphony Orchestra raised its Violin A to a frequency of 442. This caused a flurry of excitement, for since 1920 the U.S. Bureau of Standards has held that the frequency of Violin A should be set at 440. However, neither the Bureau nor the Federal Communications Commission has power to enforce such a decision. The precise setting of Violin A or of any other pitch letter is largely a matter of group decision and may vary from time to time and place to place.

Of far more interest to the musical structure, to the melody and harmony, is the ratio formed by an interval's two bounding tones. When a pipe of constant bore is cut in half, the pitch of the tone yielded by blowing across each half is an octave above that given by the original length, and the number of cycles of the pitch produced by each of the smaller pieces is twice that produced by the longer pipe. The ratio 1:2 then refers to any interval where the higher tone has twice the pitch frequency of the lower (150:300, 240:480, etc.). Multiple octaves would have ratios 1:4 (150:600, 240:960, etc.), 1:8, 1:16, and the like. The two tones of the ratio 1:2 sound well together and their psychological effects are so similar[5] that they have been given identical letter names (c and c, or d and d) since 600 A.D. when an edict to this effect was issued by Pope Gregory the Great. The absolute size of the spans is generally not of paramount importance, since a large span covering 2,000 to 4,000 cycles has many of the same psychological effects as a small span spreading from 100 to 200 cycles. Both spans cover 12 semitones in Western music, are termed octaves,[6] and can be described by the ratio 1:2. It is out of ratios that melody and harmony are constructed, and as long as the ratios remain unchanged, the notes can be raised or lowered within reason without damage to the tune. Such a change in the pitch locations, termed transposition by the musician, merely shifts the melody to another pitch level.

The octave relationship was already recognized in the earliest documents history has provided. The ratio 2:3, which covers seven semitones in Western music and is called the musical fifth (e.g.

do:sol, re:la),[7] and the ratio 3:4, which covers five semitones and is known as the musical fourth (e.g. *sol:do, do:fa*), also had early recognition. It is not surprising that these three simple ratios and combinations of the three appeared in the first Western scale considered seriously by scholars.

PYTHAGOREAN SCALE OF ANCIENT GREECE

A pattern of tones had already achieved status as an important diatonic (seven-tone) scale in the Western world at least by 350 B.C. and has been spoken of since that time as the Pythagorean. Its ratios employed only the prime numbers 1 and 3. Its whole tones invariably had the ratio 8:9 (e.g. 432 cycles to 486 cycles) and its semitones 243:256. History does not tell us how accurately the instrument makers and performers of ancient Greece tuned their pipes and strings, but it is probable that they lacked the enthusiasm for careful intonation which characterizes contemporary Western music. Hence the Pythagorean probably sounded as if it were our present scale played on a poorly tuned instrument. Even with careful tuning, the Pythagorean scale sounds to the sophisticated contemporary only slightly different from his accustomed scale.

Unfortunately the Pythagorean scale had disadvantages for both practice and theory. Its semitone was smaller than a true half-tone and the instrument makers found the semitone ratio quite awkward to manipulate. Then too it had other ratios, like *fa* to *ti* (512:729), which were even more complex. But it was the musical theorists who were probably most distressed since the scale did not possess quite all of the mathematical (to them, metaphysical) properties they wished to see in it. Their ideal Pythagorean scale was to have been formed, say some historians,[8] by placing end to end the seven white notes along with the five blacks as they appear in a succession of musical fifths (seven half-notes each). All the notes above the first octave were to be pitched at lower pitch levels so that they could be contained within the spread of a single octave. That is, if one happens to start the succession with an *f* and count up seven semitones, the next higher fifth will be *c;* then with another seven semitones comes *g*, then *d, a, e, b, f♯, c♯, g♯, d♯, a♯*, and then *f* again. Rearranged and brought down to the same octave register they become the *c, c♯, d, d♯*, and the other members of the chromatic scale. The theorists were greatly disturbed to find that the final pitch, reached by adding together the twelve musical fifths and bringing them back to the starting octave, is not an exact pitch replica of the original tone but is approximately an eighth of a tone sharp. We shall see later how perceptible this "error" really was.

PYTHAGOREAN SCALE WHERE *DO* IS SET AT 256 CYCLES

Do	Re	Mi	Fa	Sol	La	Ti	Do
256	288	324	341.3	384	432	486	512

It has been claimed by some theorists (and hotly denied by others) that another great theorist of ancient Greece, Aristoxenos,[9] tried to resolve the Pythagorean dilemma by suggesting that the ratio of each whole tone be made exactly twice the ratio size of each semitone, with the octave containing twelve of these identical semitone intervals. If this idea of tempering intervals had been immediately implemented, Western music might have been spared the horrors of sharps and flats, and transposition from one pitch register to another would have been quite simple. But because of intellectual stubbornness and since the technique of achieving equal temperament was not for many years understood by the craftsmen, this remarkable suggestion sparked no aesthetic revolution. However, the idea of giving the octave twelve semitones of equal ratio size was so obviously reasonable that Galileo and several other thoughtful persons kept it alive until the day of Johann Sebastian Bach when it finally triumphed. But between these dates other scales flourished.

SCALES OF JUST INTONATION

The Pythagorean scale spawned over the years a number of variants, the most important of which used the prime numbers 1, 3, and 5 and are termed scales of just intonation. As we have seen, there was great difficulty because of the complexity of a number of the Pythagorean intervals. To improve the situation, brave instrument tuners experimented from time to time with ratios which made use of the prime numbers 5 and 7 (e.g. 3:5, 4:7). However, ratios using the prime 7[10] were never adopted by any large number of organ builders or other tuners, and so this member of the Western scales will not receive further mention here. It is of some sociopsychological interest, however, that in the sixteenth century a taboo existed against the use in Western music of prime numbers not in the series 1 to 6. The metaphysical reason offered was that since God in his wisdom had arranged for only six directions—above, below, fore, after, right, and left—the number 6 must have metaphysical significance. To use a larger prime like 7 would be contrary to God's will. The classical Chinese had a similar rationalization although they spoke of only five "proper" directions—up, down, before, after, and center.

In developing scales of just intonation with primes 1, 3, and 5, the Pythagorean procedure of adding together musical fifths was followed. But at the time of the fourth addition the interval was made a trifle smaller so that the ratio of *do* to *la* could be changed from 16:27 to 3:5. *Do* to *mi* now changed from 64:81 to 4:5, and *do* to *ti* from 128:243 to 8:15. These changes from more to less complex ratios were most palatable to the instrument tuners, but unfortunately they made transpositions much more difficult. For in this new family of scales there were two sizes of whole tones and a semitone which was a half of neither whole step. Obviously a whole step pitched at 8:9 could not have quite the sound effect of one pitched at 9:10. To handle modulations and transpositions in these new scales the organ builders felt forced to make many additions to their banks of pipes. But perhaps in their search for tonal perfection, these tuners added more pipes than the exigencies of transposition really demanded. They apparently failed to realize how very adaptable man is, how quickly he stops being aware of minor mistunings.[11]

Happily for the viability of the just-intoned scales, a savior appeared in the form of a pseudoscientific rationalization. By the time these scales appeared, science had already discovered that sound-giving sources tend to yield complex tonal effects. An air column not only vibrates as a whole giving the so-called fundamental (also termed the first partial) tone, but a half of the air column, a third, a fourth, a fifth, and even smaller parts add partial tones (called overtones or harmonics) to the pitch conglomerate. The prime 1 and its powers (octave and multiple octaves of the fundamental) appear most often in the overtone series, the prime 3 and its powers next most often, the prime 5 and its powers next, and so on. That is, if a fundamental tone of 100 cycles is played, its octave and multiple octaves (prime 1) appear in the second partial tone (200 cycles), the fourth partial tone (400 cycles), the eighth (800 cycles), the sixteenth (1,600 cycles), etc. The musical fifth (prime 3) appears in the third partial (300 cycles), the sixth (600 cycles), the twelfth (1,200 cycles), etc. The major third (prime 5) appears in the fifth partial (500 cycles), the tenth (1,000 cycles), etc. Unfortunately one must go up to the forty-eighth partial to reach approximate multiple octaves of all the scale notes.

The thinking of the theorists was somewhat as follows. Man

unconsciously (or more rarely consciously) analyzes his physical world, and his preferences and musical scales emerge from the repeated effects of his unconscious "hearing" of (and his conscious attending to) these partials. Just-intoned scales seemed to their users to be scientifically correct with multiple octaves of the tones all appearing among the partial tones of the harmonic series. The hypothecation of unconscious perception was commonplace in those days, with architectural theorists offering a similar rationalization termed "naive geometry" for man's preferences for "golden" sections, root rectangles, and many other "good," unconsciously perceived forms. However, the modern scientist sees little to justify the belief that man can unconsciously analyze out mathematical and form relationships, and it seems particularly absurd to think that medieval man was able, even when fully conscious, to tease out and identify from what he continually heard the several partials necessary to the derivation of his just-intoned scales.

But it was the need for easier transpositions and modulations and not the emergence of modern scientific knowledge that killed the just-intoned scales. Indeed there are writers even today who maintain that they are the only "correct" musical scales. Other scales they would allow to remain only if these "compromises" offer practical gains, such as greater ease in transposition and modulation.

A SCALE OF JUST INTONATION WHERE *DO* IS SET AT 256 CYCLES

Do	*Re*	*Mi*	*Fa*	*Sol*	*La*	*Ti*	*Do*
256	288	320	341.3	384	426.6	480	512

MEAN-TONE TEMPERAMENTS[12]

We have already said that to transpose melodies easily and yet maintain the use of just-intoned scales, the listener was forced to adjust to some mistunings or else the instrument builder had to add to his sound sources to allow for a number of auxiliary tones sharper or flatter than those offered by the basic scale. Finally, however, after centuries of inconvenience with just-intoned scales, there occurred a partial implementation of what a few theorists had long been advocating—the tempering or altering of the sizes of certain intervals so that fewer auxiliary pipes and other extra tone producers would be needed. First to appear was what has come to be termed mean-tone temperament. This came into use in western Europe in the seventeenth century and was almost universally accepted during the eighteenth until equal temperament won the day. In any mean-tone temperament there is a shaving or flatting of several of the fifths so that the Pythagorean hope of a scale of musical fifths could be approximately fulfilled. With mean-tone temperaments, transpositions and modulations within a few of the most used keys were possible. It is unfortunate, however, that what today are similarly pitched sharps and flats, e.g. c♯ and d♭, were still given different pitch locations and were regarded as different notes in mean-tone temperament.

A SCALE OF MEAN-TONE TEMPERAMENT WHERE *DO* IS SET AT 256 CYCLES

Do	*Re*	*Mi*	*Fa*	*Sol*	*La*	*Ti*	*Do*
256	286.1	320	342.4	382.8	428	478.6	512

EQUAL TEMPERAMENT IN WORLD MUSIC

Equal temperament[13] in Western music was accomplished by dividing the octave into twelve *equal* semitone steps, equal so far as ratios were concerned but not in terms of the span of frequencies covered. The scale of equal temperament is the one for which J. S. Bach fought and to which the modern piano is approximately tuned. While its ratios are complex (e.g. that of the semitone is 1:1.059), the technical age was dawning and complex ratios could be more easily handled. Of paramount importance was the fact that at last one could freely move his tune up and down the pitch range without mistunings or the need for auxiliary tone makers. Equally tempered scales also developed in the Orient. The Siamese traditionally divide their octave into seven equal steps while the Javanese theoretically divide one of theirs (the slendra) into five equal steps.

WESTERN SCALE OF EQUAL TEMPERAMENT WHERE *DO* IS SET AT 256 CYCLES

Do	*Re*	*Mi*	*Fa*	*Sol*	*La*	*Ti*	*Do*
256	287.3	322.5	341.6	383.5	430.3	483.2	512

DETECTABILITY OF SCALE AND NOTE DIFFERENCES

It is tempting to believe that all tonal differences must necessarily be preceptible, at least to the trained listener, but such a
notion is simply not valid. Each listener has psychophysiological
thresholds for the several tonal characteristics, and many physical
differences are not perceptible. Being subthreshold, they do not
exist for the listener, although they may intrigue the theorist. Let us
then see which of the scale changes over the centuries were above
typical thresholds and which were below and so of no practical
significance. But first we shall need some unit of ratio measurement
to make our discussion more meaningful.

Either the octave, the whole tone, or the semitone span (termed
the semit, approximately a 6 per cent change in pitch frequency) of
the equally tempered scale could have served as a unit of ratio measurement if a relatively large unit had been desired. One theorist,
Yasser,[14] has urged the adoption of the decitone, the centitone, and
the millitone (tenth, hundredth, and thousandth of the whole tone
of equal temperament) as feasible units. The thousandth part of the
octave has also been suggested as a reasonable unit. In most general
use, however, is the *cent*[15] which is a hundredth part of the semitone
of the equally tempered scale of Western music. The octave in this
system of measurement equals 1,200 cents, the equally tempered
whole tone 200 cents, and the semitone 100 cents. For the Siamese
who divide the octave into seven equally tempered intervals, each of
these steps equals 1/7 of 1,200 cents or approximately 171 cents.
Dividing the octave into five equally tempered intervals in the manner of the Javanese gives each of their steps a value of 1,200/5 or 240
cents. The Ganda eight-string harp of Africa also makes use of the
240-cent step which in this instance is the pitch interval between
strings.

Let us now attempt to think in terms of these cent units and
examine the previously described scales to see how perceptually important the changes from one scale to the next really were. To do
this we must look at interval thresholds, at man's ability to discriminate between intervals of differing size.

Careful work by Pratt[16] and his associates shows that the threshold for perceiving changes in intervals is approximately 20 cents in
the middle range of tones. This value seems reasonable to the present author whose students hear no difference between the musical
fifths (*do:sol*) of the several Western scales, between the several
fourths (*do:fa*), or even between the major seconds (*do:re*). The

SCALE VALUES IN TERMS OF CENTS

	Do	Re	Mi	Fa	Sol	La	Ti	Do
Pyth.	0	204	408	498	702	906	1110	1200
Just	0	204	386	498	702	884	1088	1200
M.T.T.*	0	193	386	503	697	890	1083	1200
E.T. (West.)	0	200	400	500	700	900	1100	1200
Javan.	0	240		480		720	960	1200
Siam.	0	171	343	514	686	857	1029	1200

* This is the tuning used by Pietro Aron around 1523.

difference between the Pythagorean and the mean-tone major sevenths (1110–1083 or 27 cents) is most readily perceived, but occasionally other differences are recognized under optimum conditions. However, the vibrato, when present, tends to make all differences more difficult to detect. It is possible that the musicians of centuries past had even more difficulty than we do in perceiving such differences, since some of their tone-producing sources were markedly cruder than the instruments of today. But of course the theorists expected to hear differences. Believing as they did in the perfection of just-intoned scales, they undoubtedly imagined they were hearing greater differences than they actually perceived.

In our discussions up to now we have been seeing but one side of the coin, the matter of interval discrimination. Pitch discrimination, however, can also be employed in some instances in detecting scale differences, and this particular human capacity is far more sensitive than is the ability to perceive interval differences. While with interval discrimination two *two-tone clangs* are judged as "same" or "different," with pitch discrimination two *single* tones are thus compared. If for example one has just heard a tune played first in Pythagorean intonation and then in equal temperament, one can fixate on any single equally tempered tone of the melody and compare its pitch with the immediate memory of the pitch as it was played a few moments earlier in Pythagorean intonation. The use of this capacity for pitch discrimination discloses unmistakable differences between just-intoned and Pythagorean *la*'s and *mi*'s and even between just and mean-tone *re*'s. The eighth of a tone discrepancy which had bothered the Pythagoreans centuries ago is also discriminable—*barely* and only under optimum conditions if ratio discrimination alone is employed, but *readily* if pitch discrimination is allowed to enter in. Ward and Martin[17] in a study with well-trained musicians found a few "sensitives" who could detect differences of six cents if at least three of the sequence tones were "mistuned." Surprisingly enough, a number of their musicians could not distinguish just intonation from equal temperament. The present author has never found such "insensitives" among the musically trained. The musicians he has tested often commented on the absence of "roughness" and the consequent "clarity" of just-intoned intervals. Thus roughness effects became an added cue in distinguishing between the scales. If interested, the reader can, to some degree, learn how skillful he is in scale differentiation, since there are now available two commercial recordings[18] which play musical snatches pitched in the several historical scales.

Intervals may be distorted, made somewhat larger or smaller, without loss of identity. It is indeed fortunate that this is true, for otherwise the transition from one historical scale to the next might have been more difficult to accomplish. Exactly how much interval distortion can be tolerated is difficult to determine since the researches in this area are not entirely in agreement. But it does appear that for most people the uniqueness of the musical fifth's interval quality is disturbed more readily than that of the major third or sixth. It is well that the historical changes in interval size were in line with this aspect of human psychophysiology. As will be noted in the table on page 25, the fifth was kept at approximately 700 cents in all the Western scales. Even the Siamese and Javanese had scale points which might be thought of as approximating the fifth. The fourth was kept at approximately 500 cents. The other intervals varied more extensively from one scale to the next.

Western music is today tied rather closely to the piano, and pianos are tuned to fairly accurate equal temperament. Yet there are still theorists who worry because much highly rated music was composed for some mean-tone or earlier scale and is now played in equal temperament. They maintain that keen-eared musicians "sense" equal temperament to be a mere compromise scale. These sensitive people will, they hold, employ just intonation whenever it is possible to do so. The truth is, however, that most Occidental listeners and performers are quite content with equal temperament. They do not unconsciously think in terms of just intonation. Although the early scientist Helmholtz[19] describes instances where he believed violinists were reverting to just intonation whenever their playing was unaccompanied, more recent observations paint a very different picture. Greene,[20] Lottermoser and Meyer, Nickerson, Mason, and Shackford have all studied the problem and offer findings contrary to those of Helmholtz. Unaccompanied performers, it is clear, do *not* revert to an earlier scale. Of course they do not play with perfect pitch accuracy, but their pitch placements correspond rather well to what is called for by equal temperament. Yet they do tend to show a slight but consistent sharping of their tones. By and large the case for equal temperament has been well expressed by Barbour:

> This contemporary dispute about tuning is perhaps a tempest in a teapot. It is probably true that all singers and players are singing and playing false most of the time. But their errors are errors from equal temperament. No well-informed person today would suggest that these errors consistently resemble departures from just intonation or from any other tuning system. Equal temperament does remain the standard, however imperfect the actual accomplishment may be.[21]

OTHER POSSIBLE SCALES

So far we have centered our discussion on the Western diatonic scales of seven notes (with passing reference to the scales of Thailand and Java). While these heptatonic scales were basic to the music of the West, several other scales have had a substantial degree of popularity. One of these is the pentatonic where only the *do, re, fa, sol, la* are heard, i.e. spans of 2, 3, 2, and finally 2 semitone steps. A number of well-known Scottish tunes are based on this scale and many Chinese and African tunes on quite similar scales. In fact the suggestion has been made by some jazz historians that the somewhat uncertain pitch placements of the "blues" thirds and sevenths might be in part due to the African's more exclusive use of a pentatonic scale which had no *mi* or *ti* and thus to difficulties in handling these when he was later forced to use a heptatonic scale after he came to America and developed jazz.

Even at a time when the seven-tone scale was more rigidly adhered to than it is today, it was allowable to make occasional use of any one or more of the octave's five other semitones (the black notes in the key of *c*). These accidentals, as they were called, were thought to offer variety or color. When added to the more "basic" seven there was formed the dodecuple or twelve-semitone scale. These twelve notes have been more and more freely used as a scale. The rise of atonal music has greatly facilitated their acceptance as scale notes.

The employment of accidentals can also be seen in the contemporary use of the old Greek modes (seven-note scales arranged as if one were employing only white notes with the starting tone *d, e, f, g,* or *b*) and in Debussy's whole-tone music where a succession of six whole steps is used, as in *c, d, e, f♯, g♯, a♯, c.* It has been found that his whole-tone scale seems very strange to the unsophisticated who react just as Debussy hoped they would. Sensing that it is neither major nor minor they often decide that it must be Oriental. Such "thinking" allowed Debussy to compose "Oriental" music which, quite understandably, no Oriental recognizes as such. To give a distinctive character to his music, Scriabin has used a scale with a series of three whole steps, followed by a step of three-semitone size, a semitone, and a whole tone. Perhaps others will follow him in devising still other scales as their personal trademarks.

Scales made up of a variety of steps smaller than the semitone have been suggested at one time or another. One of the most bizarre was that of the fifth-century Chinese, Chien Lohtze, who proposed a 360-note scale to match the 360 days he thought made up the year. While it is not quite clear whether this was a scale in our sense or merely a set of starting points for each day's melodies, it would seem that this theorist was little acquainted with the psychology of human perception.

The Hindus have a 22-note scale which can be sung with considerable accuracy. And the Moravian musician Haba, who has advocated splitting the semitone into a number of smaller intervals, claims to be able to sing with little error spans as small as one-sixtieth of an octave. So far as the author knows, Haba's skills have never been scientifically studied, and even if he is able to do all he claims, he would certainly lack appreciative listeners.

Clearly our interest should not focus on freakish virtuosity but rather on those extensions to our present scale that could conceivably prove viable. A number of musicians and psychologists have seen the quarter-tone[22] as the next logical development, partly because our Western music system now operates on a semitone base and the quarter-tone is half of the semitone. Particularly in Europe a number of quarter-tone pianos and organs have been built and a considerable body of quarter-tone music has been written. It will be recalled that the threshold for interval discrimination is approximately 20 cents, but this is the value at which Pratt's observers could detect differences only half the time. To be completely functional, an interval should properly be discriminated not half but all the time. Pratt[23] has found the value for the smallest interval that will be perceived as different 100 per cent of the time to be somewhere near 50 cents, the span of the quarter-tone in the equally tempered scale. Thus quarter-tones are psychologically feasible, but no interval much smaller than this would seem to be acceptable except to the person of extraordinary sensitivity.[24] An interesting demonstration for the musically unsophisticated is to play one octave in quarter-tones and ask what has been heard. A common answer is that the chromatic scale of two octaves has been played. Most persons will find at least a few of the quarter-tone intervals pleasing. Generally the most pleasing quarter-tone span is the one that extends from a bass of *c* to the pitch halfway between the minor and major thirds, an interval which approximates one appearing in Siamese music. In fact this interval is typically rated as pleasanter than either of the seconds or sevenths.[25]

SUMMARY

In this chapter we have seen that the basic scale of Western music has for centuries been the seven-note (diatonic), whose precise ratios have varied from time to time. The Pythagoreans had held that their version of the scale could be derived through the addition of a succession of twelve musical fifths (ratio 2:3), with the final note approximately seven octaves higher than the starting tone and with all notes finally lowered in pitch to be within the octave of the starting tone. The prime numbers 1 and 3, which alone appear in the ratio of the musical fifth, were thus the only primes needed in the building of this scale.

It was early noted that the addition of the twelve musical fifths made a pitch range a trifle too large to squeeze into seven octaves. This fact bothered the metaphysically minded theorists who felt that a "proper" scale, to be agreeable to God, should fit without forcing or alteration. The practical tone makers were also bothered but not by theological considerations. They were disturbed rather by the complexity of the ratios with which they had to contend. This led in time to the creation of ratios composed of primes beyond 1 and 3. The first and only other prime to be rather generally accepted was the 5 (in ratios 2:5, 3:5, etc.) which appeared in what were termed scales of just intonation. The addition of this prime was accomplished by flatting the musical thirds, the sixths, and the sevenths of the Pythagorean scale. Since these new scale ratios were held to facilitate work in harmony, there developed a school of thought which subscribed to the notion that the just-intoned scale steps had been borrowed from positions on the overtone or harmonic series. It was thought that man had recognized, unconsciously or perhaps consciously, the higher tonal partials and had made use of them in creating these scales. Such a philosophy inspired theologians to call on the Deity for the blessing of His scales and led early scientists to regard just intonation as scientifically correct. This type of scale became so honored that later efforts to alter it met with tremendous opposition, and arguments for its "God-given quality" and its "naturalness" were repeated ad nauseam.

Although there were abortive attempts to bring in primes other than 3 and 5, the more lasting changes to the scale came with meantone and equal temperament. The former made limited modulation possible while equal temperament allowed for free modulation through all keys and transposition ranging through the entire tonal range. In equal temperament the octave is divided into twelve ratios of equal size. Equal temperament but with fewer scale steps was also achieved in Java and Thailand.

Taking the cent (the twelve hundredth part of the octave) as the unit of scale measurement, it was found that the threshold for interval change is approximately 20 cents. Since over the centuries most of the changes in note placement were less than 20 cents in magnitude, and because in earlier times it would seem that man took mistunings more lightly than he does now, moving from one historical scale to the next doubtless caused but little difficulty except to a few theorists and persons with extreme sensitivity. Scale changes above threshold magnitude do exist, however, and many persons can easily tell that the several scales are not identical. They are sometimes aided in this task by their capacity for pitch discrimination which is far more sensitive than is interval discrimination. Moreover, many listeners note that the equally tempered intervals sound rougher than do the just-intoned.

There is no evidence for the notion that we moderns accept equal temperament for practical reasons only, solely because it allows easy modulation and transposition, or that we do our musical thinking in a framework of just intonation. Psychological research discloses no outstanding preference for "natural" just-intoned scales. It suggests rather that whenever unaccompanied performers deviate from equal temperament in their playing, their tones are still closer to equal temperament than to any other scale but show some tendency to be a trifle sharp. On the other hand, there is no inherent reason why the scale of equal temperament must necessarily be Western music's final scale form. For as Mursell[26] says: "Any scale is a construct of the social mind, a phenomenon of social agreement." Over the years the seven-tone scale of the West has had many rivals— pentatonic, dodecuple, whole-tone, etc.—and in some circles has been modified to include quarter-tones. Quarter-tone spans of 50 cents can be heard as qualitatively distinct intervals and are therefore perceptually reasonable scale steps. But research indicates that microtones much smaller than 50 cents are more rarely perceived as qualitatively unique by the typical listener and hence are not functional for music.

A number of scale properties still remain to be considered, but they can be better understood after more attention has been given to the interval, particularly to the role the interval plays in melody. The interval and its role will concern us in the next chapter.

CHAPTER THREE   *The Interval*

IN THE PRECEDING CHAPTER it was shown that the building blocks of music are the tonal intervals. This chapter will continue the examination of these musical constituents and will pay special attention to a number of characteristics they have been said to possess.[1]

DISTINCTIVE QUALITY

It goes almost without saying that each interval has its own distinctive quality, the psychological characteristics by which it is recognized. We have already mentioned the fact that, physically speaking, the interval may be a number of things. The tones of the major sixth for example may have frequencies of 256 and 432, 256 and 426.6, 256 and 430.3, 384 and 648, or even 512 and 864 cycles, to mention only a few. But all these physically different stimulus configurations have a psychological quality in common, a major sixthness. The major sixth, like all other intervals, has stability within a margin of span tolerance.[2]

A number of researchers who are interested in phenomenological description have attempted to describe verbally the several interval characteristics. The results have not been strikingly successful. It is unlikely that an octave rendered by a flute will be described in the same terms as will the identical interval presented by a piano, a violin, or a tuba. However, the reader can check his own reactions to intervals played on a variety of instruments and see if the fifth always sounds dilute, hollow, and harsh; the fourth rich, harsh, and coarse; the second gritty and grating; the third mellow and sweet; the sixth luscious and juicy-mellow; the seventh astringent and sharp-rough; and the octave smooth, as the Edmunds and Smith observers found them.[3]

While the octave is officially defined as the interval whose size is 1,200 cents, it is standard procedure for piano tuners to make the octaves progressively sharper in the higher registers. They feel that the higher octaves sound decidedly more brilliant if they are made slightly larger in span size.

The reader will probably correctly guess that with much practice he can improve his ability to recognize the intervals.[4] He will possibly also know that descending intervals are more difficult to recognize than the ascending. If he tests himself he will very likely find that he, like Ortmann's subjects,[5] is relatively poorer in his recognition of minor intervals and particularly of minor sixths, sevenths, and thirds and, like Maltzew's observers,[6] poor also in the identification of tritones, e.g. $c:f\sharp$. Recognition tends to be best in the middle register, the tonal range most used in music. But whether the greater use of the middle range has made recognition better or better recognition has forced greater usage is as yet unanswered.

VIBRATO AND TRILL

Vibrato[7] concerns small physical spans which are not perceived as intervals. Although the instrumentalist or vocalist produces a series of definite pitch spans whenever he oscillates two tones in creating his vibrato, the listener reacts as if he were hearing embellished single tones. The latter does not hear the two pitches as such but rather one pitch midway between them, and he continues for a time to hear a single tone even though the performer may oscillate his tone over a progressively wider pitch span.

On an instrument with fixed tones like the piano the oscillation of two tones a semitone or more apart will of course be perceived as a trill. But in the case of voice and many other sorts of tones, the oscillation span must often be somewhere between three-quarters of a tone and two whole tones before the listener ceases to hear a single wobbly tone and instead perceives an oscillation between two tones, a successive interval or trill. Thus the trill emerges as qualitatively different from the vibrato. The two pitches are now heard as separate tones which can alternate, especially if sung, even at vibrato rate. In making a trill the performer often overreaches his interval. He apparently does this to compensate for the fact that his listener tends to underestimate the size of the trill just as he does the extent of the vibrato.[8]

APPARENT PITCH OF INTERVALS

After stating that an interval has two boundary pitches, it may seem paradoxical to speak of interval pitch as if the interval were a single tone. Yet each interval is an entity and as such possesses a special pitch which even naive listeners can recognize.

Many years ago while at work on the pitch of intervals, Stumpf, a German psychologist, proposed a principle which he supposed had universal application.[9] He held that the pitch of the lower component of an interval is always dominant over that of the upper; that is, that the pitch of the lower is so much more obvious that it has the greater effect on the pitch of the interval configuration. In his experiments he presented two octave intervals to his listeners, one whose frequency span was approximately from 130 to 260 cycles and the other from 260 to 520. His audience reported that it was the apparent pitch of the first interval which was more unlike the pitch of 260 cycles (approximately Middle *C*). They seemed to be attending more to the pitches of the lower components.

Stumpf's generalization seems to be in line with the dictum of the harmonists who state that the normal orientation of a tonal pattern is from below upward. To quote Watt: "Rising makes the impression of tonal recession, falling, that of approach. We begin a scale involuntarily from below, not from above, and we end it below again."[10] Perhaps this tendency toward upward movement is responsible for the fact that ascending intervals are easier to recognize than the descending.

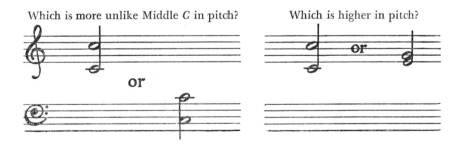

Which is more unlike Middle *C* in pitch?   Which is higher in pitch?

The British psychologist Valentine was unable to verify this principle of Stumpf's, for his subjects regarded the pitch of the higher interval as more unlike that of 260 cycles.[11] When he further asked for a comparison of the pitch of a certain octave with that of a smaller interval which lay wholly within this octave, his subjects voted for the octave as the higher in pitch. Thus it is quite apparent that his subjects were in each instance more affected by the higher pitch.

Puzzled by these conflicting sets of data, the present writer performed two experiments along similar lines, one in the early 1920's and the other fifteen years later.[12] In his researches he attempted to learn whether these divergent findings might not somehow be related to the fact that Stumpf had used musically naive men in his experiments while the majority of Valentine's subjects had been schoolchildren with some musical training. It was the author's theory that children, sopranos, and well-trained musicians generally have had so much experience in melody hunting in looking at the upper lines of their music that the higher pitches of a complex of tones now stand out for them.

To verify this idea that melody hunting is an important variable in establishing the pitch of intervals, the writer tested relatively unmusical persons, sopranos, contraltos and altos, and adult male singers. The resulting data showed that the relatively unmusical, and to some extent the adult male singers, voted in line with the Stumpfian theory. The sopranos, on the other hand, and many of the other singers of both sexes behaved as had Valentine's schoolchildren. Clearly then Stumpf's rule must be modified to embrace the effects of training in melody hunting. Stumpf was correct in stating that the pitch of the lower component of an interval is dominant, but only for the musically untrained and for some basses. For other persons it is the higher component which more markedly affects the pitch of the interval.

MAJOR-MINOR EFFECT IN INTERVALS—A FICTION

Misled by the terms "major" and "minor," many people assume that the major sixth, for example, calls forth a major or joyous affect and the minor sixth a minor or gloomy-feeling tone. It can easily be demonstrated, however, that intervals as such have no major or minor characteristics. Moreover, the major and minor chords, the musical structures which do possess such attributes, are each composed of a major and a minor interval. It would have been far better, therefore, had more writers followed the lead of Alchin and the small number of bolder harmonists who have changed the interval labels from "major" and "minor" to "large" and "small."[13] To term a sixth a "large sixth" or a "small sixth" is to impute to it no characteristic except size of span.

FINALITY EFFECTS

A simple demonstration of the finality effect can be made by running over a succession of *c*'s and *f*'s on the keyboard and asking the listeners for an appropriate stopping point. Among listeners steeped in Western music there will be little argument; the stop will almost invariably be made on an *f*. Yet the vote would have been for one of the *c*'s if the demonstration had been immediately preceded by several renditions of the *c* scale. The repeated playing of this scale with *c* as the first note will make *c* the tonic or keynote, which some have called a "magnet tone." Because of the emphasis on *c*, all melodies ending on this note, or intervals and chords with it as a bass, will seem more restful, more finished, more final. A striking example of repetition can be seen in bagpipe music with its almost continuous sounding of the drone bass. Even an ending that ordinarily is not regarded as at all restful will take on this characteristic of finality if it is listened to as an ending many times.[14] We see here then a principle of return, a desire to come back to an emphasized note.

But the reader may well ask, Why was so much emphasis on *c* needed to make it the more appropriate ending? Why was a stop on *f* otherwise the more final? The answer would appear to depend on the way Western scales are constructed. In the key of *f*, *c* is a perfect fifth above *f*; and the fifth, or dominant, is without much doubt the second most important note of the scale. *C* is the upper boundary note of both the major and minor chords (*f, a, c; f, a♭, c*). On the other hand, *f* is only the subdominant (a perfect fourth above *c*) in the key of *c* and is heard in that capacity far less often than *c* is heard as the dominant in the key of *f*. Hence experience leads us to structure *c*'s and *f*'s with *f* as the tonic with the notes in the key of *f*.

If the listener had heard a succession of unemphasized *c*'s and *g*'s, his inclination would have been to vote for a *c* as the more appropriate ending. This time it is *c* which is the subdominant in the key of *g* and *g* the dominant in the key of *c* (*c, e, g; c, e♭, g*). Therefore *c* is the more likely keynote and gives the better ending.

A second principle which operates in inducing finality effects is that of falling inflection.[15] Just as in many languages the voice rises with an unresolved question and falls with an assertion, so in Western music at least there is a feeling of resolution in the lower tone of a successively played interval or the lowest point of a descending melodic line. This phenomenon has appeared in the data of a host of researchers and is quite possibly linked to the fact, mentioned earlier, that a scale is normally begun from below and is ended as a descent. The effect of falling inflection is enhanced by a slowing of the tempo.

It also appears that size of interval is related to restfulness and finality. Thus Zener has shown that increasing the size of successive intervals from one to eleven semitones rather steadily decreases the finality effect.[16] But with chords the effect of size of span is quite different, for the larger chords may be as restful as or even more restful than the smaller.

Striking finality effects can be obtained by playing a successive interval (or broken chord or melody) where the ratio of the frequency of one of the tones is to that of the other as 2 or some multiple of 2 is to some other number. For example in the interval of the perfect fifth, whose ratio is 2:3, the 2 is the point of more rest. This power-of-2 effect is often termed the Lipps-Meyer law after the eminent psychologists Lipps[17] and Meyer,[18] who first worked in the area and postulated somewhat similar theories to explain the phenomenon.

The factual side of the Lipps-Meyer law is unquestioned, but considerable controversy has arisen over the explanation of what it describes. Is there some neurological or gestaltish reason for the phenomenon which makes it universally applicable, or should it be subsumed under the co-principles of emphasis and return and applied only to certain cultures? Many years ago the present author was inclined to accept a neurological position similar to that of the earlier theorists. In fact, in researches undertaken in the 1920's, he thought he had found lesser but still measurable finality effects associated with the ratio symbol 3, smaller effects with 5, and still smaller effects with 7.[19] In these experiments he had employed stimuli tuned in equal temperament which he hoped would approximate the symbols 3, 5, and 7. A decade later he was able to use tones pitched to just intonation, i.e. with quite exact tuning.[20] But this time these lesser finality effects did not appear.[21] His inability to validate the earlier work strengthened his belief that the neurological factor as reflected in these primes was, if it exists at all, not of major importance in finality effects.

Among those who have attempted to show that the Lipps-Meyer effect is the resultant of cultural conditioning rather than biophysical structure is Updegraff, whose research was arranged to determine whether the conventional resolution of a suggested harmony or the "power of 2" was the more influential in determining finality.[22] The former, she found, appeared to be somewhat stronger. More important perhaps was her discovery that Chinese students regarded

Chinese melodies as more finished and restful while Americans voted for their own melodies. In other words the decisive element for Updegraff's subjects was familiarity, not the pitch relationships of the endings.

Others have found that American-reared Chinese give finality responses much like those of Caucasian Americans. Orientals recently from the coast of China feel the finality effects of our Western music less keenly than American Chinese, while those from the Chinese interior, where our style of music is not so well known, do not share our notions of finality. Because of these racial-national differences in response, it would appear that cultural conditioning is the more likely explanation for the Lipps-Meyer power-of-2 effect. It is conceivable, however, that in addition to the "pulling power" which practice would give the tone symbol 2, there may also be some less important neurological, gestalt, or other biophysical causation.[23]

INTERVAL RESOLUTIONS

Harmony textbooks teach that the successively played intervals that make up the diatonic scale can be divided into those that are "restless" or unresolved and others that have repose and finality. The table below shows the traditional resolutions in the *tonic sol-fa* system. Any other intervals, such as *do-re* or *do-ti,* yield a "restless" or unresolved effect.

RESOLUTIONS	
Tonic Sol-Fa System	*Scale Letter in Key of C*
re to *do*	*d* to *c*
re to *mi*	*d* to *e*
fa to *mi*	*f* to *e*
sol to *do*	*g* to *c*
la to *sol*	*a* to *g*
ti to *do*	*b* to *c*
mi to *do* (rather weak)	*e* to *c*

Over half of the resolutions listed in the table are quite obviously examples of the principle of emphasis and return. Wherever *c* has been sufficiently emphasized to achieve keynote status, all successive intervals ending on *c*, that is, on *do*, will display the finality effect. Thus the descending major second *re-do* and the third *mi-do,* the descending fifth or ascending fourth *sol-do,* and the ascending

minor second *ti-do* all return to the keynote. If scaled in just intonation the intervals can be made to end on 2 or a power of 2 (9
to 8, 5 to 4, 3 to 2, and 15 to 16). These resolutions then can be described in terms of the Lipps-Meyer effect. It is interesting to note
that performers often sharp the *ti* a little, anticipating, as it were, the
resolution. Since the *ti* is a point of great strain it has been termed
the *leading tone,* i.e. it leads immediately to *do.* (It will be recalled
that the ratios of equally tempered scales do not employ such small
numbers. However, they approximate the values given here for just
intonation and can perhaps be described similarly.)

The chief chord in any major key is *do, mi, sol,* which occurs
not only with *do* as the bass but in two other positions as well. In
the first inversion (also called the second position), *mi, sol, do,* the
mi is the bass, and in the second inversion (also called the third position), *sol, do, mi,* the chord is based on *sol.* Hence *mi* and *sol* become
magnet tones, weaker than *do* but effective nonetheless. *Mi* "pulls"
re and *fa* to it and *sol* "pulls" *la.* Of the two, *mi* makes a stronger
ending than the *sol,* since the first inversion with *mi* as its bass is
more used in Western music than the second inversion. It is apparently for this reason that *mi* needs little resolution.

Pinkerton[24] has counted the number of times each note of the
diatonic scale appeared in 39 nursery songs. As might have been expected from our discussion of resolutions, *do* won out with a score
of 16.3 per cent. *Sol* came next with 14.9 per cent, followed by *mi*
with 13.2. These, it will be recalled, are the three so-called magnet
tones. The other percentages were: *re* 11.2, *fa* 6.6, *la* 4.5, and *ti* 3.6.
The rests accounted for the remaining 29.7 per cent.

It would be interesting to speculate about the reactions of
people who had heard music in only minor keys. The expectation
would be that since *me* (*e♭* in the key of *c* minor) would now replace
mi as the much-heard bass of the first inversion of the chief chord
(e♭, g, c), *mi* would no longer display marked finality. But there is
little probability that people will ever be so tonally confined.

TONALITY

So far we have not attempted to define tonality except to point
out that it is a musical expectancy that is culturally and perhaps also,
to a slight degree, biologically derived. Badings defines it: "Tonality is a grouping of tones which occurs in the human perception of
music around a tone-center called 'tonic.' "[25] But does all music
possess tonality?

We note the twentieth-century interest in atonality and we meet much enthusiasm for polytonality, which the layman may erroneously regard as another form of atonality. We are also aware that the Oriental, although perceiving finality in his own music, fails to sense the tonalities of our Western music. If the tonalities are really there, why does he not perceive them?

The Oriental's lack of sensitivity for our tonics simply underscores the point that tonality is, in the last analysis, what one puts into the music. It is a subjective matter. The Oriental, unfamiliar as he is with the Western music system, needs to hear our resolutions over a considerable period of time before he is equipped to appreciate our expectancies. But after a time he can learn to share experiences with us, even as we in time can learn to react "properly" to the nuances of some of the Eastern systems. Musical sensitivities are culturally (but not racially) bound.

In creating his earlier atonal or keyless music, Schoenberg tried to insure that no tone would be emphasized above its neighbors and so acquire keynote status. His method for achieving this atonality barred the repetition of any one of the chromatic scale's twelve tones until the other eleven had all been played. As Schoenberg had hoped, this self-imposed rule yielded music which seemed, at least on the first few hearings, to possess no tonality; it led to no feelings of finality. Yet many persons have saturated themselves with Schoenberg's music to the point where they have begun to read a modicum of tonality into his music. Atonality, regardless of what Schoenberg may have thought, is a relative matter after all.

Milhaud and others have for some time been composing polytonal music. Although to many it sounds keyless, from two to six keys are functioning at once in the several melodies of the musical fabric.[26] Attention to any one melodic line will disclose an obvious tonic. Yet the lay listener may focus his attention on the complex, not on a single strand, so that to him the music is virtually atonal.

Although we speak somewhat carelessly of the evolution of music, it is more accurate to talk simply in terms of cultural changes. We know that "primitives" the world over tend to have more weakly structured music systems and that they have somewhat less feeling than we for Western tonality.[27] Of our own early music we know little or nothing. By the time the records of the Western world were such that its music system could be described with reasonable accuracy, polymodality was already in vogue. But over the years the modes gradually disappeared until only the major and minor remained. Late in the sixteenth century the stage was set for strong tonality as we now know it. Tonality is still with us in spite of the endeavors of the atonalists, but whether it will be with us several centuries hence in its present strength is anyone's guess.[28]

CONSONANCE AND DISSONANCE

Textbooks on harmony state quite arbitrarily that the octave, the fifth, and the fourth are "perfect" intervals and are the most consonant; the thirds and the sixths are not "perfect" but are yet concordant or consonant; while the seconds, sevenths, and all diminished and augmented intervals are discordant or dissonant. These books, however, have little or nothing to offer the student who quite properly asks what makes the minor seventh dissonant or the minor third consonant. The student may know that he prefers the dissonance of the minor seventh to the concordance of the minor third.[29] He may also realize that a musical detective can generally find some musical context in which almost any dissonance will seem highly agreeable. It is clear that the traditional conceptions of consonance and dissonance do not so readily apply to the present, and that there can in fact be no fixed definition of either.

Among the rationalizations offered for the consonance-dissonance classification, the most accepted (perhaps because of the prestige of the theorists) has been that proposed by Helmholtz and even earlier by Sauveur.[30] According to Helmholtz, the consonant intervals are those whose fundamentals and/or overtones are free from the roughness caused by beats.[31] Smoothness, then, is the Helmholtzian criterion of consonance. Krueger has offered a somewhat similar theory of beating difference tones.[32]

It is remarkable how these theories have persisted in the face of numerous refutations. One need only arrange for one of the two tones of the interval to be piped to the left ear and the other to the right to see that all psychological effects are largely unchanged even when the possibility of air-borne beats has been eliminated. Moreover, no beats can be created by the sounding of successively played intervals. Yet even Helmholtz classified these latter just as he did the simultaneously sounded ones. Here is an example of name magic, for an interval without beats is branded as dissonant simply because the same interval with beats is termed dissonant.

Stumpf's theory of fusion can be objected to on somewhat similar grounds.[33] When he says that the consonant interval tends to fuse into a unitary impression which defies analysis, he is quite obviously speaking solely of the simultaneously sounded interval. Successively played intervals can be fairly easily separated into their component tones by the musically untrained as well as the trained, and the listener is almost always certain that he is hearing two tones. But with the simultaneously sounded interval, with the well-fused octave particularly, there may be moments of doubt for many persons.

A theory stressing the unconscious perception of the internal structure of the interval was proposed by Lipps.[34] According to his view, which is essentially a restatement of older theories put forth by Pythagoras and Euler, the consonant intervals are those with simple ratios, and the dissonances those with the more complex ratios. Thus the consonant fifth has the simple ratio of 2:3 and the dissonant seventh the more complex 8:15. A variant of the Lipps theory is that offered by the composer Schoenberg[35] who holds that consonance depends upon distance in the overtone series. Thus the octave is the most consonant because it appears in the first overtone.

There are many difficulties with Lipps's theory and its variants One of the most serious perhaps is its failure to cover the fact that the consonant interval can within limits be stretched or squeezed, and the ratio be made more complex, without an apparent change in the interval quality.[36] If the interval is still recognizable as, say, the perfect fifth, it will be rated as consonant no matter how much larger or smaller it has been made or how complex its ratio has become.

The hypothesis of adaptation, that consonance depends on the number of times one's ancestors and the listener himself have heard a given interval, has been supported both by Ogden[37] and by Moore.[38] Although the two men differ in the details of their theories, they agree in employing in an explanatory sense the once popular but now discarded biological doctrine of the inheritance of acquired characteristics.[39] Hence we shall not consider this aspect of their ideas further except to note that they have both suggested the possibility that consonance is not absolute, fixed once and for all, and that it can be affected by personal experience. If these suggestions were followed, the theorists might then go a step forward, drop the consonance-dissonace dichotomy, and replace it with a continuum. This would indeed be a gain for musical theory.

So far we have considered theories which have identified consonance with smoothness, with fusion, with simplicity of interval ratio, and with stage of cultural and individual adaptation. These four criteria appear to be so dissimilar that one wonders whether their proponents had the same phenomenon in mind. That not all of them did has been quite well demonstrated by several studies in which persons have been asked to judge intervals first in terms of smoothness, then for blending, and later on for fusion.[40] Three quite different sets of judgments emerge. They are so different, in fact, that the early Seashore *Sense of Consonance Test,* whose directions asked for judgments on all three criteria at once, proved quite unworkable and was abandoned.[41] The test subjects became hopelessly confused and ended by rating the intervals in terms of their agreeableness. This settling on some sort of affective evaluation in judging consonance is not limited to contemporary Americans or to the days of the first Seashore music test battery. It can in fact be seen among Europeans even today.[42]

In their studies of consonance, the theorists of the past largely ignored the fact that the human organism is capable of learning. Inherent in their theories was the assumption that a given interval should call forth identical responses in all people regardless of the extent of their musical training. But as Cazden says: "The difficulties in the study of consonance and dissonance dissolve as soon as we realize that these qualities are not inherent in perception as such but are learned responses, adaptations to an existing pattern of the social group."[43]

A successively sounded major third is perceptually different from a simultaneously played third. A major third in a Bach work is quite different from a major third in a whole-tone composition. A major third has a different effect on a Hottentot than on a European theatergoer. A major third is not an abstraction. It is composed of two tones which may be played together or one after the other, which may be played as a part of this composition or that, and which may be heard by a person of our own or some other culture.[44] But to speak of the major third (or of any other interval) as consonant is to do no more than parrot a dogma. Musical science would be the better were this concept dropped from the scholarly literature.

SUMMARY

The music student knows that all but extreme mental defectives and the tone-deaf can readily learn to recognize the several intervals of the diatonic and chromatic scales. What he may not know is that each interval span can within certain limits be stretched or squeezed without harm to its distinctive interval quality. He will find that interval uniqueness is only one facet in the composite of psychological effects on the listener. The register of the interval, the rate and loudness of its playing, the timbre of the instrument on which it is played, and the melodic and harmonic contours it helps to form all have their part in creating what each listener has learned to want. Hence the interval as an abstraction or in isolation has only slight musical significance. What is of real importance is the interval in some specific musical context.

The simultaneous playing of two tones forms, by definition, a simultaneous interval, and the sounding of first one tone and then another a successive interval. When the two tones are rapidly alternated yet still perceived as two tones, a trill is produced. The trill differs from the vibrato in that the latter is heard as a single pitch. The trill then is a successive interval, while the vibrato is perceptually but an ornamented single tone.

Although composed of two easily localized tones, each interval is felt to possess a definite pitch level. If the listener has been trained to "melody hunt" among the higher voices, the top boundary tone is more likely to give the interval its pitch location. But if the listener has been attending to lower registers or is quite unsophisticated musically, it will be the lower boundary tone which provides the pitch.

Intervals possess a number of perceptual characteristics but, although certain intervals are traditionally labeled "major" or "minor," no one of them displays major or minor effects. Such effects appear only as phenomena of chords and modes.

In Western music a number of intervals are regarded as restful, as yielding the effect of finality, whereas others are looked upon as unresolved. Certain theorists tend to be impressed by the fact that wherever the frequency of one tone is to another as 2 to some other integer (as in 200 to 300), a melodic ending on the tone bearing the 2 relationship will call forth the greater feeling of finality and rest in persons steeped in Western music. These men regard finality effects as physiologically engendered even though members of other cultures often fail to find the well-resolved intervals of the West to be restful. Other more sociopsychologically minded theorists have offered habituation as their main explanatory principle. At the moment, however, the issue is still unclear. The formalists[45] and those given to gestalt and biological explanations may be correct in their belief that the human organism is natively geared to feel certain endings to be more restful. But it is a fact that continued experience with a so-called unresolved ending will lead to a growing feeling of rest and finality. Even atonal music becomes somewhat restful in time.

Most theorists and composers are beginning to see that an interval can be evaluated only in terms of its context and that labeling certain intervals consonant or dissonant is a stumbling block to musical creativity and appreciation. No interval is per se unmusical even when it cannot be formed from diatonic or chromatic notes. But since the listener of any culture is to some degree a traditionalist, he must be taught to like the rarely used and the unfamiliar, and these must be presented with caution. Indeed music history is in large part the story of the handling of innovations, of the gradual acceptance of what was once musically unacceptable.

CHAPTER FOUR ✄ *Melody*

ALTHOUGH INTERVALS have great musical significance, one must usually present a somewhat larger configuration of tones before the listener will feel that music as such really exists. At least for the musically unsophisticated the basic element of music is a series of tones he terms a tune or an air. It is what he can recall and name. He tends to regard most other musical phenomena as the tune's embellishments. This chapter will consider in some detail the tune, what musicians call the melody.

Melody, like so many other concepts in music, is very difficult to define. But it is clear that a melody is made up of successively sounded intervals and must have some sort of organization. The nature of that organization has puzzled both the musical theorists and the experimentalists. In the literature is the frequent statement that a melody is a tonal sequence displaying optimum variety within unity. Such a description may have some validity; yet it tells us too little. We still need to know how optimum unity and variety can be identified.

In 1933 G. D. Birkhoff[1] offered a mathematical scheme for assessing unity and variety, and Sir Cyril Burt[2] suggested a somewhat different formula for achieving the same end. Both approaches might seem at first glance to be easy to employ, but the experience of a number of persons including the present writer indicates that they are essentially unusable except for the simplest of aesthetic materials. Beebe-Center and Pratt,[3] who tried out the Birkhoff formula in one set of experiments, have expressed a belief in the usefulness of the scheme but have published nothing further. All in all it seems safe to say that the formalistic approaches of Birkhoff and Sir Cyril have not captured the interest of any substantial number of aestheticians.

The formalists attempt to state their definitions entirely in terms of tonal configurations. Certain tonal sequences, they say, are by their very nature properly unified and show optimum variety. There are more than a few formalists who feel that intuition tells them what is proper and optimum, but the majority fall back on the practices of their favorite composers. Only what approved eighteenth- or nineteenth-century composers regarded as properly melodic can be accepted. These formalists would freeze music at one of its periods. When they are reminded that musical practices are in the process of continual change, they either hold firmly to the rules followed by the earlier elite and frown upon later composers, or shift models with the thought that absolute principles are only gradually revealed. Absolutes, they say, are implicit in the tonal stimuli and so are fixed and eternal. But man must search them out with the expectancy of only partial success.

The relativistic position, the one accepted by most social scientists, favors a definition in terms of human learning.[4] It holds that a listener comes to regard a sequence as forming a unity only through hearing it over and over again or because it resembles some already accepted melody. Not every sequence of course will have the chance of repetition. For all of us live in a social organization which brings to our attention certain sequences and ignores, if it does not actively frown upon, others. But culture is never static. As it changes, its sanctions change. Hence what was once regarded as properly unified and optimally varied may later be thought of as hackneyed, and what once had too much variety may eventually take on unity.

Many years ago Emerson, employing intervals smaller than our semitones, constructed what might be called microscopic melodies.[5] The sequences seemed to possess little tonality as the musician of the West knows the term. Yet Emerson's subjects learned to regard these unusual patterns as unified and to develop certain expectancies concerning them. Emerson had in effect established a tiny musical subculture. Another researcher, Werner,[6] has shown that after a sequence is once accepted as a melody, it can be drastically changed without complete loss of identity. His procedure was to reduce all intervals proportionately until they were of microtone size. Somewhat similar in aim was the study by White[7] who distorted well-known songs but kept them in the conventional scale. He did such things as multiply the intervals by a positive integer, subtract or add an integer, or make certain nonlinear transformations. This last-mentioned change made the recognition most difficult, but even here the correctness was above the chance level.

A melody then seems best defined in terms of learning. Like any other pattern we learn to recognize, a melody can stand considerable warping and still preserve its identity. It is a personal thing, a matter of expectancy. Theoretically speaking, any sequence of tones could conceivably constitute a melody for some culture group. But at any one time and place only a fraction of the many possible will receive official approval. In spite of this, the nonconformist will persist in experimenting with unapproved patterns until, for him at least, these become melodies. The extent to which the radical can convince others that they should accept these sequences is a mark of his greatness.

PRINCIPLES OF ATTENTION AND LEARNING

Ortmann has shown that the principles of primacy, recency, and emphasis, which educational psychologists have found so helpful, also hold for melodies.[8] First and last notes he found to stand out prominently. They often become focal centers for the melody and aid the listener in his quest for unity and coherence. The highest and lowest notes were also seen as attention-getting. Moreover, any one of the remaining notes of the melody could, he found, be made equally or even more prominent by giving it more loudness or emphasizing it in some other way.

Ortmann's conclusions can easily be verified by analyzing responses to Seashore's *Measure of Tonal Memory*.[9] In this test three- to five-note sequences are played twice, with one of the notes changed on the second rendition. The task is to recognize the change. It might be guessed that the three-note melodies would always be the easiest to remember and the five-note the most difficult. But the problem is not so simple, for the difficulty in recall is in part a function of the prominence of the note which has been altered. Altering the first or the last tone, or the highest or the lowest, may produce a conspicuous change in the tonal configuration regardless of the number of tones in the sequence.[10]

The principle of frequency is one of the most important principles in melody formation. The themes of the musical radical who is composing in some new and unfamiliar idiom seem tuneless, i.e. unmelodic, until they are heard a number of times. The layman who is forced to listen to such material may cry for the good old-fashioned melodic music of the past, without realizing that some of what he now calls melodic music his great-grandfather once described as tuneless. Repeated hearing over the years has led to acceptance and with it the feeling that this kind of melody now possesses adequate unity and coherence.

Many American laymen and psychologists are hard put at times to understand why so many musical theorists seem so blind to the importance to their art of the principle of frequency, ignoring so completely the function of learning. The explanation appears to be that music theory stems pretty largely from European philosophy which was long dominated by the great formalist Kant. This or that is so, said the formalists, because *inherent* in the *stimulus configuration* are the qualities that make it this way. The formalists ignore the possibility that reasons may lie in frequency of association, in cultural inheritance.

The present author quite obviously does not hold to the formalistic position. He feels that many, perhaps even the majority of, explanations necessary for understanding the phenomena of music must be looked for in the habits of the listener, in what he has learned from his personal and culture history.

MELODY AND PITCH LEVEL

Now and again one may hear of a small child who, after hearing his customary evening lullaby, will complain that "Mama didn't sing my song tonight." Mama of course will insist that the song was the same as on previous nights. And so it was, except that it was sung at a pitch level slightly higher or lower than the usual one. For this child and for a tiny fraction of the population, precise pitch level is an important part of melody. A melody whose *do* has customarily been pitched at, say, 440 cycles will for this extremely small number of persons be psychologically different if *do* is perceptibly raised or lowered.

There was a time when most of the authorities considered the ability to play on command any desired pitch or to identify pitch level (termed "absolute" or "positive" pitch) the resultant of some Mendelian principle of inheritance and an infallible index of musical precocity. But the facts of the case are not quite as the early theorists described them.[11] We now know that no person can identify by letter with complete accuracy every tone given him or can sing or play with absolute correctness any demanded pitch. Varying with a number of circumstances, his accuracy will probably be better for tones whose timbre he knows best. It will for example be good for piano tones (exceptional ability here is termed "absolute piano") and poorer for the purer tones from a tuning fork or some laboratory instrument.[12] It will be better for tones in the middle range, in the registers most used in music. It will be poorer for the lesser used black than for the more employed white keys.

A small boy of five, who was studied in the Stanford Psychological Laboratory, began while still in kindergarten to notice the pitch level of his mother's songs and to "correct" her when her *do*'s were as little as a semitone away from their accustomed pitch level. At this age, however, he could not make such fine discriminations with piano tones, even with those of his home instrument. But in about two years he showed great skill when tested on his own piano, and in another year's time he could do as well on the very different laboratory piano. Still later his skill became phenomenal with violin and clarinet tones. Here we see a growth in pitch-level skills paralleling growing experience with a variety of timbres.

Pitch level skill among musicians appears to be distributed in a continuous fashion, not dichotomously. That is, there are musicians who are very poor in this ability, others who are poor, average, or moderately good, and still others who are very good. Persons claiming absolute pitch generally display more skill in recognizing pitch level than do other musically minded persons who make no such claims. Yet the overlap in ability between those willing to claim the ability and the more modest is large.[13] Without practice the high scorers usually decrease in skill. Those lower in ability can vastly improve their status with assiduous practice.[14]

After hearing a pitch of 256 cycles frequency, most of us could play or sing a 512-cycle pitch with reasonable accuracy. Or if given some kinesthetic cue, if allowed to probe for the lowest or highest note we can sing, some of us could roughly figure where 512 should be. But we definitely would need some sort of reference point. We would be reacting in terms of relative, not absolute, pitch, or so said the early writers. In absolute pitch, on the other hand, there is no need for auditory or kinesthetic reference points, for the reactions are allegedly "intuitive"; the faster they are, the more accurate they will be.

The reader may still be convinced that absolute pitch is a matter of biological inheritance.[15] Such a stand is in line with that taken by the majority of European psychologists who have been largely trained to think in Kantian nativistic terms, while their American peers more generally favor learning as the chief causative factor. Perhaps then it is his American heritage which, in part at least, forces the present author to feel that absolute pitch is either an extreme and early-learned form of relative pitch or, if it and relative pitch are qualitatively different, that at least both are greatly dependent on training of some sort.[16]

The notion that relative and absolute pitch are somewhat different, qualitatively speaking, is favored by Aizawa[17] who has demonstrated that schoolchildren do not necessarily display more absolute pitch facility as they mature yet are prone to become more skilled in relative pitch. It may well be, as Jeffress[18] has suggested, that absolute pitch ability can best be thought of as the result of early training similar to the imprinting of baby ducks and other young animals. A number of writers have speculated that, because relative pitch rather than absolute pitch judgments are more often reinforced in our culture, much of the absolute pitch behavior young children may possess is gradually trained out of their learning patterns.

It is a fact familiar to all psychologists that in learning a motor skill an individual at first makes use of a variety of cues or crutches.[19] As the skill improves, less and less attention will be paid these cues. By the time the person has achieved real mastery over his task, he can and does forget his earlier aids. In fact, if he tries to use them, he will be likely not only to slow his performance but seriously to harm its quality. He does his best if he behaves in an unthinking, "intuitive" fashion. Thus it is with the formal learning of absolute pitch.

Many years ago the author improved his own accuracy in recognizing Violin A (440 cycles) to the point of approximately an eighth-tone error. At first he found it necessary to hum the lowest note he could manage, taking this note as a point of reference to "figure" the Violin A position. After many weeks of effort, the need for the audible humming disappeared, but for a time he still needed to imagine the humming. Later this need also vanished and Violin A could be sung immediately or the A string of the violin could be tuned without outside reference.

It has been said that many "primitives" possess absolute pitch. While this claim has not been adequately verified, it is reasonable to suppose that a person whose tonal experiences were confined to a *do* of constant pitch would rather quickly develop a relatively good feel for pitch level. Certainly better pitch-level responses should be expected more in an area where all persons agree on the pitch setting of Violin A than in another area where a variety of standard pitches are used. Many German schools do not teach the movable-*do* system so common in America. They follow the "tone-word" method which, by assigning a singable name to each tone of the chromatic scale, gives a more nearly absolute frame of reference.[20] It is not surprising that children so taught make fewer errors in pitch level.

So far we have not delimited the term absolute pitch. Seashore would reserve it for abilities with errors of a tenth of a semitone (10 cents) or less.[21] Bachem's criterion is almost as stringent.[22] Still others would allow a much greater margin of error, since persons who make errors of only 10 cents no longer seem to exist! It is likely that the earlier workers thought their subjects to be far more skillful than they actually were. At any rate no census of the general population has ever been made to find the percentage possessing absolute pitch. If one is ever undertaken it is obvious that the figures can be made large or small depending on the strictness of the criterion adopted for absolute pitch.[23]

It is safe to conclude that only a person extremely interested in pitch level or one who has been indoctrinated with the notion that each melody has its "proper" key will be greatly upset by melody modulations of small magnitude. The great majority of us think musically in terms of intervals, not single tones of fixed pitch. Therefore, unless a melody is raised or lowered to a relatively unmusical register, its basic characteristics will not be greatly affected by changes in pitch level.

Pitch range also has its psychological importance. Thus when Silbermann and a team of associates[24] queried persons in some 42 Parisian dance halls, it was found that people of age 30 or more preferred compositions with a tonal range fairly well restricted to the middle or lower registers, while younger persons desired ranges which included many notes from the higher registers. Silbermann has also shown that, other things being equal, the listener tends to react against music whose pitch range is not somewhere near his own vocal range.

Believing that a Violin *A* of 444 cycles gives a more brilliant tone than the more commonly accepted 440 or 435, the officials of the Boston Symphony Orchestra have for many years used this higher reference pitch. That the effect is perceptibly more brilliant is, however, questionable. Over the past two hundred years or so the musicians of the Western world have set Violin *A* at pitches ranging from 422 to 455 cycles, usually rationalizing their choices by claiming better psychological qualities for the pitch reference they are employing at the moment.

MELODY AND LOUDNESS

Melodies with unconventional skips and harmonies are noticeably less bizarre when played at low intensities. No doubt increases in loudness call attention to what otherwise would tend to slip by unnoticed. Dynamic contrast often can be shown to be a major factor in ratings of the overall excellence of band and orchestral performances.[25]

The table below shows a typical set of preferences obtained from college students for intervals based on Middle C.[26] Note that by and large the softer renditions are the more preferred.

RELATION OF LOUDNESS TO INTERVAL PREFERENCE

1	4th soft	13	minor 3rd soft	25.5	4th loud
2	major 3rd soft	14	major 6th loud	25.5	minor 6th loud
3	octave soft	15.5	major 6th medium	27.5	tritone loud
4	tritone soft	15.5	octave medium	27.5	minor 7th loud
5	minor 6th soft	17	4th medium	29	minor 3rd loud
6	minor 7th soft	18.5	major 7th soft	30	major 2nd loud
7.5	major 6th soft	18.5	minor 6th medium	31.5	major 7th medium
7.5	major 3rd medium	20	5th medium	31.5	minor 7th medium
9	5th soft	21.5	major 2nd soft	33	minor 2nd loud
10	tritone medium	21.5	octave loud	34.5	major 2nd medium
11	major 3rd loud	23.5	5th loud	34.5	minor 2nd medium
12	minor 3rd medium	23.5	minor 2nd soft	36	major 7th loud

If made sufficiently loud, a pitch in the middle register may appreciably change in apparent pitch. While estimates differ, one good experimentalist claims to have observed a change as large as a minor third.[27] Ordinarily an increase in the loudness of a low- or middle-register vocal tone tends to increase its pitch, of a very high tone to decrease the pitch. Soft tones are generally flatted.[28] The blaring discordance then may, because of its extreme loudness, have pitch relationships slightly different from those the composer intended. Indeed it is conceivable that on very rare occasions the shift in pitch might lead to less discordance.

Much that is invalid has been written about the control of loudness in playing the various musical instruments. There is for instance the assumption on the part of many piano teachers that an almost infinite number of tone qualities can be elicited simply by varying the way in which the fingers strike the piano keys. But Ortmann[29] and others have shown that the mechanics of piano action allow for very little tone variation. The few effects that do obtain are made possible through hammer velocity, impact and hammer noises, and pedal—nothing else. Most of the effects allegedly brought about by striking the keys in various ways are illusory.

As anyone with only a passing acquaintance with the modern

piano knows, there are at least two and sometimes three foot pedals. These are the sustaining or loud pedal, the soft, and, particularly in American-made instruments, the sostenuto. Scores for pedal effects like those for intensity generally are in a rather primitive state. Even so it is surprising that professional pianists are in so little agreement as to the "proper" use of the pedals. Heinlein, who did extensive research in this area, found marked disagreements among the performances he examined.[30] As a matter of fact, no performer he studied was able even to duplicate the pedal performance he himself had made ten minutes earlier. Heinlein found music teachers to have little precise knowledge of just what the pedals can and cannot do.

It should be noted that performers do not follow their pitch scores exactly. They intentionally (and unintentionally) sharp and flat slightly and they employ a variety of melodic ornaments. Yet these deviations from the pitch scores are relatively slight. "Inaccuracies" in intensity control, on the other hand, are far more extensive. With intensity-score indicators so crude and knowledge of finger and pedal possibilities so meager, it is no wonder that the control of loudness often mirrors the idiosyncrasies of the performer more than it does those of the composer.

Because of terminological inadequacies it is difficult for the musician to designate a particular loudness. There is available, however, a unit of loudness, the phon, which appears to be enjoying some use. The number of phons is equal to the number of decibels a tone of 1,000 cycles is above the reference intensity when judged equal in loudness to the tone in question. The phon is approximately the smallest increment of loudness that can be noticed under ordinary circumstances. The table below gives some idea of the average loudness of various noises.

Type of Noise	Phons
Loud thunder or painful sound	120–130
Riveting machine 35 feet away	102
Pneumatic drill a few feet away	90–100
Conversation	60
Quiet suburban street	40
Quiet whisper	20

The contemporary conductor Leopold Stokowski is said to interpret his scores as follows:

ppp = 20 phons	p = 55 phons	ff = 85 phons
pp = 40 phons	mf = 65 phons	fff = 95 phons
	f = 75 phons	

MELODY AND TIMBRE

It is unfortunate that authorities write at times as though a perfect fifth, a minor chord, or a melody will have identical characteristics whether sung or played on a marimba, a harmonica, a tuba, or an old Cremona violin. They are neglecting the differences in timbre, the constellations of partial (harmonic and inharmonic)[31] tones each voice or instrument adds to the fundamental tones.[32] The tuning fork and certain organ pipes will yield the purest, simplest tones one can meet outside an acoustics laboratory, for their tones are relatively free of overtones. The air columns around them vibrate largely at only one frequency for each pitch. But orchestral instruments by and large give very impure tones. In some, certain of the overtones even match the fundamentals in loudness.[33]

Flute tones and soprano voices are relatively pure; tones from soft horns, soft male voices, pianos, and strings are richer and more complex; tones from woodwinds (except the flute), loud male voices, and loud brass (in this order) are still more complex and may be described as brilliant, cutting, blaring, or even strident. The tones of the clarinet emphasize the uneven-numbered partials and are usually regarded as hollow and nasal.[34] Melodies in a low register have richer quality than those of high pitch.

Many of us associate melodies of bagpipe timbre with things Scottish, the fife-drum combination with the military, the oboe family with the Oriental world, and the pipe organ with church. To many people the music of woodwinds sounds "whimsical" while the tones of the brass family seem "majestic."[35] Because we in the Occident often associate the male falsetto with buffoonery, a serious melody sung in falsetto may lose much of its serious quality. Yet for the Cantonese whose classical stage employs no female voices, the male falsetto replaces the female voice and so warrants serious listening.

There are those who feel that music should always be played precisely as its composer played it. To these people it is a sin to play Bach on a modern organ or to arrange his music for the present-day orchestra. One can only wonder how many of these conservatives really prefer Bach on the baroque organ and how many are victims of their own intellectualizing. However, there is no question but that the psychological effects of Bach's polyphony depend in some degree on the type of organ employed.

It is a bit disheartening to find that as one grows older the timbre of what is heard progressively changes. The human ear becomes gradually deafer, especially for tones in the highest registers, and the higher overtones cease to be heard. The average thirty-year-old hears almost as well as he did a decade earlier, but the man fifty years of age is likely to be appreciably deafer, particularly for tones of 2,048 cycles and above. By seventy years the deafness may extend as low as the 1,024-cycle level.[36]

Another way of looking at this age decrement is to compare the hearing of several age groups at one pitch level, say at 8,192 cycles. In the decade from the early twenties to the early thirties there is little change, but by age forty there is often a ten-decibel loss. The testable loss tends to grow to approximately 25 decibels by age fifty and to more than 40 decibels by age sixty.[37] These loudness losses have little relevance to the hearing of the melody's fundamentals, but they bar the older person from hearing the full richness of the overtone matrix.

Many instruments have important resonance areas in the higher pitch reaches. The partials in these areas are lost to the older listeners. In consideration of these hearing losses we should perhaps be more considerate toward crotchety old music critics. When one such critic maintains that the tones of a certain orchestra or virtuoso performer are not so full and rich as they once were he is quite correct; for to his aging ears the tonal mass truly is less rich. What he fails to realize is that the time has come for him to leave to his younger colleagues the evaluation of tonal effects.

We saw earlier that the "timbre effects" elicited from the playing of old Cremona violins are in part illusory. There are other situations where the alleged timbre effects are better attributed to some other sense than the auditory. An instance of this sort concerns what is said to be the coldness of Heifetz's violin performances. In one study[38] it was first demonstrated that Heifetz is indeed regarded as one of the coldest of concert performers. But whenever his recorded performance of a particular composition was compared with another's recording of the same piece it was frequently the latter's playing that was rated as the colder. Morini and Elman were thought to be quite definitely colder, and Totenberg and Milstein at least as cold. Only Szigeti seemed occasionally less cold. Of course in these experiments the listeners were *not* told the names of the violinists. It would appear, then, that the Heifetz coldness is probably due to the visual effects of his stiffer posture and/or lack of facial expression. Since Heifetz's manner of playing looks colder, we imagine that it also sounds colder.

In addition to the harmonic partials (tones twice, three times, four times, etc. the frequency of the fundamental) inharmonic over-tones can also be detected in musical effects. Thus Fletcher and his colleagues[39] have demonstrated that for a piano tone of 27.5 cycles the thirty-third overtone is sharp from the harmonic series by as much as four semitones. These researchers believe that it is this lack of harmonicity that gives the piano its characteristic quality, especially for the low-pitched tones below Middle C. If these inharmonic overtones were not present much of the lively piano-like timbre would be lost. They also point out that the starting and stopping characteristics of a piano tone must be considered under the caption of timbre or perhaps sonance.

MELODY AND SONANCE

Tone quality and timbre appear as synonymous terms in most musical treatises. But as Metfessel points out, timbre usually refers only to *instantaneous* pictures of the sound complex.[40] Under the broader caption of tone quality must also be considered the *progression* of the complex for which Metfessel has coined the word "sonance." Sonance, as the term is now used, refers to the progressive changes and fusions which take place within the tone from moment to moment. Like timbre, sonance furnishes a setting for melody and can greatly affect its psychological characteristics.

The most worked-over area of sonance is that of the vibrato, a melodic ornament described elsewhere (Chap. 1). It will be recalled that in employing the vibrato the singer or instrumentalist varies his tones periodically from those of the score. Sonance also appears in nonperiodic and erratic tone fluctuations.[41]

C. E. Seashore has been much impressed by the fact that a melody is never sung or played precisely as scored. The introduction of the vibrato and of glides and the intentional sharping or flatting of tones illustrate how the performer can stamp his individuality on the music. Seashore has generalized from these data to the point of formulating an aesthetic rule: Beauty lies in artistic deviation from the rigid and regular. He has offered the analogy of the photograph which, with its too faithful copying of an object, is not so highly rated as the less representational painting. But whether or not the deviation principle should be elevated to the position of an artistic law, we must agree that the "horizontal" impurities of the vibrato and of the erratic and the nonperiodic fluctuations of tone are, musically speaking, extremely important. Sonance then must be considered along with those "vertical" impurities we term timbre.

MELODY AND NOISE

We have seen that a melody shows different psychological characteristics when it is played on instruments of dissimilar timbre. Noise too attaches itself to melody and aids in the creation of most musical experiences. Noise has been defined as "a sound either so complex, or so irregular, or both, that it seems to have no tone when heard by itself."[42] There is no definite boundary between noise and tone, for experts can sometimes detect a pitch while laymen hear only a conglomerate of unpitched sounds.

The rubbing of the bow, the tapping of the fingers on piano keys[43] or on the fingerboard of a violin, the hissing of the breath in playing the flute, and the plucking sounds necessary to harp-playing all serve as excellent examples of noise in music. As Ortmann[44] points out, it is the noise component which occurs at the beginning and end of a violin tone which largely differentiates the playing of a Kreisler from that of a mediocre violin student. Contrary to the belief of some, noise is not unpleasant per se, nor is it to be avoided at all costs. On the contrary, it is often deliberately sought to give pleasure.

That beating effects add to the fullness of tonal experience can be observed by listening to the pipe organ. This versatile instrument assigns more than one pipe to each pitch but does not achieve for them precisely the same pitch. The beats so created help to give the pipe organ its characteristic quality, an effect which is much missed in the thinner sounding and more exactly tuned electric organ. There are organs which achieve the effect of massiveness and awe by possessing pipes whose frequencies are below the human threshold of audition. While these slow periodicities cannot be heard as tones, they can be felt as building vibrations and sometimes heard as faint rattlings.

The violinists in a symphony orchestra do not and should not play exactly in unison. The beats their tonal divergencies yield give a richness to the musical sound. Were they all playing precisely on pitch, the only gains from hearing more than one instrument would be a mere increase in the loudness and some broadening of the timbre. Another example of the aesthetic utility of beats can be seen in Balinese gamelan music. Here gongs are traditionally arranged in pairs (termed the male and the female). Each pair member is tuned a few cents off from its mate. This technique of tuning creates the shimmer effect so characteristic of gamelan music.

The modern orchestral composer often feels the need for more noise effects than the traditional instruments can provide. He may excite and shock his audience with his use of apparatus which yields rhythmic grunts, siren wails, noises usually associated with the factory, and even more unusual sounds. The late Henry Cowell, a leading composer of midtwentieth-century American music, has put noise to work in his piano compositions. His plucking sounds arise from a harplike picking of the piano strings. An eerie, wailing effect comes from a light stroking or massage of the strings. Following Dandrieu, who in the early 1700's expressed the cannon's roar by striking the lower harpsichord notes with his fist, Cowell developed with great precision "tone-clusters" where the fist, the flat of the hand, or even the entire forearm simultaneously depressed all or many of the keys it could encompass. Cowell's techniques were especially effective for program music.

MELODY AND TEMPO

It is a matter of common observation that the tempo or speed with which a melody is played is often an index of its function. A composition set to walking speed may well be a march, another at very slow speed a dirge, and still another at some intermediate speed a waltz. As we shall see in the next chapter, the tempo of a melody is an important determinant of its activeness, of whether it is reacted to as major or as minor.

Some years ago a Duo-Art player-piano, made by the Aeolian Corporation, was used in an attempt to learn if college students had one specific tempo well fixed in mind for waltz time.[45] The subjects were blindfolded and told to move back and forth a large speed lever until the playing of the composition they were hearing was at the rate they deemed proper. The lever settings given by this group were generally in the neighborhood of 116 quarter-notes to the minute, just what the Aeolian Corporation regarded at that time as proper. The fox-trots were usually set at a considerably faster tempo —approximately 143.

Further research on dance tempo was carried on six years later by Lund with a similar sample of college students.[46] Lund found that faster speeds were by this time considered proper, 139 for the waltz and 155 for the fox-trot. Lund noted that many dance-orchestra leaders recognized two waltz times, a slower one that approximated the value uncovered in the earlier study and the so-called concert or faster style whose tempo was about the figure his subjects considered proper. The fox-trot also had several tempo variants, of which two, the Charleston and the Black Bottom, had considerable popularity for a time. These studies point to the possibility of a sort of "absolute tempo" derived from years of dance experience.

Conductors and performers often alter the tempo in order to develop some particular effect. In one movement of the *Eroica Symphony (The Funeral March)*, Beethoven's own marking was set at 80. Koussevitzky cut the speed to 74 for his conducting, Beecham to 62, and Toscanini to 52. Wagner once complained that the *Tannhauser Overture* took twelve minutes under his own baton but as long as twenty under certain other conductors. There is also the possibility, often mentioned but never proved, that the tempo of a composition set by the composer is correlated with his walking speed while the performance tempo is related rather to the walking speed of the conductor or performer.

Music seems to have more than its share of nomenclature difficulties. Confusion abounds in this tempo area where terms such as time, tempo, periodicity, takt, true beat,[47] and rhythm are variously defined. In the next section we shall discuss the relation of melody to rhythm. The reader should be warned that other authors might have included portions of the discussion on rhythm in this section on tempo. But although tempo and rhythm are obviously very closely related, they are by no means identical.[48]

MELODY AND RHYTHM

Rhythm is more than the periodicity resulting from the continuous repetition of a simple sequence such as *do, re, mi, fa, do, re, mi, fa,* etc. To elicit rhythm, one element in the sequence must be emphasized in some way to make it stand out from its fellows. If the *do* tone alone were made more intense, if it were held longer than any one of the others, or if it were somehow made qualitatively unique, say given a very different timbre, then the sequence would possess what has been termed objective rhythm.

All three of these modes of emphasis are used in music, often simultaneously. The pianist, in striking more strongly the first note of a rhythmic pattern, not only makes the tone louder but automatically alters its timbre slightly as well. Unwittingly he also breaks the regularity of his timing and tarries longer than he thinks he does on the stressed tone.[49] Thus in trying to use intensity as a means of emphasis the pianist has also employed both timbre and timing to create his rhythms. The organist of course cannot so easily control his intensity relationships and must depend more on timing in his attempts to bring about emphasis.

Rhythms serve the listener by increasing his perceptual span, dividing up patterns of melodic material so that larger units can be more readily grasped. When the rhythmic emphasis is on the important positions of the scale, e.g. on the tonic, dominant, etc., the tonality structure is made more obvious and the listener's anticipations are whetted. By shifting the accent to a tone which is normally not accented in a given rhythmic pattern, that is by syncopation, the listener's anticipations are strengthened even more and the intensity of the adjacent time-keeping beat is intensified.[50]

The most obvious gift rhythm brings to music is its invitation to motor activity. This activity may reach only the covert stage with movements too slight to be casually observed, or the rhythms may induce overt nodding, foot tapping, and still other activities, such as often occur while jazz music is played.[51] The early church, with its stress on contemplation rather than on action, looked askance at rhythm and endeavored to eliminate it as far as possible.[52] The earthy, activity-inducing quality of rhythm is well demonstrated in work music. Simple labor, such as that of unskilled workmen passing heavy loads down a line, is made easier because of the highly rhythmic chanties they sing. And although many lay dancers pay little or no attention to the rhythm of the music to which they are dancing, the more skillful do dance in time with the music and are guided by it.

Combing through the work of the past, Mursell has tentatively concluded that there are only seven unit groups among the musical rhythms.[53] In the table below, the dash designates the emphasized element in each case. The reader can readily find illustrations of the iamb, trochee, dactyl, and probably the amphibrach, although the last is much the least frequent. Handel's *Dead March* from *Saul* illustrates the single beat, and Chopin's *Opus 53* the tremolo. Lundin offers the rumba as an example of the anapest.[54]

UNIT GROUPS IN MUSICAL RHYTHMS

— accented, ∪ unaccented

∪	—		Iamb	∪ ∪ —		Anapest
—	∪		Trochee	∪ — ∪		Amphibrach
—	∪	∪ Dactyl		∪ ∪ ∪		Tremolo
		| — | — |	Single Beat			

According to the experimentalist Dunlap, music with short rhythmic units tends to possess a joyous quality and that with longer units seems more somber.[55] It would appear, however, that Dunlap is referring less to rhythm than to tempo, and we have already noted that faster music seems more active or major, while slower tunes appear more somber or minor. The available evidence indicates that the affects given melody by rhythm depend very much on either cultural conditioning or personal experience. In our culture we do not rush a corpse to its grave but carry it slowly and with measured tread. Hence rhythms with single beat may seem funereal. Infantrymen usually favor one or the other foot, so the trochee may well take on a march flavor. Other illustrations of our associations could be gathered, but they would be somewhat different from those of a people of an alien culture.

We have already commented on the fact that Western music has specialized, so to speak, on the rather simple rhythmic patterns— the 2-beat, 3-beat, 4-beat, and to a lesser extent the 6 and 8. The 5 and 7 occur so rarely that laymen are usually ignorant of their existence and fail to appreciate them. These rarer rhythms do occur in the Orient and could enjoy more use in the West if dances or drills were devised which forced movements in these patterns. Modern jazz composers occasionally seem willing to try at least the 5-beat rhythm.

It is fortunate that the ability learned by one set of muscles "crosses over" in some degree to other sets. A rhythmic pattern, say a 5-beat one, learned through drill with the right hand, is in actuality learned by the entire organism. The left hand, either foot, or in fact any mobile part of the body can beat out the rhythm. After the pattern has been thoroughly mastered it can be superimposed, as it were, upon a sequence of events which physically has only periodicity. Such a superimposition is termed "subjective rhythm." A person asked to hear a metronome beat first in 2-beat rhythm, then in 3- and later in 4-beat can readily do as requested even when he knows that there is no rhythmic pattern in the physical stimuli. But he could not hear a 5-beat rhythm unless of course he had had considerable contact with 5-beat music or had been subjected to laboratory drill with this rhythm. If a melody possesses a strong and familiar objective rhythm, the listening is in terms of that rhythm. But if the objective rhythm is very weak, the listener may supply his own subjective rhythm.

A number of the early missionaries to Africa brought back the surprising tale that the natives seemed poor in rhythms and often beat randomly on their drums. Since drumming was a sort of telegraphy as well as musical behavior and so was a highly skilled activity, such a report did not seem very reasonable. More careful observations proved the missionaries to have been quite mistaken. These later studies showed the rhythmic patterns to be extremely precise but too complicated for Western-trained laymen to follow. The African drummers, it was found, were simultaneously tapping in several patterns, i.e. 2 against 3, 3 against 4, 2 against 3 against 5, etc.

Western music has not entirely neglected polyrhythms. They can be observed for instance in MacDowell's *Tragic Sonata* or in Chopin's *Nocturne in D Flat*. Certain twentieth-century composers, notably Henry Cowell, have employed cross- or polyrhythms rather extensively, and composers of several varieties of jazz have traditionally superimposed rhythmic cycles of three beats on the fundamental rhythm of two or four beats.[56] But the majority of conservatories and schools of music offer no special training for their mastery. It is assumed that somehow the student will be able to play these polyrhythms on the occasions he finds the need.[57]

The schools that do teach the handling of polyrhythms employ one of two procedures or some combination of these. The most obvious procedure is the kinesthetic method, by which the hands (or feet) are separately trained in two or more rhythms. This is supposedly the scheme featured by Jaques-Dalcroze in his dance system of eurhythmics.[58] The method was also used by the late pianist Arthur Hardcastle, who on being tested by the author some years ago was found to be very skillful. Hardcastle could tap 2 against 3, 3 against 4, 3 against 5, 3 against 7, and 4 against 7 with less than a 10 per cent error.

A second approach to the mastery of polyrhythms is by counting to oneself the least common multiple (or fraction of this) of the rhythms to be played. For example, in learning to play 2 against 3, one counts from 1 through 6 and taps with one hand on the 1, 3, and 5, and with the other on the 1 and 4.

One Hand		Other Hand
x	1	x
	2	
x	3	
	4	x
x	5	
	6	
x	1	x

Where the multiple becomes large it can be split into parts. When playing 3 against 5, one hand taps on the first and fourth counts of the first group of five, on the second and fifth counts of the second group, and on the third count of the third group. The other hand taps on the first count of each group of five. The composer Henry Cowell was quite adept in his use of this method.

One Hand		Other Hand
x	1	x
	2	
	3	
x	4	
	5	
	1	x
x	2	
	3	
	4	
x	5	
	1	x
	2	
x	3	
	4	
	5	
x	1	x

At Stanford University there has been devised a third, or gestalt, procedure which appears to have an advantage over the other methods in that complicated patterns can be learned almost as readily as the simpler. The scheme necessitates cutting a player-piano roll or pressing a phonograph record. In presenting the polyrhythms, say the 2 against 3, the roll or record is made to offer a succession of tones, say Middle *C*'s, in 2-beat rhythm and a series of some other tones in 3-beat. The learner merely listens and attempts to duplicate what he is hearing at some higher or lower piano register. If the piano roll is employed, the beginner has additional cues from watching the keys as they are automatically depressed.

HARMONY

Singing in unison is undoubtedly as old as music. But when pre-adolescent children and men (or women and men) join in singing the same melody, the natural differences in the lengths of the vocal folds make it easier for the men to sing an octave below the others. The octave span was probably adopted for perceptual reasons as well. Its two tones fuse so completely that the musically untutored often imagine the singing to be all in unison. This confusion is likely to occur less often with any of the other intervals.

Another early breakaway from unison singing came with the drone bass. Here one tone is continuously sung or played for the duration of the melody. In effect the drone becomes a keynote which adds greatly to the stability, i.e. to the tonality, of the musical structure. At times the *sol,* or dominant, is additionally employed as a drone. Nowadays the drone bass is most readily heard in bagpipe music, and the pipe organ has a place for it in the pedal, so called because the foot sustains the drone.

Many of the world's music systems went no further along the road to harmony. Their major innovations were often in rhythmic development, an area in which Western music has done relatively little. But the West, perhaps during the ninth century, took a logical next step in developing the organum in which there were now added, in addition to the octave, voices a fourth below and a fifth above, both moving parallel to the theme. Here then is a type of harmonizing, although one with little variety.

After several centuries the monotony of parallel octaves, fifths, and fourths finally drove composers to the scheme of opposing motions, where two melodies moved in opposite directions. At first the only intervals officially recognized were the same three "perfect" ones, but since the very mechanics of opposing motion necessarily created other intervals, thirds and sixths gradually came into vogue. With these innovations simple parallel motion gradually dropped in favor to the point where later harmonists proscribed its use. It was in fact not until fairly recent times that composers once again dared employ it to any considerable extent.

It is a fact of music that the composing habits of any era tend to become rigidly codified. The rules take on the character of taboos which keep all but the braver composers from experimentation. Yet each great composer establishes his own school by breaking at least a few of the rules which have fettered music up to his time. By this process of breaking old rules and making new ones, simple opposing motion gradually broadened into polyphony in which several melodic stands were simultaneously sung or played. Although polyphony's great rival homophony appeared during the Renaissance and gradually won a dominant position in Western music, it never entirely replaced polyphony. In fact much contemporary music is quite polyphonic in character.

During the heyday of polyphony, any simultaneously sounded interval or chord was more or less a fleeting, fortuitous affair which happened with certain juxtapositions of the several melodic lines. In homophonic writing, however, a single line became the focus of attention and the other parts took on a decidedly secondary aspect. These latter became the clothes, the ornaments, for the melody. The effect was music as the present-day layman hears it. Chords and intervals became important in their own right, and arguments about which ones were allowable were heard. But gradually the harmonic rules changed until, as the reader well knows, almost every chord has by now had its day of glory.

SUMMARY

Although in the past it was taught that, to be a proper melody, a tonal pattern must have inherent unity and coherence, it now appears that the unity is not in the tonal line at all but is literally read in by the listener. It is naturally difficult to feel unity in patterns which are virtually impossible to sing or play. Yet even such tonal contours, if heard sufficiently often, become increasingly familiar so that the hearing of any one of the tones arouses the feeling that this should be followed by the next tone in the sequence. It is this expectancy then that characterizes our conception of melody.[59] Melodies are perceptual phenomena which obey the principles of learning.

Melodies are far more than familiar sequences of tones. To the few persons with "absolute pitch," a melody may appear to change its characteristics if the pitch register is altered by an above-threshold amount. But for the great majority of the musical public, melodies can be modulated freely without much change in psychological effect. Relative and absolute intensities, on the other hand, are important to almost all listeners. Since this is so, it is unfortunate that the staff signs for loudness variations are extremely crude and that the control of loudness changes by vocalists and instrumentalists is incredibly poor. For loudness nuances may make just the difference between the acceptance of a melody or its rejection. Perhaps in the years to come, musicians will develop symbols which will permit more exact notation. It should be noted that finer units of measurement, e.g. phons, already are available to the musician.

Pure tones have no place in music. Indeed each musical culture features a variety of tonal impurities—timbres, sonances (e.g. vibrato), and noises—and trains its public in their appreciation. New timbre effects are accepted slowly and grudgingly. For centuries this conservatism in Western music could be readily excused, but now that the innovator can draw on the almost inexhaustible resources of modern electronics there is less justification for timidity. The job is largely a propaganda one of convincing the public that all worthwhile timbres were not discovered by the old masters.

The older person often imagines that if he turns up the volume of his radio or phonograph he will hear his favorite melodies just as he heard them when he was younger. But deafness tends to be selective, with the higher registers affected earlier than the lower. Hence the elderly miss much of the tonal complex and perceive their melodies as having a less rich timbre. Deafness then is more than a weakness in loudness sensitivity.

Tempo and rhythm often cue the listener to the melody's function. With one temporal arrangement a waltz is indicated, with another a dirge. The proper use of syncopation can whet the auditor's anticipations. Although certain other cultures have made great use of rhythmic complications, the West has not. A few courageous contemporaries have attempted to free their music from the tyranny of the quarter-note by the use of polyrhythms, but music teachers have made little effort to train their students in the execution and appreciation of such "novelties." They fail to realize that they are bypassing a rich source of aesthetic enjoyment.

Slow though the Occident has been in experimenting with rhythmic materials, it has led the world in melodic improvisation. From the stage of unison singing, the West slowly moved to the use of drone basses, the organum, opposed motion, polyphony, and finally to homophony with its chordal structures. It should be noted that music systems do not necessarily evolve. The music of a people may remain relatively static, it may proceed along one line or another, or it may turn back toward an earlier set of forms. The composer's task is to keep his public from satiation, a goal which can be achieved in countless fashions.

In the present chapter we have concerned ourselves largely with the anatomical side of music—with its flesh and bones. We shall continue in the next chapter with our discussions of melody, but there we shall emphasize its more dynamic aspects. Several facets of the language problem will interest us.

❧ *Language Aspects of Music*

WE HAVE ALREADY SEEN that to some people a melody sometimes presents at least a small message. It may "talk about" an eerie feeling, a restlessness, an Oriental atmosphere, a march time, or communicate still other impressions. Granting all this, can it be said that music is a language in any strict sense of the word? To answer this question we must first agree on what we mean by language and then examine the research material of the area.[1] We must also be careful to distinguish between the messages the composer may desire to send and what he actually does send; the messages received by the conductor, the performer, or both and what they in turn may send; and the messages finally received by the listeners.[2]

DESIRE FOR COMMUNICATION

Before the language process can be said to exist, there must be persons who desire to communicate their thoughts and emotions.[3] If this were the only earmark of a language, music would qualify; for many composers, convinced that the world needs their favored religious, economic, political, or other ideologies, feel that they must share their beliefs through the medium of their musical creations. An occasional performer or conductor can be found who believes that he too has a share in the communication process through his unique way of handling musical materials. His thoughts, he insists, add to or modify what the composer has to say. It should be noted, however, that the confidence of composers, conductors, and performers in what they think they can do is no proof that they can successfully employ musical elements as linguistic signs, that they can tell the stories they are so anxious to tell. The matter of success constitutes quite a different problem.

EMBODIED MEANING (GRAMMAR OR SYNTAX)

A second major earmark of language has to do with the formal relations among signs. Every language has its grammar or syntax, its embodied meaning, to use a term given us by L. B. Meyer. So does music, with its detailed rules governing the use of its melodic and harmonic signs. But no grammar is fixed once and for all. The use of "none are" would have been banned without question by any editor a few years ago. Now this phrase commonly gets by on the rationale that frequent usage by well-educated persons eventually comes to mean "acceptable usage." Thus it is with the rules of music. What was not allowed some time ago may now be viewed as acceptable, and some of the presently accepted usages may be frowned on in a later period. It is clear then that the rules of grammar change. Even so, there has been a grammar for every school of musical composition.

Although music by its very nature can arouse imagery of a very personal sort, not all music is intended by composers to point to nonmusical phenomena, to possess designative meaning. An extreme example can be seen in serial music where it is expected that the affective experiences which are elicited will depend largely on the nature and musical background of the listener, on his interest in the grammar of what he is hearing. The more he understands the musical syntax of, say, Schoenberg's music, the more likely it is that the grammar, its embodied meaning, will delight him. Here grammar becomes virtually all-important.[4] At the opposite pole is the grammarless "music" composed by tossing dice or by the use of random numbers. It is conceivable of course that some particular piece of "chance music" may someday develop a devoted following. If this should occur, one might expect that musical specialists will dutifully study its "structure"!

In one sense of the word any composition, except perhaps chance music, has some meaning to persons reared in the culture of the composer. Cazden[5] calls this aspect of meaning "realism," which he defines as "the totality of concrete references to the common experience of human beings as embodied in all the formal elements of musical art." "We cannot leave our social biographies behind in listening to music," he says. *This* phrase has traditionally appeared in waltz music, and *that* snatch in martial compositions. No music then is ever truly pure or "absolute," for its elements possess connotations derived from the musical culture.

It is becoming increasingly popular to measure the amount of information transmitted by a language system in terms of units (termed "bits") more familiar to the communications engineer than to the aesthetician. Articles are beginning to appear in which music is so treated. So far, however, the amount of labor necessary to describe a snatch of music is so astronomical and the conclusions offered up to the present time appear so meager that a detailed account here of the technique would seem unprofitable. Yet in the future, the application of engineering procedures to the riddles of musical grammar may prove of great worth.[6] Already it has proved possible to abstract rules employed by some particular composer, feed them into a digital computer, and in effect create a "new" composition. The resultant may be a "poor" but perhaps recognizable creation in the style of the composer in question who may in fact be long dead.[7]

DESIGNATIVE MEANING

Few but professional musicologists and experts in communication theory take much interest in the grammar of music. It is a highly specialized area to be studied by the historically minded. More attention is likely to be given to the desire for communication. What motivates a composer to create or a conductor or professional performer to reproduce music arouses a deep-seated curiosity on the part of many of us. Yet even motivation and creativity do not as a rule excite as much interest as does the problem of designative meaning, the story that music allegedly tells and the moods it elicits. The remainder of this chapter will be concerned with music's designative meanings.

It has already been suggested that the existence of a desire to send a particular communication does not of itself guarantee that it can be sent. A hungry monkey may wail and screech in his attempts to communicate with his mate in a nearby food-filled cage. While the first monkey may interest the second with his antics, his vocalizations will normally not tell her to give him food. So far as she is concerned, his vocal behaviors are not specifically meaningful although he is obviously striving to make them so. The problem now before us is to see to what extent musicians are communicating and in what degree they, like the hungry monkey, are deluding themselves into believing that others must somehow understand them.

The composers themselves are sharply divided on this issue. At the one extreme stands Stravinsky who has said: "For I consider that music is, by its very nature, essentially powerless to *express* anything at all, whether a feeling, an attitude of mind, a psychological mood, a phenomenon of nature. . . ."[8] Copland agrees only in part when he says: "Heaven knows it is difficult enough to say precisely what it is that a piece of music means, to say it definitely, to say it finally so that everyone is satisfied with your explanation. But that should not lead one to the other extreme of denying to music the right to be 'expressive.' "[9] Mendelssohn stands in complete opposition to Stravinsky. "People usually complain that music is so ambiguous; that it is so doubtful what they ought to think when they hear it; whereas everyone understands words. With me it is entirely the converse. . . . The thoughts which are expressed to me by a piece of music which I love are not too indefinite to be put into words, but on the contrary too definite."[10]

ALLEGED MODE AND KEY EFFECTS

In Grecian times, long before the day of free modulation and tempered scales, a melody was supposed to reflect the unique psychological character of the mode in which it was written. If it was in the Dorian mode with its arrangement of a half-tone, three whole tones, a half-tone, and two whole tones (as in *e, f, g, a, b, c, d, e*), dignity, manliness, courage, and self-dependence were the qualities thought to be expressed. But if the Lydian mode was used, the melodic message was considered one of softness and self-indulgence. Because he believed that hearing the Lydian mode could be harmful to man's character, Plato banned it from his "Ideal Republic."[11] It should be noted that the internal arrangement of the Lydian mode is that of our current major scale!

There is no doubt that there were ancient scholars who heard or at least imagined they heard these psychological (i.e. "meaning") effects. But it is also clear that no person of the present day is apt to be so affected unless he is told what effects he "should" hear.[12] Man is highly suggestible in this area as in many others, and it is not much of a trick to make him "hear" what he should hear.

It is of considerable interest that this notion concerning modal effects persisted even after the modes had been shaken down to two—the present-day major and minor. In fact the idea was further extended to the several keys of the major and minor modes. Thus the key of *f* major was said to be the key of the pastoral idyll (e.g. Beethoven's *Pastoral Symphony*); keys with five, six, seven, eight, or nine sharps made men think of heavenly matters; while the keys of *f* minor and *f♯* minor were the tragic ones. The so-called Lavignac Table of Key Effects associates the key of *d* major with the qualities gay, joyful, and brilliant; *e* minor with sorrowful and agitated; *f* minor with sullen, angry, and energetic; and *a♭* with tender and caressing.

It is not difficult to speculate on how, before the advent of equal temperament, one key or mode was associated with Heaven, another with the farm, and still another with tragedy. For, as was shown in Chapter 2, a melody whose *do* is to *re* as 8 is to 9 (e.g. 800 to 900 cycles) will not sound precisely like one whose *do-re* ratio is 9 to 10 (e.g. 900 to 1,000 cycles). It would have been a simple matter to attach psychological qualities to these differences, but whatever was attached would have been pretty much pure whimsey. Of course there would come in time a codification of the rules of this school of thought. Pastoral music *must* be written in the key of *f* major, the rules would read, and tragic music in *f* minor or *f♯* minor. And all "sensitive" people would begin to "hear" pastoral effects whenever they knew that the key of *f* major was employed.

It may strike the reader as odd that even today there are composers who try to find the "proper" key for their melodic message. For with equal temperament, where *do* to *re* has the same ratio in every key, there is little possibility that key differences of a psychological character can exist. It is true that the listener with absolute pitch may know whether a melody is being played in *e* or *f*, and if he is versed in these traditional expectancies he may feel that the keys are vastly different. Other possible differences arise from differential fingering and from the fact that equal temperament is almost never quite secured by piano tuners. Weak fingers may be given too great a task in certain multi-blacknote keys. But such slight stimulus differences can hardly be expected to yield psychological effects such as those described above. It seems safe to conclude, therefore, that no key (as distinguished from modal) effects of any importance exist for the typical modern listener.

MAJOR AND MINOR MODES

We have already seen that intervals are major or minor only in the sense that the so-called major intervals are of larger span than the minor. Centuries ago these modal labels were erroneously attached to intervals of the major and minor chords where they remained as curiosities of nomenclature. But with chords and melodies there is more reason to apply these terms.

There are three positions of the major chord—in the key of *c* they are *c, e, g; e, g, c;* and *g, c, e*—and all were thought by the early theorists to have something in their structure which aroused in the listener a happy mood. The three positions of the minor chord—in the key of *c* they are *c, e♭, g; e♭, g, c;* and *g, c, e♭*—with their different structure were thought automatically to elicit somber moods. But what in the structures causes these opposing feelings has never been satisfactorily stated. One of the few helpful suggestions has come from Max Meyer,[13] who points out that in the just-intoned scale the major is well balanced with its structure of 4 to 5 to 6 (e.g. 400 to 500 to 600 cycles) in that the tones with cycle symbols 5 and 6 both achieve resolution on the tone of symbol 4. On the other hand, the minor with its 10 to 12 to 15 structure has more ambiguity in that the 15 "points" both to the 10 (3 to 2) and to the 12 (5 to 4). See the discussion of the Lipps-Meyer law in Chapter 3 for an elaboration of this. Meyer has also suggested that the smaller ratio symbols of the major chord may, neurologically speaking, make it more stable.

There may be much of worth in Meyer's suggestions, but two sets of facts have been uncovered during this century which lead to a somewhat broader view than that of the earlier theorists: (1) The ability to distinguish major from minor is not nearly so good as the older statements would have us believe. (2) The structural difference between major and minor chords is not the only variable which suggests "majorness" or "minorness" to the listener. Let us then examine further the findings which cast doubt on the invariance of the correspondence between chordal structure and modal affect.

Shortly before World War I, Valentine, an English psychologist, began to question the idea that a particular chordal or melody structure automatically called forth a particular modal name.[14] His subjects, he found, made many errors in their attempts to separate the major from the minor. About fifteen years later, Heinlein made a similar observation.[15] Heinlein's much more extensive research showed that even his musically trained subjects labeled as minor more than a third of the major chords he presented to them, and labeled major approximately 12 per cent of the minor chords. Furthermore, Heinlein located a number of compositions in a major key which sounded minor to his subjects, and others in minor mode which were reacted to as major. Thus a Sousa performance of Handel's *Largo* from *Xerxes* and the first theme of the largo movement from Dvořák's *Fifth Symphony,* both in major keys, seemed minor; and *Anitra's Dance* from Grieg's *Peer Gynt Suite,* written in minor mode, was described as bright and happy. A Kreisler rendition of his own *Caprice Viennois* was labeled melancholy by many and cheery by many others. Hevner, however, found that her musically trained group and even her relatively untrained subjects usually did rather well in separating the major from the minor melodies (as distinguished from simple chords).[16]

It has been noted that both the whole-tone chord—*c, e, g♯*—and the chief Siamese chord (which is about halfway between our major and minor) tend to be classified incorrectly by American laymen as minor.[17] There seems to be a fairly widespread misconception that whatever is not major must be minor or Oriental. So much then for the invariance of the structure-mood relationship.

Modern research has brought to light other variables which can affect the success with which people distinguish major from minor. The most important of these are loudness, pitch level, tempo, and the temperament of the listener. Thus Heinlein noted that the louder and/or higher-pitched chords seemed more major and the softer and/or lower-pitched ones minor.[18] Possibly because falling is customarily associated with unpleasantness and rising with alertness and achievement, falling intervals call forth more sad than happy affects while rising intervals tend more often to be labeled exhilarative.[19] Flatting and wobbling the thirds and sevenths are tricks employed in the blues and later popular music to induce minor effects. Characteristic of much American Negro music is the alternation of ordinary major thirds and sevenths with "blues" (slightly flatted) thirds and sevenths. This flatting may conceivably be due to the clash of pentatonic and septatonic scale traditions, to the Negroes' earlier difficulties with the diatonic scale and their unwitting attempt to equalize the interval sizes. The two half-steps would be enlarged by flatting the *mi* and the *ti*. Other techniques to create a sad atmosphere are found in some jazz compositions—*Beale Street Mamma,* for instance—where there is an avoidance of the leading tone. The tonic is approached at a cadence through a blues third, the sixth from below, or more rarely the blues third and the second.[20]

That tempo is an important variable can easily be demonstrated if the reader will simply drag the timing of some otherwise major-sounding melody or play rapidly some typical dirge. His classification of what had been a happy-sounding tune will now more likely be minor, and of the erstwhile dirge, major.[21] Another factor leading to atmospheric effects but which is obviously not under the control of the composer, conductor, or performer is the temperament of the listener. Reasonably enough, the person who is characteristically cheerful is far more prone to regard the music he hears as major and cheerful than is his neighbor who sees the world through dark glasses.[22]

We conclude that the problem of identifying the major chord or major melody is far more complicated than was once thought. It is admitted that major chords and melodies are typically employed, in Western culture at least, on joyful occasions, but the relationship is by no means invariant. Moreover, the effect can be nullified by deliberate changes in tempo, loudness, pitch level, or by still other means.

COLOR-TONE LINKAGE

Music has chromatic (i.e. color) notes and a chromatic scale. It also has timbre, which in German is *Klangfarbe,* that is, sound-color. Music has color then in a figurative sense. But is there a further literal sense in which tone points to color? Is there a necessary connection between any particular frequency, interval, chord, timbre, key, or melodic sequence on the one hand and some given color? Many musicians and poets of the past and even an occasional scientist have thought so. The great Newton saw such a connection in the "fact" that both the diatonic scale and his own classification of colors had seven names. But since the days of Helmholtz it has been known that there is no finite number of colors. Newton might just as well have named eight or only four colors. Nevertheless, the idea that there is some inherent connection between color and tone has persisted and has led to the construction of a number of instruments which "play" colors (e.g. the clavilux and several Russian instruments)[23] and sometimes tones as well.

In the table on page 77 are contrasted the key-color associations of two eminent Russian composers.[24] It should be noted that they agree only slightly.

It is the general lack of agreement among those having tone-color associations which attests the absence of inherent connection between the two senses. There is often some similarity among the associations of the members of a family, but this much agreement can be expected because of common family experiences.

That color-tone associations are very common has been shown by many investigations. In one of Omwake's surveys of college students, 60 per cent reported that they had color-tone associations.[25] But less than 1 per cent of the general population has color imagery of hallucinatory intensity when stimulated by particular

Key	Rimsky-Korsakov	Scriabin
C major	White	Red
G major	Brownish-gold, bright	Orange-rose
D major	Yellow, sunny	Yellow, brilliant
A major	Rosy, clear	Green
E major	Blue, sapphire, sparkling	Bluish-white
B major	Somber, dark blue shot with steel	Bluish-white
F♯ major	Grayish-green	Bright blue
D♭ major	Dusky, warm	Violet
A♭ major	Grayish-violet	Purple-violet
E♭ major	Dark, gloomy, bluish-gray	Steel-color with a metallic luster
B♭ major	————	Steel-color with a metallic luster
F major	Green	Red

tonal signals.[26] The behavior of this tiny fraction of our population has been termed "colored hearing," or chromesthesia, one of several possible types of synesthesia.

If one can trust the introspective reports of chromesthetics, it would appear that some see a colored haze whenever they are stimulated by a particular auditory stimulus. Thus when the nineteenth-century musician Joseph Raff heard a cornet, he viewed the world through a greenish haze; the flute produced in him an experience of azure blueness and the oboe yellowness. The trumpet called up a scarlet haze, the French horn purple, and the flageolet gray.

Chromesthetic behavior tends to run in families, but this does not necessarily imply biological inheritance. Chromesthesia occurs most frequently in persons with vivid imagery and is facilitated by fatigue, shock, and the presence of certain drugs (e.g. mescaline).[27] The reactions so far reported are one-way, with color never calling up a tonal hallucination. In chromesthesia higher tones are usually tied to lighter colors.[28] As a rule chromesthetics either cannot recall the date of the peculiarity's first appearance or place it in the years before age 7. They often tend to regard colored hearing as inborn and universal and to look upon those who claim not to have it as insensitive individuals who are not realizing their potentialities. One study shows women to be more often chromesthetic than men.[29] This is of some interest since women typically claim the ability to recall earlier experiences than do men. One Negro woman is recorded as having observed the birth of her chromesthesia at age 3![30]

So far as the author knows, no one has ever been able to induce a true chromesthesia under controlled scientific conditions. Kelly did what he could along this line, even going to the extent of giving his subjects peyote and physical shocks in the hope that these added stimuli might help elicit the effect.[31] But not one of his subjects even after 2,000 associations of tone and color (even 3,000 for one subject) became a chromesthetic. Had his subjects been preschoolers instead of teen-agers and persons in their twenties, it is possible if not probable that Kelly might have created a chromesthetic.

In an ingenious experiment by Howells, subjects were given either a high or a low tone along with a green or a red light.[32] Most of the time the high tone and green light were given together and the low tone and the red, but occasionally the experimenter reversed the pairings. The subjects were told that their jobs depended on doing well and so were strongly motivated. They kept their eyes closed until the tones were heard. Then they examined the lights and quickly named them. Of considerable theoretical interest is the fact that there was a gradual increase in the number of naming errors made at the times of the unusual (high tone/red and low tone/ green) pairings. But whether this rise in the error curve indicates the creation of a chromesthesia or of only a pseudochromesthesia is problematical.

The reason for the presence of chromesthetic behavior in a few persons and its absence in most others is still not known.[33] Anatomical, physiological, and psychological theories have been suggested, but no one theory seems entirely satisfactory. Of course there is the possibility that the correct answer may involve more than one theory. It is conceivable that the chromesthetic is one whose brain structures and/or physiological functions are such that he makes tone-color conditioned responses more readily than do most of us. But he would also need to be a person for whom some accident of environment had allowed the tonal and color stimuli to occur together so that the conditioning could take place and a given tonal configuration could come to "mean" a certain color. Here then is one hypothesis. Whether it is correct or incorrect, the fact remains that no aspect of tone per se has a universal color-meaning.

"LANGUAGE OF THE EMOTIONS"

We have seen that by means of a variety of devices music can be made to play on one's emotions. The fact that it can so act has led an occasional theorist to speak of music as the language of the emotions. But perhaps it is time to consider a warning sounded on several occasions by C. C. Pratt,[34] a psychological aesthetician who sees a fundamental ambiguity in this description. Pratt notes that to many writers this expression appears to mean that the emotional character of music is a subjective commotion within the listener. To others, including Pratt, the emotional character is an objective property of the music itself. The confusion arises, thinks Pratt, in that the same words have quite properly been employed to describe the objective as well as the subjective events. Both John Doe and a certain musical composition may seem agitated, or calm, or passionate, or sentimental. But in Doe's case the affair is one of *kinesthetic-organic* forms, while with the music it is a matter of *tonal* form.

The attempts of the formalists to keep these two sets of phenomena separate should not deny the possibility that on occasion agitated music may stimulate agitation in the listener. Some authors take a somewhat superior attitude and imply that the real sophisticate does not allow his moods and emotions to intrude while he is listening to the "best" in music. But the rank and file of us are not functioning at such an "elevated" level and know of many occasions when joyous-sounding music has improved our mood or when a sad-seeming composition has elicited a sad affect.

Quite different in appearance but not essentially opposed to Pratt's position is the stand taken by Zink[35] who attempts to differentiate between the perceiving, the understanding, the appreciating, and the feeling of emotions. He prefers the term "dynamic emotion" for an intense kinesthetic-organic pattern like blind rage "in which the person is aware of little more than the violent throb of his organism." Zink posits a continuum running from this sort of emotion to "an extreme of quality, as in the aesthetic objectification of emotional experience in life."

A danger greater than that of denying the possible influence of music on mood lies in the assumption that tonal forms invariably arouse the moods and emotions whose names they share. Psychiatrists and clinical psychologists would no doubt rejoice if all they needed to cure the schizoid, the depressed, or the maniacal were access to a variety of compositions whose "moods" had previously been carefully catalogued. Therapy under such circumstances could be administered in truly engineering fashion—composition X for one disturbance and Y for another. But music's effects are not so invariant, and the listener is after all no simple machine. He has a personal as well as a cultural history which makes his reactions to any piece of music, to some degree at least, unique and therefore difficult to forecast.

Years ago the great Thomas Edison was so concerned at what he considered the whimsicalness with which composers titled[36] their compositions that he hired a panel of experts to catalogue his 589 available Edison recordings according to "mood." Out of these the panel labeled 112 "true mood music." Fifteen were guaranteed to stimulate and enrich imagination, 14 to bring peace of mind, 10 to make one joyous, and 8 to elicit moods of wistfulness. Ten were kept in the list for jolly moods and good fellowship, 9 for more energy, 11 for love, 10 for moods of dignity and grandeur, 12 for the mood of tender memory, 13 for the mood of devotion, 9 for stirring the spirit, and 16 to "catch the childish fancy and make it merry with glee."

No doubt hearing the Edison recordings worked wonders on the more suggestible. Yet Anna Case's singing of *Home, Sweet Home*, supposed by Edison's panel to bring peace of mind, might well have made the homesick person more distraught. And while some of the more religious-minded no doubt found Schubert's *Ave Maria* conducive to the peace of mind Edison had guaranteed, it is doubtful if even all the religiously minded so benefited. And one could be almost certain that the forced hearing of this composition would make the confirmed Communist more irascible.[37]

The mood elicited by the music will depend not only on the tonal configurations the listener hears but also on a variety of factors external to the music itself. Among the more important of these variables are the listener's personality structure,[38] the mood held just preceding the listening period, the word-meanings of the libretto if there is one, and the attitudes built up in the listener toward music in general and toward the piece in question. Although musical compositions can quite properly be placed into mood categories, they will not invariably arouse the moods in terms of which they have been described. We are thus forced to conclude that music can be regarded as a language of moods and emotions in a very limited sense only.

ADJECTIVE LISTS FOR CLASSIFYING MUSIC

Research by Schoen, Gatewood, Mull, and others has demonstrated beyond the possibility of doubt that synonymous words will be employed with some consistency to describe the character of much of our Western music whenever the listeners are drawn from roughly the same subculture.[39] The degree of agreement is little affected by differences in listener intelligence, tested musical aptitude, musical training, or age level (if above the sixth grade).[40] As might be suspected, listener agreement is greater where the concern is with pro-

gram music.[41] It is relatively poor for passages which are characterized in terms of "yearning," "tenderness," and "calm."[42] "Defiance"
is more easily identified than "rage" or "fear."

A more systematically constructed adjective checklist than any
used in the past has been developed by Hevner.[43] It contains 67
words arranged in eight clusters. The mood quality expressed by
the adjectives within any one cluster has been assumed to be almost
identical. Hence the characterization of any bit of music is typically
made in terms of a profile of the eight clusters and not of the 67 adjectives, although the listener is urged to check every word he regards
as appropriate. The clusters are arranged like the dial of a clock
on the supposition that as one proceeds from any given cluster
around the dial, the mood similarity steadily decreases until the opposite cluster is reached; from there back to the starting cluster the
resemblance increases.

The utility of the checklist for the aesthetician can be illustrated
by data from the files of the Stanford Laboratory. In one experiment 200 college students were asked to listen to a number of brief
tonal patterns. It will suffice for our purposes to show the responses
to two of these musical passages. Only the adjectives checked by one-
half or more of the listeners will be listed. For the first 12 measures
of the First Movement of Franck's *Symphony in D Minor* (allegro
non troppo) all but one of the adjectives were from cluster 2—heavy,
gloomy, dark, solemn, and mournful. For the first 26 measures of
Debussy's *Clair de Lune,* on the other hand, the adjectives checked
were quite different. Here two were from cluster 5, one was from 3,
and two were from 4—delicate, graceful, dreamy, soothing, and
serene. These checkings were quite reliably and consistently made.
It is to be expected of course that the responses would have varied
somewhat had there been changes in the manner in which the passages were played.

Winold[44] has used the Hevner list in studying what he terms
gross harmonic tension. Music with mostly consonant sonorities he
finds to be rather generally characterized as dignified, spiritual, triumphant, or majestic. Somewhat dissonant music is more likely to
be termed calm, dreamy, gentle, sentimental, dainty, lyrical, happy,
or light. Extremely dissonant sonorities tend to call forth the descriptions tragic, depressing, frustrated, humorous, whimsical, agitated, or
exciting.

Hevner's checklist has been revised with a rearrangement of the
adjectives so that the new clusters have considerably more mood
consistency than the older clusters had.[45] In the course of the research

6
bright
cheerful
gay
happy
joyous
merry

7
agitated
dramatic
exciting
exhilarated
impetuous
passionate
restless
sensational
soaring
triumphant

5
delicate
fanciful
graceful
humorous
light
playful
quaint
sprightly
whimsical

8
emphatic
exalting
majestic
martial
ponderous
robust
vigorous

4
calm
leisurely
lyrical
quiet
satisfying
serene
soothing
tranquil

1
awe-inspiring
dignified
lofty
sacred
serious
sober
solemn
spiritual

3
dreamy
longing
plaintive
pleading
sentimental
tender
yearning
yielding

2
dark
depressing
doleful
frustrated
gloomy
heavy
melancholy
mournful
pathetic
sad
tragic

it was found that one of the adjectives, "pathetic," fitted almost equally well two of the revised clusters. The adjective "frustrated" did not fit any of the clusters and so stood alone. It was found that neither the original Hevner nor the revised clusters could be placed in exact clock-face arrangement although the new clusters came closer than the old to satisfying such a scheme.[46] No doubt as time goes on this much-used Hevner list will be added to and further improved.

MODIFIED ADJECTIVE CHECKLIST

A	B	C	D	E
cheerful	fanciful	delicate	dreamy	longing
gay	light	graceful	leisurely	pathetic
happy	quaint	lyrical	sentimental	plaintive
joyous	whimsical		serene	pleading
bright			soothing	yearning
merry			tender	
playful			tranquil	
sprightly			quiet	

F	G	H	I	J
dark	sacred	dramatic	agitated	frustrated
depressing	spiritual	emphatic	exalting	
doleful		majestic	exciting	
gloomy		triumphant	exhilarated	
melancholic			impetuous	
mournful			vigorous	
pathetic				
sad				
serious				
sober				
solemn				
tragic				

VARIABLES WHICH GIVE MEANING TO MUSIC

Of the variables which give meaning to music, tempo plays the largest role. According to Hevner, who has carried on numerous experiments in this area, modality is probably second in importance.[47] Pitch level seemingly ranks third. Harmony and rhythm are of far less importance, and whether the melody is ascending or descending carries relatively little meaning to the listener. In other words, the listener is most likely to change the affective terms with which he describes a piece of music whenever its tempo is appreciably slowed or hastened. Other alterations of the musical matrix change less strikingly how he will describe the music he is hearing. The relative importance of these variables can be seen in Hevner's table reproduced below. There is no need to consider here the statistics by which she derived her weights; for our purposes it is enough to say that they indicate the relative importance of the variables. The following example indicates how to interpret the table: For music described as dignified and solemn the most important variables appear to be firm rhythm, slow tempo, and low pitch. Major mode, ascending melody, and simple harmony are of little importance.

RELATIVE IMPORTANCE OF SIX VARIABLES *(Hevner Data)*

Musical Factor	Dignified Solemn		Sad Heavy		Dreamy Sentimental		Serene Gentle	
Mode	Major	4	Minor	20	Minor	12	Major	3
Tempo	Slow	14	Slow	12	Slow	16	Slow	20
Pitch	Low	10	Low	19	High	6	High	8
Rhythm	Firm	18	Firm	3	Flowing	9	Flowing	9
Harmony	Simple	3	Complex	7	Simple	4	Simple	10
Melody	Ascending	4	—		—		Ascending	3
Musical Factor	Graceful Sparkling		Happy Bright		Exciting Elated		Vigorous Majestic	
Mode	Major	21	Major	24	—		—	
Tempo	Fast	6	Fast	20	Fast	21	Fast	6
Pitch	High	16	High	6	Low	9	Low	13
Rhythm	Flowing	8	Flowing	10	Firm	2	Firm	10
Harmony	Simple	12	Simple	16	Complex	14	Complex	8
Melody	Descending	3	—		Descending	7	Descending	8

Gundlach has made a somewhat different analysis of the variables which give meaning to music. He factor-analyzed data obtained from asking listeners to characterize a considerable number of melodies.[48] Out of this process emerged a factor which dealt with tempo, smoothness of rhythms, and loudness. A second factor had to do with orchestral range and the use of certain intervals, particularly firsts and seconds. A third factor was related to the use of large intervals. Gundlach found music carried by woodwinds to be characterized by terms such as "mournful," "awkward," and "uneasy"; by brasses as "triumphant," and "grotesque"; by the piano as "delicate," "tranquil," "sentimental," and "brilliant"; by strings as "glad."

Two tables constructed by Gundlach[49] seem worthy of reproduction here. They contrast the connotation of certain variables in
European style music with those in the music of a number of American Indian tribes.

PITCH, RANGE, AND TEMPO *(Gundlach Data)*

High pitch	European	sentimental, whimsical, animated, glad
	American Indian	happy love, recitative
Low pitch	European	mournful, somber, tranquil, dignified, grotesque
	American Indian	general war, organization of war party
Wide range	European	uneasy, animated, grotesque, brilliant, glad
	American Indian	general war, organization of war party
Narrow range	European	tranquil, dignified, delicate, mournful, awkward, somber
	American Indian	healing, scout, warpath
Fast	European	brilliant, animated, uneasy, glad, whimsical, flippant, grotesque
	American Indian	general war, organization for war
Slow	European	dignified, somber, tranquil, melancholy, mournful, delicate, sentimental
	American Indian	in battle, sad love

From the Harvard Laboratory of Social Relations comes an interesting study in semantics.[50] Metaphorical terms employed to describe voice qualities were taken from the writings of George Bernard Shaw and three contemporary music critics. These were offered
to musically naive subjects for use in describing nine operatic voices.
There appeared to be far better than chance agreement among the
judges and a tendency to lump the descriptive terms into three categories—one having to do with evaluation, another with potency, and
a third with activity. The baritone voice was often termed "dull,"
"coarse," "closed," "dark," "heavy," "rough," "hard," and "thick";
the tenor "bright," "thin," and "light"; and the soprano "coarse,"
"soft," "light," and "thin."

Another attempted use of factor analysis for studying the meaningful elements of music can be seen in the researches of Henkin.[51]
The items to be intercorrelated were the preferences of college stu-

RHYTHMS AND INTERVALS *(Gundlach Data)*

Factors	Characterization of Musical Phrases	Appropriate Situations for Amer. Indian Songs	European Folk Songs
Many rough rhythms	grotesque uneasy	after killing warrior scout song, victory	victory war march
Many uneven rhythms	delicate sentimental dignified exalted somber	disappointment in love parting happy love	death of lover description of, or song to, love
Few uneven rhythms	flippant animated grotesque brilliant	after killing warrior recitatives victory	victory
Many smooth rhythms	brilliant animated flippant glad	war medicine parting death of lover healing, happy love	lonesome or sad gay or playful
Many 1sts and 2nds	uneasy mournful awkward	war medicine death of lover healing, recitatives warpath	sentimental or serious love lonesome or sad absence or parting
Many 3rds	triumphant	absence of lover after killing warrior war organization	victory
Many large intervals	glad, exalted delicate	disappointment in love lonesome, scout	gay or playful lonesome or sad death of lover, war dirge

dents who had listened to ten pieces representative of (a) baroque, preclassic, and classic, (b) romantic, and (c) modern styles. Two independent meaningful factors emerged which Henkin designated as a melodic and a rhythmic factor. There was also the possibility of a third factor, orchestral color. When Henkin was deciding on his ten compositions, he searched for recorded music written in a "purely harmonic idiom" but was unable to find a single example. It was this lack of records with strong emphasis on harmony, he feels, that kept a harmonic factor from appearing in his final data.

The data of a slightly later study led Henkin to believe that the melodic and rhythmic factors are independent both mathematically and psychologically. These factors appeared to be relevant variables in eliciting the galvanic skin response. Musical style, dynamics, orchestration, timbre, and other compositional variables seemed to have no significant relationship with this physiological measure of affective response.

EXPRESSION OF TENSIONS

A number of researchers have felt that to characterize the meanings of music solely in terms of the Hevner mood adjectives is to oversimplify. These theorists prefer to describe what music signifies in the framework of conflict, of the arousal, growth, change, and resolution of tensions. While granting that unfamiliar music designates no concrete goals and no specific universally agreed-upon imagery, they hold that it can carry a message of goal-seeking, goal-blocking, and goal-finding. We have already seen an illustration of the resolution of tensions in the discussion of the keynote. Fay[52] has pointed out that music tensions can be produced by "dissonance and diminution of dissonance, intensification of a rhythmic pattern, intensification of a note or chord, sequential building of phrases or motives, change in dynamics, alternation of unfamiliar material with familiar material, enlargement and elaboration of material already presented, addition of new harmonies or of melodic and rhythmic counterpoints."

Rogge is one who has become impatient with the earlier highly analytic studies of music's linguistic potentialities. To test the possibility that music can communicate in terms of human tensions, she developed a clever experimental design. Bloch's *Schelomo*, Ravel's *Daphnis and Chloe*, and Stravinsky's *L'Histoire du Soldat* were chosen for study. She first played these pieces to a group of eighteen college students who differed somewhat in musical training and for whom the compositions were unfamiliar. After these students were carefully queried about the imagery the music elicited, the interview material was analyzed to extract similarities in content. Taken arbitrarily out of the content similarities, two different stories of paragraph length were constructed for each of the three pieces. These six descriptions were termed the "correct" descriptions.

Other students were then called in to read these six paragraphs and to decide which of Hevner's adjectives most adequately characterized the three mood patterns.[53] When agreement was reached, two new stories were composed for each piece. These differed from the "correct" descriptions as to narrative, i.e. in concrete imagery, but could be characterized by the same Hevner adjectives. Hence they were termed "correct in mood only." This meant that Rogge now had four paragraphs for each piece, two "correct" ones made up from interview imagery material and two "correct in mood only," constructed to fit the Hevner adjectives. To make the procedure clearer the four for *Schelomo* are given below.[54]

Correct

He wants to see her open her eyes, to see her looking at him. He wants to see that she remembers too. Remembers the years they had been apart, searching, following one another from border to border. He wants to see her remembering now the last few years they've been together. If he could whisper just once more how much he loves her, how the memory of her love for him is deep inside him. Her forehead is cold. Her eyes glass over. He cries out, begging her to return. Once again he is alone. He can't believe it. Then holding her hand, he begins to feel the strength of their love. He knows it will be strong enough to help him go on alone.

Correct

As he watches the shore fade away he wants to sit on the deck and sob. He can never return to that land he loves. He is exiled. Forever. Why hadn't they believed him when he had pleaded? Had there been one voice to defend his act? No, not one. Now, as the shoreline lies dim on the water he grips the rail. Had they all been blinded to his love by their own hate? Persecuted, suffering in loneliness, can he condemn them? Can he fear his future now, regret his love for his country? No, for so long as he knows that what he has done was right, will benefit his people, then he can somehow endure the coming years.

Correct in Mood Only

The pigeon flies back through the cold gray sky. The storm has passed, and she is anxious to return to the safety of her nest. When she is over a village she hears a bell tolling. She wants to stop, to descend and rest, but more than anything else she wants to reach home. She passes over another town searching for the building where she knows her nest lies strong and secure, and as she sees the chimney, she circles and begins to settle. As she alights on the ledge, and folds her wings, she sees that the storm has dislodged her nest and the three eggs.

Correct in Mood Only

As he approached her house he wondered if she had forgotten that night on the lake. He straightened his well-clad shoulders. How would she react to his success? Oh, he wished she might open the door and be as she was before, as she was that night on the lake. Going up the steps he remembered. Twenty years. Oh, if she still had that strong, direct warmth. She would probably shout his name when she'd see him. He heard footsteps inside. He held his breath.

The door opened. As he saw the stooped old woman he closed his eyes. It can't be true. This wasn't her. He wanted to open his eyes, telling himself he'd been mistaken. But his eyes refused to open.

The table below indicates how a third group of some ninety students reacted to the descriptions while listening to the three compositions.[55] They had been asked to select the three descriptive paragraphs which best matched the three pieces of music. If chance alone had operated, seven and one-half votes (90 ÷ 12) would have been

ROGGE DATA

Description	Bloch	Ravel	Stravinsky
1	**16	1	1
2	0	1	*4
3	0	0	*3
4	6	**28	0
5	2	*1	0
6	*11	0	1
7	2	*3	0
8	1	3	**49
9	**25	0	0
10	15	**48	3
11	1	1	**27
12	*11	4	2
Total	90	90	90

cast for each of the twelve descriptions. But that the voting was not a chance affair is suggested by the concentrations at the double-starred positions, which indicate the "correct" descriptions. The single stars show descriptions which were "correct in mood only." These descriptions received relatively few votes.

Naturally the Rogge study, like all pioneering experiments, can be criticized. One wonders for instance how the votes would have fallen had three pieces more alike in mood been selected. A good guess would be that Rogge maximized her effects by her choice of compositions. It is also quite possible that the votes for the "correct-in-mood-only" paragraphs might have been more numerous had the mood been judged directly from the music instead of from reading the "correct" descriptions.

In spite of certain inadequacies in the Rogge experiments, it is probably safe to conclude that unknown compositions may be described not only in terms of the Hevner adjectives but sometimes also in the language of goal-striving, goal-blocking, and the resolution of tensions.[56] Of course a descriptive narrative with its specific imagery may not be the same for any two persons, but any narrative with patterns of stress parallel to the tension episodes of the music will be appropriate to describe the musical action.

A tension parameter was also made use of in an experiment by Tyrrel.[57] Here the 52 short (8 to 15 sec.) musical snatches which served as stimuli were derived from five sound-effect combinations, six small samples of African music, six Oriental and Polynesian fragments, seven percussive and five folk music excerpts, nine western orchestral and eight piano bits, and four popular items. Two stimulus sequences were duplicated. "Normals" and mental cases were asked to rate the stimuli on two 5-point continua: happy-sad and tense-relaxed. The test as a whole separated the normals from the abnormals to a promising degree. In fact all but six of the individual items aided in the separation.

A purely musical analysis in this area is that by Ferguson[58] who holds that tone-stress and ideal motion are the primary elements of expression. The former is said to be the musical portrayal of nervous tension and the latter the motor impulsive or rhythmic aspect of emotional experience. There are also secondary factors such as timbre, register, tempo rubato, vibrato, shading, and phrasing.

MUSIC AS A UNIVERSAL LANGUAGE

We have seen that the major chord communicates its "proper" message only under rather limited circumstances and that, while our major scale may have symbolized decadence to Plato, it does not affect us in such a fashion. Although the Siegfried motive may be perceived by the devotee of the *Ring* cycle in the approved Wagnerian manner, it will have quite different meanings to those who have not been taught Wagnerian symbolism. Are there then no configurations which have similar meanings throughout the arts or music forms which appeal similarly to people of widely dissimilar culture?[59]

Knapp and Ehlinger[60] believe in what they term "general stylistic consonance" which exists, they say, between restless and troubled music, turbulent and diffuse abstract art, and curvilinear architectural forms. After considering the data of his tables presented in a preceding section, Gundlach concluded that there is at least some slight similarity in the meanings the cultured European and the American Indian attach to the musical variables he had studied. But whether the similarities are extensive enough to raise them significantly from chance is a question.

Morey played Schubert's *Doppelgänger* and the love duet from Tristan to members of the Loma culture in Liberia and found these "emotionally charged" compositions to have little emotional effect on the African natives.[61] Yet the argument has been made that had he played other sorts of European music he might have stirred their emotions.

When Dartmouth psychologists asked laymen to draw forms suggested by hearing a series of twelve short, simple clarinet selections, there was more than chance similarity among the forms produced under the stimulation of any one of the selections.[62] Cowles in one study and Wehner in another also found some agreement among subjects who had been asked to select a particular picture to match a given musical selection.[63] Reversing the experimental procedure, Willmann found a degree of correspondence among musical themes composed under the stimulation of four designs, e.g. a sawtoothed form.[64]

The commonality of response which appears in these experiments can be explained, in part at least, on purely practical grounds. It would hardly seem reasonable to expect a mother to scream a lullaby to her baby, regardless of the culture to which she might belong. She would be likely to employ soft tones, monotony, and anything else she and other mothers the world over had learned was sleep-inducing. Similarly a piece of extremely fast tempo could scarcely mean "march" to any human. In line with Pratt's argument, one might hazard a small wager that were a Chinese, a Loma Negro, and an Italian forced to listen to a series of tones all of the same pitch and then told to draw whatever seemed appropriate, they would be more likely to draw horizontal lines than vertical or wavy ones.

PSYCHOANALYTIC SYMBOLISM

The early psychoanalysts claimed to have discovered a symbolism which is universal in its sweep but largely unknown to the individual until made manifest through psychoanalysis. The force of the claim for universality was somewhat tempered, to be sure, by the inability of the Freudian and the less orthodox analysts to agree among themselves on what symbolizes what. Yet this lack of agreement did not deter the bolder of them from extending their dogmas to embrace most if not all human activities. For illustrative purposes only a few of the claims pertaining to music need be given here, since very little has been done by way of scientific check. Thus Montani holds that minor modes containing the diminished [sic] third express feelings of the suffering, chastisement, and pain which characterize reactions to the castration complex.[65] According to Mosonyi primitive and noninstrumental music signifies narcissism, and "good" harmonies "mass ecstasy."[66] On occasion the symbols reflect obvious associations, e.g. certain rhythmic patterns and sexual intercourse; in other instances only an analyst will see a logical connection. Other psychoanalysts believe that the act of artistic creation makes restitution or atonement for innate destructive impulses.[67] And Hannett likens "haunting lyrics" to the "voice of the preconscious."[68]

In an attempt to demonstrate sexual values in motion-picture music (nonvocal), Beardslee and Fogelson[69] chose two sorts of stimuli—what they called the "arousal" sort where the rhythm was very obvious and there were large tonal ranges and gradual build-ups to a climax, and the "neutral" where there was evenness in melody and in overall construction and little rhythmic emphasis. Two pictures were viewed at the time the music was played and themes were written by the college subjects. The presence of sex symbolism in the stories was decided by clinical intuition, aided by ratings the clinicians made of such psychoanalytic favorites as (1) motion of the body below the head and arm, (2) rhythm of over one repetition, (3) peak (increase of tension or activity followed by a letdown), and (4) penetration (entrance into or movement through a resisting surface). The sex activities of the stories were classified as primary where there was explicit or implied evidence of sexual intercourse; secondary where there was kissing, dancing, or fondling; and tertiary where mention was made of sweethearts, love, dating, and the like. The differences in the stories elicited from the women by the two kinds of music were greater than those found in the men's stories. The latter's contained more primary sex activity while the women's writings showed more of what the authors call sex symbolism.

What was in some respects a continuation of the Beardslee-Fogelson study was the Wallach-Greenberg research[70] linking symbolic sexual arousal to personality functions. Using a modified Beardslee-Fogelson technique to measure arousal they also measured what they called the traits of social and emotional introversion and manifest anxiety. They concluded that persons describing themselves as socially introverted and with high anxiety level will show a much greater degree of symbolic sexual arousal to music than will those calling themselves socially extraverted. The study fits well the Freudian party line but of course stands or falls on the validity of Freudian assumptions which are tentative at best. In a later study Wallach[71] found that "degree of liking for esthetic [musical] materials is positively related to the degree of symbolic sexual arousal in response to these materials." Working in this same area Sopchak feels that eroticism increases with familiarity with a particular piece of music.[72]

Altshuler[73] and Tilly[74] have also suggested that music possesses sexual symbolism and feel that the symbols are, to some degree at least, recognized even by laymen. Their interest in such symbolism stems from the belief that music can be employed therapeutically. According to them, a "manly" patient who has emotional difficulties should be approached with music different from what must be employed with a man of more "feminine" personality. In other words some music is "masculine" in character and other music is "feminine."

Handschin made use of a masculine-feminine parameter (Note 21, p. 240). The ancient theorists of China also saw sex qualities in music. In the Lin Lun system of approximately 2700 B.C. in the reign of Emperor Huang-ti there were the *lu* (Yang) or masculine family of scale notes and the *lui* (Yin) or feminine. The gamelon music of Indonesia also has sex tuning, but here the sex pairs of pitches differ by only a few cycles so that when they are sounded together the beating effect which ensues gives a shimmer which is pleasing even to many Occidentals.

A number of psychologists have attempted to set up experiments with the aim of indicating to what extent music can be described in terms of a masculine-feminine continuum.[75] As a result of these studies it seems clear that, *if forced to it,* laymen and musicians will agree in selecting certain composers as the creators of predominantly masculine music and others as the originators of rather feminine compositions. Thus Wagner, Beethoven, Shostakovich, Bach, and Rimsky-Korsakov are typically regarded as having created music most of which was masculine in character; R. Strauss, Chopin, Debussy, Brahms, and Schubert are classified as writers of more feminine music. By and large the march, loud music, and the music of the drums, bass viols, trombones, and trumpets are thought of as the more masculine; "decorative" music, soft music, and that rendered by the harp are classified as feminine.

These findings should not be taken to mean that certain musical phenomena necessarily function as sexual symbols.[76] Rather the data appear to show that in the American subcultures polled, individuals are sometimes willing to use "masculine" and "feminine" as category headings if these names are suggested to them and that there is considerable consistency in the way they employ them. But the making of such forced choices should not be interpreted as proving that Beethoven's music is inherently and universally masculine in any true sense of the term. The raters presumably have associated loud and low-pitched tones with men, marching rhythms with male soldiers, soft music with women, etc. When queried, the raters generally maintain that they would have much preferred to use other categories than those of "masculinity" and "femininity."

Attention should be called to one study[77] of persons who were plagued by obsessive songs and song lyrics. Interestingly enough it was found that their conflicts, while severe, were largely nonsexual. This was true even though the lyrics of these obsessive tunes were filled with what the Freudians traditionally term sexual symbols, e.g. bananas, coconuts, pistols, and the like.

SUMMARY

Music has a grammar, a syntax, except perhaps when it follows a random-probability system.[78] Its performers, conductors, and composers, the orators and authors of music, often believe they have much to say. To this extent then music behaves as a language. But does music convey detailed messages which are understood similarly by large groups of listeners from diverse cultures? This is a question that has aroused the most extended argument.

Key effects, at least for the modern listener, do not exist in any objective fashion. Nor is there a natural tone-color linkage although many persons associate a particular color with some pitch or timbre and a few have associations of hallucinatory intensity. However, major and minor chordal effects are real, at least in certain cultures. Chordal structure, tempo, loudness, pitch level, and the temperament of the listener have been shown to play a part in eliciting the words "happy" and "sad." Moreover, there are a number of other affective and tension responses which music can convey to the relatively unsophisticated listener. Some music can even be described as masculine or feminine, although this sort of categorization seems to have little significance and certainly none that would excite any but the Freudians. All told then, it is clear that the "messages" of music are more in the affective[79] than the cognitive realm. Music stimulates little detailed imagery of a sort that is universally shared. The paragraph given below illustrates rather well the fallacy in the thinking of those who would make music a language in the sense that English or French is a language. These notes, taken from a program of the Boston Symphony Orchestra, describe some of the varied reactions to Beethoven's *Seventh Symphony*.

Mark what commentators have found in the Seventh symphony: One finds a new *Pastoral* symphony; another a new *Eroica*. Alberti is sure that it is a description of the joy of Germany delivered from the French yoke. Dr. Iken of Bremen saw in it a political revolution. Nohl shakes his head and swears it is a knightly festival. Marx is inclined to think that the music describes a Southern race, brave and warlike, such as the ancient Moors of Spain. An old edition of the symphony gave this programme: "Arrival of the Villagers; Nuptial Benediction; The Wedding Feast." Did not Schumann discover in the second movement the marriage ceremony of a village couple? D'Ortigue found that the Andante pictured a procession in an old cathedral or in the catacombs; while Duerenberg, a more cheerful person, prefers to call it the love-dream of a sumptuous odalisque. The Finale has many meanings: a battle of giants or warriors of the North returning to their country after the fight; a feast of Bacchus or an orgy of the villagers after a wedding. Ulibichev goes so far as to say that Beethoven portrayed in this Finale a drunken revel to express the disgust excited in him by such popular recreations. Even Wagner writes hysterically about this symphony as "the apotheosis of the dance," and he reminds a friend of the "Stroem-karl" of Sweden, who knows eleven variations, and mortals should dance to only ten of them: the eleventh belongs to the Night spirit and his crew, and if any one plays it, tables and benches, cans and cups, the grandmother, the blind and lame, yea, the children in the cradle, fall to dancing. "The last movement of the Seventh symphony," says Wagner, "is this eleventh variation."[80]

As Rigg phrases it: "Music is *sui generis* and autonomous."[81] The images music ordinarily arouses are far more specific to the unique experiences of the listener than is true of the verbal languages.[82] If several listeners have had similar experiences, are trained in the same school of imagery (e.g. the motive-hunting Wagnerians), their images will quite naturally be more alike. On the affective side there is more commonality of response, at least partly from the fact that, as Pratt states it, music sounds the way the emotions feel.[83] Music can be used to indicate the buildup and release of tensions. It can of course be given almost any desired meaning if time is taken to stamp in the proper associations. Such specificity of designation, however, is not generally encouraged, for to most people the real essence of music lies in the fact that it gives each person an opportunity to project his private experiences through his own personal images or even to listen without trying to elicit images of any sort.[84] Everyone can appreciate the grammar, the melodic and harmonic rules of the school to which the music of his immediate interest belongs. But he is not listening to a language in the fullest sense of that term.[85]

CHAPTER SIX ✣ *The Nature of Musical Taste*

A PERUSAL of the current definitions of artistic taste would lead one to believe that there is no definition which can be taken as authoritative. Even Runes's *Dictionary of Philosophy*[1] offers two statements which are quite different in meaning. Its first is "the faculty of judging art without rules, through sensation and experience." The second, "the ensemble of preferences shown by an artist in his choice of elements from nature and tradition, for his works of art," would appear to be acceptable to the social scientist interested in music if the term "artist" is broadened to include *all* men making judgments in the field of art. The term "preferences" should not be limited to momentary pleasures but should refer to overall typical sets of emotionally oriented attitudes, perhaps even including the strivings for appreciations not yet gained. Thus the person who is endeavoring to achieve an appreciation of Bach's music, but who so far does not enjoy contrapuntal music, has taste different from that of his friend who casts Bach aside as the creator of seemingly endless scamperings up and down the keyboard.

Musical taste then can be very roughly described as the overall attitudinal set one has toward the phenomena which collectively comprise music. The communication expectancies one has—the attitudes built up in oneself toward composers and toward the modal, finality, key, and other musical effects—all quite clearly form a part of one's musical taste. In the present chapter we shall examine this larger attitudinal picture called taste in an effort to understand at least a little of its nature.[2]

The fact that several of one's friends may enjoy only jazz and other colleagues receive their greatest pleasure from the music of Beethoven is often brushed aside with an airy "What's one man's poison, *signor,* is another's meat or drink." The assumption seems implicit in this statement that taste is whimsical and thus without pattern of any sort. But the diametrically opposed view—and quite possibly the more common one—is that musical taste obeys some absolute and unchanging set of laws. According to this view, the musically elite—the critics, the genius composers, and the musicologists—have discovered or are on their way to discovering what constitutes "good taste." One's jazz-loving friends have taste of a low order; a higher order of taste is possessed by the man who loves the music of Mendelssohn but not that of Beethoven or Bach; and a still higher status has been reached by those who are more attracted to the works of Beethoven and Bach than to those of Mendelssohn.

Laws can be either absolute, eternal, and unchanging, or relative, culturally derived, and stable for only limited areas and periods of time. The professor of music who attempted to keep his students from being "polluted" by the music of Mahler and Bruckner—action which really happened—was more than likely following the absolutist's conception of musical taste. His colleague was more of a relativist when he said to his students: "I much prefer the music of the eighteenth and early nineteenth centuries to that of later periods. Yet it would be well if you would become familiar with music of later periods, since who can tell what level of regard this newer music will have achieved by the days of your grandchildren."

The absolutist in musical theory holds that musical creations are good either because they follow metaphysical rules or because they are in line with certain of the principles of natural science. For a sample of the metaphysical approach we can refer to the classical Chinese, who justified their pentatonic scale on the grounds that there were five planets;[3] five elements—metal, wood, water, fire, and earth; five social and political relationships—father and children, husband and wife, brothers, friends, and ruler and subjects; and five political terms—king, official, people, governmental affairs, and wealth.[4]

Closer to our own culture was the western European sixteenth-century taboo against music ratios employing prime numbers not in the series 1–6.[5] A reason offered was that space has six directions —above, below, fore, after, right, and left. To make use of a prime not in this series was thought to be contrary to the will of God. Even in our own time there are many who believe that "good" aesthetic taste is inherent in those of us who happen to have been born under a propitious sign of the zodiac. But these astrology-lovers are often a little vague as to just which sign is most influential in predetermining musical taste although most favor Libra. Whatever the astrological answer, however, it does not check with experimentally tested facts; for, as was stated in Chapter 1, the distribution of the birthdays of the musically great is not different from that of the less gifted.[6] In their birthdays the artistic and the inartistic have been favored by the same astrological signs.

Although it is quite probable that only the more credulous today would believe in such metaphysical principles as the above, the idea that a gestalt principle or some other law of natural science underlies taste is still held by many theorists. A number of the important textbooks persist in describing the pre-Bach scale of just intonation as the scale of nature and our contemporary equally tempered scale as a compromise affair, simply because the former can be derived, in theory at least, from the overtone series while the latter cannot be so rationalized. These overtone enthusiasts seem to forget that other cultures have enjoyed equally tempered scales, some of them even further removed than ours from the possibility of such rationalization (e.g. the Siamese and the Javanese). Although the physics of horns, reeds, and strings doubtless did help condition the early use of the octave and perhaps a few of the other intervals with simple ratios, it seems unjustifiable to restrict our explanations of present-day taste to oversimple physical principles.[7]

Attention has already been called to the interesting neurological speculations of Max Meyer and to the gestaltish theories of Mursell, particularly as they relate to finality effects. So long as these theories are not formulated to exclude habituation they would not appear untenable, although in the present primitive state of neurology it does not seem currently to furnish much help to the understanding of the nature of taste. A firmer statement can be made about the alleged relation between the true beat in music and body pulserate, for there are experiments to show that the latter cannot possibly account for the diversities of true beat. It is true of course that the capacities of the biological organism set the general limits within which man's ears and muscles react. But that they can affect his taste without the mediation of cultural forces has never been demonstrated. All the facts so far accumulated by the musicologists and social scientists seem to point in a different direction, toward a cultural explanation of taste.

The hypothesis that contemporary taste in music is largely culturally derived can be demonstrated through the data of anthropology, sociology, history, and experimental psychology. It has been shown that the Occidental love for simple rhythms, careful tuning, fixed tonal steps, harmonies, the tonic effect, and the diatonic scale is not shared the world over. As we saw earlier, the African predilection for more complicated rhythmic patterns was so far out of line with the taste and perceptual abilities of many of the early missionaries that they commonly reported the Africans to be arhythmical. The Chinese of the "backward" heartland of mainland China often appear oblivious to mistunings; they love music which has little harmony in the Western sense of the word, and their taste in fiddles is not usually shared by Western man. Yet Orientals can learn to love Occidental music and indeed, with continued residence in Europe or America, come to appreciate Western musical principles and gradually to develop facility in the perception of small auditory differences. Conversely the people of the Western world often learn to love alien music forms and to master more complicated rhythmic patterns. When constantly subjected to poor tuning, the American slowly loses his pitch sensitivity and his taste for pitch exactitude.

It is well known that the people of each culture area are likely to regard their art forms as God-given and superior to those of their neighbors. But the theorist who would accept the mythology of racism and believe that the composers of his group alone have discovered the "true" standards of musical taste will receive no support from the social sciences.

Some form of the absolutist view is often accepted by professional musicians. It is among the relatively untutored, on the other hand, that the whimsey view of taste is more likely to be found. As a matter of fact the evidence which can be gathered supports neither of these conceptions. First let us see why we cannot accept the idea that taste is without pattern. We shall start our scrutiny by noting the degree of agreement to be found in judgments on relative eminence.

EMINENCE

The most eminent composer is not necessarily the best known or even the man whose works are most preferred. Yet the relationship between these three categories—eminence, knowledge, and preference—is a very close one. Moreover, while eminent composers are assumed to be geniuses or at least near-geniuses, not all geniuses can be called eminent. Only a few live up to their potentialities or create that which is honored by their fellows. Others have traits of character or are subjected to situational pressures which preclude great achievement; or perhaps they are not born at the "right moments" in the development of their art.[8] We can readily accept the traditional dictionary view of eminence as "an elevated condition among men; a place or station above men in general," adding that the elevated status is the result of social evaluations which are relative to particular times and places.

The patience of the listener along with the conventions of the classroom and lecture hall force each lecturer on music history to confine his talk to an hour or so. Written work is similarly restricted to what the author and editor, if no one else, consider a reasonable number of pages. These limitations function to reduce the number of composers who can receive critical attention and to decrease the extent to which those regarded at the moment as of lesser importance can be treated. By these means eminence hierarchies are in effect created, with as many such lists appearing as there are musicologists at work. Each scholar has his individual biases produced out of national, school, and teacher loyalties. If eminence as a measured entity is to have stability, each selection of the eminent must be balanced by the choices of many others. Fortunately the polling of individual decisions furnishes just such a balancing mechanism and cancels out many of the eccentricities in the choices.

Eminence Rankings. The unsoundness of the view that taste is just a matter of whimsey can be demonstrated in a variety of ways. Our first evidence is that the members of the American Musicological Society, one group of elite, agree among themselves extremely well in their selections of eminent musicians. In 1964 these specialists were written to and asked for the names of the ten composers born in the 1870's or later who presumably had the best chance subsequently of achieving great eminence, of producing compositions most worthy to be called to the attention of children and lay contemporaries, and so to be preserved as a part of the musical heritage.[9] As the ballot sheets were received they were put alternately into two piles, the first ballot going into pile 1, the second into pile 2, the third into pile 1, etc. Thus with two piles of the same size (350 ballots in each pile), two rankings of eminence could be constructed by tabulating the number of checks each composer received from the ballots in each pile.

The table below shows that the first fourteen names chosen by the two subgroups of musicologists were identical and were ranked in almost the same order. Of course if the table had been lengthened to include composers who received relatively few votes, the two columns would not resemble each other quite as much as they do now. Just as almost all of us relish roast beef and apple pie but disagree more with regard to tripe and cottage-cheese pie, so practically all musicologists treat with high regard Stravinsky and Bartok but do not agree quite as well on the importance of composers of the order of Grainger and Ibert. Yet even the top 35 names were ranked in almost the same order by the two groups of musicologists. Where a correlational value of 1.00 would have indicated that the two halves of the AMS membership gave identical rank orders, the actual value for the agreement on these top 35 names was found to be .97. This extremely high value indicates that there is a very stable and common expectancy as to the future eminence of composers born since 1870. No doubt each member of the American Musicological Society had his own peculiar reasons for making each of his ten choices, but when the group as a whole was considered, the individual idiosyncracies of judgment tended to cancel out and a highly stable group feeling clearly emerged. These data unmistakably show that the votes were not made whimsically.

EMINENCE CHOICES OF MUSICOLOGISTS POLLED IN 1964*

	Composers Born Since 1870	
Rank	Pile 1	Pile 2
1	Stravinsky	Stravinsky
2	Bartok	Bartok
3	Hindemith	Hindemith
4	Schoenberg	Schoenberg
5	Berg	Berg
6	Prokofiev	Prokofiev
7	Ravel	Webern
8	Britten	Ravel
9	Copland	Copland
10	Webern	Britten
11	Vaughan Williams	Vaughan Williams
12	Milhaud	Ives
13	Shostakovich	Shostakovich
14	Ives	Milhaud

* See Appendix A for the combined rank order of the first 50 names.

These musicologists were also asked in 1964 to scrutinize lists of 207 composers whose birth dates were before 1870. They were to check the 25 they deemed most worthy to be called to the attention of children and lay contemporaries. When the same two-pile scheme was employed, the top 23 names in each pile were found to be identical and in approximately the same order. In fact when the rank orders yielded by the two piles of ballots (425 in each pile) were compared, there was a rank correlational value of .98, again indicating that the voting was surely not capricious.

EMINENCE CHOICES OF MUSICOLOGISTS POLLED IN 1964*

Composers Born Before 1870

Rank	Pile 1	Rank	Pile 2
1	Bach	1	Bach
2	Beethoven	2	Beethoven
3	Mozart	3	Mozart
4	Haydn	4	Brahms
5	Brahms	5	Haydn
6	Handel	6	Debussy
7	Schubert	7	Handel
8	Debussy	8	Wagner
9	Wagner	9	Schubert
10	Chopin	10	Chopin
11	Monteverdi	11.5	Monteverdi
12	Palestrina	11.5	Palestrina
13	Verdi	13	Verdi
14	Schumann	14	Schumann
15	Des Pres	15	Des Pres
16	Berlioz	16	di Lasso
17	di Lasso	17	Purcell
18	Purcell	18	Berlioz
19	Tchaikovsky	19	Mendelssohn
20	R. Strauss	20	R. Strauss
21	Mendelssohn	21	Vivaldi
22	Mahler	22	Tchaikovsky
23	Vivaldi	23	Mahler

* See Appendix A for the combined rank order of the first 99 names.

The members of the American Musicological Society had been first contacted in 1938 and were asked at that time to list the ten musicians of history whom they regarded as having contributed most to music. A total of 92 composers were named in this survey. Letters were again sent to the AMS members in 1944, in 1951[10] and, as already noted, once more in 1964. The ballots received in 1944 were placed randomly into two sets. Special attention was paid to the ranks achieved by the 92 names mentioned in the original (1938) survey. The correlation (*rho*) between the two-pile orders came to the high value of .97. The same technique employed on the 1951 and 1964 data yielded *rho*'s of .96 and .97 for those born since 1870 and .98 (in both surveys) for those born before this date. It is apparent that even at the lower levels of eminence there was considerable agreement between the two subgroups of contemporary musicologists. Thus it can safely be said that the judgments of this group of musically elite are following some sort of principle or lawful pattern.

The reader may say, however, that it is one thing to prove that considerable agreement in taste exists among musical specialists and quite another to demonstrate it among lay groups. To answer this reasonable objection, the procedures which were employed with the musicologists were used in 1938, 1945, 1958 and again in 1962–63 with college students taken from psychology classes at Stanford University, and in 1945 with 105 nearby senior high-school students and with 100 sixth-graders and 100 fifth-graders. Here again each group was split into two and the scheme was followed of correlating two eminence lists compiled from the ballots cast for the composers (regardless of date of birth) voted as most eminent. While no correlations quite as high as the .98 of the musicologists appeared, the highest university value was found to be .95, the high-school .93, the sixth-grade .88, and the fifth-grade .76.[11] It is not assumed that these groups are typical of all college, senior high, or grade-school groups even in California. But it is logical to believe that since all the above groups showed marked communality of taste, other fairly similar lay groups would also show fair agreement among themselves.

For illustrative purposes the fourteen names receiving the highest number of college votes from a 1962–63 balloting are shown here. Below the fourteenth rank the disagreements between the two rank orders became steadily larger.

It is of interest that Dutch symphony attenders display attitudes fairly similar to those expressed in the tables above. In one study[12] 468 subscribers to the Utrecht Symphony Orchestra series were classified as upper-, middle-, or lower-class members and interviewed in their homes. The group contained 22.7 per cent who were 30 years of age or younger and 40.7 per cent who were 51 years of age or older. Mahler and Bruckner received relatively more votes from the upper classes than American musicologists or college students give them, and Wagner appears not to have recovered from the much publicized love Hitler had for Wagnerian music. Tchaikovsky's high rank with these Dutch music lovers is similar to that given him by American college students.

The fact that American musically elite, university students, Dutch symphony attenders, and even high- and grammar-school stu-

EMINENCE CHOICES OF 200 UNIVERSITY STUDENTS POLLED IN
1962–63

Composers Born Before 1870

Rank	Pile 1	Rank	Pile 2
1	Beethoven	1	Beethoven
2	Bach	2	Bach
3	Chopin	3	Mozart
4	Mozart	4.5	Chopin
5	Brahms	4.5	Brahms
6	Tchaikovsky	6	Tchaikovsky
7	Wagner	7	Handel
8	Handel	8	Wagner
9	Schubert	9.5	Schubert
10	Debussy	9.5	Debussy
11	Liszt	11	Liszt
12	Mendelssohn	12	Mendelssohn
13	Haydn	13	Haydn
14	Schumann	14	Schumann

CHOICES OF DUTCH SYMPHONY SUBSCRIBERS*

	Upper Class		Middle Class		Lower Class
1	Beethoven		Beethoven		Beethoven
2	Mozart		Mozart		Mozart
3	J. S. Bach		Chopin		Tchaikovsky
4	Tchaikovsky		J. S. Bach		Schubert
5	Brahms		Tchaikovsky		Chopin
6	Chopin		Brahms		Dvorak
7	Mahler		Schubert		J. Strauss
8	Bruckner		Dvorak		J. S. Bach
9	Debussy		Mahler		Haydn
10	Haydn		Handel		Handel
14	Dvorak	13	Bruckner	12	Brahms
15	Handel	14	Haydn	16	Debussy
17	Schubert	15	Debussy	20	Mahler
31	J. Strauss	22	J. Strauss	—	Bruckner (not mentioned)

* Note that the names below the line appear among the top ten in at least
one of the other columns.

dents agree so well in their selections of eminent composers can only be interpreted as showing that this facet of taste is patterned and is not a matter of whimsey.

Eminence hierarchies of considerable stability also appear when people of similar culture are queried about the composers of the "popular classics." The next table shows the top nine names given by two university groups of approximately 40 each, questioned in 1954. Each subject had been given a list on which were the names of 108 composers and had been told to rank the ten most eminent from 1 to 10.

FIRST NINE CHOICES OF 80 UNIVERSITY STUDENTS POLLED IN SUMMER OF 1954

	Composers of "Popular Classics"		
Rank	Pile 1	Rank	Pile 2
1	George Gershwin	1	George Gershwin
2	Cole Porter	2	Irving Berlin
3	Jerome Kern	3	Jerome Kern
4	Irving Berlin	4	Richard Rodgers
5.5	Richard Rodgers	5	Cole Porter
5.5	Stephen Foster	6	Stephen Foster
7	Hoagy Carmichael	7	S. Romberg
8	S. Romberg	8.5	Hoagy Carmichael
9	J. Strauss	8.5	Sir Arthur Sullivan
10.5	Sir Arthur Sullivan	10	J. Strauss

Changes in Eminence Rankings. If taste behaves as do other folkways it should be possible to perceive changes over the years. That such changes do occur is shown by the fact that, although the eminence ranks yielded by the votes of the American Musicological Society's members in 1964 correlated .95 with the ranks obtained in 1951, they correlated only .78 with the ranks derived from the polling of 1938.

RELATIONSHIPS BETWEEN FOUR POLLINGS OF THE AMERICAN MUSICOLOGICAL SOCIETY

	1944	1951	1964
1938	.77	.85	.78
1944		.95	.90
1951			.95

EMINENCE RANKS OF THE MUSICOLOGISTS

Rank	1938	Rank	1944	Rank	1951	Rank	1964
1	Bach	1	Bach	1	Beethoven	1	Bach
2	Beethoven	2	Beethoven	2	Bach	2	Beethoven
3	Wagner	3	Mozart	3	Brahms	3	Mozart
4	Mozart	4	Wagner	4	Haydn	4	Haydn
5	Palestrina	5	Haydn	5	Mozart	5	Brahms
6	Haydn	6.5	Brahms	6.5	Schubert	6	Handel
7	Brahms	6.5	Palestrina	6.5	Debussy	7	Debussy
8	Monteverdi	8	Schubert	8	Handel	8	Schubert
9	Debussy	9	Handel	9	Wagner	9	Wagner
10	Schubert	10	Debussy	10	Palestrina	10	Chopin
11	Handel	11	Chopin	11	Chopin	11	Monteverdi
12	Chopin	25	Monteverdi	15	Monteverdi	12	Palestrina

Below are the rank orders of the top ten names as given by Stanford University students in 1938, 1945, 1953, and 1962–63 and their intercorrelations.

RELATIONSHIPS BETWEEN FOUR POLLINGS OF STANFORD
UNIVERSITY STUDENTS

	1945	1953	1962–63
1938	.88	.81	.90
1945		.88	.85
1953			.87

EMINENCE RANKS OF UNIVERSITY STUDENTS

Rank	1938	Rank	1945	Rank	1953	Rank	1962–63
1	Beethoven	1	Beethoven	1	Beethoven	1	Beethoven
2	Bach	2	Wagner	2	Bach	2	Bach
3	Wagner	3	Mozart	3	Chopin	3	Mozart
4	Mozart	4	Bach	4	Mozart	4.5	Chopin
5	Brahms	5	Chopin	6	Brahms	4.5	Brahms
6	Tchaikovsky	6	Tchaikovsky	6	Tchaikovsky	6	Tchaikovsky
7	Schubert	7	Brahms	6	Wagner	7	Handel
8	Chopin	8	Mendelssohn	8	Liszt	8	Wagner
9	Mendelssohn	9	Schubert	9	Schubert	9.5	Schubert
10	Debussy	10	Liszt	10	Handel	9.5	Debussy
11	Liszt	11	Handel	11	Debussy	11	Liszt
13	Handel	12	Debussy	17	Mendelssohn	12	Mendelssohn

Reverence for the Past. The sociologist and aesthetician John Mueller[13] has written that for a variety of reasons the musicians of Haydn's time were fairly well in rapport with the musical audiences of their day but that the same cannot be said of contemporary composers of serious music and their audiences. What Mueller has termed the "aesthetic gap between consumer and composer" has caused an occasional cynic to remark that "The older a composition the more highly will it be regarded nowadays," or, "Music of the quality of Mozart's compositions but written in the twentieth century will not receive wholehearted acceptance." Unfortunately the complete facts which could prove or contradict these statements are not at hand. Yet data are available which bear at least indirectly on the problem.

In one pertinent study the time which had elapsed since the birth of each of the 92 composers mentioned as most eminent in the 1938 polling of the American Musicological Society was carefully tabulated.[14] The rank order which these time periods yielded was then correlated successively with each of more than 20 eminence ranks obtained through a variety of methods. The coefficients of correlation were found to range from $+.21$ to $-.36$, with the median coefficient falling at $-.15$, a value not significantly different from zero. Had time from death been used in the tabulations instead of time since birth, the values would have been almost precisely the same, since the two time series correlate .99 one with the other. The overall picture disclosed no significant relationship between the relative eminence of the men in this highly selected list and elapsed time since birth or death.

In a second study the relation of the year of birth to eminence was observed by plotting the birth years of the 92 selected composers and then finding the central tendency. The median birth year was found to fall in the decade of the 1720's.[15] Next the birth years of a larger number of less rigidly selected musicians were analyzed to determine the effects of broadening the concept of "high eminence." For this part of the research the original list of 92 composer names was expanded to include 118 other composers mentioned as eminent by current musicologists in their articles and books. The median birth year of this less highly selected group fell in the first decade of the 1800's. Finally, to study the effect of broadening the selection still more, the birth years of all the musicians mentioned in two current encyclopedias of music, the *Oxford Companion to Music* and the *International Cyclopedia of Music and Musicians,* were examined. For these two large groups the median birth years were in the late 1820's and the early 1850's respectively. In each of the four lists examined the mode was found to fall several decades after the median.

Another view of the working of the same principles can be obtained by studying the birth dates of the hundred or so who ranked highest in the American Musicological Society's eminence lists. The five persons who achieved top status in the 1944 survey were found to have a median birth year of 1756. For the top 11, the median figure was 1770; for the top 15, 1809; top 25, 1813; top 100, 1820. The comparable medians compiled from the data of the 1951 survey showed a somewhat similar move toward the present: top 5, 1756; top 11, 1770; top 15, 1797; top 25, 1810; top 100, 1818. The analyses were not carried beyond the first hundred ranks because of the poorer reliability of the lower rank positions. In the 1951 survey 23 composers born since 1870 appeared among the top 100 in the "eminent composers of all time" list. In the 1964 poll only six appeared among the "all time" group because no "born since 1870" list had been presented to the raters and hence there was no visual reinforcement of the names of the more recent composers in the minds of the musicologists. The effect of this of course was to push back the median birth years in the top 15, top 25, and top 100 groups. Although the top 5 in the 1964 poll had a median birth year of 1756, there was essentially no move toward the present when more than the top 11 (1770) were considered.

From the data of these researches we can conclude that, in considering musicians of great eminence, there is little or no tendency to bestow most honor on those who have been longest dead. It is clear, however, that the higher the selection of those we call eminent, the greater the chance that they will not be close to our own day. In fact the data show that it is far easier for a composer of a century and a half or so ago to achieve a placement in a music encyclopedia than it is for one born toward the end of the last century or later. The composer of recent years has not had the requisite time to become as familiar to his listeners, to build up a school of supporters. His peer of many centuries ago is also at a disadvantage, for his works are too far removed stylistically from the contemporary scene. The latter's chances of being rediscovered become progressively slighter as his birth date recedes further and further from the 1700's. The most honored then must be the intermediate groups, the composers of the eighteenth and early nineteenth centuries.

This tendency to love the older (but not too old) composers was not nearly as marked in Haydn's day since, as Mueller points out, the composers were "more musical," i.e. they shared in marked degree the taste of their audiences. While these eighteenth-century composers were innovators as well as polishers, they did not attempt by and large to push their listeners so rapidly into what the latter could only regard as extreme violations of the "fundamentals" of music. Their audiences could usually "understand" what they were hearing. Contemporary audiences, on the other hand, leave the concert hall all too often saying: "If what I just heard was music, my dog can sing!"

ENJOYMENT

For those who refuse to believe that the measurement of eminence is an adequate measurement of contemporary taste, there is pertinent information to be considered which concerns the closely related variables of enjoyment and knowledge. Enjoyment and eminence ratings are positively correlated, but their degree of relationship varies with the musical sophistication of the subjects, being higher with the more sophisticated.

The data on enjoyment shown in the table below were obtained from students from Stanford University who were asked to scrutinize a list of 207 composer names and indicate (not rank) the ten composers whose music they most enjoyed. The 140 ballots were split into two piles and each was tabulated separately. The correlation between the two rank orders of the names came to .87, a high value but one somewhat below that found for eminence ratings. While Bach's music is apparently enjoyed in very high degree by these students of a topflight university, it has been shown that groups of lower socioeconomic status tend to rate their enjoyment of his compositions far lower than they rate his eminence. Thus one junior college ranked him eleventh. The West Coast critic Alfred Frankenstein has also found Bach relatively lower in the enjoyment lists he has assembled by interviewing many college students in different areas of the United States.[16] However, by the end of 1968 there was reason to think that Bach's music was being increasingly favored by young Americans (see Dec. 27, 1968, issue of *Time*). The reasons for this attitude change seem reasonably clear—recognition of structural similarities between Bach's music and certain types of jazz, and the ease with which Bach's works lend themselves to jazz arrangements.

Ratings for enjoyment and eminence apparently overlap enormously but are by no means identical. The latter reflect the mores more exactly and so are more similar from one rater to another. Enjoyment is somewhat more personal.

PREFERENCES OF 140 UNIVERSITY STUDENTS POLLED IN 1965

Rank	Pile 1	Rank	Pile 2
1	Beethoven	1	Beethoven
2	Bach	2	Tchaikovsky
3	Tchaikovsky	3	Mozart
4	Mozart	4	Bach
5	Chopin	5	Chopin
6	Brahms	6	Brahms
7	Handel	7	Wagner
8	Debussy	8	Handel
9	Mendelssohn	9	Debussy
10	Dvorak	10	Rimsky-Korsakov
11.5	Wagner	13.5	Mendelssohn
11.5	Rimsky-Korsakov	21	Dvorak

As another example of how similar groups will show similar preferences, let us examine the ballots collected from members of the Philadelphia Orchestra and the Boston Symphony Orchestra in the early 1930's by Folgmann, a former symphony player.[17] The members of these orchestras were asked to exclude from their preference ratings of composers any biases based on their knowledge of the relative greatness of the composers. As can be seen from the accompanying table, the first nine names are identical, although the order is somewhat dissimilar for the members of these two great orchestras.

PREFERENCES OF SYMPHONY PLAYERS

Rank	Boston	Philadelphia
1	Beethoven	Beethoven
2	Wagner	Brahms
3	Bach	Bach
4	Mozart	Mozart
5	Brahms	Wagner
6	Debussy	Schubert
7	Schubert	Haydn
8	Haydn	Debussy
9	Schumann	Schumann

The enjoyment of sections of compositions,[18] of the simpler phrases, and even of chords and intervals is also rather consistent for similar groups. Let us compare the order of preference established for students at the University of Minnesota[19] and in Great Britain[20] in the years before 1929 with the order found at Stanford University in 1933.[21] While there is some slight variation in the order of preference, there is essential agreement as to which intervals are preferred, which are regarded as neutral, and which are disliked.

PREFERENCES FOR INTERVALS

Rank	Univ. of Minnesota	Stanford	England
1	major third	major third	major third
2	minor third	minor third	minor third
3	minor sixth	minor sixth	octave
4	major sixth	fourth	major sixth
5	fourth	octave	minor sixth
6	tritone	major sixth	fourth
7	fifth	tritone	tritone
8	octave	fifth	fifth
9	major second	major second	major second
10	minor seventh	minor seventh	minor second
11	major seventh	major seventh	major seventh
12	minor second	minor second	minor seventh

Some years ago while making studies of the *Measure of Consonance* from Seashore's well-known music-test battery and of Kwalwasser's *Melodic and Harmonic Sensitivity* tests, an analysis was run of the "errors" made by two large groups of subjects.[22] In these experiments the *Measure of Consonance* was treated as a tonal-preference test, just as were the two Kwalwasser records. The "errors" (i.e. the disagreements with the "correct" choices) of two groups of 100 subjects correlated in this order: Consonance, .96; Melodic Sensitivity, .98; Harmonic Sensitivity, .99. A later similar study of the Kwalwasser-Dykema *Test of Melodic Taste* yielded coefficients of correlation of .78 for fifth-graders, .92 for eighth-graders, and .91 for college students.[23] The corresponding values for the Kwalwasser-Dykema *Test of Tonal Movement* were .91, .91, and .98 respectively. Here again we see almost perfect agreements, this time in the liking for intervals, for simple phrases, and for certain resolutions as well.

KNOWLEDGE OF COMPOSERS

Like enjoyment, knowledge of composers seems to be a factor in musical taste. Even though we generally like only what we know (and say we know what we like), the best-known composers do not always appear at the top of the eminence listings, and when knowledge and eminence ranks are correlated, the value may run as low as .65. The next table shows the top nine composers as they appeared on certain college ratings of professed knowledge. When 212 names were considered, the rank orders of the two piles correlated at .75.[24]

FAMILIAR NAMES, JUDGED BY 126 JUNIOR-COLLEGE STUDENTS
POLLED IN 1954

Rank	Pile 1	Rank	Pile 2
1	Chopin	1	Chopin
2	Beethoven	2.5	Beethoven
3	Mozart	2.5	Mozart
4	Schubert	4	Schubert
5	Brahms	5	Tchaikovsky
6	Tchaikovsky	6	Brahms
7	R. Strauss	8	Schumann
8	Schumann	8	Bach
9	Bach	8	Mendelssohn
10	Mendelssohn	10	R. Strauss

PROGRAMS

By this time the reader may be saying to himself: "So far the behavior under observation has been purely verbal. Why not discuss taste from the standpoint of action? Does any one of our great orchestras, for example, ignore many of the more eminent composers and concentrate consistently on playing the music of certain others? Do the programs of the several great symphony orchestras of the world tend to resemble one another?

To give a partial answer to the first of these queries a study was made of the frequencies with which the compositions of each of the 92 composers (mentioned in 1938 by the musicologists) have been listed in the programs of the Boston Symphony Orchestra. The tabulations made by decades show rank-order correlations from one decade to the next averaging in the nineties (.90 to .98). In the table below are given the names of the five composers whose music was played most frequently in each of five decades. Again we can make the statement that the top names are practically the same. The major exception is Sibelius who rose to high rank and then fell precipitously. In 1950 there was published[25] a frequency list of the programs of the Boston Symphony from 1881 through 1948, compiled for the *Boston Evening Transcript*. Beethoven, Wagner, Brahms, and Mozart topped the list (in that order) while Bach held only eighth place. This Bach placement is in line with other findings which show that, relatively speaking, Bach's name has not as often appeared on the programs as his extremely high eminence status might suggest it should appear. Comparisons with the 1935–45, 1945–55, and 1955–65 lists make obvious the fact that Wagner's music must have been played far more in the very earliest decades of the symphony's history.

PROGRAM CHOICES OF THE BOSTON SYMPHONY ORCHESTRA

Rank	1915–25	Rank	1925–35	Rank	1935–45	Rank	1945–55	Rank	1955–65
1	Beethoven	1	Beethoven	1	Beethoven	1	Beethoven	1	Beethoven
2	Mozart	2	Brahms	2	Brahms	2	Brahms	2	Mozart
3	Wagner	3	Wagner	3.5	Mozart	3	Mozart	3	Brahms
4	Brahms	4	Bach	3.5	Sibelius	4	Bach	4.5	Bach
5	R. Strauss	5	R. Strauss	5	R. Strauss	5	Wagner	4.5	R. Strauss
*12	Bach	7	Mozart	7	Wagner	8	R. Strauss	9.5	Wagner
*12	Sibelius	8	Sibelius	10	Bach	15.5	Sibelius	15	Sibelius

* Tied with Tchaikovsky.

Furthermore, supplementary information shows that the programs of the great orchestras do resemble each other in large part in spite of the biases of the conductors who choose them. Mueller and Hevner have constructed a "popularity pyramid" from the pro-

SEVEN AMERICAN SYMPHONY ORCHESTRAS, 1936–41

Rank	Composers
1	Beethoven
2	Brahms
3	Mozart
4	Wagner
5	Tchaikovsky
6	Sibelius
7.5	R. Strauss
7.5	Bach
9.5	Ravel
9.5	Schumann

grams played during 1936–41 by seven of our leading American symphony orchestras.[26]

Thus it appears that this operational or action aspect of taste shows consistencies just as does the more verbal side which is generally studied through balloting.

To learn whether or not the broadcast programs of recorded music also show consistency, an analysis was made by the author of the Pacific Gas and Electric Company's programs of "serious music," which for a period of years were broadcast nightly over KYA from 8 until 10 P.M. The years 1941, 1942, and 1943 were chosen for study.[27] Ranks for each of these years were constructed by counting the number of times the works of the great composers were broadcast. Great consistency was found, shown by the fact that the average of the intercorrelations of the three ranks was .95. If other radio hours of this type show similar program hierarchies, and there is no reason to suspect that they do not, it can be said that the choice of recorded music for broadcasting purposes also follows some sort of lawful pattern.

PACIFIC GAS AND ELECTRIC COMPANY BROADCASTS					
Rank	*1941*	*Rank*	*1942*	*Rank*	*1943*
1	Beethoven	1	Beethoven	1	Beethoven
2	Tchaikovsky	2	Tchaikovsky	2	Brahms
3	Brahms	3	Bach	3	Mozart
4	Mozart	4	Mozart	4	Bach
5	Sibelius	5	Brahms	5	Tchaikovsky
6	Bach	6	Sibelius	8	Sibelius

Changes in Programs. Fluctuations in musical taste can be seen clearly in program trend lines. If taste were a matter of the slow discovery of absolute values, one might reasonably expect that the great orchestras would gradually discard from their programs the works of all but the "best" composers. This progressive elimination would show itself in upward swings on the curves of the chosen few. However, when Mueller and Hevner examined the 1876–1941 programs of several of the great American symphony orchestras, curve fluctations and plateaus rather than persistent climbs or falls seemed to be the rule.[28] Brahms was shown to be slowly climbing in favor, but the curves for Mozart and Bach were quite flat. Beethoven, who started at the top in favor, was still in this position, though his curve dropped speedily at first, then less rapidly and finally leveled off. Wagner started second in popularity, then had a dip in the late 1880's, climbed back into second place with a peak about 1910, and later fell markedly. Tchaikovsky's curve appeared to resemble Wagner's but at a lower level of popularity.

These researchers have conducted many other interesting studies on taste, among them an analysis of the relative popularity of Beethoven's nine symphonies as program material. For illustrative purposes let us describe the popularity curves of the *Fifth* and *Ninth*. The former had fairly high status in the earliest years, dropped a bit in the late 1880's, climbed in popularity rather rapidly until World War I, and then fell slowly, though at the time of the study it was much preferred to any of the other symphonies. The *Ninth* started somewhat below the *Fifth* and rather steadily fell in rank until by 1940 it was lowest in favor.

In the course of a later study, Mueller assembled additional data to show the cultural nature of taste.[29] Just as social attitudes tend to strike different world areas at somewhat different times, so, he finds, do trends in musical taste. Thus while Beethoven's curve of popularity was found to be much the same whether plotted for the London or the New York orchestras, any given position on the curve was reached by the New York orchestras approximately five years later than in London. For Wagner the lag appeared to be in the same direction but fifteen years in length.

We have seen that the relative frequencies with which the works of eminent composers appeared on the programs of the Boston Symphony Orchestra for the decade beginning in 1915 are similar to those for the next decade. The data of the following table indicate that the resemblances tend to be greatest between contiguous decades. Program shifts are slow and irregular but definitely present.

DECADE INTERCORRELATIONS FOR THE BOSTON SYMPHONY ORCHESTRA

Period	1925–35	1935–45	1945–55	1955–65
Decade starting in 1915	.98	.90	.90	.89
Decade starting in 1925	. . .	.90	.90	.90
Decade starting in 1935	. . .	. . .	.90	.90
Decade starting in 1945	. . .	. . .	. . .	.96

NUMBER OF RECORDINGS

The relative number of new recordings also mirrors contemporary taste. Thus if one counts the number of "classical" and "semi-classical" recordings mentioned in *High Fidelity* in 1965 as listed in the 1966 edition of its *Records in Review* (counting a stereo and a mono of the same composition pressed by the same recording company as only one piece), there appear the same top names we have found leading in the polls and other measures of taste. Bach, Mozart, Beethoven, Haydn, Brahms, and Schubert appear in that order. It can be guessed that these names would also emerge, but possibly in slightly different order, from top listings of other recent years.

SPACE ALLOCATIONS

Another operational or action aspect of taste concerns the relative amounts of space allotted to composers in histories of music and in general and music encyclopedias. As it is obviously out of the question to permit the insertion in these books of articles of considerable length on *all* of the world's musicians, there must be selection in considering the composers to be mentioned and the amount of space each composer is to receive. Our children cannot be informed about the lives and works of all who have composed. Are selections made in accordance with some principle, or is it largely a matter of chance which composers are included in a music history or an encyclopedia?

To throw light on this problem, histories and encyclopedias published in English in the early 1900's were studied, as well as others published in each decade from 1920 on. It was found that these publications agreed among themselves quite well; that is, they devoted almost the same relative amounts of space to the musicologists' favored 92 composers.[30] This high degree of agreement along with what was reported earlier shows clearly that musical taste is not whimsical.

Changes in Space Allocations. We have just seen that the relative amounts of space given the eminent composers tended to be fairly similar from decade to decade. Although similarities are to be found, it should also be noted that these allocations, like other social judgments, typically change at least a little with time. Here then is further small evidence for the cultural determination of musical taste.

ALLOCATION OF SPACE IN SCHOLARLY WORKS

HISTORIES OF MUSIC

Before 1920		1920's		1930's		1940's		1950's		1960's	
1	Bach	1	Bach	1	Wagner	1	Beethoven	1	Bach	1	Bach
2	Wagner	2	Wagner	2.5	Beethoven	2	Wagner	2	Mozart	2	Beethoven
3	Mozart	3	Beethoven	2.5	Mozart	3	Mozart	3	Beethoven	3	Mozart
4	Handel	4	Mozart	4	Bach	4	Bach	4	Wagner	4	Wagner
5	Beethoven	5	Handel	5	Haydn	5	Brahms	5	Handel	5	Schubert
10	Haydn	6	Haydn	7	Handel	6.5	Haydn	6	Haydn	6	Haydn
11	Schubert	10	Schubert	9	Brahms	8.5	Handel	7	Schubert	7	Handel
12	Brahms	13	Brahms	10	Schubert	8.5	Schubert	11	Brahms	12	Brahms

MUSICAL ENCYCLOPEDIAS

Before 1920		1920's		1930's		1940's		1950's		1960's	
1	Wagner	1	Beethoven	1	Wagner	1.5	Beethoven	1	Beethoven	1	Beethoven
2	Mendelssohn	2	Mozart	2	Bach	1.5	Wagner	2	Mozart	2	Mozart
3	Beethoven	3	Schubert	3	Beethoven	3	Mozart	3	Wagner	3	Wagner
4	Schumann	4	Mendelssohn	4	Schubert	4	Liszt	4	Haydn	4	Haydn
5	Schubert	5	Wagner	5	Mozart	5	Bach	5	Liszt	5	Schubert
6	Mozart	6	Schumann	6	Schumann	6	Schubert	6	Bach	6	Bach
9	Haydn	8	Bach	9	Mendelssohn	7	Mendelssohn	8.5	Schubert	7	Schumann
10	Bach	10	Haydn	12	Haydn	8.5	Schumann	8.5	Schumann	8	Mendelssohn
26	Liszt	31	Liszt	13.5	Liszt	10	Haydn	11	Mendelssohn	10	Liszt

GENERAL ENCYCLOPEDIAS

Before 1920		1920's		1930's		1940's		1950's		1960's	
1	Wagner	1	Beethoven	1	Beethoven	1	Beethoven	1	Bach	1	Bach
2	Beethoven	2	Wagner	2	Bach	2	Bach	2	Beethoven	2	Beethoven
3	Bach	3	Bach	3	Wagner	3	Mozart	3	Wagner	3	Wagner
4	Mozart	4	Mozart	4	Handel	4	Wagner	4	Mozart	4	Mozart
5	Brahms	5	Handel	5	Schubert	5	Mendelssohn	5	Schubert	5	Schubert
7	Mendelssohn	6	Brahms	6	Mozart	6	Schubert	6	Handel	6	Handel
8	Handel	7	Schubert	8	Mendelssohn	8.5	Handel	8	Mendelssohn	8	Brahms
9	Schubert	8	Mendelssohn	11	Brahms	12.5	Brahms	9	Brahms	9	Mendelssohn

INTERCORRELATIONS IN SPACE ALLOCATIONS

	Histories of the				
	1920's	*1930's*	*1940's*	*1950's*	*1960's*
Histories of the 1900's	.90	.88	.78	.86	.82
Histories of the 1920's	...	.90	.88	.91	.89
Histories of the 1930's	...	...	.90	.94	.92
Histories of the 1940's	...	...	...	.94	.94
Histories of the 1950's	...	...	...	...	.96

	Music Encyclopedias of the				
	1920's	*1930's*	*1940's*	*1950's*	*1960's*
Music encyclopedias of the 1900's	.77	.74	.72	.75	.82
Music encyclopedias of the 1920's	...	.91	.89	.88	.87
Music encyclopedias of the 1930's	...	...	.95	.94	.94
Music encyclopedias of the 1940's	...	...	...	.94	.96
Music encyclopedias of the 1950's	...	...	...	...	.97

	General Encyclopedias of the				
	1920's	*1930's*	*1940's*	*1950's*	*1960's*
General encyclopedias of the 1900's	.90	.88	.88	.92	.88
General encyclopedias of the 1920's	...	.94	.91	.95	.91
General encyclopedias of the 1930's	...	...	.93	.96	.93
General encyclopedias of the 1940's	...	...	...	.96	.93
General encyclopedias of the 1950's	...	...	...	...	.97

INDIVIDUAL AND GROUP DIFFERENCES

In the earlier portions of this chapter, the similarities rather than the differences among aesthetic responses were stressed. While such an emphasis does not need to be justified, we should not forget that any given social pressure does not stimulate all people in the same way. Even if musical taste obeys social principles, individual differences of considerable magnitude will of necessity be present in this behavioral area, just as they are in all other socially significant realms of human response. In any social group there will be those who respond to a particular social pressure with almost complete passivity and compliance. Others will be more resistant, and a few will be extremely unconventional.

Although the pooling of items is necessary if trends are to be established, this process tends to mask whatever individual differences are present and may give an erroneous impression of the extent of the agreement between people, books, programs, or whatever the items may be. To avoid all possibility of misinterpretation it might be wise to study the diversity of the elements which make up a typical pool. To illustrate this process, 126 randomly selected university students were presented (late in 1946) with a list of over 200 composers born since 1860. They were asked to rank on a scale of 10 to 1 the names of those they regarded as the ten leading composers. The response sheets were divided by simple alternation into two equal piles, labeled A and B.

The table shows the detailed distribution of the votes cast for each of the twelve composers who received the greatest number of votes. The number at the top of each column shows the ascribed rank, and the numbers below (opposite the names of the composers) show the number of votes cast for each composer under each rank. Thus twelve of the students in Pool A gave Debussy a rating of 10, five a rating of 9, etc. To figure the final ranks, the number of votes received by each composer was multiplied by the respective rank-value, the products were totaled, and the sums so obtained were arranged in order of size and ranked. For Debussy (Pool A) the figuring proceeded as follows: 12 times 10 plus 5 times 9 plus 12 times 8, etc. Note that even Debussy, who achieved the top position in each pool, received a number of 4-, 3-, 2-, and 1-order votes. Thus the examination of the inner structure of the two pools reveals enormous individual differences among the judgments of the raters. Yet a view of the two rank orders shows almost unanimity of opinion (correlation of .96) when the voters are considered as groups rather than as individuals.

POOL A

	Order of Choice											
Composer	*10*	*9*	*8*	*7*	*6*	*5*	*4*	*3*	*2*	*1*	*Sums*	*Rank*
Debussy	12	5	12	4	5	4	3	2	3	1	364	1
Kreisler	1	0	3	4	2	3	4	2	4	1	120	11
Sibelius	7	7	9	6	1	2	6	2	0	4	297	3
Ravel	1	8	3	2	2	4	4	2	1	0	176	9
R. Strauss	7	8	3	5	4	4	3	3	1	0	268	5
Paderewski	4	2	6	2	2	5	4	1	3	4	186	7
Prokofiev	0	3	1	4	7	2	2	2	1	1	132	10
Rachmaninov	7	12	6	11	5	2	1	3	0	2	358	2
Shostakovich	6	4	4	4	8	5	3	1	2	3	251	6
Stravinsky	2	2	3	5	5	1	4	8	4	3	183	8
Gershwin	7	6	7	1	4	5	3	4	3	5	271	4
Schuman, W.	0	0	0	1	1	4	4	1	3	2	60	12

POOL B

Order of Choice

Composer	10	9	8	7	6	5	4	3	2	1	Sums	Rank
Debussy	16	7	10	5	1	5	3	3	2	1	395	1
Kreisler	1	1	4	1	4	1	5	4	5	5	134	11
Sibelius	7	7	5	5	2	4	2	4	8	0	276	5
Ravel	0	8	6	5	8	4	5	2	4	3	260	7
R. Strauss	9	7	5	5	2	4	2	4	8	0	296	4
Paderewski	0	8	7	6	3	1	1	6	5	4	229	8
Prokofiev	1	3	6	7	3	1	2	2	3	0	177	10
Rachmaninov	14	8	8	4	10	2	3	2	0	1	393	2
Shostakovich	5	5	3	5	6	5	9	3	1	2	264	6
Stravinsky	2	7	2	4	2	8	7	2	5	2	225	9
Gershwin	9	3	5	9	7	6	7	3	2	1	334	3
Schuman, W.	0	2	1	1	1	1	2	3	4	3	72	12

It has just been shown that individual musical tastes differ much as do other individual behaviors governed by social pressures. Moreover, characteristic differences as well as similarities also can be detected among the programs of the leading American symphony orchestras. In their careful study of orchestral idiosyncracies, Mueller and Hevner have given us a wealth of information, from which are presented here a few illustrations of the characteristic program styles their researches have disclosed.[31]

During its years under Koussevitzky the Boston Symphony Orchestra changed from lowest to highest place in the amount of Russian music it presented. But this great organization has never, except for a five-year period under the batons of French conductors, favored French music. Moreover, it has given less attention to Wagner than have most other top orchestras. Surprisingly enough when its foreign-born personnel is considered, it has always been a proponent of American music. From 1920 at least until the time of the study (early 1940's) it has been an outstanding leader in the presentation of music of the modern period.

Since the time of Stransky the programs of the New York Philharmonic Orchestra have reflected less interest in Russian music than have the programs of the other leading American orchestras. But they have indicated more than average interest in German music, an interest held throughout World War I. French and American music on the other hand have been rather neglected. The program trends of the sister organization, the New York Symphony Orchestra, were the most irregular and difficult to characterize of the entire study. The programs of this orchestra have been weak in German and American music but strong in French.

The programs of the Philadelphia Orchestra have reflected almost an average interest in the music of all the chief Occidental nationalities with the exception of the British. There is less than average interest indicated for the music of Beethoven, Mozart, Mendelssohn, Liszt, Handel (except from 1925 to 1930), Schumann, D'Indy, Rachmaninov (except from 1915 to 1920, 1925 to 1930, and 1937 to 1940), Saint-Saëns, Berlioz, and Glazunov. In contrast, more than average attention has been paid to Haydn, Bach (up to 1936), Brahms, Wagner, Debussy, Stravinsky, Sibelius, and Mahler.

The opera in New York and Chicago also has been scrutinized by these two researchers, with the result that certain characteristics for each geographic area have been uncovered. This research on the opera companies and that on the orchestras make it clear that, while the hierarchy of composer prestige is roughly similar from one organization to another, conductors, directors, and perhaps others stamp their individualities on the programs.

CRITERIA AND CONDITIONERS OF TASTE

With the Seashore dictum that beauty consists in artistic deviations from the regular or rigid no one need quarrel, for illustrations of this phenomenon are legion in all of the arts.[32] The painter never paints with completely photographic accuracy; the vocalist and the violinist make great use of that deviation from the regular known as the vibrato. But if one should desire to make specific use of this generalization in forecasting which future compositions will be accepted and which will be rejected, he will find it of little help. For what is considered an artistic deviation in one generation may not be so regarded in another. To be called artistic, a deviation must be acceptable to some particular culture group, and the reasons for its acceptance may be difficult to ascertain.

Howes and others have maintained that a person's taste in music is good whenever he chooses the sincere; avoids the shallow, the sentimental and the cliché; and is not deceived by base motives and emotions.[33] Some writers have implied that somehow the listener comes to appreciate the composer's motives and so eventually develops good taste.

A careful examination of this position shows that no one can ever be absolutely certain of a composer's motives—not even from a study of his life, and certainly not from a mere scrutiny of his music.

In fact the musical genius may not understand his own impulses and if asked about them will answer with rationalizations of the most unrealistic sort. Was Wagner's music insincere because Wagner hoped it would bring him fame, and because he forgot his earlier democratic ideals? Is boogiewoogie shallow and sentimental per se or because of the associations we have with it? Although one may be quite certain in one's own mind that some particular style of musical expression, say "soul" music which arose from the tribulations of the American Negro, is eminently sincere, such an evaluation lacks objectivity and is not of great help to one who desires to study taste.

And as for the cliché, it need only be said that while there is a tendency to eschew the hackneyed, clichés are matters of personal and group experience, and the musical cliché of one period may become acceptable music in the next (and vice versa). Thus parallel fifths were popular at one time but became clichés later. Their excessive use in this second period brought on a ban which was in force for many decades. To the listener born in this century, parallel intervals do not constitute hackneyed material but may be regarded as alluring and strange. Thus Howes's criteria, we are forced to conclude, are not adequate for our purposes. Only the cliché has utility as an explanatory concept, and even it has very definite limitations.

In considering the phenomena which are basic to the appreciation of music, Staffelbach has stressed the feeling tone he believes to be implicit in rhythms and auditory sensations; the associations formed between music and persons, places, things, and previously expressed affective states; the lure of the familiar and the novel; the stimulation of the imagination; the possibilities of self-expression; and the pleasures to be derived from the genius and good craftsmanship of composers and performers, from facts about the lives and works of these artists, and from the belief in one's ability to interpret what artists are attempting to express.[34] Seashore, a pioneer in the scientific study of music, has said:

> Why then do we love music? Among other things we love it because it creates a physiological well-being in our organism; it is built from materials which are beautiful objects in themselves; it carries us through the realms of creative imagination, thought, actions, and feelings in limitless art forms; it is self-propelling through natural impulses, such as rhythm; it is the language of emotion, a generator of social fellowship; it takes us out of the humdrum of life and makes us live in play with the ideal; it satisfies our cravings for intellectual conquest, for isolation in the artistic attitude of emotion, and for self-expression for the joy of expression.[35]

Whether or not we agree with all of these carefully considered reasons for the love of music, it should be clear that the topic needs further review. It is time then to examine in some detail the theories which purport to explain the reasons behind some of our current preferences. Not all of the facets of the situation are yet known, but sufficient data have been assembled to prove the great importance of both formal training and incidental learning in the building up of taste norms.

One might suspect that persons of very different personality structures might react dissimilarly to music, and data are at hand which point to this conclusion. Thus Wallach[36] found a low but positive correlation (r of .33) between preference for jazz and social extraversion. No relationship was visible between the latter and liking for the music of Ravel and Debussy. Keston and Pinto[37] also found the social extravert to show a preference for jazz.

Using a parameter of close-mindedness or, if one prefers, dogmatism, Mikol[38] found that open- and close-minded college students, on hearing for the first time a rather conventional composition (by Brahms or Saint-Saëns), appeared to show equal amounts of enjoyment. Their enjoyment increased with repeated hearing. However, a relatively unconventional and unfamiliar piece by Schoenberg, while disliked by both groups, was reacted to much less favorably by the close-minded. This dislike on the part of the close-minded grew on repeated hearing. The open-minded on the other hand expressed less distaste for the Schoenberg number after hearing it a few times. It is apparent that close-minded persons are not very receptive to what to them are violations of musical tradition. In the experiment just discussed, a piece by Bartok was found not to follow the Schoenberg pattern; i.e., the close- and open-minded reacted similarly to it. Although sometimes thought to be rather radical, it apparently still fell within the limits of what the close-minded regarded as the "rules of music."

In some respects no doubt the personalities of elementary school children are more rigidly structured than are those of older children. Yet Hornyak[39] seems to have shown that the former, perhaps because their taste is not so well established, are more ready to listen to unfamiliarly styled music. It should be noted, however, that mere familiarity with a composer and his music does not automatically insure acceptance of his compositions.

Cultural Derivations. If taste is culturally derived rather than innate, one would expect to find the taste of the child approximating more and more closely that of the adult as he grows older. Such a convergence does occur in judgments of eminence. In an early study in which several groups had been asked to assess the relative eminence of 92 composers, fifth-graders were found to agree only moderately with the members of the American Musicological Society (a *rho* of .33), but sixth-graders were somewhat closer to the musicologists in their judgments (*rho* of .52). The similarity was more marked for some high-school students (.68), and still more for Stanford University sophomores (.79). Musicologists contacted later (in 1951) and university students polled (in 1954) agreed to the extent of a *rho* of .77, while the most recently (1964) polled musicologists and the university students interviewed a year or so earlier agreed to the extent of a *rho* of .83. Here we see a steady climb in the degree of agreement as the groups become more alike in age and in training.

In 1913 Valentine reported on some of his experiments with British schoolchildren.[40] He had found that by age twelve or thirteen there tended to be a decided change in the preferences for tonal intervals, so that the intervals preferred by adults were also enjoyed by these adolescents. Another psychologist, Dashiell, had observed that, although American kindergarten children did not have precisely the adult preferences for the diatonic intervals, they already rated the thirds high and the sevenths and seconds low.[41] Aizawa, who had examined the songs most enjoyed by Japanese schoolchildren, noted that agreements in preference of children and adults increased as the school years advanced, being particularly marked among children of the upper classes.[42]

The Kwalwasser-Dykema *Test of Melodic Taste,* in which 20 items are considered for their suitability as concluding phrases, can be employed to yield data which reflect the learning of folkways. While the university subjects in one study of this test showed agreement with the "correct" responses on 15.4 out of 20 items, eighth-graders gave the "correct" responses 13 times, and fifth-graders only 12.2 times on the average. Similarly, when data of the Kwalwasser *Test of Harmonic Sensitivity* were analyzed, it was found that an unselected group of university students averaged 25.4 "correct" scores out of a possible 35, eighth-graders 24.1, and fifth-graders 21.2. As the ages became more similar the responses became more like those of the experts, i.e. more like the "correct" responses.

In the areas of tempo and rhythm, it is noteworthy that subjects show consistent preferences but differ considerably among themselves.[43] Although one writer feels that this "intra-individual consistency" is solely the result of inheritance,[44] there are the previously mentioned data which clearly show that tempo preferences are at least in part functions of cultural conditioning. Foley, it will be recalled, found that subjects studying trades in which activity proceeds at a slow pace (e.g. dressmaking) favored andante tempo; those working with power machines, a slow allegro; while his typists preferred a fast allegro bordering on presto.[45] Other experimenters have found that college students prefer their dance music to be played at about the speed they have heard it rendered traditionally. In fact these students have demonstrated a sort of absolute or positive tempo quite comparable to absolute pitch.

Somewhat similar to the work of Foley but broader in its scope was the study by Schuessler.[46] Eight phonograph recordings were played to large groups of subjects who had been divided according to occupation into six job levels. On the five-point preference scale which Schuessler employed, great differences of scores occurred between the levels. Occupational level was also studied in Tasmania and found to be far more important than sex or age in determining musical taste.[47]

A study of preferences for popular music among teen-aged girls[48] revealed the presence of neighborhood norms which were reflected more in the "popular" than in the "unpopular" girls. Preferences were shown to be anchored in relatively small groups of friends. The saturation point for each teen-age hit was usually reached in six months. In a fairly broad gauge study of preference change made by Rogers,[49] four types of music—classified as seriously classical, popular classical, dinner music, and popular music—were given to 635 children from the second through the twelfth grades in six schools. Popular music was found to be the overwhelming favorite. "Classical" music was liked relatively more by those high in socioeconomic status. Acceptance of "classical" music declined with age as did intragroup variability.

In still another study of teen-agers Baumann found[50] "classical" music to be increasingly liked as age increased. Students from relatively high socioeconomic levels showed far more preference for "classical" and "string" music than did students from lower-class families. A confounding variable here of course is educational status which correlates highly with socioeconomic status. Since intelligence is also closely tied to education, it is difficult to interpret the findings of Gerren[51] who has reported a correlation of .43 between intelligence and sophistication of musical preference. Are bright people per se more sophisticated or is this characteristic merely a reflection of their generally better education?

One of the most extensive studies made so far on the development of musical taste in college students, that by Erneston,[52] found that length of time spent on musical activities was quite significantly related to "level" of taste (as measured by formal tests of attitude toward music, musical preferences, and ability to discriminate musically). Although variety of musical experience is of course related to length of time spent on music, the data suggested that variety by itself was conducive to taste growth. Mental ability seemed of little importance in the early stages of taste development but grew in importance as taste developed.

Climatic Cycles and Taste. According to one of the climatic determinists, R. H. Wheeler, world climate fluctuates "in rhythms within rhythms which tend to follow multiples of the sunspot cycle of 11.3 years."[53] Whether long or short, these rhythms "tend to follow a similar pattern of phase sequences, the phases being cold-dry, warmwet, warm-dry, cold-wet, then cold-dry again, in that order." Phases of warm weather are supposed to bring into being musical taste for (and so creativity in the area of) the serious opera, the symphony, the sonata, the concerto, chamber music, swing, jazz syncopation, masses, anthems, oratorios, dissonance, and atonality. Warm weather is also said to be conducive to the rise of choruses, orchestras, and bands. Cold spells on the other hand somehow put us temperamentally in tune with light and comic operas, program music, tone poems, folk music, ballads, madrigals, and counterpoint—according to the Wheeler doctrine. During cold periods occurs the heyday of castrati and musicology. However, the "golden ages" of music were neither warm nor cold but rather were periods of transition from cold to warm.

Just before 1940 (when Wheeler was writing) we were supposedly in a cold-wet phase which is to last until 2000 or 2010 except for possibly one ten-year warm period. Since such swings were held by Wheeler to be the rule of nature, he believed that we need merely to study weather cycles to forecast the taste of any future time period. The only escape from these predetermined swings would seem to be in universal air-conditioning!

No scientist would dare say that the Wheeler doctrine may not eventually be found to have some very slight validity. Yet it would be surprising, to say the least, if the relatively insignificant temperature changes the world has endured during the past few centuries should have caused huge changes in aesthetic interests and taste while the far greater climatic differences of, say, Minnesota and southern Florida are apparently unrelated to musical taste.

Taste Created by the State. It is popular in some quarters to believe that good taste in music is indicated by special reverence for those compositions which mirror the times. Some would go so far as to say that good taste insures the honoring of only that type of music which has a propaganda value for the furthering of "good" causes. Ordinarily, little is done to promote the acceptance of compositions which are so regarded. But in lands under police control, this doctrine is often so rigidly held that only compositions which are felt to mirror the times or which follow the state's approved pattern can be heard.[54] The fact that the leaders may be deluding themselves as to the timeliness or propaganda worth of their approved compositions is beside the point. If only certain musical works can be heard, and it is healthier to honor these than to laugh at them, they will quite likely come to be accepted by the masses.[55] This is one way to create taste.

Training. Little by little, data are being accumulated which demonstrate the potency of both auditory and visual training in the creation of musical taste.[56] As Tyler[57] and C. L. Stone[58] have shown, we are trained to think of music in terms of stereotypes. Even the relatively unsophisticated college student has been taught to tie the names of Mozart, Beethoven, and Schubert to certain styles of composition. Italian music he associates with the light and the airy, Russian music with the somber and the gloomy, and German music with the heavy and the philosophic. The studies reported in previous chapters also tell of training in stereotyped thinking. American grade-school children surely have few facts to go on when they place Beethoven and Bach so high on their eminence lists. They answer not from deep conviction but rather in accordance with their teaching. The situation is analogous to their placing of Jesus, Washington, and Lincoln at the top of their lists of the most eminent men of all time.

J. Stone[59] and Robinson[60] have studied the sociopsychological aspects of war music. Stone points out that during the American Civil War, the soldiers' songs reflected their common traditions and not their war alignments. Although noting that the music of each war to some slight extent mirrors the times, Robinson stresses the common subjects soldiers of all wars sing about: bad food, insect pests, war terrors, the enemy, sweethearts and other loved ones, and the desire to return home.

Gardner and Pickford have demonstrated by experiment what absolutists have difficulty in accepting: that perceived dissonance varies with (1) the listener's experience, training, and traditions, (2) the musical "intent" of the passage as a whole, (3) the physical composition of the chord.[61] The effect of the listener's recent experiences on enjoyment has also been shown in an experiment in which Beethoven's *Fifth Symphony* and Stravinsky's *L'Histoire du Soldat* were presented to several groups of college sophomores. When the playing of the Beethoven composition preceded that of the Stravinsky, the professed enjoyment ratings were 73.8 and 27.4 respectively (a rating of 100 equaled "greatest possible enjoyment"). When the order was reversed, the values became 34.5 for the Stravinsky number and 79.1 for Beethoven's *Fifth*. Note the depressive effect on the less enjoyed when it followed the better liked, and the enhancement of the latter when it was played second. The effect which can be elicited by varying the order of recent experience was also demonstrated by Wynn-Jones[62] who found that, while 87 per cent of his subjects preferred the octave to the fifth when the former followed the latter, only 41 per cent preferred the octave when it preceded the fifth. No doubt the tonic effect was responsible in large part for this difference in preference.

Wiebe found that the extensive playing of popular songs over the radio did not appear to increase his student subjects' liking for them.[63] However, lack of "plugging" seemed to result in a decrease of preference. Suchman on the other hand concluded that the broadcasts of radio station WNYC in the 1930's did much to develop an interest in music among its listeners and to establish taste norms.[64] Broadcasts it would seem make music more accessible; they extend the range of musical experience; they repeat the musical stimuli; they supply commentators and occasionally program notes[65] and other educational literature. A possible liability which may be inherent in radio taste training is the development of a dependent attitude of listening attentively only to compositions which are sponsored by the broadcasters of the favored radio station; there may be little carryover of interest to other somewhat similar compositions. It should also be noted that where the exposure comes from courses in music appreciation, the effect may be to encourage intellectual analysis of music far more than enhancement of emotional response to music.[66]

A number of researchers have attempted to telescope history by forcing their subjects to hear the same musical stimuli many times within a relatively short period.[67] Although the conclusions of the several studies are not in complete agreement, it seems safe to say that a composition with little variety reaches maximum acceptance quickly and then as speedily declines in popularity. Music with more complexity tends to gain acceptance more slowly and to become hackneyed less rapidly. In one paper it has been suggested that the continuous repetition of musical material has a stronger effect on the listener than would the same number of well-spaced hearings.[68] Mull has made the interesting discovery that the preferred parts of musical compositions tend to become larger on rehearing. Since the spread of preference usually is greater at the anterior end of the focal region, Mull has suggested that this phenomenon may be a case of what psychologists call "goal gradient." As she phrases it:

> Might it not be that learning to like a composition has features similar to those involved in an animal's learning to run a maze—that is to say, in the case of our experiment, an original high spot (corresponding to the maze goal) may be thereafter anticipated and a pleasure gradient extend backward? Thus, pleasure would actually spread from a focus, rather than appear *de novo*. Once the climax is reached, there would be relaxation of interest and some tendency for the pleasure to drop off.[69]

Leonard Meyer[70] has described the changes in affect which come with repeated listening to a musical composition in terms of his "kinetic syntactic" theory of musical meaning, the notion that the cardinal characteristics of a musical event are functional rather than formal. In Meyer's terms, the listener with practice comes to change his musical expectancies, his "internalized probability system." Meyer's hypothesis ties in with what is now called "information theory" and gives a clever and (to this author at least) fairly reasonable set of explanations of what happens on hearing the same composition a great number of times. However, his heavy emphasis on decreasing expectancy and surprise has been criticized by Marco,[71] who points out that perceiving is more than mere discovery and notes that most persons still greatly enjoy certain pieces after innumerable hearings when surprise is no longer possible. Significance in art, he holds, is not only a function of observer surprise. In support of Meyer it can be said that he has left room in his theory for a variety of cultural factors which might cause increases in pleas-

ure with almost innumerable rehearings. Among the more important
and obvious of these are religious and patriotic feelings which may be
aroused whenever church or national hymns are rendered and which
may become even stronger with time.

On several occasions mention has been made of Seashore's principle that deviations from the fixed and the regular are per se pleas-
ant. More recent theorists have subsumed this principle under a
broader "law" which states that man habituates to what he repeatedly
senses until an adaptation level is reached. He then reacts to slight
deviations from this level with pleasure. As the deviations become
progressively larger the degree of pleasure is likely to increase for a
time and than rapidly decrease. Part of the performer's skill rests
in discovering how much he can safely deviate from his listeners'
adaptation levels without inducing unpleasantness and hence losing
these persons as an audience.[72]

A peculiar situation developed for a time in the area of phonograph and radio listening, in which tones of relatively "poor" quality, i.e. with timbres unlike those of the "live" instruments, were
preferred to those of more realistic quality. Apparently, long-con-
tinued informal training was the responsible agent. We had developed one set of taste habits for listening to the phonograph and
the radio and another to function when in the presence of orchestral
instruments.[73] Chinn and Eisenberg, two of the investigators of
this phenomenon, found this type of preference among the musically
sophisticated as well as the naive; it persisted even when the listener
was told that a wider tonal band yielded tones closer to the sounds
of real life.[74] For many years the lay preference had been for an
unusually strong emphasis on the bass. Presumably this preference
arose from the fact that the engineers early achieved reasonable
realism in the lower tonal ranges but only later brought in the very
high frequencies at all adequately. As a matter of fact, the early
attempts of RCA Victor to produce "high fidelity" led to such poor
audience response that this manufacturer continued for some years
with an overloaded bass.

The Hi-Fi Hall with its incredibly short reverberation time has
necessitated further taste adjustments.[75] Long accustomed to the
deadening effects of most auditoriums, the listener is here called
upon to react to greater brilliance, to tone that is "acoustically
naked." While the hi-fi enthusiast has little difficulty in learning to
appreciate this "drier" effect, persons more attuned to the older
home sets are at first somewhat startled, to say the least.

Some of us learn to pay more attention to the associations music can call up than to the music itself. Schoen terms this extreme sort of response "extrinsic" listening,[76] Myers "associative,"[77] and Ortmann "imaginal."[78] Those who pay more attention to the music than to its associations Schoen calls "intrinsic" listeners. Such persons are often said to have taste of a high order. Myers subdivides this group into "objective" if there is great concern with the objective features of the music, "intrasubjective" if the attention is on real or apparent changes within the listener's own body, and "character" if the listener imputes moods, traits, and activities to the music itself. Ortmann divides this group into "sensorial" and "perceptual." While these classifications may to some readers look suspiciously like fixed types,[79] it is clearly not the intent of these theorists to create typologies. Rather they are emphasizing the different things people have learned to perceive in music, and they realize full well that few if any listeners belong to a single pure category.

We hardly need proof to be certain that taste develops out of experiences gained in home, church, club, and school and out of contacts with the concert stage, recordings, radio, television, and the printed page. These agencies of education, propaganda, and censorship help us to revere certain composers and their compositions and to take less seriously other men and their works. We come to have several standards of taste: for the concert stage, for the dance hall,[80] for church, and for school—to mention some of the more important. Age, intelligence, and special training all can be important variables in this process of taste formation.[81] But it is difficult to be specific about all this since there seems to be some difference between taste as it is observed in everyday life and the sort of taste people are willing to admit they possess.[82]

If we take as our aim the inculcation in our children of the standards of taste that adults of our culture regard as "good," checks on the success of this endeavor with groups of children can be made through the use of taste and attitudinal tests, interviews, and other methodologies. Care should be taken, however, that the standards set up are not made too narrow and that they are not thought of as absolute and unchangeable. For if taste training is to be directed toward the widening of the possibilities for the enjoyment of music, it would seem obvious that a standard of taste which embraces only a few composers of top eminence will be less effective than a more catholic standard which leads to an interest in many styles of composition.[83]

SUMMARY

The first thesis considered in this chapter was, "Is musical taste a matter of whimsey or is it in some way lawful?" The answer was clear—taste is lawful. It was noted that the musically elite have surprisingly similar tastes in their selections of eminent composers. Even more astonishing is the high agreement on eminence found to exist among college and high-school groups. Enjoyment too is shared, with the music of certain composers given top billing by the elite and the lay public alike. If knowledge of composers is accepted as forming at least one facet of musical taste, knowledge also must be mentioned as lawful, for a man known well to one segment of the population tends to be equally well known to the members of other similarly chosen samples. Analyses of musicians' nonverbal behavior further attest to the fact that musical taste is not whimsical. Thus the composers whose works are most recorded and appear most often on the programs of symphony orchestras are with few exceptions those regarded as most eminent. Moreover, they are likely to be the men whose biographical sketches occupy most space in histories of music and in general and music encyclopedias.

The second question the chapter posed was that of learning whether the laws of taste are absolute or relative. Here too the answer was unequivocal. Taste follows no absolute, metaphysical rules. Even if natural science variables are among the several determiners of taste—as they may well be—they can be of only secondary importance. All the evidence so far gathered points rather to the relativity of taste, to the fact that it is culture-bound, not culture-free. The descriptions sociology gives of mores fit taste exactly. Change with training and individual differences in the acceptance of standards, both characteristics of musical taste, are earmarks of mores and folkways. Thus the teaching of taste is essentially a process of indoctrination, and the material to be learned differs somewhat from culture to culture and from period to period.

CHAPTER SEVEN ❧ *The Measures of Musical Taste*

WE HAVE SEEN that taste in its several manifestations has considerable stability. Moreover, it has been shown that taste behaves like other social phenomena of our culture and not as if it were obeying some absolute law.[1] It is now time to consider the measurement of taste.

VARIETY OF MEASURES

Experience has shown that no one measure of musical taste can hope to tap the ensemble or totality of attitudes and preferences. Several procedures are needed, each to paint a partial picture. Though the measures we are about to describe are of many different types, they can for convenience be divided into two main categories: (1) the formal tests and (2) the approaches which do not employ such standardized procedures. The tests in turn can be split into auditory and purely paper-and-pencil types. The less standardized methods include the techniques discussed in the previous chapter— the interview and the counting of ballots, the measurement of space allocations,[2] and the analysis of programs—as well as the tabulation of phonograph record listings.

AUDITORY TESTS

One of the earliest of the standardized music tests was Columbia record number A7539, designed by C. E. Seashore as a measure of the "sense of consonance," rather than as a test of taste.[3] However, the directions proved to be impossible of execution, and the term "consonance" was seen to be so ambiguous that the test was dropped from the later revision of the Seashore battery. The record has since been more suitably employed by some researchers as a preference test for tonal intervals. In giving the test 50 sets of simultaneous dyads are presented in pairs, with the second of each pair to be judged as "better" or "worse" than the first. Since the reliability of the measure is, by a very conservative estimate, only in the neighborhood of .65 for adults and considerably lower for children, its use should be limited to group work.[4] It should be noted, however, that this reliability figure, low as it is, at least equals the values reported for a number of the other tonal appreciation tests.

The early Kwalwasser battery consists of two tests of 35 items each. The *Melodic Sensitivity Test* presents two-measure melodic progressions, and the *Harmonic Sensitivity Test* presents harmonic progressions of three chords each. The stimuli are to be rated as "good" or "bad."

> Bad melodic progressions result from the following: bad resolutions, incompatible tones, awkward rhythms, failure to turn after a wide skip, lack of design or purposiveness, distorted balance, incompleteness of melody or rhythm, etc. Authorities agree that bad harmonic effects result from parallel fifths and octaves, wrong doublings, bad-sounding voice movement, bad part omissions, digressions, unprepared modulations, unresolved dissonances, voice distribution over too wide a range, etc.[5]

Scores on these two Kwalwasser tests intercorrelate best at the fifth-grade level with a value of .40. The corresponding value for the eighth grade is .29 and for college .24. With reliabilities of only .42 and .21 (adult level), these two tests must be rated as of questionable value except possibly for studying group trends. The measures have the disadvantage of offering stimuli which are completely out of musical context and of scoring the answers on the basis of rules from a day now past. To a greater or lesser extent many of the other tests described below suffer similarly.

The somewhat later Kwalwasser-Dykema battery has among its tests two that appear to be directly concerned with taste. The *Melodic Taste Test* measures, "on the basis of general music appeal, sensitiveness to structure, balance, and phrase compatibility."[6] Each test item consists of two melodies of two phrases each. The opening phrases of the two melodies are identical, but the second ones are unlike. The latter are to be compared for their suitability as concluding phrases. The test has only 10 items. As this number of stimuli is too small to allow the test much reliability, its usefulness is definitely limited.[7] The second test having to do with taste, the measure of *Tonal Movement,* offers 30 patterns, each consisting of four tones. The patterns are incomplete melodically, and the listener must supply mentally a fifth tone, reporting whether it is *above* the fourth tone or *below* it. With its reliability for adults in the .80's, this test is statistically the best of the K-D battery.[8] There is a correlation of .40 between the scores of college students on the two K-D tests, but the scores of grade-school children show only chance resemblances.

One of the earliest tests of appreciation which employed music is the one by Courtis in which the child is asked to recognize moods and rhythmic movements. Typical of the directions is the following:

It was Saturday morning and the sun was shining. John's mother gave him a pail and sent him into the woods to pick berries. The music will tell you how John felt about going. Listen to the selection and underline the words which best express how the music says John felt.[9]

After listening to approximately 30 seconds of Victor record number 74711 *(Sérénade Mélancolique)* or 25 seconds of number 74581 *(Perpetual Motion),* the child states whether he thinks that John felt glad, sorry, angry, or busy. The test is very short and so has little reliability. However, for training purposes it may have a real function.

A higher-level test with somewhat the same basic idea is the Schultz *Test of Listening Power in Music.*[10] Admittedly more than a taste test, it calls for the playing of phonograph discs followed by 32 multiple-choice questions similar to those in achievement tests. Reliabilities range from .75 for junior high-school students to .81 for college adults.

Themes from 20 selected works constitute the *Gernet Music Preference Test.*[11] The compositions include both "serious" music and jazz. The stimuli are arranged in pairs for simple preference judgments, forming a test which has a reported reliability of .55.

Short themes from 20 selected works are also the elements of the *Bower Musical Moods Test.*[12] The items of this test, which was arranged for seventh- and eighth-graders, were prejudged by 17 music instructors whose answers are assumed to be the correct ones. The task is to designate the one or more sets of adjectives which describe each of the themes. No reliability data are reported for this test, which has little relation to the so-called "tonal capacity" tests.

A similar measure is the *Keston Music Preference Test* in which

120 musical excerpts, each 45 seconds in length, are arranged for judging in groups of four.[13] Twelve "music authorities" decided the relative worth of each excerpt. As was to have been expected, the twelve rated the "serious classics" as best and the swing as worst. In the *Keston Music Recognition Test* the subject is asked to match a list of 34 composers with 30 snatches of "serious" music.

The point has been made that it is sometimes virtually impossible for the testee to shift around his attitudinal sets as speedily and frequently as a test like the *Keston Music Preference Test* demands. Lifton[14] took another approach which lessens this difficulty by presenting only four pieces in his *Music Reaction Test*—the Second Movement of Prokofiev's *Concerto in G Minor (Op. 63)*, Bach's *Allemande from Suites Françaises (Suite #1 in D Minor)*, 59 measures of Puccini's *Suor Angelica*, and the Fourth Movement of Debussy's *String Quartet #1*. Subjects were told to write what the music meant to them and the judges rated these statements as to their reflection of "sensitivity." When seniors in a college music curriculum were asked to rate each other on this same criterion, a correlation of .53 was obtained between the judges' and the students' evaluations. The test correlates at .63 with scores on a test which supposedly measures empathy.

A reliability of .81 has been obtained from one of the more recent of the measures of musical taste, *The Erneston Preference Record*.[15] Sixty-four musical excerpts, each 30 seconds in length and prejudged as either excellent, good, fair, or poor in quality, make up the test. The items which must be ordered for excellence are arranged in groups of four.

The *Kyme Test of Esthetic Judgment of Music*[16] offers 53 pairings of recordings and has a reported reliability of .80. Used also as an aptitude test it correlates .29 with the *Thurstone Test of Primary Mental Abilities*, .26 with the amount of the student's formal musical instruction, and in the .70's with the teacher's estimates of his students' musical levels.

The *Adler Music Appreciation Tests* present compositions by Brahms, Chopin, Mozart, Rameau, Ravel, and Weber recorded on player-piano rolls.[17] Besides the original version of each piece there are three distorted forms—a sentimental, a dull, and a chaotic version. The subject indicates which are his most and least preferred versions and attempts to guess the names of the composers.

Phonograph records give the stimuli for the *Mohler Scales for Measuring Judgment of Orchestral Music*.[18] Sixteen compositions of jazz and serious music, prejudged as to merit by 368 critics, were assembled into groups whose small size precludes a reliability of more than .51. The measure is now of historic interest only as several of the record discs are unavailable. Semeonoff, following the Mohler procedure, has also offered sets of phonograph records for preference judgment.[19] In one study he also asked his subjects to check from four possible interpretations the mood intended by the composer.

An ambitious attempt to measure musical taste has been made by Cattell and Saunders.[20] Snatches of 120 compositions averaging 20 seconds in length were given to 188 persons confined to a mental hospital and to 196 who were assumed to be normal. The data were factor-analyzed and eleven factors were teased out. Unfortunately the phonograph recording was badly done. But if it can be assumed that this imperfection did not unduly affect the subjects' judgments, and if it can be further granted (as many will not grant) that the emerging factors all have meaning, the data become of interest. One factor was found to concern liking for popular jazzlike structure, rhythmical emphasis, fast tempo, individual interpretation, discordant harmonies, and joyful but agitated mood. A second factor apparently involved "an attachment to classical music, of a sentimental, introspective but cheerful nature, with a tendency to color harmonies." Another factor seemed to stress a liking for "warmth and gentleness," and another a preference for "lush, romantic, fairly conventional harmonies, with a flourish." The nature of still other additional factors was not entirely clear. A master's thesis study by Schultz[21] shows that there is at least some stability of preference over a two-month period. In her study the retest correlational values for eight of the eleven factors ranged from .31 to .86.

The easier of the *Oregon Music Discrimination Tests* (constructed by Hevner and Landsbury) can be used to learn whether or not a subject can differentiate between short musical compositions deemed to possess merit and versions of these compositions with distorted melody, rhythm, or harmony.[22] The test consists of 48 pairs of "meritorious" and altered compositions. Scoring credit is given for recognition both of the unaltered versions and the type of distortion of the altered version. The reliability of this measure ranged from .47 for children of the fifth and sixth grades to .63 for junior high-school groups, .78 for pupils in senior high school, and .86 for adults. A second more difficult test comes in two forms, each of which contains 40 items. The subject indicates his preferences and his degree of confidence, the latter being taken into account in the scoring. The test's reliability has been found to fall in the neighborhood of .80 (college population).

Hevner has constructed another measure, the *Test for Musical*

Concepts, to assess the subject's comprehension of compositions as complete wholes.[23] While hearing a rendition of Tchaikovsky's *Sixth Symphony,* for example, the listener answers a set of true-false questions of this type: "The melody of the middle section is taken from the original theme; it is varied, however, and is played in faster tempo." After three hearings of the symphony, the listener checks one statement in each of four pairs of statements which have largely to do with mood. Preliminary forms of this test have reliabilities which run as high as .81.

Somewhat similar to the *Oregon Music Discrimination Tests* is Hoffren's *Test of Expressive Phrasing in Music.*[24] Deciding that the ingredients of expression are rubato, smoothness, articulation, phrasing, unity, continuity, dynamics, and dynamic and agogic accentuation, Hoffren presents on tape 40 pairs of musical excerpts, approximately one third of which are played by a clarinet, one third by an unaccompanied trumpet, and the rest by an oboe. Each pair of items consists of two versions of the same excerpt with one of them deficient in one or more of the elements of expression listed above. Correctness of answer was judged by the faculty and graduate students of the University of Illinois School of Music. Reliabilities of from .53 to .66 are reported, and there is a positive but rather small relationship (around .35) with scores on the somewhat similar Wing subtests (see below).

Wing has devised four tests which have to do with judging the appropriateness of the style of playing a tune.[25] In each test a recorded tune is repeated either in identical or altered style. The notes played by the left hand in the "harmony" test may or may not be altered during the second rendition. The subject must listen for the possibility of a change and then decide which of the two harmonizations (if there are two) is the more appropriate. In the test of "rhythmic accent" the accents may or may not fall in a different place in the second rendition. The possibility of change and, if there is a change, the more appropriate style of playing are to be checked. The two other tests in this series concern loudness patterns and phrase groups. The four tests are not very reliable individually, but when taken as a battery and combined with several other tests of music ability, a reliability in the neighborhood of .90 is achieved. The Wing battery appears to be having considerable use in Great Britain.

Tests of taste have been constructed by Schoen,[26] Lowery,[27] Drake,[28] and others. Schoen's *Tonal Sequence Test* supposedly reveals the listener's sensitivity to the fitness of the tones of a melody.

For fitness Schoen suggests five criteria: balance, "belonging-to-getherness," unity, variety, and finality. In the test each phrase is followed by four terminal phrases which must be assigned values of 0, 2, 4, or 6 for fitness. In Lowery's *Cadence Test*, the second of each pair of cadences heard must be judged as more or less complete. Drake's *Test of Intuition* probes for the ability to supply endings to unfinished themes. This ability is thought to be concerned with phrase-balance, key-center, and time-balance. The listener judges whether or not the second phrase of each stimulus pair makes a satisfactory ending to the first phrase. Lowery, Drake, and Schoen have constructed other measures of abilities[29] which border on the area of taste.

Little is known about the degree of overlap among the areas covered by these formal auditory tests. However, with the stimuli often quite divergent, the reliabilities typically low, and the test philosophies occasionally rather dissimilar, it would be surprising if all of the test intercorrelations were found to be very high, i.e. for all of the tests to be measuring very similar variables. Moreover, it should be remembered that the criteria of the tests for "correct" answers are based on social judgments. Naturally then a fraction of the "correct" answers of today will be "incorrect" tomorrow.

PAPER-AND-PENCIL TESTS

On the theory that general musical information should be related to appreciation, Kwalwasser has published a *Test of Music Information and Appreciation*.[30] Its arrangement is that of the typical school-subject achievement test, with queries about composers and compositions, the production of tone by orchestral instruments, etc. The test requires some 40 minutes for its administration. Its reliability has been found to be approximately .84 for Stanford students. A more difficult form of this test has been constructed by Young,[31] and another modification of it is by Semeonoff.[32]

A novel sort of measure with a reliability around .85 is the *Test of Musical Taste* developed by Vernon.[33] Here the subject is asked to record his reactions to 30 wholly imaginary programs of music. On the assumption that the experts Vernon has chosen to prejudge the programs possess taste (he has chosen as experts a panel of six musicians), the score is defined in terms of the resemblances between what the subject records and what the experts have previously checked as the ideal.

Using a slight modification of the Thurstone method for the

construction of attitude scales, R. Seashore and K. Hevner have developed a *Test of Attitude Toward Music* with a reliability for college students of about .90.[34] While this measure may not, strictly speaking, be a true test of taste, it surely bears rather closely on the problem. The test is composed of statements about music with which the subject is asked to agree or disagree. Scale values are obtained from the ballots of a large group of people. Each item can thus be placed on an attitudinal continuum which stretches from 1 (extreme of favorableness) to 11 (extreme of unfavorableness), and the testee's score is the average of the scale values of the items with which he agrees. The scale values shift a bit over the years since they reflect changing cultural (semantic) attitudes towards music.[35] An example of an item whose acceptance would indicate a mildly favorable but not enthusiastic attitude toward music is, "I believe strongly in the beneficial and pleasurable effects of music, but do not care to take an active part in it myself." As each test item was prejudged by a large group of people, the testee's verbal attitude can readily be assessed by this instrument. In 1962–63 when the test was restandardized,[36] this item was found to have a scale value of 4.8.

Self-rating scales have been developed to measure interests in "serious" music and in several sorts of "popular" music.[37] An important feature of these scales is the placing of prejudged behavioral characterizations along the rating lines as points of reference. Thus in the case of a one-line scale 24 cm. in length, where a check at the extreme left indicates "extreme dislike of music" and one at the right end "strongest possible interest in music," the two most extreme characterizations are, "I listen to music only when my parents or teachers make me listen to it" (placed 2.7 cm. from the extreme left) and, "I spend most of my free time listening to or playing music" (placed 21.3 cm. from the left end). In an assessment of one of the scales, seventh-graders and their mothers were asked to check independently the musical interests of the former. The coefficient of correlation between the ratings of the mothers and their children was found to be .80, indicating a fair degree of validity for the scale. It should be added, however, that the mothers tended to believe that their children had more interest in music than the latter admitted to having.

Another more informal measure of taste involves the use of a list of composers described in Chapter 6.[38] Those whose taste is to be assessed are given this list with the request that they check the most eminent ten, fifteen, or so. The extent of the agreement with the ordering made by the members of the American Musicological Society determines the score. It should be noted that any such list becomes out of date in the course of time. To be of worth it must reflect contemporary attitudes.

The more formal tests are obviously concerned with individual taste. With their reliabilities and validities generally mediocre or poor, they would appear to have a rather limited future. So far they seem to have stimulated relatively little interest or research. The techniques next to be discussed are in no sense rivals, for they aim to measure what might be termed "collective" or group taste.

POLLING

This book has already considered at some length data obtained through polling, which is obviously not a perfect psychological tool.[39] Samples polled in past studies have sometimes proved to be but poor representatives of the populations with which the researcher was really concerned. The questions which have at times been asked have all too often been shown to be ambiguous or impossible to answer. And pollsters have occasionally misinterpreted their own data. Yet polling data in the musical area, inaccurate as they sometimes are, have been found to yield roughly the same picture of collective contemporary taste as have the more operational procedures. Thus polling would appear to possess a degree of validity and research utility.

ORCHESTRAL PROGRAMS

Attention has been called to the fact that the Boston Symphony Orchestra in its programs favors roughly similar composers decade after decade. It is of interest too that this orchestra's top choices[40] tend in the main to be the ones also favored by the musicologists. This can be shown by the correlational figure of .65 between the musicologists' rankings obtained in 1964 (American Musicological Association membership) and other rankings derived from the relative frequencies with which compositions (of the composers mentioned as most eminent by musicologists in 1938) were played by the Boston Symphony Orchestra in the decade 1955–65. The fact that this great orchestra chose to give certain contemporary and late nineteenth-century composers a frequent audience even before the musicologists were ready to award them top status kept the correlation from being even higher. Thus Prokofiev and Ravel were played about as often as Wagner, Richard Strauss considerably more often, and Honegger and Hindemith almost as often. Schubert and Handel were rarely played. The comparable correlational value with college student ranks obtained in 1962–63 was .72. The program rank order correlated with ranks obtained from measurements taken from musical histories, musical encyclopedias, and general encyclopedias published during the decade of 1960's at .71 for each.

BOSTON SYMPHONY'S TOP FIVE FAVORITES COMPARED WITH THOSE FROM OTHER SOURCES

Rank	Boston Symphony (1955–1965)	Rank	Musicologists (1964)	Rank	College Students (1962–1963)
1	Beethoven	1	Bach	1	Beethoven
2	Mozart	2	Beethoven	2	Bach
3	Brahms	3	Mozart	3	Chopin
4.5	Bach	4	Haydn	4	Mozart
4.5	R. Strauss	5	Brahms	5	Brahms
7.5	Haydn	8	Schubert	8	Wagner
12.5	Wagner	9	Wagner	9	Schubert
13.5	Schubert	10	Chopin	13	Haydn
23.5	Chopin	19	R. Strauss	17	R. Strauss

Rank	Histories of Music (1960's)	Rank	Musical Encyclopedias (1960's)	Rank	General Encyclopedias (1960's)
1	Bach	1	Beethoven	1	Bach
2	Beethoven	2	Mozart	2	Beethoven
3	Mozart	3	Wagner	3	Wagner
4	Wagner	4	Haydn	4	Mozart
5	Schubert	5	Schubert	5	Schubert
6	Haydn	6	Bach	8	Brahms
12	Brahms	11	Brahms	10	Haydn
13	Chopin	13	Chopin	16	Chopin
15	R. Strauss	20	R. Strauss	20	R. Strauss

BROADCASTS OF RECORDINGS

A number of years ago when a series of the Pacific Gas and Electric Company's broadcasts were analyzed in an effort to learn whose compositions were most often played, it was found that the favorites over a three-year period coincided remarkably well with those of the Boston Symphony Orchestra (*rho* of .90) of the same time period. Here Sibelius' and Tchaikovsky's broadcast ranks were the most markedly out of line (using the musicologists' ballots as the frame of reference). The rank order of composers favored in the broadcast programs correlated well (*rho* of .85) with the eminence ranks established from the votes of the musicologists (1944) but somewhat less well (*rho* of .71) with the eminence ranks derived from the ballots of a group of Stanford sophomores. The hierarchies based on the relative amounts of attention paid the musicologists' 92 composers in the histories of music and in the music and general encyclopedias of the 1940's yielded *rho*'s of .81, .81, and .68 when correlated against the rank order derived from this utility company's programs. A glimpse at the table will give approximately the same picture of current taste as will an inspection of some of the other barometers (barring Tchaikovsky's high placement).

PACIFIC GAS AND ELECTRIC COMPANY'S BROADCASTS
1941, 1942, AND 1943

Rank	Composers
1	Beethoven
2	Tchaikovsky
3	Brahms
4	Mozart
5	Bach
6	Sibelius
7	Wagner
8	Schubert
9	Schumann

RECORD LISTINGS

The composers favored in the programs of the Boston Symphony Orchestra and the Pacific Gas and Electric Company broadcasts tend also to be the ones with the most recordings to their credit. Thus the rank order of the record-listing frequencies of the early 1940's correlates .88 with the symphony's rank order in the same time period, and .91 with that of the utility company's broadcasts. When compared with the eminence ranks obtained from the histories, the music encyclopedias, and the general encyclopedias of the 1940's, the correlation values were found to be .87, .88, and .69 respectively. The musicologists agreed to the extent of a *rho* of .90, but the college students' value was lower (.75).

The scores for the disc listings were obtained by noting the distribution of recordings mentioned in each of four books. Those used in counting the discs were Kolodin's *A Guide to Recorded Music* (1941), Hall's *The Record Book* (1943), Haggin's *Music on Records* (1943),[41] and *The Gramophone Shop Encyclopedia of Recorded Music* (1942). The four books agreed very well among themselves on the number of recordings associated with the 92 composers. The pool of any two of the book lists against the pool of the other two yields a *rho* of approximately .95. Incidentally, the agreement between the 1936 and 1942 and between the 1942 and 1948 editions of the *Gramophone Shop Encyclopedia* is roughly of the same order of magnitude.

In the latest study of phonographic recordings now available, the ranking derived from the most recent polling of the musicologists was found to agree substantially (*rho* of .75) with the rank order established from counting the long-play recordings listed in the October 1967 issue of the *Schwann Long-Playing Record Catalogue* (W. Schwann, Inc., Boston). The counting, made by Richard M. Grant as a class project, was of the recordings of the 50 top-producing composers of the Schwann list who had been born before 1870. The most notable disagreement occurred with Telemann who was fifteenth as a current producer of recordings but near the bottom of the list of 50 in the eyes of the musicologists. Other instances where musicological status was not nearly as high as production rate included Johann Strauss, Grieg, and Saint-Saëns. Composers with far fewer recordings than their musicological status would seem to warrant were D. Scarlatti, Monteverde, Schütz, Corelli, and Purcell.

SCHOLARLY TEXTS

Since histories of music and encyclopedia articles on the composers are written by musicologists or their peers, it is not too much to expect that the allocations of space in scholarly works will follow the taste patterns of the authors' subcultures. Of course the editors of encyclopedias must usually limit the overall space, and, as we have said earlier, this necessity must in turn lead to a restriction of the number of composers whose names can appear in such publications. But the relative amounts of space devoted to the names which do pass the selection will tend to reflect cultural attitudes.

It must be granted of course that the allocations will mirror more than taste. The perfectionist who composes relatively little and the important composer whose life-span is short may both receive less space than they deserve, while the controversial and notorious character, particularly if blessed with a long life, may receive undeserved space. Moreover, the author of the history or article may possess biases of his own which at times can reach serious proportions. But if the data of many histories and encyclopedias are pooled, the author biases will tend to cancel, or at least will distort the picture less. The validity of the space allocation method is also affected by a sort of group parochialism. In work done in 1968 the author has demonstrated that scholarly treatises tend to favor their own nationals. Thus *Grand Larousse* and *Larousse de la Musique* pay far more attention to French composers than do comparable English-language treatises. *Groves Dictionary* on the other hand gives relatively more space to English composers and the *Encyclopaedia Britannica* to the Americans.

Before the turn of this century, Cattell employed the space-allocation method in an attempt to discover the thousand most eminent men of history.[42] Although the names of the encyclopedias he used cannot now be determined, it may be guessed that the *Encyclopaedia Britannica* was quite probably the major or perhaps the only one. There are some ambiguities in his list because no initials were added to the surnames to aid in distinguishing which of the several famous Webers and Strausses Cattell intended. Hence some of the composers who bear these names may or may not have been in the list. Of those whose identities cannot be questioned, Mozart is the first musician, with a rank of 93 in the general array (Napoleon topped the list with a rating of 1). Beethoven had a rank of 220, Handel 261, Haydn 300, Rossini 326, Wagner 337, Mendelssohn 404, Palestrina 471, and Bach 475. No other composers appeared among the first 500.

It was to have been expected that the editors of the general encyclopedias would allocate less space to composers than to the military heroes and to the eminent of certain other fields. Hence the absolute ranks of these musicians tell us very little. Yet the fact that these nine composers received the lion's share of the space allocated to musicians is surely indicative of their relative status during the period just prior to Cattell's researches. It is of interest that all of these names with the exception of Rossini's appear high on the later lists compiled by the present author. The space devoted to this Italian composer has decreased slowly but steadily in both the music and general source books written in the English language during this century.[43] Rossini was not mentioned by a single musicologist in the 1938 survey and received few votes from the musicologists in the later polls. Bach on the other hand improved in status rapidly and soon became one of the top-ranking masters.

It is unfortunate that in recent years the *Encylopaedia Britan-*

nica has not always maintained the high quality that marked its earlier editions and printings. By the early 1960's[44] it no longer yielded a faithful reflection of elite attitudes in the area of contemporary music. The 1967 printing, however, gives recent composers considerably more attention, and the composers born before the 1870's are well handled on the whole. But it seems clear that if one desires to make the most of space measurement as a reasonably valid research procedure, the more specialized documents, i.e. those devoted wholly to music, make much the better vehicle.

Although an eminent composer is normally discussed in but one section of any given encyclopedia, histories typically mention a number of composers on a single page and repeat mention of the same composer on a number of widely separated pages. Hence exact space measurements are usually not feasible in work on histories, and the only practical technique so far found to be serviceable is that of the tabulation of page-mentions. Fortunately the number of page-mentions and the exact amount of space have been found to correlate so highly (*rho*'s in the .90's) that for most purposes they may be considered as a single technique.[45]

It has already been demonstrated that the rankings of composers determined on the basis of exact space measurement and page-mention frequencies are quite similar to the eminence rankings obtained from the preference orders taken from the programs of the Boston Symphony Orchestra and the Pacific Gas and Electric Company, and to the order of frequencies secured from record listings. Furthermore, the three sorts of scholarly endeavor—histories of music, music encyclopedias, and to a lesser degree general encyclopedias—devote rather similar amounts of attention to our group of 92 composers. When the decade of the 1960's is considered, the rank order obtained from the histories correlates .93 and .88 respectively with those constructed from the music and the general encyclopedias. The ranks secured from the two kinds of encyclopedias agree to the extent of a *rho* of .92. The ranks obtained from these three sorts of treatises of the early 1960's correlated with the American Musicological Society's 1964 rank order as follows: histories, .90; music encyclopedias, .84; general encyclopedias, .77.

BOREDOM

While no one has probably ever attempted seriously to measure taste by testing for musical boredom, the *New York Herald Tribune* during March of 1954 asked its readers to name the ten compositions they regarded as most boring.[46] It would seem likely that the New York list is unique, that it should in all probability not resemble one assembled either in Minneapolis or in San Francisco since local conditions would be quite dissimilar in these three locales. Each area would have its own particular irritations, brought on in part by the too-frequent hearing of certain pieces and by the fact that other compositions may have recently been badly played.

One wonders if it is not a relatively small number who would react so strongly to clichés and nuances of rendition. As the critic Alfred Frankenstein has said, there is a considerable group of listeners who are passive followers and honor what they have been taught to honor.[47] For them, boredom, even if present, would have less effect on basic taste. Only the sophisticated listeners might be seriously affected. Of course most persons tire rather rapidly of specific jazz pieces and other examples of less serious music. And Rachmaninov's *Prelude* must be shelved occasionally to keep it reasonably in favor. Boredom, however, has a place in music in that it may be deliberately used within a composition for contrast effects.[48]

In a somewhat broader sense of the term, boredom is clearly related to taste. Any school of musical composition, no matter how much it is in favor at any one time, sooner or later begets some reaction against itself. Although it may later return to favor, at least in modified form, it must pass through a period of partial or total eclipse. Here is a phenomenon found in all but the most static cultures, a sort of collective boredom.

SUMMARY

In this chapter attention was first called to the formal tests and to the fact that, except for a few, they measure individual taste with relatively poor reliability and validity. To disclose the taste of classes and interest groups, other techniques have been more successful. Polling, program analyses,[49] the counting of recordings, and examinations into the relative amounts of attention paid composers in scholarly works on music all have disclosed similar group favorites among the composers. These "barometers" have been found to be, in considerable degree, internally consistent. They furnish ways of studying collective taste as it exists here and elsewhere, and even as it existed decades ago.

CHAPTER EIGHT *The Nature of Musical Abilities*

IN THE preceding chapters, the notion of capability has been freely employed but in rather loose fashion. To discriminate between intervals, to differentiate major from minor, to sense strain or relaxation in a melody, or even to develop a taste for a particular kind of music presupposes musical abilities of some sort. But whether or not these capabilities are largely inborn and whether only one general ability or several must be assumed are questions which have so far not been considered. It is time then that these and other important questions about the functioning of our musical capabilities be examined.

ABILITY—APPROPRIATE DESCRIPTIVE TERM

In their work of describing musical capabilities, the psychological testers have employed a variety of terms without complete agreement as to exact meanings. To some authorities musical talent has meant innate capability for musical performance. Others have used the term more broadly to include musical appreciation. The term "capacity" also seems to bear the connotation of innate ability. Capacities of course are never directly observed but are inferred from behavioral manifestations such as test scores. The term "aptitude" is somewhat less controversial in that the inferred ability is generally assumed to be only in part innate. It tends to imply potentiality rather than achievement, ability largely undeveloped before formal training has taken place. The term "ability," suggesting the power to act but indicating nothing about the heritability or congenitalness of inferred potentiality, is the broadest and safest of all of these terms. As we shall soon see, nature and nurture invariably function jointly, and it is erroneous to say that any act is the sole result of either the one or the other. Hence in the discussions of the present chapter, conservative usage will be followed and musical ability will be the focus of attention.

GENERALITY OF ABILITY

Almost everyone who has attempted to forecast musical success has met persons who show great promise along some musical lines and extreme weakness in other areas. Here is a sixth-grader who scored in the top percentile on standardized tests of tonal memory and of pitch and intensity discrimination but had only chance scores on measures of time and rhythm. A monotone of mature years who came to the laboratory for aid in overcoming his disability was found to score quite well on time, intensity, and rhythm tests. But his pitch weakness was so complete that he could detect only a slight difference between the highest and lowest tones of the piano. The vocalist Galli-Curci, while proficient in most musical endeavors, had such a poor "musical ear" that she needed an accompanist who could be called upon to transpose at a moment's notice. There also are weaknesses in the affective realm, e.g. a kettledrummer in one of America's great symphony orchestras who privately admitted that he abhorred all music in which the kettledrums were not frequently called into action. It was his abnormally strong interest in rhythms which early led him to work with the percussion choir. Cases such as these would seem to yield evidence for the existence of several rather independent musical abilities rather than a single all-embracing one.

Certain of the statistically minded have attempted to answer the question of the generality of ability through recourse to tables of intercorrelations. They point out that most music tests now at hand intercorrelate very poorly indeed. If it can be assumed that the tests are valid measures of musical capabilities, this evidence also refutes the notion of a single musical ability.

The factor analysts have tried to probe more deeply into the problem. Unfortunately, however, the several different methods of factor analysis now available are based on somewhat dissimilar philosophies and therefore do not always lead to identical conclusions. It is hardly an exaggeration to say that the English, who are prone to believe in the existence of general factors, tend to find them in almost every set of test intercorrelations, while the Americans, with their different theories, more commonly find several group factors but no general one. In his earlier researches the British-trained Drake thought he found a general musical factor when he studied tests covering the areas of tonal memory, pitch, rhythm, intensity, tonal movement, and general intelligence.[1] While scrutinizing his own English-made music tests, Wing also found a general factor which accounted for 40 per cent of the total variance.[2] There were two additional group factors, one being bipolar and apparently having to do with analysis and synthesis, and the other concerned with harmony and melody. Another Briton, McLeish, who gave both the Wing and the Seashore music batteries to some 100 students, found the same general cognitive factor in each.[3] Still another Briton, Vernon, feels that the American-built tests of Seashore which stress sensory capabilities have little to do with music ability.[4] He quotes the data of Manzer and Marowitz to bolster this view.[5] He himself has studied tests such as the *Oregon Music Discrimination Tests* which make use of actual musical materials, and he thinks these test a general factor. Vernon's attitude toward the sensory tests is partly shared by Franklin, who has factor-analyzed a battery of tests including several of the Seashore, the Wing, tests of intelligence and vocabulary, some visual perceptual tests, and his own relatively unstandardized music tests. A study of the factors which emerged convinced him that musical ability has two aspects, one being the mechanical-acoustic (e.g. pitch, timbre, time, and intensity discrimination) and the other, on a far higher level, he terms the judicious-musical. The latter reaches its highest levels in creative musical talent.[6]

In an analysis of factors involved in learning a simple musical theme, Burroughs and Morris[7] identified four which they regarded as most pertinent. These were memory for melody, recognition of musical shape, verbal intelligence and interest, and rhythmic accent. The most extensive factor study of basic music abilities so far undertaken has been that of Karlin, an American who investigated 32 tests and found eight group factors.[8] No general factor emerged from the statistical manipulations. The most important factors involved pitch, memory for musical passages as a whole, and recall for isolated musical elements. A still later American study by Bower also disclosed no huge general factor but rather three group factors.[9] Bower's first factor was a complex one which had to do with tonal memory, pitch discrimination, melodic taste, and rhythm discrimination. Her second concerned mood, loudness, and time discrimination. Her third featured rhythm discrimination and tonal memory. The reader will probably agree that conclusions based on research using factor analysis must be quite tentative at best. Factors are obviously products of the tests used. Therefore, if there is no test covering some important area of musical activity, the picture disclosed by the factor analysis will reflect this imbalance. When two studies employ different sets of tests, it is quite possible that they will report different factors. After all, factor analysis is only a way of describing with some economy a matrix of correlations. Since the factors depend upon the measures used, they will be meaningful only as the tests are meaningful. With present-day music tests still in a somewhat primitive state, it follows that factor analysis can yield no definitive answers. We are left then with whatever conclusions case studies and intercorrelational analyses can yield, and with the notion that there probably are several poorly correlated music abilities.

ARE ABILITIES IN MUSIC RELATED TO OTHER ART ABILITIES?

Another aspect of the problem of general musical ability has to do with the hypothesis that there may exist a broad ability which embraces all the arts. But here again the experimental evidence is largely opposed. In an extensive study with a variety of special aptitude and taste tests, Morrow could find no correlations of any size between the music and art measures.[10] Strong[11] found that the male artist score as measured by his well-known *Vocational Interest Test* correlates .69 with his male musician performer score but only .17 with that for the male music teacher. He also noted that the male artist score correlates more than .69 with the following occupational scores: psychologist, physician, architect, and author-journalist. The male musician performer score, he found, correlates above .69 with both the psychologist and the physician score. The Strong data, it would seem, give little support to the notion of a general art interest. Nor could White in a study of the versatility of 300 eminent men find much trace of a general aesthetic type of interest or ability.[12]

It is true that certain British psychologists[13] have seen a general aesthetic factor in the low positive correlations they have found between the appreciation scores obtained in the several arts. This interpretation of their data, however, has been strongly challenged,[14] partly on statistical and partly on philosophical grounds.

One small area in which musicians do resemble artists is in the average length of life of their eminent fellows. In one study the life-span for both musicians and artists was found to be approximately 67.5 years (it is undoubtedly longer now). That of eminent engineers on the other hand was slightly over 71, and for educators it was somewhat more than 72.5 years.[15] Just why artists and musicians should be alike and musicians and educators different in this regard is not clear. But the fact that two occupational groups have similar longevities is most certainly no justification for hypothesizing a commonality of abilities.

ACADEMIC INTELLIGENCE AND MUSICAL ABILITIES

It has been argued that academic intelligence is an important component of musical abilities.[16] At least the fact has been established that the musically great men of history possessed far better than average intelligence. J. S. Bach for example had an estimated IQ somewhere between 125 and 140, Beethoven's was between 135 and 140, Haydn's between 120 and 140, Handel's between 145 and 155, and Mozart's between 150 and 155.[17] And there are studies which show children with high music-test scores to be significantly brighter than their low-scoring colleagues.[18] For the other side of the argument, it must be said that scores on the better-standardized music tests, when given to groups of limited age range, show little correlation with those on tests of academic intelligence, although the slight correlations which are found are usually positive.[19] It should also be noted that children of high IQ tend to yield music-test scores appropriate to their chronological ages but not to their IQs.[20]

Other evidence against the notion that intelligence and musical abilities are invariably related can be seen in data gathered on those peculiar individuals, the idiot savants. Traditionally this term has been applied to persons who test relatively low in intelligence but who possess some well-developed special ability. Typical is a child of four years who could barely articulate "papa" and "mama" but was able to sing over 50 melodies. It is now believed that many of the cases thought earlier to fit the idiot-savant classification could better be called schizophrenics. Others have been found to be much higher in IQ than had first been estimated,[21] while still others, admittedly low in intelligence, have been shown to be musical or artistic in only a relative sense. They were imbeciles perhaps in academic intelligence but average or a little deficient in the special ability, not really superior. There seem, however, to be at least a few cases who come close to fitting the classical picture of the idiot savant. When Rife and Snyder addressed inquiries to 55 American institutes for the feeble-minded, they unearthed eight mental defectives who appeared to show somewhat better than average musical ability.[22] Anastasi and Levee[23] have more recently described an adult with exceptional musical ability. His Binet IQ was only 67 but his WAIS verbal score was 92. There was some evidence of brain damage due to encephalitis. The authors suggest that the case of each idiot savant is different from that of every other, and explanations fitting one may not fit another.

But true idiot savants, while small in number, are sufficiently numerous to refute the hypothesis that slightly better than average musical ability must invariably be accompanied by high intelligence. As we have seen, the music test data indicate that within the range of school populations, academic intelligence and the several tonal abilities have at best only a slight positive relationship.[24] Yet the fact remains that if one is to reach the highest level of musical success one needs an intelligence considerably above that of the average.[25]

HERITABILITY OF MUSICAL ABILITIES

The present-day formulation of the nature-nurture relationship is not one which would have appealed to the extremists of the 1920's and 1930's. Whether they were hereditarians or environmentalists, the older theorists blinded themselves to the obvious in their attempts to maintain their one-sided positions. It is now clear that neither nature nor nurture alone can make a musician. Both must be present before musical and other abilities can emerge. The person who has excellent tonal and rhythmic sensitivities but who is in unmusical surroundings will not be as likely to achieve in music as will another with similar sensitivities who finds himself in a more propitious environment. Questions which ask for the relative potencies of nature and nurture in creating a musician are unanswerable. They are as meaningless as questions on how much of the speed of a particular automobile is due to the gasoline and how much to the make of the car, or what percentage of the area of a rectangle is attributable to its length and what percentage to its width.

Certain people seem to be so constructed that they react far more positively than most to tonal stimuli. Even for these cases there must be fertility of environment if the early interest is not to be turned in other directions. Erwin Nyiregyhazi, a prodigy who was studied most carefully by Révész, sang melodies before he could speak and began to improvise during his third year.[26] Yet he did not achieve the renown which might reasonably have been forecast for him. But Mozart, who "learned" the clavier before age four and composed little pieces at age five, although perceptibly no more precocious, reached musical heights almost no one else has attained. The differences in the successes of Mozart and his fellow prodigy must be due at least in part to dissimilarities in environmental pressures.

A warning should be given on the possibility of confusing musical ability with motor skills. History reveals youngsters whose hands were excellently formed for piano work, who were willing to practice long hours and so mastered many difficult piano techniques, and who had parents or teachers to tell them precisely what to play and when and how to vary their playing from the mechanically exact. These children admitted to no real love of music or yearning to perform or to compose. The "performance expressiveness" of their playing was not their own but was imposed on their playing by others. Were these children musical geniuses or were they merely persons of unique build on whom optimal pressures from the surrounding environment led to the development of remarkable motor skills?

The more tonal abilities[27] appear in the child at an earlier age than do the rhythmic.[28] With practice, preschool children make spectacular gains in singing tones, intervals, and phrases but less improvement in time-keeping. Greatly enhanced skill in the last mentioned appears with training at a somewhat later period, as soon as better motor coordination permits. Some of the unevenness in musical growth then is apparently due to differences in maturational readiness for the activities in question.

It is reassuring to know that pitch sensitivity can be improved by training. Wyatt and a number of others have shown that enormous changes can be produced by the use of proper training procedures.[29] After training, Wyatt's music-school students had moved on the Seashore pitch norms from the seventh up to the second decile. Her subjects who were not enrolled in a music school had with pitch training risen from the seventh decile to the third or fourth. This growth in sensitivity was not just a coaching effect but was apparent at tonal ranges where no training had been attempted. But is the improvement so far demonstrated a matter of enhanced attention and mental concentration, a mere upping of cognitive limits as Carl Seashore has maintained,[30] or is it something more basic? If Seashore's thesis were valid, one would expect children of high IQ with their better powers of concentration to score higher than their more normal fellows on tonal tests. But as we have already noted, the two groups make similar scores.[31] Hence it seems safe to assume that the effects of pitch training on ability are rather basic. It might be added that even if sensitivity changes had not been demonstrated so dramatically there would still be no reason to suppose that training methods developed later might not be effective.

The view of nature and nurture to which our considerations so far have led us is briefly that an ability is always the resultant of the interplay of heredity and environment. The organism limits or facilitates achievement in many ways. The environment likewise aids or inhibits. From these two sets of interacting limitations and facilitations abilities develop. Musical abilities seem in general no more nor less inherited than abilities in many other areas.

Musical Abilities and Family Lines. Like begets like only to a limited extent. But even where the offspring closely resemble the progenitors in abilities, it is impossible to determine the exact causes of the resemblance. D.A.R.-like studies of family stock are of little or no value to the problem of unscrambling the roles played by heredity and environment in the creation of musical abilities.[32] It should come as no surprise to find that where a man has had two wives, only one of whom was musical, his two broods of children usually resemble their own mothers more than their stepmothers. Whether the resemblance is due to the biological inheritance of genes transmitting musical potentiality, to a complex of mother fixations or stepmother rejections, or to some combination of biological and sociopsychological causes, the analyses cannot disclose.[33] Whether a person is wedded to the idea that musical ability is wholly a matter of inheritance or entirely due to excellent training, he can be made happy by the same family-line analyses. If the genealogical research proceeds far enough back in time, the musician who believes in heredity can always find a musical ancestor from whom his musical ability may have come, while the environmentalist can relish the absence of musical abilities among his immediate ancestors and point to some unrelated musician or teacher as the "source" of the environmental pressures which have antedated the musical achievements.

The musical Bachs and the members of other families of famous virtuosos have been carefully counted generation after generation but with no great benefit to science.[34] For who can tell whether the eventual eclipse of certain of these families was due to dilution of the musical heritage; to changes in the social, economic, and political milieu which made other occupations more attractive to the members of later generations; or to some combination of biological and economic forces? Genealogical research may indeed be quite necessary for those who crave to belong to the socially elite, but it throws no light on the problem of the origin of special abilities.

MUSICAL ABILITIES AND PHYSICAL AND MENTAL STRUCTURE

Much of the folklore about the effects of physique on musical ability is an outgrowth of "common sense" and primitive logic.[35] One such folktale is that angular ears predispose the owner to unmusical existence since sound waves are not angular but curvilinear. A person fortunate to be gifted with long, thin, muscular fingers and wide handspan has per se the ability to be a violinist, a pianist—or a thief. Extremely even front teeth and certain textures of lip are allegedly related to the ease of playing one or more sorts of wind instruments, and a protruding lower jaw makes its owner especially suited for playing the oboe or bassoon.

So far no one has bothered to check on the relation of ear shapes or jaw protrusion to musical abilities, but work has been done on finger length and slenderness, tooth evenness, and thickness of lips.[36] Admittedly it is easier to play the violin or the piano if the hands are "properly" constructed. Yet no correlations of moment have been found between finger, lip, or tooth measurements and ability to master violins, horns, or clarinets. Although the pianists and violinists of college age so far examined do have slightly wider than average hands and longer fingers,[37] a study of still younger pianists showed these beginners to have shorter than average fingers.[38] Apparently a dedicated musician like the great violinist Ysaye, who had extremely stubby fingers, simply worked harder at his task to reach skills as great as those his better-fingered colleagues could more easily achieve.

The racial determinists have had much to say about musical abilities.[39] Ordinarily Nordic-lovers, they have been willing to grant the Alpines, Mediterraneans, Semites, and sometimes American blacks prominence in one or more of the nonliterary arts because they regard ability in literature as belonging to a higher order of creativity than capability in music, painting, and the other arts. Most racists base any alleged superiority on obscure elements of physique presumably caused by differences in genetic structure. A very few have offered sociopsychological explanations; e.g., the musical achievements of black Americans and Jews are overcompensations for their unhappy minority status.

It would seem wise to check on the facts of race before searching for reasons for the supposed superiority of some one "racial" group. It is true of course that music has blossomed at certain times and places and has withered at other periods and in other areas. But is the blossoming correlated with the rise or fall of any particular race? The question would have more meaning if there were general agreement as to what constitutes a race. After decades of argument the physical anthropologists are in the process of discarding the term except perhaps for use in separating a half dozen (or fewer) groups. The ancestry of most Europeans and Americans shows such diverse strains that it can be described only in terms of national and cultural unities. To explain a person's musical abilities by saying "X is musical because he is a Slavic Jew" can mean little more than that X probably came from a culture area where there were excellent teachers and where music was especially honored and furnished one of the few outlets for occupational success.[40]

As was mentioned earlier, research in music testing has proved of little worth for "racial" assessments,[41] even for the comparisons of whites and blacks.[42] In the several studies on racial difference, sometimes one and sometimes the other of these two American groups has achieved the higher mean test score. The most that can be said is that whatever the mean score differences are, they appear to be due largely if not entirely to factors of the testing situations and not to basic differences associated with racial stock.

He who would uncover genetic differences between "racial" groups must first find culture-free tests. But, to quote Goodenough and Morris, "the search for a culture-free test, whether of intelligence, artistic ability, personal-social characteristic, or any other measurable trait, is illusory, and . . . the naive assumption that the mere freedom from verbal requirements renders a test equally suitable for all groups is no longer tenable."[43]

The explanation of sex differences in musical ability is much the same as that for "racial" differences except of course that there is no difficulty with the term. Music tests cannot be guaranteed to award the higher mean score consistently to either sex.[44] On the achievement side there is no question but that the male has so far taken almost all prizes. In a man's world this is hardly to be wondered at, for the environmental pressures to succeed are largely exerted in his direction. Such observations, however, have not dissuaded Vaerting,[45] Schwarz,[46] and others from the thought that woman is naturally less creative and is inherently defective in whatever may be the biological bases for the several musical abilities.

Moreover, the eminent psychologist and determined hereditarian Carl Seashore has declaimed: "Woman's fundamental urge is to be beautiful, loved, and adored as a person; man's urge is to provide and achieve in a career."[47]

The statements of the hereditarians are not backed by evidence of any strength. Far more basic data must be gathered before sex differences can be properly explained. Unfortunately these cannot be gathered until there emerges a culture in which the two sexes have equal opportunity and equal motivation to achieve in the arts. Then and only then will the comparisons have real meaning. At the moment even well-educated women tend to see men as somehow more creative and properly so.[48] In our culture relatively few women have been allowed and encouraged to engage in creative activity in really serious fashion. But this historic fact should not be taken to signify that men are "naturally" more creative.

It probably would not occur to most musicians that there might be a connection between handedness and musical abilities. Yet the psychiatrist Quinan has maintained that musicians display more than the normal amount of sinistrality.[49] Sikes, a music teacher, has also considered the presence of left-handedness a cue for the prognostication of later musical achievement, in this case success with the piano.[50] However, there is little support from piano teachers for Sikes's theory.[51] Indeed there was the feeling that Sikes may have been unduly affected by the skillful left-hand work of her more promising students. In piano-playing the left hand has an important load to carry, a fact which most beginners fail to realize. A more nearly ambidextrous person or one who early recognizes the inadequacies of his left hand and assiduously practices this weaker member would have an advantage although he was not left-handed.[52]

There is the implication in the writings on sinistrality that left-handedness is associated with mental and emotional abnormality and that musicians have more than their proper share of such deviant behavior. It is true that an occasional musician may assume a Hollywood-like personality which has many deviant elements, but there is no reason to believe that one must have an unstable nervous system before he can achieve in music.[53] In one study elementary-school children were rated by their teachers and music supervisors for promise in music, handedness, and speech adequacy.[54] The data showed that those rated as most musical possessed only the normally expected number of speech troubles and amount of left-handedness. In another unpublished study of college students, the most musical and most unmusical were compared on standard personality tests.

Here again there was no evidence that musical abilities are in any way tied to mental or emotional abnormality. Moreover, the work of Miles and Wolfe on the early life histories of fifty of the great geniuses of history discloses no unusual concentration of mental or emotional abnormality.[55]

Keston has compared the personality profiles of students who scored high on a music preference test of his own construction with others who scored low.[56] His two groups of female subjects made quite similar mean scores on the Minnesota Multiphasic Personality Inventory. But his more musical men scored significantly higher than did their less musical fellows on the feminine subscale. The fact that musical men scored more like women on the MMPI is in line with the finding that they also scored more like women on the Strong Vocational Interest Test. Keston speculates that, with music looked upon in America as a relatively feminine interest area, only men with slightly deviant personality patterns can be expected to show great interest in this art. It is too early to know whether further researches along the line of Keston's work will yield similar findings. Even if they do it is not to be expected that the deviations will be large enough to justify the branding of male musicians as psychoneurotics.

ADLERIAN VIEWS ON ABILITY

It is well known that defects often spur an individual to extraordinary achievement. The stuttering Demosthenes of antiquity became a famous orator. The illegitimate Smithson showed the world that though he suffered from social inferiority he was superior to the majority of his generation in many areas of achievement. And the partially deaf Beethoven, perceiving that his affliction was progressive, composed at a faster and faster rate in an attempt to hear his own compositions before complete deafness could overtake him.

The theories of at least a few of the more dedicated followers of Alfred Adler go beyond the simple idea described above.[57] It is granted that a man may be spurred by his inferiorities to new heights, but instead of seeing this mechanism as one of the many wellsprings of virtuosity, these Adlerians see it as one of few, often as the major wellspring. Thus Rosenthal views the Jew as possessing a "racial tendency" toward defective hearing and becoming through his overcompensation to this sort of inferiority far more musical than his fellow Gentile.[58] And the deafness of the genius Beethoven is looked upon as antedating all signs of his musicality. Had he not been deaf he would not have become a musical giant, these extremists declare. Needless to say, Rosenthal's "proofs" are of the anecdotal sort. Moreover, it is quite well demonstrated that Beethoven was well on the road to musical success when infection led to his hearing difficulties.[59]

There has been surprisingly little experimentation on the subject of the Adlerian theory of musical ability. In 1937 comparisons were made of the auditory acuities of two groups of school children chosen by their teachers as either the most musical or the most unmusical of a group of 1,169.[60] The acuities were measured at seven pitch levels, for each ear alone and for both ears together. Of the 21 comparisons only one—that for the right ear at 1,900 cycles—was what one might regard as a really significant difference and this favored the Adlerian formula; that is, the unmusical group showed more acuity for this pitch with the right ear. With all other comparisons showing insignificant differences it was concluded that these two groups of young children had very similar acuities.[61] The acuities of college students were tested at the same seven pitch levels some years later.[62] At this age the more musical had consistently better acuities. Along with the acuity tests the students were also given the older Seashore battery of music measures. The acuities of those who placed at 67 percentile or above on the Seashore were compared with the hearing scores of those who scored at 33 percentile or lower. Except in the areas of rhythm and consonance the higher Seashore scorers had the better acuities. A similar study of junior high-school students but undertaken in a different context was that by Bower.[63] She states: "There is some evidence here that those with superior and average hearing did better in the tests of pitch, rhythm, and tonal memory than those with defective hearing."

The data gathered in these studies are not incompatible with the notion that *occasionally* a somewhat deaf person may overcompensate in a musical direction. But this is not to say that *all* musical persons (or "races" which show a high incidence of musical achievement) are musical because of overcompensations to felt auditory defects. More often the more musical possess the better acuity.

JUNGIAN VIEWS ON ABILITY

A onetime collaborator and later opponent of Freud, C. G. Jung, has written extensively of what he has termed "archetypes." These are primordial images, psychic residua of experiences which have happened not to the individual but to his remote ancestors.

These psychic residua allegedly act as unconscious forces which are basic to the appearance of musical and other artistic abilities.[64] Unfortunately for the Jungians, the theory of the collective unconscious is out of line with the thinking of most present-day biologists since it involves the concept of the inheritance of acquired characteristics. In other words it can be subsumed under the now discredited Lamarckian theory of evolution.

It was Jung who gave the world the terms "introvert" and "extravert." The introvert is said to be introspective, tending to be preoccupied with his own attitudes and mental processes. The extravert attends more to external events and objects. These terms have had a difficult history with almost every researcher holding to his own unique usage of the words. Thus Szucharewa and Ossipowa have held that the extreme extravert is rarely musical although he may possess a good sense of motor rhythm.[65] Gross and R. Seashore with a somewhat different conception of the extravert found quite the reverse to be true, at least in America.[66] Here the more musical college students they tested and ten American composers as well were found to be more extraverted than were the less musical. Keston and Pinto have painted still a different picture of the extravert.[67] They found him not unmusical per se but preferring popular to serious music. Wallach and Greenberg saw the social introvert with high manifest anxiety as showing a greater degree of symbolic sexual arousal to music than his more extraverted and less anxious peer.[68] Wallach found a correlation of .33 between preference for jazz and social extraversion but no relationship between the latter and preference for excerpts from Ravel and Debussy.[69] Keston and Pinto[70] also found the extravert to show a preference for jazz. Rankin, using a standard test for the measurement of anxiety, found a slight relationship with the Seashore time, timbre, and perhaps the loudness test, but he suggests no rationale for the relationship he may or may not have uncovered.[71] To find disagreement between research findings is not surprising at a time when the various measures of extraversion now available agree so poorly with each other. What is really needed is a better way of describing personality.[72]

FREUDIAN VIEWS ON ABILITY

Perhaps because their master had slight musical interest, music has received less attention from the Freudians than have its sister arts. But the basic psychoanalytic assumptions seem roughly similar throughout the aesthetic fields. The perplexing problem of the

Freudian symbol was considered in Chapter 5. The other elements of Freud's system are equally difficult to handle.[73] Explanations in terms of instincts tend to be tautological, and Freud's explanations seem to be no exception. Moreover, such concepts as sublimation are slippery.[74] The Freudians and everyone else who is not blind can see sex in the cancan, but in explaining this dance form there is no need for the concept of sublimation. Where sex is not obvious, the only "proof" that the energy source is basically sexual comes from the process of psychoanalyzing. And unfortunately the psychoanalytic interview is (in great part at least) a process of indoctrination, a putting into the mind of the analysand what the analyst later takes out as his proof. Such a process of course adds up to no proof at all. So while psychoanalysis at its present stage may have therapeutic utility, it has not yet provided a consistent set of scientifically verified explanations for the origin of the several artistic abilities. It must, if it is to be accepted, be taken largely on faith.

IMAGERY AS A SOURCE OF ABILITIES

Sir Francis Galton, one of the first scientists to work with mental imagery, thought he had discovered pure image types. Later researches convinced the psychological fraternity that most persons have images of considerable strength in several sense fields, with the strongest in the visual area and the next most vivid in the auditory. Musicians of course tend to have more intense auditory images than do the unmusical and may be above average in the tactual and kinesthetic areas as well.[75] Von Weber for example, was a musician with extraordinarily strong visual and auditory imagery.[76]

One of the most extensive comparative studies of imagery has been that by Agnew who has carefully rated the "mind's ears" of many run-of-the-mill musicians, psychologists, and children[77] as well as of great composers.[78] She has developed an imagery questionnaire which has enjoyed some use.

The German scientists particularly have noted the existence of imagery of hallucinatory intensity which they have termed "photographic" or eidetic." Imaginal material appears to the eidetic almost as in normal perception. Virtually unbelievable tales have been told of the abilities of eidetics who, by reading a book or a musical score only once, or by listening to one rendition of a symphony, could then without obvious cues reproduce the material as if rereading or rehearing.[79] Mozart, Gounod, Cowell[80] and Berlioz were undoubtedly eidetics, and so presumably is the contemporary pianist Artur Rubinstein. Mozart's famous "theft" of the *Miserere* after visiting the Sistine Chapel only twice was accomplished through the aid of his eidetic imagery. Eidetic images are known to be far more common among children than among adults, many of the latter having lost their eidetic potentialities through lack of practice. The early appearance of strong auditory imagery in the child may serve as a predisposing factor to subsequent ability with and interest in tonal materials. The evidence so far collected indicates that images can be cultivated and that the absence of a functioning sense organ from an early age, e.g. as in complete deafness, is always paralleled by absence of imagery in that sensory area.

DEVELOPING ABILITIES

It is possible for the organism to respond to sudden, loud noises thirty days or more before normal birth time. Several instances have been observed where the fetus has jerked convulsively when tones of high intensity were sounded close to the mother. Unless there is anatomical impairment, the child normally shows considerable sensitivity to tone shortly after birth, and by the eighth day he will usually stop feeding at the sound of a gong.[81] Quite naturally the small infant's reactions to tone will depend to some extent on his physiological condition of the moment, e.g. whether or not he is sleepy or hungry.[82]

There is some evidence that children 9 to 31 months of age react most strongly to the rhythm factor in music, next most strongly to melody, less to the harmonic factor, and least to dissonant music.[83] The first two-note cadences sung by the very young child tend to be descending fourths and major thirds, according to Platt.[84] Werner agrees that the early cadences are the descending ones but feels that the minor third appears first.[85] The octave is less frequently attempted and the ascending and other descending cadences are tried less often. As the child matures and is presented with scale progressions and chord figures, he learns the former with far greater facility than he does the latter.[86]

When singing voluntarily, children four and a half to eight years of age employ mean pitch levels significantly lower than those arranged for them in many of their song books; the mean of their voluntary pitch range, approximately 9.5 semitones, was in 1933 found to be smaller than that demanded of them by their printed songs, which averaged about 10.5 semitones.[87] But without much strain young children can, if they really try, cover a considerably greater tonal span, as Fröschels has shown.[88] His four-year-olds had a range of 8 semitones, his five-year-olds 10 semitones, his six-year-olds 11, his seven-year-olds 14, and his eight-year-olds 16 semitones. Jersild and Bienstock found even higher values—age four, 13 semitones; age five, 17; ages six and seven, 22; and age eight, 24 semitones.[89] These researchers report that with some practice there can be expected at least a 30 per cent gain in the number of tones three-year-olds can sing.[90]

Outstanding musical abilities are often noted considerably before age seven. In fact the studies of Garrison, [91] of Cochran,[92] and of Brown[93] would lead one to suspect that at least by age seven the typical child has matured to the point where piano lessons may be profitably begun. Unusual ability in painting usually appears at a later age, presumably because the motor skills necessary for handling art tools are not sufficiently developed until after the seventh year.

For some time a Japanese violin teacher, Suzuki, has been manufacturing tiny violins, some even 1/16 size, and has been successfully motivating children as young as two and a half or so to practice these instruments. While the greater discipline traditional among the Japanese may aid in making the Suzuki system more workable in his country, he is convinced that it would work reasonably well in other countries.[94]

Petzold,[95] in an extensive study of children in the first six grades, has found that tonal and rhythmic abilities, at least their perceptual aspects, depend largely on musical training and experience and reflect school grade level. No significant sex differences were demonstrated in his study.

The typical child must be nearly nine before he will show a decided preference for the traditional concordances, and then only if he has been subjected to Western culture.[96] But just how old he needs to be before he will get the full import of the major-minor dichotomy is not clear. Walker, who like many Continentals delights in complicated typologies, has drawn a most involved picture of the growth of the modal discriminatory powers.[97] His data at least make it clear that the child only gradually develops a feel for these affective associations. Particular trouble comes with the minor, which at first seems merely dull and perhaps slightly unpleasant. Only much later does it begin to take on a clearly sad affect.

That the growing child steadily improves his discriminatory powers in the several tonal areas is shown by the fact that music testers like Carl Seashore found it necessary to offer several sets of age norms. In his earlier music test battery, Seashore presented separate norms for the fifth grade, for the eighth grade, and for adults.[98] His current battery offers one set of norms for the fourth and fifth grades, another for the sixth, seventh, and eighth grades, and still another for grades nine through sixteen.[99]

Attention has already been called to the peculiarly thin tone of the preadolescent male soprano, a tone with less than normal vibrato. The female appears to pick up this ornamentation much earlier than the male, possibly because she matures faster than he does.[100] In both sexes there is a change in tonal quality and a widening of the pitch range at the time of puberty, slight in the female and quite marked in the male. It goes almost without saying that puberty in the male is a period of considerable musical strain. Not only is his voice under less firm control as he shifts from a higher to a lower register but his status has changed. He has begun to assume an adult role and will from now on be compared with other adults. Prodigies particularly suffer from this shift in frame of reference, and many such exceptional children leave the musical spotlight shortly after this period. For it is one thing to be compared with other child performers but quite something else to be rated on a continuum along with a Heifetz or a Rubinstein.

TRAINING METHODS: GENERAL PROBLEMS[101]

Musical learning might be expected to follow in general the rules of all learning.[102] Questions regarding whole versus part learning, motivation, overlearning, prestudy and mental rehearsal, distributed versus massed practice, beta learning, and retroactive inhibition are encountered here as elsewhere. In addition there are other problems met solely within the music area.

Under what conditions for example is *whole learning* more efficient than *part learning?* Should one go over the material as a whole, time after time, or is it wiser to break it up into smaller sections with practice restricted pretty much to these smaller portions? Research on music materials checks rather well the work in other learning areas. Where the material to be learned seems very long to the memorizer so that he tends to become discouraged and lose morale, the part method is superior.[103] But where the learner's prior habits are not too tied to the part method and he is not overawed by the length of the score he must learn, the whole method tends to win out.[104] The student's aim should be to work with as large a portion of his score as makes a manageable unit for him. For most persons this means that, as learning proceeds, longer and longer scores can be treated as a single unit.

The literature reveals but one experimental study in the musical area on *motivated* versus *unmotivated* music learning, and this one would appear to be quite limited in applicability. In each section of the Rubin-Rabson study, one of three different sorts of incentives was operative.[105] In the first of the experimental situations the only incentive was what the learning process itself provided. No verbal encouragement or other goad was employed. In a second there were many exhortations from the experimenter. In a third there was promise of money payment if improvement became especially good. Rubin-Rabson's data revealed no differences among the three stimulus situations in the number of trials needed to bring the skill up to a previously agreed-upon level of achievement.

It should be noted that the Rubin-Rabson study does *not* prove that learning efficiency will be the same irrespective of the type of incentive. What it does demonstrate is that rather forceful incentive changes must obtain before the slope of the learning curve will be much affected, more forceful than any that Rubin-Rabson employed. One is reminded of an adult monotone who was being taught to discriminate pitches. His improvement had been unmistakable and quite steady, but it remained exasperatingly slow until his hat was knocked from his head during the singing of the national anthem. At this point his learning curve swept sharply upwards and maintained for some time much of its new slope. Any music teacher of long standing can undoubtedly recall somewhat similar instances among her pupils where spurts in learning speed occurred as soon as "proper" incentives were come upon.

To learn an act, say the educational psychologists, practice should be continued beyond the trial where the material can for the first time be reproduced correctly. The material in other words must be *overlearned*. Valid as this principle seems to be in most areas, it did not hold in the extensive musical studies of Rubin-Rabson who forced her subjects to practice 50, 100, and even 200 per cent more than was necessary for bare learning.[106] Nothing was measurably gained by all this added effort. Rubin-Rabson explains her finding with the notion that, while it is conceivable that overlearning might affect favorably sheer motor performance on the piano, it should not so affect the learning of piano music since the activity here is much more a matter of meaning and insight. Consequently, once memorization is achieved, it "needs only to be restored to its original clarity on subsequent occasions."[107] With no other studies to contradict those of Rubin-Rabson, her conclusions must be at least tentatively accepted.

Although Kovacs, as early as 1915, attempted to ascertain

whether careful inspection of a score before keyboard practice actually takes place might not benefit the subsequent learning of the score, his experimental controls were so poor that no generalizations could safely be drawn.[108] Hence we must rely again upon the researches of Rubin-Rabson as no other psychologist or educator has apparently worked in this area.[109] The questions Rubin-Rabson attempted to answer were in brief: (1) Is *mental prestudy* of benefit to subsequent learning? (2) If it is, will *mental rehearsal* be of value at other periods in the learning process? Affirmative answers were found to both questions. The best period for mental rehearsal was found to be a time roughly midway among the keyboard practice sessions. Thus it would appear that the ambitious piano student should not only analyze and study his scores before he starts his formal keyboard practice but should take time considerably before his top skill is reached to rehearse mentally what has been going on.

With limited time to spend on learning something, is it wiser to allocate all to one continuous session or to split the effort between several sessions? This is the problem of *massed* versus *distributed* practice. In one investigation of this issue,[110] college students with no prior training on the clarinet were split into two groups with one receiving two weekly group lessons and the other having four weekly meetings. After a month and a half the two groups were rated as equal in ability. This is not in keeping with the usual teaching of educational psychologists who generally favor some sort of distribution or spreading of the practice trials. Rubin-Rabson's data[111] on the learning of piano music, on the other hand, fall in line with the more usual generalization. She set an interval of one hour between trials for her first group of students and 24 hours for the second. Admittedly far more than two time intervals must be experimented with before it can be said just what allocation is best for any given situation. But with some labor a music student can, if he will, find the optimum time spread (if there is one) for each sort of material he desires to master.

Common sense warns against the practicing of one's mistakes. Repeated again and again, the making of these errors will grow into habits which become difficult to eradicate. But is this belief in the power of practice really sound? Would it not be more accurate to say that almost all practice is a matter not of avoiding but of repeating mistakes? For if an act can be done perfectly, why practice it at all? The fact that practice is needed shows that errors are still being made even though the learner may not recognize them as associated with the individual skills he wishes to acquire. In ordinary learning then there is practice of errors along with a rehearsal of the correct elements.

Why not force the practicer to become acutely aware of his errors? asks the psychologist Dunlap.[112] Why not have the learner single out his mistakes and rehearse them alone but do so with the ever-present desire that they can and should be eliminated? This procedure Dunlap called *beta* learning in contradistinction to the more ordinary form in which the learner does not restrict his practice to his errors but drills himself on a medley made up of both correct acts and mistakes in the hope that the latter will gradually be eliminated. While McGeoch and Irion categorically state that beta learning has proved effective "in correcting errors in piano-playing," they cite no studies to support their contention and, when contacted by the present author, could not recall just why they had made so positive a statement.[113] Moreover, the only published report of the use of the beta technique in the entire music area, that by Wakeham on the elimination of errors in organ-playing, tells us only of its failure.[114] It might be added that the present writer has twice tried beta practice on musicians who were bothered by persistent performance errors and was quite unsuccessful in both instances. Perhaps Wakeham and the author unwittingly failed to carry out some detail of Dunlap's methodology. Or it may be that performance errors in music are somehow unlike typing errors where the scheme has proved so successful. But in any event, there is no reason as yet for replacing the more ordinary procedures with the beta variety.

Educational psychologists have long been interested in *feedback,* ways in which the learner can quickly be informed both of his improvement and his possible lack of progress. In one experiment[115] in which students were learning to match the pitch of a standard tone, it was found that prompt auditory feedback (immediate rehearing of the standard tone) was far more helpful to learning than either somewhat delayed auditory feedback or immediate visual feedback (seeing the errors recorded on a visual scale).

There is the distinct possibility that the learning process may be thrown badly out of gear should the learner practice two tasks more or less concomitantly. Evidence from a number of areas suggests that this possibility becomes practically a certainty whenever the two tasks are quite similar. The learning of the one somehow inhibits the learning of the other task, a phenomenon called *retroactive inhibition.* It behooves the music educator then to ascertain how important this principle may prove to be for keyboard learning.

To obtain at least a partial answer, Rubin-Rabson observed the behaviors of 18 highly trained musicians in a number of situations. Happily no important inhibitory effects were detectable when two tasks were learned concomitantly. To quote Rubin-Rabson:

> [My] conclusions are not unexpected. The experimental procedure was only a repetition of a learning situation familiar to these subjects for many years. The mechanics of piano study had long since accustomed them to learning much new music concomitantly while retaining material already learned to various degrees. No confusion develops transferable from one learning to the other because the organizational skill of these learners is highly trained and specific and because rarely are two bits of music so similar in key, rhythm, melodic or structural details as to make involuntary transfer feasible. There is here, furthermore, a favorable task-set engendered by the prestige factors implicit for musicians in a music-learning situation.[116]

It would be a bit premature to suggest that the Rubin-Rabson research has completely settled the problem. While its conclusions will probably be found to hold for well-trained musicians generally, they may or may not apply to beginners. Further research at this lower proficiency level must be undertaken before a final answer can be given.

TRAINING METHODS: SPECIAL PROBLEMS

While it has long been known that practice with the right hand will, to some extent, also train the left hand, this fact has certainly led no one to limit his practice to his right hand. Yet certain music teachers have believed that practice first with one hand and then with the other would result in quicker learning than drill with the two hands in coordination. The notion seemed to be that while one hand was resting it would be absorbing more skill from the hand that was practicing than if it continued to practice with its mate and then rested with it. However, the facts do not support this idea. There are at least two studies available which demonstrate beyond question the superiority of the *coordinated* technique as opposed to the *unilateral*.[117] It has also been demonstrated that rhythms are learned faster when played by two hands than by one hand.[118] Hence the student is advised to attempt hand coordination from the very beginning of practice.

Rare indeed is the specialist in learning and motor skills who is also a competent performer on some musical instrument. Clyde E. Noble is one of these unusual people, a behavioral scientist and a cornet player of no mean ability. He has written *The Psychology of Cornet and Trumpet Playing*[119] in which attention is paid to embouchure techniques, breath control and tone quality, articulation, reading and playing with style, and the psychological principles underlying rewards, practice, memorization, and the development of confidence. The reading of this book should be rewarding to musicians generally, since many of the problems which are discussed are met in a variety of musical situations.

Proper imagery is most important for music training. The imagery needed for "good" voice quality is particularly difficult to achieve but, according to Bartholomew, training in this area can be effective.[120] The kinesthetic "feel" and auditory "image" of a tonal quality represented by strong resonance at 500 and 2,800 cycles are essential for the male singer and at approximately 3,200 for the female vocalist. Good kinesthetic imagery is also needed by the violinist, particularly when he begins to practice double stops.[121] At this stage in his learning, auditory imagery is no longer as effective a guide as it was when he was learning to play on a single string. In his earlier practice on the single string he could by careful listening almost instantly adjust his finger position whenever it was incorrect, but with two fingers breaking the strings it becomes difficult to know which finger to change. So now he must rely on kinesthetic images which refer specifically to a single finger. Too much emphasis, however, must not be placed on imagery. Indeed direct sensory cues are often more essential. Thus beginners on the piano learn more slowly if they are kept from looking at their hands and the keyboard than if allowed to look where they will.[122] The Russians too have studied the learning process in music. In one experiment they have found that violin students were markedly helped by imaging or singing while they played, or by silently fingering as if they were playing.[123] This and other somewhat similar findings follow the basic principle which states that, other things being equal, the more the sensory cues available at the start of learning, the faster the learning.[124]

An equal amount of factual information was learned in one experimental session[125] where the members of one group of fifth-graders were exposed to a self-initiated listening experience with phonograph, earphones, and supplementary visual materials while the others were given a group-listening period and a discussion about composers. It was felt, however, that the first group showed "more positive attitudes toward music."

As it has in many other areas of learning, programmed instruction in music has made its appearance felt rather strongly since the late 1950's. It is to be hoped that both the advantages and disadvantages of programming will become much more obvious with time. At the moment one can safely say that this method of instruction shows much promise.[126]

Several excellent studies on *sight-reading* are available. Although space here allows for but few comments, the serious student will find an examination of the original articles cited in the bibliography of this chapter most worthwhile. The exposure of musical material on cards offers one approach to the study of sight-reading, and photography of eye fixations furnishes another excellent source of data. In certain of the studies, the moving hands and the hammers within the piano have been photographed.

Bean warns piano teachers to allow their pupils to gain reading speed in the early stages of learning even at the expense of occasional errors.[127] He finds all too many persons reading slowly and attending to single notes when they should be attending to musical patterns, that is, to short phrases. Reading individual notes is akin to attention to individual letters while reading literature, and this is behavior typical of extremely poor readers. By the judicious use of flash cards the reading of most students can, Bean says, be speeded up appreciably and be made considerably more accurate. Ortmann points out that the teacher who knows what her pupils' eyes can and cannot do will be better equipped to suggest proper training methods.[128] Research by Hargiss[129] on elementary teachers emphasizes the importance to sight-singing ability of overt singing.

As a result of their researches, Lannert and Ullman believe that the piano student should be taught early to read ahead of the measure being played and should be forced into considerable sight-reading practice.[130] The arrangement of the keyboard must become so well known that little visual attention need be paid it. Lowery also stresses the great need for sight-reading practice and the early achievement of smooth eye-hand coordinations.[131] He notes that reading music is far more complicated than reading European letter print, since musical symbols are not arranged on lines or columns but are scattered both horizontally and vertically. The eye often fixates on areas between notes or even between staves. Music reading is made even more difficult because of our unscientifically arranged staff and symbols. The work of Wheelwright[132] for example clearly shows that the spaces between notes and rests should, for purposes of better reading, be proportional to the represented time values.

A wealth of material on the reading and playing of music can be found in the excellent reports of Weaver,[133] of Van Nuys and Weaver,[134] of Jacobsen,[135] of Hammer,[136] and of Hargiss.[137] Only a few samples of their findings will be given here, however, since this book is not the place for an extended coverage of all that might be found helpful to the music teacher.

The reading of music should start with diatonic intervals and not with chromatics and accidental signs which are more difficult to perceive. Music in the bass clef and that written on leger lines cause much reading difficulty which can only be overcome by extensive practice. Surprising as it may seem, practice on reading words is often more needed by the beginning music student than practice on note reading. Immature students should be introduced rather early to scale runs and only much later to arpeggios. Emphasis should be on speed reading rather than on accuracy since the habit of slow reading is difficult to break. On the average it is the fast music reader, not the slow one, who is the more accurate. Jacobsen ended his advice with the pessimistic comment that much of the note-reading material available for beginners up to 1941 was not well adapted to their reading level and should be replaced by scores better geared to their perceptual capacities.

While most of the attention in training studies has been focused on the improvement of poor performers, it has been shown that competent players can also be aided by proper procedures. In one experiment advanced woodwind players were given training in the analysis of tonal relationships, the use of imitation, important intervals, repetition of motives and phrases, and rhythmic patterns. The memorizing ability of these performers improved quite markedly over that of an untrained group.[138]

CREATIVITY

No one really understands the intricacies of the creative processes as they function in any particular composer, not even the composer himself. This fact, however, has not stopped several musicians from introspecting and retrospecting on these interesting processes. For example the composer Henry Cowell, stimulated by his psychologist-mentor L. M. Terman, has described in some detail how he believed he composed.[139] Deciding early to be a composer and for a time having little access to musical instruments, Cowell diligently practiced imagining the timbres he had heard. He was aided in this labor by the possession of eidetic imagery. With practice he put together in his "mind's ear" many different timbres, finally getting imagined effects not offered by any instrument played in the traditional manner. Later when a piano was available to Cowell, he experimented with it to elicit some of the bizarre effects he had been imagining. In this fashion were born his tone clusters, his string massage, and the other Cowellian timbre novelties. Whenever Cowell was commissioned to compose, he employed effects which seemed to him appropriate to the occasion, realizing, however, that he was offering his listener no clear-cut musical message.

One composer[140] tried the novel experiment of allowing a psychologist to meet with him in regular sessions while he composed a fugue. Everything said or played during these sessions was recorded on tape. An analysis of this ongoing creative act was then made in terms of the framework provided by what psychologists call the General Problem Solver, a type of model which simulates in a formal manner what an individual does when he attacks a problem. While up to now little that is definitive has emerged from this and other such pioneering studies with simulation models, this approach to the study of creativity may yield heavily in time as the models become more refined and closer to real life behavior.

Research which many composers might not consider entirely realistic was that performed by Benham when, in the interests of an experiment, he composed a series of nine-measure melodies (average time between 60 and 70 seconds).[141] He found his auditory imagery strongest at the emergence of each musical idea. During the development there were motor sensations and other types of imagery. The major danger in this and other similar experiments of course is that the overly analytic mental set necessitated by the experiment may have interfered with the experimenter's creative powers or have given them rather different qualitative flavor.

Observations somewhat similar to those of Benham were made by Bahle, who sent questionnaires to 32 well-known European composers in an effort to learn how they believed they composed.[142] Their replies were later checked against autobiographical documents left by a number of the greatest European composers of the past three centuries. In one of his many studies on the problem of creativity, Bahle asked his composer respondents to set poems to music and to introspect and retrospect on the process. Unfortunately his data, extensive as they are, have led to few generalizations which could not have been made before the studies were undertaken. In some respects Bahle's problem was like that of asking centenarians about the reasons for their long life. Many and varied are the convictions that are aired—yet no one knows with certainty the degree of validity of any one of the theories offered to explain either the longevity of an indivdual or his creativity.

Thirty of the "world's foremost creative jazz musicians" have been studied clinically by three psychiatrists.[143] The study focused on the musicians' recollections of their early interpersonal relationships. Common to the group were the lack of adequate father figures, great parental pressure to seek a unique position in the community, and frustrations in peer relationships leading to isolation and withdrawal. There was great need to identify with legendary jazz heroes and to use jazz as a mark of rebellion against family and society.

Rudáš holds that composers can be divided into several creative types. Many seemed "predominantly endowed acoustically," e.g. Mozart, Dvořák, and Chopin. With others, e.g. Bach, Wagner, and Beethoven, visual endowment seemed of somewhat greater importance. Still others like Rimsky-Korsakov were more mixed in the relative strengths of their sensory capabilities. Rudáš' speculations are certainly of interest, but one wonders how they can be validated.[144]

By comparing better and poorer students of composition, Gross and R. Seashore have helped confirm the commonly held belief that facility in composition comes in part at least from toil and sweat.[145] Formal and informal training and knowledge of good work habits appeared in this study as extremely important for all who would compose. Whittaker and his associates also found compositions to reflect the particular composer's informal training.[146] Musical creations were shown to be generally in line with the traditional and folk art of the immediate culture and the rather narrow interests of the community in which the composer lived.

The sociologists Lastrucci[147] and Becker[148] have studied the way of life of dance-band musicians and the effects on creativity and performance which stem from their extremely atypical living habits. Dance musicians feel forced to compose and perform in idioms and manners appreciated by their audiences. Such pressures from the "ignorant" lay public they often resent and compensate for by striving to produce, at least in jam sessions, what they regard as higher-level material.

Hutchings[149] holds that a musician with only an average talent to compose can, by the exercise of his inventive capacities, gain considerable facility in the jazz arts. While the evidence for this statement is not impressive, it would appear that standards of composition in this area are only slowly gaining acceptance.

The sociologist Nash has studied the socialization of the serious composer.[150] He feels that there must be an "ability to work in the face of social non-support, ability to assume certain other vocational roles at the same time, and ability to pursue considerable solitary activity."

It is popular in some quarters to point to a reified unconscious as the major wellspring of artistic inspirations. Thus the musicologist Max Graf asserts that the greater part of musical formation takes place in the unconscious mind, which to him is a mystical entity that science cannot measure or explain.[151] Graf does admit, however, that the composer's childhood memories and his lifelong environmental pressures affect his style of composition.

Jancke makes the point that most if not all creativity is preceded by psychological tensions which are often unconscious.[152] In some degree the act of composing relieves these tensions. To the composer then even more than to the listener, music is autistic and personal. Hence when the composer listens to one of his own earlier compositions, it may take on a quite different meaning from what it originally had for him, since at this time it serves to lessen what is perhaps a rather different tension.

To make his own unconscious at least somewhat recordable, Loar deliberately fatigued himself and went without his normal sleep.[153] Then he attended concerts where he drowsed. When Loar later attempted to record his dreams and reveries he found that no repressed wish or inhibited desire could be recognized among his fantasies. Instead there appeared in fictionalized form memories which Loar had formed from his reading of the composer's life and times. However, in fairness to analytic theory it must be admitted that Loar's technique was probably not one which could uncover repressed wishes.

Why some composers create "beautiful" music and others "unbeautiful" is explained by Ehrenzweig on a Gestalt-psychoanalytic basis.[154] Aesthetically good Gestalts, i.e. beautiful tonal materials, belong to the surface layers of the mind. The "depth mind" or unconscious on the other hand is "Gestalt-free." Hence it is from the unconscious that the poor Gestalts, the ugly and the distorted, come. Although the modern composer's unpleasant music may seem highly sophisticated, his art, thinks Ehrenzweig, represents a retrogression to the least differentiated modes of infantile "thing perception."

The composer may honestly believe his compositions to be novel, to be born from an unconscious that has had little or no traffic with the music of his contemporaries or of the past. But the fact is that the composer forgets (and sometimes wants to forget) the origins of much of the material he will later use in his creations. This material has come from a variety of sources and is unconscious in the sense that it is not immediately recallable. As time goes on it will be elaborated into the form in which it will later be produced. Just how much of the rearrangement of items goes on below the verbal threshold is not known. However, the amount must often be considerable as certain composers, Haydn and Schumann for instance, seem to have done their creative work without much effort, and Hindemith has claimed to see in a flash a new composition in its entirety. But others like J. S. Bach typically scratched and erased and followed extremely rigid rules. There would appear to be a continuum then along which composers fall—with the "intuitive" at one end and the "nonintuitive" at the other, with the former yielding his finished product almost without considered thought and the latter only after much careful deliberation and conscious elaboration.

Biographical studies of the great composers usually stress their personality structures, their psychological abnormalities and sociological uniquenesses, as well as the cultural forces which seem to have been in part responsible both for the style of composition they have embraced and for the fact that they chose composing as a career.[155] Luck, special body build, extreme vitality and joy of living, outstandingly good or extraordinarily poor health, pressures from relatives or friends, an IQ of at least 120,[156] extreme tonal and rhythmic facility, vivid imagery, abnormally fine memory, past mental and physical suffering, much greater than average ambition and persistence, ability to make others work on one's behalf, love of complex rather than simple solutions to problems, poorly controlled emotions, inherited talent for composing,[157] readiness to forego present pleasures for future gains, and even willingness to be a melody thief have all been mentioned by one or another biographer as necessary for creative genius. While many theorists of the past have favored a "madness" basis for all creativity, this notion seems to be losing favor. In fact Maslow even goes so far in the opposite direction as to say: "My feeling is that the concept of creativeness and the concept of the healthy, self-actualizing, fully-human person seem to be coming closer and closer together, and may perhaps turn out to be the same thing."[158] Biographical research is fascinating work which may indeed pay big dividends in the years to come; yet at present its methods are too crude to allow for valid generalizations. A biographer is all too likely to conclude that some one of his many biographical items has great causal significance simply because his biases encourage him to select out and emphasize this item. It can be expected perhaps that over the years biographer biases will in some degree cancel each other, but until that happier day arrives only hunches and very tentative conclusions can be safely drawn from this type of research material.[159]

It is interesting to note that the period of life when neuromuscular coordinations are at their best was found by Lehman to be the time when eminent composers of the past were at the peak of their creativity.[160] Of course temporal coincidence does not necessarily indicate causality. Yet the correspondence between decade of maximum creativity and years of best motor coordination exists in so many areas—athletics, painting, writing, science, mathematics, and philosophy as well as musical composition—that it may have considerable significance. However, Bjorksten, while agreeing that motor skill and creativity must be somehow related, asks us not to forget that middle-aged and older men, particularly those in academic life, simply do not have as much free time to devote to creative work as do their younger brethren.[161] Hence the data of maximum creativity are to some extent determined by available time. Wayne Dennis[162] seems to find that topflight workers who live long keep producing to an advanced age with surprisingly little letup.

In a study by Lehman and Ingerham of the compositions of eminent deceased musicians, the half-decade from age thirty-five to thirty-nine was shown to be the most productive for grand operas, cantatas, and orchestral and symphonic works of "superior" quality.[163] This research team continued its study with contemporary American composers but apparently met with great difficulty in deciding what compositions should be placed in the "superior" category. Perhaps this uncertainty makes less meaningful the finding that the peak creative half-decade for this group fell much later —in the years from fifty to fifty-four. The peak for music of high quality was found in both studies to come earlier than that for sheer quantity.

Dennis[164] has also studied the variability in amount of creativity. Taking a bibliography of secular music published in America during the eighteenth century, he picked at random 200 names of composers. He found that the most creative member was responsible for 10 per cent of all the compositions produced by the group. The number of compositions of this top man equaled the combined output of the lowest 100 of this group of 200.

In an interesting essay on "What Causes Creative Epochs in the Arts?" Munro concludes that there must be "(a) innately potential geniuses; (b) materials and conditions adequate to implement and channel their voluntary energies into some artistic medium; (c) artistic heritage; and (d) other persons with taste, power, and will to appreciate artistic merit and help to give it wider recognition."[165]

The importance of finding performers willing to attempt the more "advanced" compositions is stressed in an article by the violinist Szigeti.[166] This virtuoso implies that present-day composers who are rarely heard cannot escape having their creative output dammed or at least drastically diminished. Szigeti's statements clearly demonstrate how vital is the interdependence between composition, performance, and audience reaction.

It must be admitted that the above discussions of creativity leave us with a deplorable lack of closure. It is quite possible that the answers sought in this area have been as unrealistic as they have sometimes proved to be in certain other areas. Rarely is a phenomenon of nature found to have a single cause. If the process in question is broad in scope and appears in many different contexts, it is bound to be related to a host of variables. We now know for example that the several sorts of leadership demand different psychological qualities, although for years researchers sought a single set of psychological characteristics that would be typical of all. Without doubt the creative processes too show multiple causality.[167] The blossoming of creativity is surely dependent in considerable part on circumstances unique to particular situations. The trigger which actually sets off the creative process in one man may be quite dissimilar from that needed for another, particularly if he is of a different personality or school of composition or from another culture or age.

SUMMARY

The layman often speaks of his friends as extremely musical, as moderately musical, or perhaps as not at all musical. He implies that there is one general musical or even broader art ability which one may possess to a greater or lesser degree. The evidence, however, points to a contrary conclusion—to the existence of a number of semi-independent musical abilities no one of which seems particularly related to abilities in the other arts. While top achievement in music as in most other areas calls for academic intelligence of a high order, the correlation in the school years between music test scores and IQ is slight. In fact a few rather stupid persons have been located who are much less stupid in the musical realm. These are the idiot savants.

In the main, spectacular musical achievement seems unrelated to anomalies of gross body musculature. This should not be taken to mean that there are not neural constitutions and body builds admirably suited to musical endeavor. Yet these are largely wasted if proper environmental pressures are not operative. We are all well aware of the constitutional misfits who struggle in vain toward musical accomplishment. But we are less apt to note the numerous prodigies who sooner or later drop out of the musical picture because of the infertility of their musical surroundings. It is the view of modern science that the course of development of neither group can be predicted from scrutinies of their family lines. Indeed the interweaving of nature and nurture is far too complicated for the successful use of such a simple device as genealogical analysis. Achievement does not invariably follow from high potentiality, and the fact that one man has achieved more in music than another, or men in general more than women, or members of one national or racial group more than of another cannot be transcribed into capacity terms. A wide range of achievement can be derived from similar potentialities.

To describe a person as "arty" is in some circles to brand him as psychoneurotic. It is true of course that history reveals musicians who have been neurotic or even psychotic, but the connection between musicality and abnormality, if there is one, is extremely slight. Standard personality tests and ratings disclose no close relationship between the two. A possible exception to this generalization concerns the jazz performer, whose way of life typically encourages unstable relations with his family and other deviant behaviors as well. The highly musical male, though not necessarily neurotic, may often in our culture be regarded as somewhat effeminate, due partly at least to the feminine connotation traditionally given the arts.

In this chapter the claims of Adler, Jung, and Freud have been scrutinized for their bearing on musical abilities. It was concluded that while auditory insufficiencies can on rare occasions facilitate musical creativity, such weaknesses are certainly not essential to composition and performance of high order, even though the Adlerian extremists would have us think so. Jung's view that abilities arise as psychic residua of ancestral experiences was dismissed as out of line with current biological belief, being a variant of the Lamarckian notion of the inheritance of acquired characters. The Freudian notion of sublimation was regarded as of little explanatory aid. What are needed are operationally sound hypotheses susceptible to eventual verification. Sublimation seems not to be a concept of this sort but rather something to be accepted as an act of faith.

While all musicians have auditory imagery of more than average strength, a few, the eidetics, possess auditory pictures of hallucinatory intensity. The presence of such images could well encourage a child to enter a musical career. He might enter anyway, however, for the possession of eidetic imagery is not a *sine qua non* of musicality.

To some degree the rules of learning as formulated by the educational psychologists are found to hold for the learning of musical materials. But each field of learning has its unique problems, and music is no exception. Overlearning for example is not as beneficial to music learning as it has been found to be in many other areas, presumably because the activities here are more a matter of insight and meaning than of sheer motor performance. Music learning is of course facilitated by proper increases in motivation although not by the slighter goadings found of value in many other sorts of learning. Beta learning, the intentional practice of errors which works so well in the elimination of typing errors, seems to fail with musical materials. And, at least with well-trained musicians, retroactive inhibition does not appear to be the hazard it is in some fields of learning.

Students of musical creativity are gradually giving up the idea that the abilities of the composer come from a common wellspring and are independent of the social setting. Unfortunately, however, most authorities are little beyond the stage of enumerating possible essentials to creativity and then of playing up a few as special favorites. The more mystically minded theorists sidestep the problem with their positing of the unconscious mind as the receptacle from which creativity is alleged to spring full blown. Gradually, however, a few data are being assembled which may later yield a clearer picture of creativity than is now available. Introspection, retrospection, biographical analysis, personality testing, and statistical treatment of age data are techniques now being used.[168]

With all our concern with precocity and creativity we should not forget that every musician must reach at least a minimum of proficiency in a number of basic abilities. In our next chapter we shall consider those capabilities assumed to be needed, since their measurement has long been one of the aims of the psychological aesthetician.

CHAPTER NINE ☙ *The Measurement of Musical Abilities*

MUSICAL ABILITIES can be measured in a variety of ways. For persons already proficient in some phase of music, achievement tests are appropriate. These may be measures either of verbal knowledge, of appreciation (see Chap. 7), or of nonverbal musical skills. For use before the person to be tested has had much formal training (and later also), there are the aptitude tests. In the latter, music is usually broken into its various components and tests are constructed in each of these component areas. In a sense, aptitude tests are also measures of achievement, although they usually aim to test informal learning and potentiality rather than the effects of formal training.[1]

TESTS OF VERBAL KNOWLEDGE

Music achievement tests based on verbal knowledge are generally geared to school performance and attempt to measure how well certain musical abilities have been taught. They tell us nothing about what should be taught and so do little toward altering the musical status quo. Achievement tests typically possess high reliability.

The earliest published tests of verbal knowledge are the *Beach Standardized Music Tests,* which cover a wide area of musical abilities.[2] There are parts devoted to notation, the elements of "time and tune both in isolated form and in melodies," recognition of fundamental structural elements, pitch differences, memory, sight-singing, and the writing of music. The title is something of a misnomer as the battery has not been well standardized.

Beach's battery was followed by the *Musical Achievement Test* developed by Gildersleeve and Soper.[3] This has five parts designed to measure recognition of compositions from notation and as played by the examiner; ability to detect changes in pitch, meter, key signature, and meter signature; knowledge of instrumentation, theory, history, note values, time signatures, and transpositions from one clef to another; and ability to use accidentals, to locate *la* in six different keys, and to write key signatures. Designed for grades four through eight, it has a reliability of over .90 at each age-grade.

The *Torgerson-Fahnestock Music Test* is another of the older achievement measures.[4] Part A taps knowledge of note and rest values, time signatures, pitch and syllable names, expressive marks, major and minor key signatures, repeat bars, slurs, *do* placements, clefs, and natural and harmonic minor scales. Part B tests ear training through four subparts which are concerned with the writing of syllable names, time signatures, and notes as well as with the detection of pitch and time errors.

Quite possibly the most used of the early achievement measures was the *Kwalwasser-Ruch Test of Musical Accomplishment.*[5] This battery attempts to test the following phases of public-school music from grades four through twelve: knowledge of musical terms and symbols, pitch and letter names in bass and treble clefs, time signatures, key signatures, note values, rest values, and familiar melodies from notation; and detection of pitch and time errors in a familiar melody.

An achievement measure very similar in most respects to the *Kwalwasser-Ruch* is the *Strouse Music Test,* which covers the same areas except for detection of pitch and time errors and adds tests of pitch height and time length.[6] The Strouse measure takes longer to administer and must be accompanied by a piano or singer. There are three forms which can be used in grades four through twelve.

Number 1 of the *Hutchinson Music Tests* is a measure of tonal imagery.[7] Snatches from 25 well-known melodies are presented along with the names of these and of 25 additional songs. The purpose of Hutchinson's measure is to test "silent reading and recognition." Norms are available for grades seven through twelve.

The *Knuth Achievement Tests in Music* are well characterized by their subtitle, "For Recognition of Certain Rhythmic and Melodic Aspects."[8] In presenting the stimuli for the test, the examiner first strikes a chord to sound the key and then plays four measures which represent one of the four scores the student has in his hands. The Knuth has three levels, one for grades three and four, another for five and six, and the third for grades seven through twelve.

The *McCauley Experiment in Public School Music,* arranged for grades four through nine, is much like the older test by Gildersleeve and Soper but so much longer that it takes more than one session to give.[9] There are measures of knowledge of syllable and letter names, of note and rest values, meter and key signatures, chromatics, sight and aural identification of melodies, types of compositions, musical instruments, famous names in music, and musical terms.

A somewhat more limited measure is the *Providence Inventory Test in Music*.[10] Its ten sections have to do with naming notes, note values, key signatures, measure signatures, rest values, syllables, melodies, bass-staff syllables, and symbols; and placing *do*. Like most of its rivals, it has but one form. It is intended for grades four through nine.

A rather different kind of achievement test is the musical vocabulary list developed by Pressey.[11] The so-called "fundamental vocabulary" words appear in capital letters, fairly important supplementary words in italics, and words of no great importance but often found in textbooks are in ordinary type.

Ear Tests in Harmony are measures suitable for use in any standard course in harmony.[12] They test "active musical experience in the world of sound." Sound combinations of many sorts including the rather unusual are treated in this battery.

Among the somewhat more recently published achievement batteries is one devised by Kotick and Torgerson.[13] Their *Diagnostic Tests of Achievement in Music* are intended for grades four through twelve. The topics covered include diatonic syllable, chromatic syllable, and number names; time signatures; major and minor keys; note and rest values; letter names; signs and symbols; key names; and song recognition.

A contemporary measure which is enjoying some success is the *Farnum Music Notation Test*.[14] Forty four-measure melodies are presented by means of a phonograph record. The student follows along with a printed score and selects for each melody the one measure in which the pitch, rhythm, or time is handled differently. Sets of norms are available for grades seven, eight, and nine and for the two sexes separately. The test correlates appreciably with a number of the standard measures of musical aptitude and with scores on certain instrumental performance scales.

So far in preliminary form is Swinchoski's *Standardized Music Achievement Test Battery for the Intermediate Grades*[15] which presents items in the areas of singing, rhythms, listening, creative activities, instrumental performance, and music reading. While the test seems to have some validity, modifications must be made to insure adequate reliability.

The *Jones Music Recognition Test*[16] is an unstandardized measure, Part 1 of which (80 items) is intended for use by students of elementary grades and junior high school, and Part 2 (100 items) by senior high and college students. Well-known musical excerpts in groups of ten are played via piano. The student must select the title of each excerpt from a group of twelve. For the items of Part 2 the composers' names must also be given. A much shortened form (50 items) of this test was tried out by Wing[17] in England and shown to have a reliability of .73 and a correlation of .60 with Wing's own test when the test was given to training school students.

A test primarily for college students not majoring in music is the *Bailey Test of Listening Skill.*[18] In its final form it was standardized on 769 subjects from thirteen southern American colleges. A reliability of .87 is reported. The student hears musical excerpts and responds to multiple-choice questions in the areas of tonality, melody, rhythm and meter, texture, media (instrument), expressive devices, structure, and style.

The battery of achievement measures by Aliferis and Stecklein has apparently been well received by music educators. Each test's tonal stimuli can be given either by piano performance or tape recording.[19] The *Aliferis Music Achievement Test: College Entrance Level* has melodic, harmonic, and rhythmic sections. The total test is said to correlate with music grades in the .50's and .60's. It is quite reliable and has been extremely well standardized with separate T-scores for each of the four major geographical sections of the United States. The *Aliferis-Stecklein Music Achievement Test: College Midpoint Level,* as the subhead indicates, is for use in reexamining music majors at the end of the second college year or at the beginning of the third. Taken as a unit, it has a reliability of .92, with that of the rhythm subtest being the poorest. Total scores correlate .41 with honor point ratios of music education majors in music courses.

Typical forms of the *Music Education: National Teacher Examinations*[20] contain 105 questions, each with five "plausible" answers. The test is intended as a sort of "board" examination for prospective music teachers who in most portions of the test check what they regard as the best answers. In the last section they are asked to check the "least plausible" answers. The test forms have plenty of top and reliabilities in the .80's and .90's. Since the measure is purely a music information test and does not cover personality or music aptitude, it quite naturally correlates well (.78) with the test generally taken at the same time, the *National Teacher Common Examinations,* which attempts to measure professional information.

English expression, information in social studies-literature-fine arts and science and mathematics, and nonverbal reasoning.

In 1951 a music achievement test was added to the well-known and much used *Graduate Record Examinations, Advanced Tests*.[21] Requiring 105 minutes to take, it has 160 multiple-choice items. Areas of concern are form and analysis, theory, and history of music. There are a few questions on instrumentation and orchestration. The test correlates well with the verbal score of the *Graduate Record Examinations Aptitude Test*.

TESTS WHICH STRESS NONVERBAL MUSICAL SKILLS

The earliest of the semistandardized tests of musical performance (1923) was the *Hillbrand Sight-Singing Test*, a measure devised for fourth-, fifth-, and sixth-grade pupils.[22] The test contains six songs which the student studies for a few minutes and then sings without help or accompaniment. The examiner listens with an ear to notes wrongly pitched, to transpositions, notes flatted, notes sharped, notes omitted, errors in time, extra notes, repetitions, and hesitations.

Hillbrand's scale was followed two years later by the *Mosher Test of Individual Singing*.[23] Twelve exercises, arranged in order of difficulty, are presented and sung back by the pupil. The score is the tally of the measures rendered tonally and rhythmically correct. In 1932 Mosher was coauthor of a second performance scale entitled the *O-M Sight-Singing Test*.[24] This measure is structurally like the earlier one. The items "progress through most of the major keys and introduce the minor mode. Some of the exercises in the latter part of the test begin on scale steps other than the tonic." The test has high reliability and is reasonably objective in the sense that any two examiners will agree fairly well on the ratings which should be given.

A considerable body of data has been accumulated on two sight-singing tests developed by Thostenson.[25] The first to be constructed, the *CSS76 Criterion Sightsinging Test*, is a 30-minute individually administered measure which has four sections to test skill in singing: (1) the 12 simple intervals, (2) 24 four-note pitch phrases without rhythm obligation, (3) 20 two-bar rhythm phrases without pitch obligation, and (4) 20 two-bar melodic phrases with both pitch and rhythm obligations. When used with either undergraduate or graduate students in music the test's reliability is around .95. The *CSS76 Criterion Sightsinging Test* has been found to correlate at .85 with a later-developed group measure termed the *PRM 78 Dictation Test*. The latter, whose reliability is approximately .88, includes 30 pitch items constructed as short melodic phrases whose rhythm factor is unchanging, 24 rhythm items made up of melodic phrases whose pitch factor is unchanging, and 24 melodic items formed from short phrases whose pitch and rhythm content each differ from foil to foil. The task is to listen and then select the foil whose notation correctly represents the sound heard. Both this group measure and the slightly more reliable individual test are weakest in their measurement of the rhythm factor.

Gutsch[26] has issued a preliminary report on two forms of a promising-looking test of the ability to sight-read rhythm while performing on a musical instrument. The theoretical aspects derive from the Schillinger System of Musical Composition.

Watkins' *Performance Test for the Cornet or Trumpet* consists of a scale of fourteen melodic exercises.[27] Two scores are usually obtained, one as the test is administered to the pupil at sight and the other after he has had a week's time to practice the material. The scores are built up from a tabulation of pitch, time, change of tempo, expression, and slur errors; and the mishandling of rests, holds, pauses, and repeats. An adaptation of this performance scale for the cornet or trumpet is the *Watkins-Farnum Performance Scale*[28] which may be used for any band instrument. The fourteen exercises are so graded that while the first is intended for those who have had lessons for approximately three months, the fourteenth will be found difficult by the student who has studied for several years. The reliability is good as is also the correlation with teacher ratings. (That the reliability of teacher ratings can also be made high has been shown by Alluisi[29] who got instructors of woodwinds and brass to agree on the abilities of their students to the degree represented by a correlation of approximately .85.)

Relatively unstandardized achievement tests keep appearing from time to time.[30] A few of these owe their birth to the idea that the music curricula of the public schools are still too local to justify national norms. Hence each large school system can with profit construct its own test battery, although at present the majority of music achievement tests do not meet the standards of good test construction. Without doubt the fluid and uncertain state of school music has made the task of devising achievement tests in music more difficult than in, say, the scientific areas. Perhaps at some later date there will be more general agreement on what children should know about music by the end of each grade. When this time arrives, even better achievement tests can be devised for the area of music.

UNSTANDARDIZED APTITUDE TESTS[31]

We have seen that the music achievement tests largely reflect current curriculum practices and give little help in isolating the basic musical abilities. Attention must be shifted, then, to the musical aptitude tests in the hope that they may yield more pertinent information.

Stumpf was one of the first psychologists to interest himself in the basic musical abilities.[32] In his work with the young genius Pepito Areola, he stressed the following: possession of absolute pitch; unusually good pitch and timbre discrimination; excellent musical memory; ease in judging pitch intervals; and ability in transposition, in improvisation, and in producing dissonant chords and series of "unmelodic" tones. Stumpf saw four basic abilities in musicality: to tell whether a clang was composed of one or two tones, to discriminate pitch differences, to judge degrees of consonance as to pleasantness, and to sing correctly. Pear modified Stumpf's ideas very slightly by testing for pitch aptitude, ability to sing, ability to analyze a clang, and consistency in reporting the clang analyses.[33]

Meyer has developed a number of ingenious devices to assess musical talents.[34] His obe-imeter measures "how echotheratic (sound-hunting) the subject is." The task in this test is to listen for an auditory stimulus which is not easily followed since it is partially masked by other tones and noises. The concertometer shows how well a musician can play with other musicians in concert. The rhythmometer, which resembles the motor rhythm test R. H. Seashore independently developed, measures how well a person can follow a rhythmic pattern and reproduce it. The terpometer presents major, minor, and mistuned chords which are to be classified as either active, sad, or neutral. The last member of the battery, the hymnometer, is in essence a tonal memory test. Both the terpometer and the hymnometer make use of a specially devised quarter-tone reed organ.

During his early research, Révész appeared to regard absolute pitch as the most important element of musicality. Chord and interval recognition; ability to compose, improvise, and transpose; and keen memory were also deemed to be basic musical abilities. All of these Révész found to be present at an early age in the wonder-child Nyiregyhazi, whose achievements he described in *The Psychology of a Musical Prodigy*.[35] In his more recent theorizing Révész has differentiated between (1) aptitudes which he feels have to do with fitness for performance and (2) talents which refer to capacities far above the average in some special field.[36] Musical talents for him are of two distinct types: creative and reproductive-interpretative. The latter type is subdivided into instrumental-virtuoso talent and talent for conducting. Révész would now measure the "lower grades of musicality" through tests of rhythmic sensitivity, regional pitch, ability to analyze two-tone clangs and chords, and ability to grasp and sing a melodic line. For the "higher grades of musicality" he would give tests suited to the measurement of relative pitch, harmonic apprehension and response, creative fantasy, and ability to play familiar melodies from memory.

For Rupp the list of basic abilities included: interval recognition, absolute pitch, chord analysis, harmonic feeling, melodic recognition and reproduction, and sensitivity to rhythms and time differences.[37] Billroth[38] and von Kries[39] had briefer lists. The former's included ability to remember, recognize, and reproduce short melodies; the latter's contained sense of rhythm, musical memory, and musical ear. For Mjön[40] the five most important abilities appeared to be: to compose, to possess absolute pitch, to play by ear, to improvise a second voice, and to sing a second voice.[41]

Haecker and Ziehen obtained the bulk of their data on musical abilities by sending out 11,000 questionnaires.[42] Exceptional tonal memory seemed to them best to distinguish their more from their less musical respondents. An excellent prognostic sign for later musicality turned out to be precocity in things musical. They found vocal skill, a motor ability, to be little related to the several sensory skills, e.g. pitch discrimination.

Lowery has devised three tests—one of musical memory, another in which it must be decided which of two cadences is more complete, and a phrase test in which the problem is to tell whether or not a phrase has been repeated.[43] Ortmann has a battery of seven tests which has enjoyed use at the Peabody Conservatory of Music.[44] The members are: pitch memory, rhythm memory, melodic memory, harmonic memory, fusion, pitch discrimination, and time discrimination. Schoen too has offered a battery of tests.[45] These are for the measurement of relative pitch, where one must judge the difference in distance between two successive pitch intervals; tonal sequence, in which four two-phrase melodies are given with alternative endings; and rhythm discrimination, where a rhythm may either be repeated or reappear in somewhat altered form. A tonal movement test of considerable promise is Franklin's *TMT*. Twenty-five unfinished melodies are presented to the testees with requests for the best final tone for each. Retest and split-half reliabilities in the .80's are reported for an adult music student population. By the use of the

TMT it is apparently possible to select the better from the poorer students at a level considerably better than chance.[46]

Crude measures in the pitch, tempo, rhythm, harmony, and tone recognition areas are offered by the *Conrad Instrument-Talent Test*.[47] Novelties on this test are the hand type, lip, and jaw charts. By rule-of-thumb procedures the student is advised on the basis of these "types" as to the instrument which will best suit him.

Among those who have used achievement tests as measures of aptitude is Madison, who has made an extensive study of the ability to discriminate intervals.[48] Since interval discrimination is basic to all musical perception, it would seem that Madison has specialized on a most important musical ability. Scores on Madison's measure have been found to correlate from .46 to .72 with grades in theory at the Juilliard School, and from .39 to .71 with indices of musical ability at the secondary-school level. Lamp and Keys[49] have also studied aptitude by way of achievement. They trained pupils for several weeks on brass instruments, then on woodwinds, and later on strings (the order varied). After these weeks of training, ratings were made for achievement on each family of instruments. The authors hoped through such ratings to learn which of the three sorts of instruments was best suited to the aptitudes of each of their pupils. They appeared to enjoy mild success in their prognostications. These teachers also attempted without success to forecast later achievement through analyses of tooth evenness, lip thickness, and length and slenderness of fingers.

No well-standardized tests have so far been developed to measure control of pitch intonation, loudness, time, or rhythm. But a record of pitch control can be obtained through the use of instruments such as the tonoscope[50] and other standard stroboscopic devices[51] now on the market which show visually the accuracy of a person's vocal or instrumental attempts. Intensity meters and instruments to study dynamic control are available.[52] Ability to control time and rhythm can be studied through the Max Meyer "rhythmometer," mentioned above, or by means of R. H. Seashore's "rhythm meter," which is a phonograph with contacts imbedded in the turntable at various points.[53] A number of different rhythmic patterns can be provided for the subject, who must make his taps on a telegraph key coincide with the clicks he hears.

Carl Seashore and his students have felt that the ability to imagine tonal material is an important aspect of musical aptitude.[54] Their way of testing imagery is to present lists of questions which it is hoped will elicit images in the eight most important sensory areas. Naturally their list for children differs from that appropriate to adults. The subjects, whatever their age, must introspectively and retrospectively evaluate the strengths of their images on a seven-point scale.

A Freudian twist to the assessment of imagery has been given by Bergan, who feels that he has demonstrated that the capacity to make accurate pitch judgments is related to the ability to experience vivid auditory images, and that the latter ability is contingent on the activation of regressive behavior. He considers this regression to be adaptive and not pathological—what one analyst has termed "regression in the service of the ego."[55]

ORIGINAL SEASHORE BATTERY

The first really standardized aptitude tests were those devised by Carl Seashore,[56] who discovered in the second decade of this century what has been shown still to be true[57]—that American school music teachers agree but little on methods suitable for selecting children for vocal and instrumental training. For this reason Seashore developed his famous aptitude tests as an objective way of evaluating musical potentiality. Seashore argued that since music is in essence a matter of pitch, intensity, time, memory, consonance, and rhythm, discrimination tests in these areas should make it possible to pick out the potentially musical, with those having the best acuities being expected to give the greatest musical promise. Seashore believed that his tests tapped basic physiological capacities which were inborn and could not be influenced by training. He admitted that his test battery was limited, that there were other capacities he was not measuring.

Seashore's test philosophy has been criticized on a number of counts.[58] Many psychologists and musicians have condemned its atomistic and unmusical orientation.[59] They have emphasized that the Seashore tests get at psychophysiological, and not necessarily at musical, differences. What is the good, they say, of a performer's being able to discriminate pitches which differ by as little as one or two cycles if his listeners can only discriminate pitches which are five or more cycles apart? If the performer is a pianist, why need he bother with differences smaller than a half-tone? Other psychologists have been made unhappy by the Seashore claim that test scores reflect pure native capacity and cannot be improved by practice.[60] It has not proved possible to entice all music testers away from Seashore's hereditarian camp, but there has been amassed an impressive array of data which demonstrate beyond the possibility of doubt that the Seashore scores can be enormously improved if proper training procedures are employed.

The original *Seashore Measures of Musical Talent* offered scores for sense of pitch, sense of intensity, sense of time, sense of consonance, and auditory memory span (tonal memory).[61] Six years later a sense of rhythm measure was added. Because of the many criticisms of the sense of consonance test it was later dropped. Norms for each member of the battery were made available for adults, for eighth-graders, and for fifth-graders, who were at that time thought to be the youngest age group which could properly attend to the tonal stimuli of the tests.

There have been a number of attempts to improve the battery. Several have found that the norms, at least for the intensity test, vary somewhat with the type of phonograph employed. Others have advocated simplifying the directions which are quite difficult for young children to comprehend.[62] Salisbury and Smith have modified the pitch test so that all of the items are scaled from less to more difficult instead of from less to more and then more to less as in the original measure.[63] Hattwick has also modified the pitch test with the aim of adapting it to children of the first five grades.[64] Gaw, deciding that the time and tonal memory tests were too difficult for fifth-graders, dropped the most difficult items of these tests.[65] These changes did improve the tests somewhat, although the Gaw-modified tests are now a little too easy.[66] California adult norms for the rhythm test have been developed, since it has been found that West Coasters make better scores on this measure than do Iowans.[67] O'Connor would modify the tonal memory test by (1) better scaling of item difficulty (2) greater temporal spacing between items, and (3) the use of the whole-tone as the minimal interval.[68]

TILSON-GRETSCH TEST FOR MUSICAL APTITUDE

Created to replace or at least to serve as a second form of the original *Seashore Measures,* the *Tilson-Gretsch Musical Aptitude Test* played into bad luck in appearing shortly after the revised (1939) *Seashore Measures.*[69] The Tilson-Gretsch test features the areas of pitch, intensity, and time sensitivities and tonal memory. It is recorded on two phonograph records whereas its older rival was spread over six. Its directions are considerably more communicable than Seashore's but its items are too easy. Its reliabilities are approximately the same as Seashore's at the fifth- and eighth-grade levels but are considerably poorer in the adult range. This battery now has little excuse for continued existence.[70]

1939 REVISION OF SEASHORE MEASURES OF MUSICAL TALENTS

Only minor changes in the Seashore test philosophy are reflected in this newer battery.[71] Musical "talent" has become musical "talents," and there is no longer an attempt to measure consonance. The stimulus term "intensity" is replaced by the more appropriate response term "loudness." Sensitivity to timbre is recognized as of sufficient importance to justify the construction of a test to measure it. But the bulk of the objections raised in connection with the earlier edition still pertain. Two forms of the battery, A and B, were constructed, one an easier and the other a more difficult series, but Form B was later withdrawn from sale. Three sets of percentile norms are now available for Form A—for the fourth and fifth grades, for the sixth, seventh, and eighth grades, and for grades nine through sixteen.

The basic tones of the pitch test are set at 500 cycles.[72] Each of the 50 items in the test consists of two tones which differ only in pitch. The subject's task is to state whether the second of each pair is higher or lower than the first. The test opens with differences of 17 cycles, moves to differences of 12 cycles, then to 8, 5, 4, 3, and finally to 2 cycles. The reliability, one of the highest of the battery, ranges from .82 in the lower grades to .84 for grades six to eight and for adults.

The 50 items of the loudness test are also arranged in pairs. Here the subject must decide whether the second tone of each pair is weaker or stronger than the first. The range of loudness differences is from four decibels to a half-decibel. The reliabilities run from .85 in the lower grades to .74 at the adult level.

In the time test the subject judges whether the second tone of each pair is held a longer or shorter time than the first. Starting with differences of .3 second, the test becomes progressively more difficult: .2, .15, .125, .10, .075, and finally .05 second. The time test's reliabilities range from .72 in grades four and five to .63 in grades six to eight and .71 in the adult reaches.

Each item of the rhythm test consists of two patterns which may have either identical or different rhythms. With only 30 true-false items, the reliability of this test is rather poor—.67 in grades four and five, .69 in grades six to eight, and .64 in the higher levels.

The measure of timbre also uses the "same-different" scheme but has more items than the rhythm test. To change the timbre, the intensity of the tone's fourth partial was increased and that of the third partial was decreased by an amount necessary to keep the total intensity constant. In the first fifth of the 50 items this change is of 10 decibels. The changes in the more difficult items are first of 8.5 then of 7.0, of 5.5, and finally of 4.0 decibels. Its reliability is poor, ranging from .55 to .68.

The measure of tonal memory has 30 items and follows a multiple-choice plan. Hence its reliability is high (.81, .84, and .83). Short series of tones are given and then repeated with one of the tones of each series changed in pitch. One-third of the series are three-tone sequences, another third are four-tone, and the remaining third are five-tone.[73] While the majority of the Seashore subtests are relatively independent of one another, the tonal memory test correlates appreciably with the others.

While Seashore has asserted that his measures are, by the very nature of their construction, valid, many testers have not agreed and hence have made a number of attempts to relate the test scores to musical performance. The majority of the many validity studies on these widely used tests have been concerned with the set of recordings Seashore brought out in 1919. The criteria against which the Seashore tests have been measured are several, with teacher ratings and grades in music appearing in perhaps most of the studies. Where correlations of any size have been found—and occasionally values in the .60's and .70's have been reported—they tend to be the highest for the tonal memory and pitch tests[74] and for the battery considered as a single measuring instrument.[75] In one of the studies of the 1939 tests, Manor found that fourth-grade work in instrumental music could be forecast by the pitch test with a coefficient of correlation of .49 and by the measure of tonal memory with a correlation value of .32.[76]

Intelligence tests have been found to be of more worth than the Seashore tests in forecasting music grades in academic classes (e.g. history and appreciation of music) while the Seashore are of more value the more the classes are tonally conducted (e.g. classes in harmony).[77] Quite naturally music achievement tests do far better than the Seashore at forecasting grades in the relatively nontonal types of music courses.[78] Members of musical organizations usually make higher than average Seashore scores.[79] High scorers on the Seashore show a greater preference for "classical" music than do the lower scorers, says one study;[80] according to another their preferences lean more toward the "romantic classical" (as opposed to "light classical").[81] Persons who regard themselves as more musical than average tend to achieve significantly higher music test scores, particularly in tonal memory, than those who think of themselves as below the musical average.[82]

From the discussion so far it is apparent that the Seashore tests have at least some validity. Further support comes from data gathered at the Eastman Conservatory of Music[83] where the music tests (1919 edition) were added to a measure of academic intelligence, a case history, and a test of tonal imagery, and the combined scores were used for selection purposes. Five levels of scores were studied. It was found that 60 per cent of the persons in the top fifth succeeded in graduating, but only 17 per cent of the bottom fifth were as successful. In a slightly later study at Eastman, it was shown that course grades in musical theory correlated .59 with Seashore scores.[84] Less success was achieved with these music tests at the College of Music of Cincinnati which concluded that, although music tests are of some use, they should always be employed in conjunction with academic intelligence tests.[85] McLeish, a British psychologist, suggests that appreciation tests should also be used along with the Seashore battery.[86]

KWALWASSER-DYKEMA MUSIC TESTS

The Kwalwasser-Dykema battery, for a long time the Seashore's only serious rival, attempts to do all its competitor does and more.[87] It has measures for the Seashore-tested areas of pitch, intensity, time, quality (timbre), rhythm, and tonal memory. There are two tests of appreciation—melodic taste and tonal movement (described in Chap. 7). In addition there are tests of pitch and rhythm imagery, which are measures of achievement rather than of aptitude. The tests are much briefer than the Seashore, the test items seem more musical, and the directions are easier to follow. But except for the measures of tonal memory and tonal movement, the reliabilities are very low.[88] This poor reliability accounts in part for the fact that only the tonal memory test correlates at all well with its Seashore counterpart.

The structural arrangement of the individual tests is as follows. The measure of tonal memory consists of 25 pairs of patterns which range in length from four to nine tones. The patterns are repeated either in original or in altered form, and the subject responds with the words "same" or "different." The test of quality discrimination presents 30 items, each composed of two tones played on some particular instrument and then repeated on that or a different instrument. Like the previous test it calls for the responses "same" or "different." The stimuli of the time-discrimination test were recorded from a player-piano roll. Twenty-five tones lasting from .03 to .30 second are repeated unchanged or with a different duration. Twenty-five rhythmic patterns repeated in the same or in an altered form make up the rhythm-discrimination test. The K-D intensity-discrimination test offers 30 tones and chords and then repeats them at different intensities. The subjects judge the relative strengths of the second members of the pairs. In the pitch-discrimination test there are 40 items. Each tone, held for approximately 3 seconds, rises or falls in pitch and then returns to its original pitch position. The pitch changes range from .6 to 50 cycles. In the pitch-imagery and rhythm-imagery tests, the subjects compare what they hear with what is on the printed blanks supplied them. Each of the 25 items is to be described as "same" or "different."[89]

Extremely disturbing is the fact that only one set of norms is offered for this battery.[90] Apparently the test designers felt that all persons, eight or eighty, trained or untrained, score similarly. But that several sets of norms are needed should not surprise anyone who is at all familiar with the area of aptitude testing.

The reliabilities of approximately half of the members of the K-D battery have been materially improved by Holmes, who has changed the plan of the tests from true-false to multiple-choice.[91] This he did solely by altering the directions for administering the several measures. Thus the subject taking the Holmes-modified tonal-memory test must not only decide whether there has been a change in pattern but in addition must check whether the second pattern of each item is, if changed, higher or lower than the first. The possible responses for the quality-discrimination test are now "equal," "different," "different and heavier," and "different and lighter." For the measure of intensity discrimination they are "equal," "different," "different and weaker," and "different and stronger"; for the tonal-movement measure, "up," "down," and "same as last note actually heard"; for the measure of time discrimination, "equal," "different," "different and longer," and "different and shorter"; for the test of rhythm discrimination, "equal," "different," "different because the time values have been changed," and "different because the accent has been changed"; for the pitch-discrimination measure, "equal," "different," "different and higher," and "different and lower"; and for the melodic taste test, "A better,"

"B better," and "equally good." With these changes the reliability of the battery now reaches .91 (high-school level).

There are a number of studies in which the K-D battery has been employed to forecast teacher ratings and grades in sight-singing, ear-training, and in "all fine arts" courses. In some instances there has been little or no success reported, but in one study the astonishingly high correlation value of .83 has been claimed.[92] Perhaps the modal forecast value for the battery as a whole would lie in the neighborhood of .40, with that for the individual tests being considerably lower.

KWALWASSER MUSIC TALENT TEST

In 1953 there appeared a new Kwalwasser-developed aptitude test which requires only ten minutes to take.[93] Accompanying Form A, the more difficult of the test's two phonograph records, is one set of norms for junior high-school students and another set for senior-high and college groups. Form B is for grades four, five, and six. Form A "consists of 50 three-tone patterns which are repeated with variation in one of the following respects: (a) pitch, (b) time, (c) rhythm, (d) loudness." The pitch differences range from 5 to 70 cents, the tempo changes from 40 to 5 per cent of the standard metronomic marking of 90 to the quarter-note, and loudness varies from 10 to 2 decibels from the standard. The rhythmic changes become more difficult as the test progresses. The corresponding values for the 40-item Form B are: pitch, 15–70 cents; time, 15–40 per cent; and loudness, 3–10 decibels. The rhythms proceed from more to less difficult changes in pattern. Kwalwasser, a staunch hereditarian and former student of C. E. Seashore, closes his eyes to the research literature and maintains that training can have little or no effect on the scores made on his test. He has violated approved test practice by publishing a commercial test without reliability data of any kind.

STOREY TESTS

Another very brief phonographically recorded test (10 minutes) has been developed by C. A. Storey,[94] a public school band instructor in Longview, Wash. Questions asked the pupil are: (1) Which is the higher of two tones? (2) How many times is a given tone played? (3) Is a cornet-rendered melody repeated or altered? (4) Which of two sets of drum-beat rhythms is the faster? Since no validity data accompanied the test, the author had two of his students (D. C. Korten and T. R. Toothaker) try out the test in the Palo Alto (Calif.) area. The Storey test scores were found to correlate .66 with scores on the combined Seashore pitch, memory, and rhythm measures (.64 with pitch and memory). When the Palo Alto area data were compared with those gathered in a town where fewer of the children had had musical training or professed as much musical interest (Raymond, Wash.), the Palo Alto data yielded a considerably higher mean score.

1932 AND 1954 DRAKE TESTS

In 1932 Drake offered the musical world four partially standardized aptitude tests.[95] These covered the areas of musical memory (melody memory), interval discrimination, retentivity (memory for isolated tones), and intuition (key center, phrase, and time balance). In 1954 he replaced these with two well-standardized tests, one in the area of musical memory and the other to forecast rhythmic ability.[96] The musical memory test has two equivalent forms, A and B, and the rhythm test has an easier Form A and a more difficult Form B. The musically naive are tested on all four, but subjects with five or more years of musical training need take only Form B of the rhythm test and either form of the measure of musical memory. The two new Drake tests intercorrelate only slightly. With reliabilities in the high .80's or low .90's they yield stable scores. Norms for them are available for music and nonmusic students and for ages 11, 12, and 13; 14, 15, and 16; 17, 18, and 19; 20, 21, and 22; and 23 and over. Sex differences in scores and those associated with racial and cultural background are said to be negligible.

The musical memory test is made up of specially composed melodies which are either repeated or changed with respect to time, key, or note. The rhythm test presents the sound of a metronome beating at a certain rate and a voice which counts "one, two, three, four." The voice then stops counting and the metronome either stops or proceeds at a different rate while the subject must continue to count silently at the original rate until told to stop. His score is the difference between the metronome beat number (where the beat continued at its original rate) and his own silent count.

Drake reports a coefficient of correlation of only .17 between scores on his measure of rhythm and the Seashore test of rhythm discrimination. The two memory tests, however, are tapping more similar variables and intercorrelate at .55 (from unpublished data gathered at Stanford University). Drake's studies suggest that his newer tests have considerable validity. He draws his support from the fact that when correlations are run against teacher estimates of musical talent, the values are generally above .58 and have run as high as .91. Research by Gordon[97] indicates that the Drake test is not easily coachable; i.e., training on similar items has so far improved scores but slightly.

WHEELER BATTERY

Wheeler's battery of music aptitude tests is in some ways a cross between the Drake and an easier version of the Seashore. With its items produced by an electric organ, recorded on tape, and designed for students from grades four through twelve, the test and its subtests have adequate reliability. The test taken as a whole correlates .71 with the Seashore total score (college years). It takes a little over a half-hour to administer. The pitch section contains 30 pairs of tones which range over five octaves. The subject is asked which of each pair is the higher in pitch. The 30-item time test is constructed on the Drake plan. The first of the two tonal memory tests presents 20 items each of two brief melodies which are to be classified as "same" or "different." In the second memory test, also 20 items in length, a sustained tone is presented with the subject then guessing how many times it appears in a subsequent melody (one to five are possible).[98]

WHISTLER-THORPE MUSICAL APTITUDE TEST

The developers of the *Whistler-Thorpe Musical Aptitude Test* pride themselves on presenting musical, not just tonal, stimuli (piano music).[99] The test has two "same-different" sections dealing with rhythm recognition, one fairly easy and the other considerably more difficult. The "same-different" pattern is also followed in the melody-recognition portion. In the pitch-discrimination section, chords are given and then repeated, either with precisely the same structure or at a higher or lower pitch level. The section of the test devoted to pitch recognition is the most novel. Here a particular pitch is strongly emphasized. Then there follows a melody of four measures of 13 quarter-notes. The subject's task is to count the number of times the previously emphasized pitch has appeared. The Whistler-Thorpe test has a reported reliability of .93. It claims to correlate at .78 with teacher estimates of vocal talent. Unfortunately, bright students often make spuriously high W-T scores by voting "different" on the "same-different" items whenever they are in doubt as to the correct answer. Since there are far more "different" than "same" items they cannot help but get inflated scores.

LUNDIN TESTS

In an effort to measure musical behaviors not considered by the earlier testers, Lundin devised five rather different tests.[100] The first of these measures is in the area of interval discrimination. Fifty ascending and descending intervals make up the stimuli, which are either repeated without change or are modified in the second rendition. The responses of this and the other members of the Lundin battery are in terms of "same" or "different." The reliability is reported to be in the .70's.

The melodic transposition test offers 30 simple melodies. If on the second rendition the key alone is changed the subject responds by "same," but if both the key and the melody are altered the proper response is "different." The reliability is said to be .65 for musicians and .72 for unselected college students.

Mode discrimination is tested through the presentation of 30 pairs of chords. If the pair members are in the same mode the response is "same"; if the mode is changed the subject responds with "different." When employed on unselected students this test has the poorest reliability of any member of the battery (one of .10). For musicians the reliability value is in the middle .60's.

Each of the 30 items of the melodic sequences test contains three melodic groups which follow the same melodic order. A fourth group may or may not follow this pattern. The reliability of this measure falls in the .70's. This test sets the pattern for the last member of the battery, the measure of rhythmic sequences, except of course that in the latter, test rhythms and not melodies are involved. For musicians the rhythm test has a reliability of .60; for unselected college students the value is .72. The corresponding reliability coefficients for the battery as a whole are .89 and .85.

In one study by Lundin, when total battery scores were employed for forecasting pooled ratings of students made by six professors, the following correlation values emerged: melodic dictation, .70; harmonic dictation, .70; written harmonization, .43; general ability in theory, .63; performance, .51; and sum of ratings, .69.

Lundin found the Seashore pitch, rhythm, and tonal memory tests and the Drake musical memory measure (original form) to forecast these criteria less well.

GASTON TEST OF MUSICALITY

A test for grades four through twelve, now in its fourth edition, is Gaston's *Test of Musicality*[101] which was standardized on some 15,000 students, ages 9 through 18. Reliabilities are very good, especially for the last three grades (.90). This measure forecasts teacher evaluation fairly well. Unlike most tests Gaston's gives credit for such matters as having a parent or sibling who sings or plays a musical instrument or possessing a home piano. The tonal portion of the test features detection of rhythmic and tonal changes and pitch discrimination.

WING STANDARDIZED TESTS OF MUSICAL INTELLIGENCE

A British flavor can be seen in the Wing tests, although the measures are not so different from the much condemned American tests as one might have anticipated, knowing British attitudes.[102] Recorded on ten discs and tapes are seven tests. Although their reliabilities range as low as .65, the battery reliability is a satisfactory .93 or so. Five-step norms are available for each year from ages 8 through 17. The selection of the tests was based on factor analyses, and the author tends to believe that there is a strong general factor in music aptitude. That the battery has considerable validity was shown in a study of 333 adolescent boys who had at one time studied or were still studying some musical instrument. Wing gave his tests to these lads and classified their scores into three classes. He found that 40 per cent of the below-average group had already given up studying music. The comparable values for the average and above-average groups were 27 and 2 per cent dropouts respectively.

The Wing chord-analysis test requires the subject to count the number of notes in a series of single chords. In the measure of pitch change, chords are played and repeated either with exactly similar structure or with some one note pitched higher or lower. The memory measure presents tunes which are either repeated or altered. If they are modified, the subject must tell which are the altered notes. In the test of rhythmic accent, melodies are either repeated in identical form or with the accents rearranged. The subject notes the changes, if any, and states which versions better fit the tune. The intensity and phrasing tests are similarly arranged except that it is now the intensity or the phrasing which is altered. The harmony test presents tunes which are either repeated exactly or altered. Each item must be assessed for identity or else a decision must be made as to the better of the two versions. In a revision reported in 1962, better norms are offered and there are suggestions for eliminating certain items to shorten the test and reduce boredom. New and more impressive validity data are included in this later article by Wing.[103]

GORDON MUSICAL APTITUDE PROFILE

What appears to be the most carefully developed musical aptitude test battery now available is the *Musical Aptitude Profile,* put on the market by Edwin Gordon and Houghton Mifflin Co. in 1965. The "basic music factors" the battery purports to measure fall into three main divisions: tonal imagery, rhythm imagery, and musical sensitivity. The first two of these are represented by two subtests each, measures of melody and harmony for the first and of tempo and meter for the second. The three tests in the sensitivity category are of phrasing, balance, and style. All are on tape.

The tests have gone through at least four revisions and at the high-school level show reliabilities[104] which range from .69 for balance and phrasing to .84 for tempo. The reliability of the battery taken as a single test is .95. The *MAP* subtests intercorrelate far more than do the Seashore subtests with a low (.23) between melody and phrasing and a high (.71) between tempo and meter. There is considerable overlap with the members of the Seashore battery, the greatest being between Seashore's tonal memory and the *MAP's* melody (.56) and harmony (.57) and between the Seashore rhythm and the *MAP's* meter (.55). In a study of 65 vocal and 95 band students this newer battery did much better than the Seashore in its correlations with teacher ratings (.60 vs. .36 with the vocal group and .62 vs. .31 with the band). Other validity data also look promising.

An extensive manual[105] comes with the test battery. A table is offered for converting raw scores into standard scores. The latter can then be interpreted in percentile terms for students in each grade from the fourth through the twelfth. Parallel norms are offered for "musically select" students. Presented also are data on item difficulties and discrimination indices. Sex differences are found to be negligible.

TAYLOR TESTS

C. H. Taylor is one who feels that the best selection tools are not necessarily pure aptitude tests but rather a mixture of these and measures of appreciation and achievement. In implementing this notion he has been developing tests[106] (first battery in 1930) whose reliability varies from very poor to very good. The most reliable members of his battery are tests to identify (a) modes of accompanied and unaccompanied melodies and of chords, and (b) a variety of musical selections by title and composer. Somewhat less reliable are measures which require the counting of the beats in a measure and the determination of the presence or the lack of constancy in the tempo of certain compositions. Of very poor reliability is a test in which the subject chooses from descriptions offered the one which best fits the mood of the selection he hears. The battery is intended for all levels through conservatory, although the tempo test does not appear in the form to be given in grades four through nine. Taylor states that his test scores grow as the child matures and (what is more pertinent) as he increases in musical knowledge and sophistication.

BENTLEY MEASURES OF MUSICAL ABILITIES

While the aptitude tests so far described have all been intended for use on children as well as adults, it seems safe to say that, in their construction, less research was done with the very young than with persons of somewhat older age. And we have seen that the tests tend not to be for children in grades below the fourth or fifth. A rather different approach was taken by Bentley[107] who focused on children as young as seven. One result is that the four tests of his battery have insufficient top for the very musical and for older people. Bentley's tests appear on a ten-inch long-playing record and can be administered in less than half an hour.

The tests are in the areas of pitch discrimination, tonal memory, chord analysis, and rhythmic memory. Taken individually these measures have little reliability, but the battery as a whole, when given to children from 9 years 10 months to 11 years 9 months and repeated four months later, yielded a reliability figure of .84. That the battery has some validity was shown in the score relationship to teachers' estimates of musicality, the testees' progress in musical activities, the far higher scores of skilled musicians, and the close correspondence with ranks on school music examinations.

STRONG VOCATIONAL INTEREST TEST

A rather different sort of test and one which is only in part an aptitude measure is the Strong musician scale.[108] Strong's well-known set of questions on interests has a music performer scale for men whose criterion group was composed of 450 musicians and a normative group of 450. Their average age was 36.4, their years of schooling 13.6, and their experience 17.9 years. The corresponding scale for women was based on 290 cases with average age 34.2, education 15.5 grade, and experience 14.3 years. Music teacher scales are also available. The men's teacher scale had a criterion group of 500 and an equal number was used in developing norms. The average age was 41.4 years, education 17.0 grade, and experience 16.7 years. The comparable women's teacher scale was based on 450 cases with average age of 43.8 years, education of 16.5 grade, and experience of 19.7 years. The test scores indicate the degree of resemblance between the answer profile of the person tested and that of the criterion group. Judged by the high validity that the Strong scales achieve in other areas where validity is relatively easy to ascertain, e.g. life insurance, the Strong musician scales merit respectful attention.

FUTURE OF MUSIC APTITUDE TESTS

It would be foolish to attempt too precise a forecast of the course music tests will take in the next few years. It seems clear that the testers will make increasing use of musical materials and that their tests will not be as atomistic as are the Seashore measures. In the early years of this century, the intelligence testers tried to forecast achievement by the use of simple items at the sensory level. They then moved to an omnibus or buckshot approach with their IQ tests, and still later worked out a sort of compromise of these extremes with their measures of primary mental abilities. As we have seen, the music testers also began their labors with the aid of simple sensory materials. The progressive educators in particular condemned this approach and argued for the omnibus stand; yet they did little to make tests in this model. The philosophy of the more recent testers, however, would seem to allow as test items at least a modicum of sensory material as well as bits of real music.

Musical memory has come to be the one area which all testers agree merits the most careful attention. Other ability areas so far considered may or may not be of vital importance to the potential performer. But, important or not, each tested ability should have a name which truly describes it. Rhythm especially seems to mean only what a particular test maker wants it to mean. Thus one tester's rhythm measure may have little or no relation to another's.[109]

As was mentioned earlier, the violinist needs far better pitch discrimination than does the pianist, yet neither instrumentalist should necessarily score near the top of the Seashore range. Music testers must get away from the philosophy of "better score, better musical potential." They should follow the trail blazed by the college aptitude testers and study more intensively the minimum levels necessary for later success in the several kinds of musical skills. More and more they can be expected to add to their batteries measures of academic aptitude, interest, personality, music achievement, home enrichment, socioeconomic status, and perhaps even taste, to give a broader base to their forecasting efforts.[110] It is likely that they will pay less and less attention to the nature-nurture problem. Instead the emphasis will be turned toward the practical issue of deciding which persons will profit most, given a minimum of practice opportunities.[111]

CHAPTER TEN ⚚ *Applications of Music to Industry and Therapy*

INCREASINGLY over the years music is being employed both as a goad to increase industrial output and as a therapy for the emotionally ill. Indeed the job of furnishing music to shops and stores has already become a sizable and lucrative business and music therapy a recognized profession. Yet the student who asks for proof of the medical and industrial worth of music is offered little that he will recognize as having scientific validity. More than likely he will be fed anecdotes and legends, e.g. the Bible story of the mentally disturbed King Saul listening to young David's harp playing. He may be shown data which demonstrate unmistakable improvement in work output or emotional adjustment. Then he learns that the music was given along with a host of other therapies or changes in industrial atmosphere and he is left puzzling over the part music may have played in the process, wondering if it was really the music that induced the changes.

Four ways in which music might possibly affect behavior are considered by Taylor and Paperte.[1] It is conceivable, they say,

> that music, because of its abstract nature, detours the ego and intellectual controls and, contacting the lower centers directly, stirs up latent conflicts and emotions which may then be expressed and activated through music; . . . that music, acting *through* the ego controls, produces a rapid development of the fantasy world, thus increasing the speed at which therapy may proceed; . . . music produces emotional reactions by producing "vibrations" in the nervous system; . . . that, if the structural dynamics of the music impinging on the sensorium is similar to the prevalent psychodynamic emotional structure, the two will unite and this fusion will allow music to affect emotions directly.

The first theory is tied to the notion that the emotions stem largely from subcortical neural areas, that wordless music somehow circumvents the governing or control mechanisms furnished by the highest cortical layers. The theory is an intriguing one, particularly when considering situations in which music is played to persons out of intellectual contact with their fellows. Where words have no effect, music *may* have because it is mediated more primitively, says the theory. This hypothesis may later be found to be sound, but at the moment there is insufficient evidence for its support.

The second theory is a reasonable one since it is obvious that music can elicit an enormous amount of imagery in all but the tone deaf. The third theory seems to be a throwback to the time when neural action was not yet known to be an electrical phenomenon but was thought rather to be the passage of vibrating particles. While this theory presents an out-of-date picture of nervous conduction, it appeals to the pseudoscientist who talks glibly of "being attuned" to this or that vibration rate. One is reminded of the press releases which appear from time to time stating that plants grow better when music attuned to their natures is played. So far the agronomists have not shown much excitement over these claims.

The authors appear to favor the fourth theory, part of which has been suggested by Pratt who has held that similar words can quite properly be used to describe both musical forms and emotional, i.e. kinesthetic-organic, experience. Building on Pratt's idea Taylor and Paperte consider the possibility that, *"when the structural dynamics of music is similar to the structural dynamics of the emotions, sympathetic unison of the two results and any changes in the former will produce corresponding changes in the latter."* (Italics are the authors'.) "May produce" is clearly preferable to the "will produce" of the quotation. With this change it would seem that the first, second, and fourth theories may all be true.

PHYSIOLOGICAL CHANGES

As a preliminary step toward getting a clearer picture of the potential role of music in therapy and industry it may be well to examine what is known of its power to affect human physiology. The thesis that music can elicit and modify moods needs no further defense. But can tone and rhythm affect blood pressure, pulse, respiration rate, and other physiological manifestations of man's life processes?

It may be categorically stated that music can markedly affect the bodily processes. Yet the effects are not so striking as was once thought. It was believed at one time for instance that the heart would within limitations invariably accommodate its beat to the pulse of the music being heard. With the use of better apparatus and controls, however, it has been possible to reexamine the problem and collect additional data.[2] Of the subjects so far studied, only one seemed to show any tendency for synchrony of heartbeat and musical pulse, and even here the correspondence was so slight that it may have been a matter of chance.

Diserens and Fine, after having carefully combed the experimental literature up through the middle 1930's for studies of musical effects on physiological processes, offer the following conclusions:

> Music . . . increases bodily metabolism . . . increases or decreases muscular energy . . . accelerates respiration and decreases its regularity . . . produces marked but variable effect on volume, pulse and blood pressure . . . lowers the threshold for sensory stimuli of different modes . . . influences the internal secretions.[3]

With some modifications the conclusions of Diserens and Fine can still be accepted. It is reasonably clear that music has on occasion increased the bodily metabolism of certain people and has affected their muscular energy, respiration, and/or circulation. But generalization in this area is dangerous since humans are not automatons reacting in a push-button fashion to music. Nor is all music the same, and the effect of one composition does not necessarily resemble that of another.

The idea that music can lower thresholds (raise acuities) in other sensory areas has been held to by some contemporary Soviet experimenters[4] and a few others. However, this notion has been questioned by Dannenbaum, who found the visual acuity of each of his subjects significantly impaired, not improved, by the presence of music.[5] But whether or not music can improve visual acuity as such, it is able, according to Lowenstein,[6] to restore the size of eye-pupils which have been experimentally fatigued by many exposures to light and thus reduced in size. It should be added, however, that Lowenstein obtained this effect with "very musical people" only. He is therefore inclined to think that this "restitution phenomenon," as he calls it, is not a function of tonal stimuli per se but rather of psychological stimuli, i.e. of stimuli which have real musical significance to the listener. At any rate, here is an example of the fatigue-reducing capacity of music.

A study by Dreher[7] showed that the unmusical as well as the more musical exhibit galvanic changes[8] while listening to music, but these electrical changes were found to be much weaker in the unmusical subjects. There was a direct correspondence between the degree of galvanic change and the importance of music in the life of the listener. This finding is in line with earlier reports by Vincent and Thompson[9] and Vincent et al.[10] on blood pressure. Zimny and Weidenfeller[11] have found that so far as galvanic skin resistance measures are concerned children are more responsive than college subjects or adult psychotics. The children evidenced a shorter latency and a greater magnitude of response to the exciting music, and a greater magnitude but not a shorter latency to the calming music. Exciting music produced a decrease and calming music an increase in the electrical skin resistance. In another study these researchers found that depressives showed more galvanic skin resistance changes than did schizophrenics while exciting music was being played.[12] Further work showed that while music rated by college students as exciting decreased galvanic skin resistance, neutral and calming music elicited no change.[13] Not surprising was Winold's report that greater galvanic changes are aroused by both consonant and strongly dissonant chords than by mildly dissonant ones.[14]

Out of line with the usual finding that musicians are more affected physiologically by music than are nonmusicians are the Sears[15] data which show music having its greatest effects on the muscle tonus of nonmusicans. The effects were found to be greater on women than on men.

Thirty-six students randomly selected by Ellis and Brighouse from college volunteers in undergraduate psychology[16] listened to three recordings—Hall's *Blue Interval,* Debussy's *Prelude to the Afternoon of a Faun,* and Liszt's *Hungarian Rhapsody No. 2*—while records were made of their heart and respiration rates. Physiological records were also kept for several minutes before and for as long as five minutes after the playing of the music. These experimenters report that no statistically significant changes in heartbeat were found at any time. But increases in respiration rate were apparent in almost all subjects, particularly during the playing of the Liszt and Hall numbers. It is of interest that no respiration change lasted for longer than five minutes after the cessation of the listening session, a finding which offers little encouragement to the music therapists. In a study on the general activity level of apathetic schizophrenics, Skelly and Haslerud[17] also found musical effects to be relatively short-lived although for 90 per cent of the cases discernible effects lasted up to six hours.

It goes almost without saying that the above findings might have been greatly different if either monotones or the extremely musical had been tested, or if quite dissimilar compositions had been presented. From what is known of the testing area we should expect enormous individual differences to exist in physiological responses to music. Contemporary experiments bear out this expectation. In fact there are persons so readily affected by music that listening to certain compositions leads to epileptic attacks.[18] At the other extreme there are the pitch-deaf who can get little or nothing from music except through the kinesthetic and tactual senses. The physiological effects of music on the listener will be large or small, depending on the nature of the composition which is being heard. A number of variables are of importance here, including the presence or absence of abrupt tempo changes, the acceptability or unacceptability of the composition, and the personal associations the music has for the listener. As Miles and Tilly have demonstrated, change in tempo is the chief cause of respiratory changes.[19] While tempo change is also a factor in altering circulation, the attitude of the listener toward the composition seems to be a far more important variable. These principles hold both while the listener is alert and while he is hypnotized. As the music becomes more familiar, more "understood" and appreciated, the physiological changes tend to become more marked.

How extensive then is music's power to affect body processes? The answer one gets from the experiments so far discussed is not an easy one to make. The physiological changes music elicits, while substantial and varied in certain musical persons, are relatively insignificant in the unmusical and appear to be relatively short-lasting. Most research shows the effects to be greater the more the music has "meaning" for the listener. That is, a given composition may call forth one set of effects in a musical person and quite different changes in one not musically inclined. Or the effects may differ from one time to another in the same person depending on the training the individual has received in the meantime, on the associations he has picked up, and on his changes in mood. It would follow from these facts that no composition will be found which can be guaranteed to produce identical or even nearly identical physiological changes among the members of any sizable population. One is not likely to find any considerable degree of generality of body change except perhaps where the effects are elicited through the hearing of national and church hymns and other old favorite tunes, music most of us have known well since early childhood. With music which is less a part of the common heritage the chances of securing identical effects are slighter.

MUSIC AND GENERAL ACTIVITY

Although many of the phenomena of the laboratory cannot be replicated in "real" life, many others will carry over or at least can be made to yield cues and principles which may facilitate later work outside the laboratory. Thus Husband's finding that several rather different sorts of music all increased the sway of people who were attempting to stand still would seem to be applicable to life generally.[20] As might have been guessed, jazz caused greater sway than music of several other styles. Unpublished work at the Stanford University laboratories has carried the Husband study further to show that even thinking of jazz music can increase sway. That is, subjects told to stand as quietly as possible swayed more while they imagined hearing strongly rhythmical music than when they imagined themselves studying in an easy chair. It would seem then that the activation of either the ear or the "mind's ear" can lead to slight body movements which are of measurable size.[21] At the other extreme is the situation where the subject's position is supine and the rhythm of the music approximates that of his respiration. Under these circumstances the person is likely to become increasingly relaxed or fall into a sleeplike trance.[22]

Diserens and Fine long ago reported a series of laboratory experiments on the influence of music on behavior. As pioneer work their research should be commended. However, viewed from the vantage point of the present day it must be said that the study generalizes too freely and concerns too few subjects. Its conclusions are given here only to show the variety of areas it encompassed.

> Music tends to reduce or delay fatigue and consequently increases muscular endurance. Music has no definite effect on precision or accuracy of movement, if the rhythm is not adapted to the rhythm of the work. It reduces accuracy in typewriting and handwriting, the result being shown in an increased number of errors. Music speeds up such voluntary activities as typewriting and handwriting. It also accelerates respiration. Music increases the extent of muscular reflexes employed in writing, drawing, etc. Music reduces normal suggestibility, except in the case of direct suggestion involving color, in which case suggestibility is increased. Music seems to have a tendency to produce a shift in normal preference for chromatic and achromatic impressions, the change being toward the blue end of the spectrum and the white end of the achromatic series.

Music has a tendency to reduce the extent of illusion by acting as a distracting factor. Music influences the electrical conductivity of the human body as manifested by increased fluctuations in the psychogalvanic reflex.[23]

EFFECTS OF MUSIC ON ACHIEVEMENT

Jensen has studied the effects of jazz and dirges on typing.[24] Although jazz seemed to have no effect on the speed of his subjects' typing, it did increase their errors. Dirges on the other hand decreased the typing speed but had no effect on errors. Jensen's findings appear reasonable. Dirge time is obviously not in synchrony with good typing speed, and work accuracy would very likely be affected by factors of the environment which, like jazz, compete for attention. Music was found by Whitely to have a very small detrimental influence on the learning and retention of verbal material.[25] The effects were so insignificant, however, that with slightly changed conditions they might not have appeared at all.

It might be fitting to describe here some experiments at Stanford University in which subjects were engaged in pursuit and code-learning tasks while in the presence of attention-getting noise at approximately the 70-phon level.[26] After a number of trials half of the subjects continued their tasks with the noise still booming in their ears while the other group proceeded in relative quiet. It is of interest that no consistent or significant differences appeared between the performances of these two groups during any of the trials. Here is an example of the fact that man is a rather adaptable organism who will learn and retain under extremely trying circumstances.

Although learning can proceed reasonably well in the face of what one might think would be a considerable distraction, there are limits beyond which the disturbance becomes a real detriment to learning. Thus Fendrick showed that music could be a serious distraction to persons reading very difficult material.[27]

It may be that psychologists are minimizing the distracting effects of music through their almost exclusive use of college students as subjects. If persons sixty years of age or more were to be tested, the data might look quite different, for these older persons learned to read and study without the blaring of radio, television, or phonograph. For them music is not an integral part of the reading process. When Henderson and his colleagues demonstrated that popular music lessened only slightly the paragraph comprehension of their college subjects and did not harm vocabulary learning at all, and that "classical" music had no effect on either of these aspects of reading skill, they were presenting data which perhaps relate solely to college populations.[28] The fact that some of these latter claimed to study without the "aid" of music and still were not bothered by the music of the experiment is of interest but cannot be taken at face value. Even these atypical students are far more likely than their elders to have come from homes noisy with music from phonograph, TV, or radio. To read in the sanctuary of a quiet study is not characteristic of the modern youth.

That different personality "types" are differentially distracted by music is hinted at in an experiment[29] in which students were first separated into the "very high achievement motivated" and the "very low achievement motivated." When both groups listened to a loud rendition of Strauss' *Blue Danube Waltz* and pressed keys at what they thought were four one-minute intervals, the low achievement group increased more rapidly than did the highs their time estimates over the four intervals.

So far the discussion has centered on music as a distraction. It might be expected, however, that readers can sometimes benefit from background music, particularly if they are young and accustomed to the simultaneity of such auditory and visual stimulation. True to expectation, examples of actual gain in reading speed can be seen in the data of Freeburne and Fleischer who played jazz compositions to college students as they studied.[30] No other sort of music had a facilitating effect. Hall too found music beneficial to reading for some persons.[31] Almost 60 per cent of his junior high-school group made higher scores on the *Nelson Silent Reading Test* while hearing background music. Mikol and Denny demonstrate that music may have a facilitating effect on rotary pursuit performances.[32] Isern[33] has reported the striking finding that mentally retarded children recall more material (immediate, recent, and remote recall) after it is given to them in a song than after it is read to them as a story.

Contrary to their expectations, the Baughs[34] found that when college students were forced to learn nonsense syllables, it seemed to make no difference to the performance whether they were at the time hearing "classical," "Oriental," "jazz," or no background music. Rock 'n' roll music, however, did help the learning. One wonders how far one can generalize these conclusions. Perhaps what was proved was that the hearing of the favored music of a particular time period (in the mid 60's it was rock 'n' roll) may affect the learning of college students. However, in another study[35] of the relation of rock 'n' roll and "classical" music to the learning of nonsense syllables (30 college students) no effects were apparent. The authors suggest that any increased output of energy may have been compensated for by the distracting effect of the musical stimuli.

The data so far considered indicate that for many persons the forced hearing of music during study hours has little or no effect on reading and study habits. For others there may be adverse consequences and for still others there may be measurable benefit. The type of and preference for the music that is heard, the difficulty of the material to be read, and the study and reading habits of the person being tested appear to be the pertinent variables which account for the diversity of effects so far reported.

Repetitive Work. The proof of music's usefulness for industry has been best demonstrated for repetitive work. This is not surprising when it is recalled that Negro stevedores and laborers the world over have typically synchronized their work speeds to the tempos of music and have derived much benefit therefrom. Their morale has been lifted and their work movements have been made smoother and more efficient by the directing force of group singing. Modern shops too have work which is highly repetitive, and it was for these factory workers that "music in industry" first became big business. For them music has a number of possible benefits. It may relieve fatigue and make for smoother motor performance.[36] It supplies food for the daydreams which may occupy much of the mental life of those engaged in this class of labor. Moreover, the fact that the worker is allowed to hear music while laboring may signify to him that the management has his interests at heart and is attempting to improve his working conditions. Thus there may be a considerable raising of morale. Yet the lifting of morale and the belief that one's work output is being enhanced by the hearing of music are not necessarily associated with increase in productivity or with improvement in work quality. This has been clearly demonstrated in a study[37] in which the amount and excellence of fairly routine work in a skateboard factory were unaffected by the playing of four types of music— dance, show, folk, and popular—even though the workers liked the music and believed they were doing more and better work in its presence.

Nonrepetitive Work. With nonrepetitive factory work requiring little intellectual effort the introduction of several periods of music each day may prove quite worthwhile. But where considerable intellectual effort is involved, music is less often beneficial and may even have a harmful effect on output. In those fewer instances, usually in offices, where music is found to be of benefit to the worker who uses his brain more than his hands, the type of music found to be appropriate resembles but little the kind used for workrooms where the labor is more manual. As might be guessed, office music is likely to be far softer, less regularly rhythmic, with fewer dynamic changes and without words.

Other Claims for Music. Proponents of industrial music have at one time or another maintained that, by the proper use of music, absenteeism and personnel turnover can be reduced; and physical health, punctuality, and plant safety can be improved. There are other students of plant music, however, who have not found these effects. So far these alleged benefits have not been reported consistently in the better controlled studies;[38] yet it is conceivable they could occur on occasion. A worker might be so filled with goodwill toward a company which brought music to its workers that he would become more punctual and less prone to "play" sick or to quit his job.

Formulae Followed. The authorities are by no means in complete agreement in their musical prescriptions. They do agree, however, that care should be taken lest music be conditioned to the beginning of recess periods. That is, if music were played each day a half-hour before time to stop work, its presentation would give the workers a "going home" cue which obviously would not lead to enthusiasm for work.

Some students of industrial music take great pains to give the workers exactly what they want to hear while others feel that the preference aspect has been much overemphasized. These latter assert that research attention should rather be focused on output changes. But where preference is emphasized, folk music and operas are often played to the foreign-born workers. Orchestral music is generally preferred to chamber music, presumably because the former is more "multicolored" and more familiar.[39] The female voice is broadcast much less often than the male, since its higher register is not so appreciated. The British as a matter of fact rule out all vocal music because they have noticed a tendency for the laborer to stop work and write down the lyrics he particularly enjoys. Sex differences for the sort of music most preferred seem few in number. Generation differences loom larger, with the older workers generally preferring quieter and more serious music.

In one extensive but older study of factory music, the optimum effect on output was found to occur when music was played 12 per cent of the time for the day shift and 50 per cent for the night crew.[40] The Muzak Corporation,[41] the leading firm devoted to supplying music to industry, pays particular attention to the midmorning and midafternoon "letdown" periods in morale and industrial output. The procedure of this company is to furnish rather unobtrusive music which rarely climbs above 25 phons in loudness[42] (as compared to long-playing records' typical 50 phons). They tend not to use vocal music, jazz, classics, instrumental solos, or minor music. They offer somewhat different programs for the office, the factory, and the public area.

Limitations of Conclusions. The more precise claims made for industrial music can be generalized only with some hazard. Perhaps the most promising area is that of worker morale, for with factory workers playing an ever growing role in plant management, worker morale is becoming of increasing importance to all concerned. But even here definitive experiments are difficult to make. With so many workers calling for music in their factories, it is probable that management will continue to provide for this desire, thus giving further opportunities for the gathering of sound data. Eventually then a more adequate assessment of industrial music may be forthcoming.

PRESENT STATUS OF MUSIC THERAPY

Since music can undeniably alter both the moods and some of the basic physiological processes of many persons, it could theoretically have potential for therapy.[43] It has long been used to treat the mentally and the physically ill in both preliterate[44] and literate cultures. Why then are its curative qualities not more easily demonstrated? A partial answer can be found in the way therapy is employed in mental hospitals. It is natural that the psychiatrists should want to improve mental health to the point where their patients can be safely and speedily returned to their homes. Many mental hospitals are dreadfully crowded, and quite often far more emotionally disturbed persons are waiting to enter than can be accepted.

With the energies of the hospital staff primarily focused on cure and not on the reasons for the cure, a research program on musical or any other kind of therapy can be only incidental at best. On the curative side, a "buckshot" policy must generally be followed. That is, a variety of therapies must be tried on each patient in the hope that some one of them or a combination of treatments will effect a cure. But this multiplicity of therapies makes it impossible to tell which one is mainly responsible when the patient improves, if he does improve. As a matter of fact it may sometimes be that no one therapy by itself contributes very much to the subsequent "cure." The active agent may be the friendly supportive attention the patient has been receiving, or there may perhaps be some dynamic personality change which would have occurred even though no therapy at all had been attempted. One psychiatrist, Colbert, suggests that music and perhaps other therapeutic agents often help simply by narrowing the patient's wandering attention. But he admits that little is known of the dynamics of this hypothesized mechanism.[45]

With the situation so beclouded, the one clear fact is that definitive statements about the therapeutic value of music must await the establishment of research-oriented hospitals where first one therapy and then another can be put through its paces. But this research heaven is still some years away. Until it comes there is little one can do but examine the anecdotes which abound, the commonsense beliefs the specialists accept, and the data of a few fairly crude experiments and from them try to winnow at least a few grains of fact.

Music in Physical Therapy. Boring indeed are the exercises that the muscle- and joint-injured, the brain-damaged, the palsied, and the victims of muscular distrophy, cleft palate and certain other troubles must practice day after day. But if set to music the exercises become, if not actually enjoyable, at least considerably more endurable. It is relatively easy to find music with tempos and rhythms to fit the needs of each patient.[46] For leg injuries dancing is often encouraged. Finger exercise needs may call for the playing of the piano. If facial and throat muscles need to be strengthened, the playing of brass or woodwind instruments may be appropriate. For the leg-injured patient who possesses no musical or dancing skill, the foot pumping of a small organ may be prescribed. Time seems to pass more quickly when music accompanies the therapeutic exercises, and patient morale tends to be better maintained. This type of musical therapy is usually administered in hospitals, but it will be reasonably beneficial in the home, although here the additional benefit derived from seeing others also exercising is missing.

Establishing Contact With Reality. When someone has withdrawn into a world of daydreams or apathy, an early step in therapy must be to reestablish his contact with the world of reality. Often the psychotic will not talk or take much interest in his surroundings. Yet the patient, particularly the inhibited,[47] who earlier had a deep love of music and no frustrations associated with it, will sometimes respond to melody and rhythm when he will not react favorably to verbal stimulation. In such cases Altshuler suggests the use of his "iso" principle.[48] After first playing strident music to attract attention, the next compositions are chosen so as to be isomoodic and isotempic, i.e. to match so far as possible the mood and "mental tempo" of the patient. Thus quiet unobtrusive music is selected for the withdrawn, lively music for the maniacal, "feminine" music for a man of feminine mentality, etc. Later, after the attention has been aroused and held, a gradual shift in type of music is engineered in the hope that the patient's mental and physiological state will also change. However, a study by Gillis *et al.*[49] on schizophrenics failed to demonstrate the worth of the iso principle. Rock 'n' roll and non-rhythmical "classical" music seemed to have about equal beneficial effects on such patients. Other researches also bring into question the validity of the iso technique.[50] According to Ruegnitz, music aids the return to reality by dispelling delusions and hallucinations.[51] Romantic music, say Mitchell and Zanker,[52] favors a release of emotion, while modern impressionistic affords an escape into fantasy. And at least in the case of college students, the hearing of music appears to decrease the tendency to condone, i.e., to behave in what some therapists term an impunitive fashion, thus facilitating the appearance of more realistic responses.[53]

Pleasantness and the Feeling of Being Rested. Many of us feel more alert and rested after listening to our favorite compositions. A somewhat similar situation exists among those in mental hospitals. Among the hospitalized, listening to music has the additional advantage of helping to pass the time which can drag frightfully. Research has shown that a fairly strong relationship exists between the feeling of restfulness and the pleasantness of music (or between tiredness and unpleasantness).[54] During the course of life pleasantness and rest become associated. We should keep the fact of this association in mind and not listen to strange (and so potentially unpleasant) music at a time when we feel mentally fatigued. Striving to understand the unfamiliar is not a restful undertaking.

Music as a Resocializing Agent.[55] The psychotic can be regarded as a person who is particularly poor in his interpersonal adjustments. He badly needs music or some other resocializing agent. To supply such a need, unison group singing and dancing are encouraged in the more therapeutically oriented of our mental hospitals. These activities take a minimum of alertness. Yet they bring about vitally needed interpersonal contacts, they break the monotony of institutional life, and for a short time at least they may dissipate the personal worries which have beset the patient. While engaged in dancing or group singing the patient is once again a member of a functioning group.

While Bonny et al.[56] have demonstrated that in a group situation "normal" persons who are hearing a succession of "stimulative" and "sedative" pieces talk neither more nor less than they do in the absence of such music, Heckel et al.[57] found that when psychiatric patients hear music of fast tempo they talk significantly more to their fellow patients. This latter finding also appeared in a study by Shatin and Zimet,[58] who add that "quieting" music tends to decrease verbal participation in a group therapy situation and to adversely affect its quality.

Sense of Achievement and Prestige. Music lessons are often given in mental hospitals so the patient can feel that he is achieving a real skill, one that he can continue to enjoy after he leaves the institution. With skill in playing a musical instrument comes the opportunity to perform in the hospital's orchestra or band, or with vocal skill a place in the chorus. Such ensemble work brings a sense of achievement and what the psychoanalysts speak of as "increase in ego strength,"[59] bestows prestige on the performers, and aids in the process of socialization. Even where the patient is too regressed to take pride in a newly achieved skill, he may while supervised derive considerable benefit from making rhythmical movements to the accompaniment of music. One procedure for doing this, termed body-ego technique or BET,[60] appears to do far more for the patient than does passive listening to music.

Other Attempts To Use Music. With so many psychiatrists and musicians convinced of the existence of large physiological and psychological effects from music, it was inevitable that music should have been used in hospitals and clinics to quiet the apprehensive, to calm the hyperactive[61] (and so to reduce hospital noise), to stimulate the depressed, to reduce accidents[62] and incontinence, to help aphasics to recover,[63] and to distract those about to undergo dental work or surgery.[64] The reported successes of such uses of music vary with the enthusiasms of the therapists. Sad to relate, therapy data are rarely recorded in terms which mean much to the scientist. To what extent the perceived benefit is more properly attributable to the attention the patient gets than to the music cannot at present be estimated. The fact still remains, however, that there are patients who are visibly less apprehensive, less maniacal, less difficult to handle, or less depressed after sessions with musical therapy.

The "Musicopoeia." Although normal persons and psychotics[65] of like subculture react in a somewhat similar fashion to music, there seems to be enough dissimilarity to justify the rule that all music to be employed with psychotics should be pretested on psychotics.[66] It would seem reasonable to suppose, as do Zanker and Glatt,[67] that the music to be employed in therapy should be chosen on the basis of common musical interest rather than a common psychiatric diagnosis. These rules appear to be followed rather religiously in some quarters while in others the therapist's own feelings or those of his friends and colleagues furnish the guide for his selection of the compositions he will use. If he is psychoanalytically oriented he may start his convalescing patients on simple folk tunes, following the theory that these "seem to resupply or reactivate the mother-child complex."[68]

Each musical therapist seems to have his favored list of musical compositions. For relieving serious headaches Brown offers some 40 pieces including such old favorites as Liszt's *Hungarian Rhapsody No. 1,* Mendelssohn's *Elijah,* Mozart's *Don Giovanni,* Offenbach's *Tales of Hoffmann,* Beethoven's *Fidelio,* and Borodin's *Prince Igor;* "popular" ones like Grofé's *Mississippi Suite* and Gershwin's *American in Paris;* and more serious moderns like Khachaturian's *Masquerade Suite* and Copland's *Lincoln Portrait.*[69]

Arrington suggests the following "reassuring" compositions for use just before electroshock treatment: Largo from Bach's *Concerto in A,* Beethoven's *Moonlight Sonata,* Brahms's *Intermezzo in E Flat,* Chopin's *First Piano Concerto* (Second Movement), Mendelssohn's *Italian Symphony* (Second Movement), and Rachmaninov's *Second Concerto* (Second Movement). During the awakening period Arrington considers these as appropriate: Kern's show tunes, Fields's *The Way You Look Tonight,* Chopin's *Waltzes in A and C,* Berlin's *Eddie Duchin Album,* and Adamson's *Time on My Hands.* To Arrington these eight are musical tonics: Tchaikovsky's *Sixth Symphony* (Third Movement), Beethoven's *Egmont Overture,* Chopin's *Prelude, Opus 28 No. 1,* Liszt's *Hungarian Rhapsody No. 2,* Bizet's *Toreador's Song,* Sousa's military marches, Offenbach's *Gaieté Parisienne,* and Bach's *Prelude and Fugue in E Minor;* and these nine are musical sedatives: Mascagni's *Cavalleria Rusticana* (Intermezzo),

Schubert's *Ave Maria*, Saint-Saëns's *The Swan*, Brahms's *Lullaby*, Beethoven's *Sixth Symphony* (Second Movement) Chopin's *Nocturne in G Minor*, Debussy's *Clair de Lune*, Schubert's *Quartet in B Flat Minor* (Andante), and Beethoven's *Moonlight Sonata*.[70]

Sugarman attempts to lower "emotional high blood pressure" through renditions of a variety of compositions which include: Bach's *Concerto in D Minor for Violin*, Bartók's *Sonata for Piano*, Bruckner's *Mass in E Minor*, Ives's *Symphony No. 3*, Rachmaninov's *Isle of the Dead*, and Tchaikovsky's *Swan Lake Ballet Suite*. To accompany eating he suggests 20 pieces, among which are Bartók's *Sonata for Violin*, Ravel's *La Valse*, Debussy's *Children's Corner Suite*, Liszt's *Concerto No. 2 in A*, and Ives's *Sonata No. 2 for Violin and Piano*.[71]

To replace jealousy and suspicion with contentment, Hillard offers Anthiel's *Piano Sonata No. 4*, Bach's *Cantata No. 21*, Bartók's *Quartet No. 5*, Chopin's *Nocturne in D Flat*, Milhaud's *Suite Française*, and Ravel's *Quartet in F*. To relieve chronic hatred this same author mentions Bach's *Italian Concerto*, Haydn's *Clock Symphony*, and Sibelius' *Finlandia*.[72]

Girard claims to reduce anger with Bach's *Cantata No. 2*, Beethoven's *Moonlight Sonata*, Grofé's *Aviation Suite*, Prokofiev's *Sonata in D*, and Franck's *Symphony in D Minor*. To overcome anxiety Girard would play Chopin's mazurkas and preludes, the Strauss waltzes, Nevin's *Narcissus*, and Rubinstein's *Melody in F*.[73]

The lists above are typical of what one finds in the current literature.[74] Quite clearly they are the resultants of "rule of thumb" rather than scientific procedures. It is very probable of course that changes both in mood and in overt activity have sometimes occurred following the playing of these and other musical compositions, but the causal connections between the music and the behavioral changes are obscure. Moreover, at this stage in the history of the institutional use of music, little or no generalization from one therapeutic venture to another is warranted. The reader should not conclude, however, that music has no future in therapy or necessarily accept the extremely pessimistic conclusion of Blair and Brooking who state that "no scientific statistics are ever likely to be produced for music therapy."[75] Indeed, later research may demonstrate large benefits attributable to the music alone.[76] At the very least, it would seem that the reality training, the resocialization, and the morale lift many patients receive from this kind of treatment amply justify the effort and money involved.[77]

EPILOGUE

Music has been variously called the most mathematical of the arts, the purest, and the least universal. That it is highly mathematical we have already seen, particularly in the data of Chapter 2. In no place in the book, however, has there been the suggestion that a satisfactory mathematical formula for forecasting musical taste or beauty has been or is likely to be discovered. Since there is no invariant relationship between musical stimuli and human responses, since attitudes toward the same stimuli often change with the years, such a formula would be unthinkable. The mathematics of the Lydian mode has not been altered over the years since Plato banned this arrangement of tones as harmful to man's character. But to many people of the contemporary Western world this sequence has become the only "proper" scale.

Music is pure in the sense that it only rarely copies the sounds of nature. Music tells no clear-cut story with universal meaning; yet each listener is trained to read local meanings into what he hears. He may recognize a Wagnerian motive, a needed resolution, or a church hymn and thus share in the enjoyment of his similarly trained associates. It is, however, the very paucity of these local meanings which gives him the opportunity to implant in the music his own personal images and associations. Thus this art medium serves as an important aid to his fantasy life.

The acceptability of any musical form may grow and later diminish, but listener satiations typically build up and eventually lead to change. Sometimes the changes are in the direction of innovations, while at other times they may in part point back toward what was acceptable at an earlier time. If the new forms differ too markedly from the old they do not achieve general acceptance. But every change is a violation of some rule and is apt at first to seem undesirable to the conservative and the close-minded.

A major thesis developed in this book is the notion that music must look for its explanations far more often to social science than to physical science. It is granted that the very beginnings of music are tied to man's physical surroundings, to the presence of instrument-building materials, and to the physics of the simplest ratios. Man's psychophysiological potentialities also affect music's development. But the fact that the music of one culture has gone through certain phases that are not duplicated in another culture must be explained largely on the basis of sociopsychological and historical factors, not physical or physiological factors. Music's changes, like style changes generally, are lawful, not in an absolutistic or metaphysical sense but in the way that other social phenomena are lawful.

This book has attempted to uncover a number of the sociopsychological variables behind music change. No doubt in the years to come many other factors will be isolated. Research of the sort described here should lead to greater, not less, musical enjoyment; for it seems to be a fairly general principle that the more man understands the complexities of a pleasing phenomenon, the more delight he takes in it.

APPENDIX A ⚓ *The Musical Taste of an American Elite*

IN CHAPTER 6 it was noted that in 1938 the members of the American Musicological Society had been sent questionnaires through which it was hoped a crude measure of their musical taste might be obtained. Again in 1944, still later in 1951, and most recently in 1964 the members of this elite organization were interrogated. At the time of the last data-gathering, the 853 who cooperated were given a long list of composers born before 1870 and were asked to place x marks to the left of the 25 composers felt to have composed music most worthy to be called to the attention of children and lay contemporaries, i.e. to be preserved as a part of the musical heritage. If any musicologist believed that the 25 should include names of composers born since 1870, their names could be added. Each respondent was also asked to write on the back of his questionnaire the ten composers born since 1870 who he felt had the best chance of achieving sufficient eminence to be worthy of a future list of 25 like the one he had just checked.

After the votes were counted, the rank orders were figured and are given in the two tables below. Note that the names of only five of the post-1870 composers appear also in the all-time eminence list. It is unfortunately true that the single-list questionnaire employed in this most recent survey worked against the more contemporary composers, for the reason that respondents tend to vote more often for names they see before them than for names they must themselves recall. In the 1951 survey a long post-1870 list of composer names had indeed been sent out, but it elicited a storm of protest from the many respondents who noticed the omission of one or more of their favorites. To calm these musicologists a list of astronomical length would have been necessary. No similar protest was made over the pre-1870 list, for its names have to a great extent weathered the test of time. It seems reasonable to conclude, therefore, that, had a list of "born since 1870" composers also been mailed to the musicologists in 1964, far fewer respondents would have cooperated with the author and those who did return completed forms would have made greater use of the more recent composers in making up their lists of the most eminent 25.

BORN SINCE 1870*

1. Stravinsky	11. Vaughan Williams	21. Boulez	31. Rachmaninoff	41.5 Cage
2. Bartók	12. Ives	22. Villa-Lobos	32.5 Orff	41.5 Cowell
3. Hindemith	13. Shostakovich	23. Menotti	32.5 Harris	43. Reger
4. Schoenberg	14. Milhaud	24. Piston	34.5 Walton	45. Foss
5. Berg	15. Barber	25. Sessions	34.5 Hanson	45. Martinu
6. Prokofiev	16. Poulenc	26. Stockhausen	36. Kodaly	45. Thompson, R.
7. Ravel	17. Honegger	27. Bloch	37. Schuman	47. Krenek
8. Webern	18. Dallapiccola	28. Varese	38. Scriabin	48. Berio
9. Copland	19. Gershwin	29. Falla	39. Chavez	49. Holst
10. Britten	20. Carter	30. Messiaen	40. Respighi	50. Kirchner

ALL-TIME EMINENCE**

1. Bach, J. S.	26. Machaut	50.5 Fauré	77. Prätorius
2. Beethoven	27. Schütz	52. Dowland	77. Borodin
3. Mozart	28. Liszt	53. Bach, K. P. E.	77. Gounod
4. Haydn (F.) J.	29. Mussorgsky	54. Rimsky-Korsakov	79. Haydn, (J.) M.
5. Brahms	30. Corelli	55. Perotinus	80.5 Sousa
6. Handel	31. Scarlatti, (G.) D.	56. Wolf	80.5 Sullivan
7. Debussy	32. Gabrieli, G.	57. Bartók	82.5 Bellini
8. Schubert	33. Couperin	58. Grieg	82.5 Janácek
9. Wagner	34. Gluck	59. von Weber	85. Donizetti
10. Chopin	35. Puccini	60. Gibbons	85. Webern
11. Monteverdi	36. Franck	61. Sweelinck	85. Willaert
12. Palestrina	37. Dvořák	62. Schoenberg	87. Offenbach
13. Verdi	38. Buxtehude	63. Strauss, J., Jr.	88.5 Ravel
14. Schumann	39. Bruckner	64. Saint-Saëns	88.5 Delius
15. Des Pres	40. Sibelius	65.5 Telemann	91. Elgar
16. di Lasso	41. Rameau	65.5 Lulli	91. Hindemith
17.5 Purcell	42. Frescobaldi	67. Landino	91. Satie
17.5 Berlioz	43. Okeghem	68. MacDowell	93.5 Cherubini
19. Strauss, R.	44. Stravinsky	69. Bach, J. C.	93.5 Foster
20. Mendelssohn	45. Scarlatti, A.	70. Leoninus	95. de Rore
21. Tchaikovsky	46. Dunstable	71. Gabrieli, A.	96.5 Boccherini
22. Vivaldi	47. Bizet	72.5 Carissimi	96.5 Franco of Cologne
23. Mahler	48. Gesualdo	72.5 Pergolesi	98.5 Clementi
24. Byrd	49. Rossini	74. Marenzio	98.5 Tartini
25. Dufay	50.5 da Vittoria	75. Smetana	(The next 4 are tied)

* See "Musicologists Look to the Future," *Music J.*, 1965, *23*(7), 44, 46.
** See "Musicological Attitudes on Eminence," *J. Res. Music Educ.*, 1966, *14*(1), 41–44.

ability. Skill of any sort; relative importance of inheritance and environment not considered. Cf. *capacity, talent.*

absolute or positive pitch. Ability to locate a pitch without the need of a reference tone; the allowable error is very slight, perhaps less than 10 cents.

accidental signs. Signs indicating sharps, flats, double sharps, double flats, naturals.

arpeggio. Tones of a chord played in rapid succession.

atonality. Absence of key in music.

beats. Throbbing effect elicited when two tones very close together in pitch are simultaneously sounded.

beta learning. Negative practice; that is, the errors are deliberately practiced.

cadence. Melodic or harmonic figure which has come to have an association with the ending of a phrase, a section, or composition.

capacity. Basic potentiality; importance of heredity is stressed.

cent. Tonal span of 1/1200 of an octave.

chromesthesia. Color image of hallucinatory intensity aroused by some auditory stimulus. Cf. *synesthesia.*

coefficient of correlation. Measure of correspondence between two sets of measurements; values vary from 1.00 (perfect correspondence) through zero to −1.00 (completely inverse relationship). Cf. *rho.*

decibel. Logarithmic unit of intensity so chosen as to be equal, under certain conditions, to one just-noticeable difference in loudness. The decibel is sometimes used as a unit of loudness.

designative meaning. The story the music allegedly tells and the moods it elicits. Cf. *embodied meaning.*

This glossary attempts to define certain psychological terms for the musician and musical terms for the psychologist. It is to be expected that the psychologist will prefer to see the terms of his craft described in more exact language, as will the musician his.

difference tone. Tone sometimes elicited when two tones separated in pitch are simultaneously sounded; its frequency is the difference of the frequencies of the other two.

double stopping. Fingering two strings of a bowed instrument at once.

drone. A tone held for the duration of a melody or at least for a considerable period of time.

eidetic imagery. Imagery so intense that the person behaves as though he were directly perceiving the imagined musical stimuli.

embodied meaning. The grammar or syntax of the music. Cf. *designative meaning.*

extravert. A person who attends more to external events and objects than to his own attitudes and mental processes. Cf. *introvert.*

factor analysis. Method of resolving a set of interrelated variables or tests into a few "factors" which are regarded as being the fundamental variables underlying the original complex of variables.

fifth. Span of 7 semitones.

fourth. Span of 5 semitones.

fugal form. A round; each new voice chases the preceding one.

galvanic skin response. Change in the electrical resistance of the skin whenever, during emotional states, perspiration is produced on the skin surfaces.

goal gradient. Change in degree of motivation with distance to a goal.

harmonics. Cf. *overtones.*

homophony. Music in which the voices move in step, e.g. hymn.

idiot savant. Person of very low IQ who has above average achievement in some specialized area.

interval. Pitch span between two notes played simultaneously or successively.

    augmented. Perfect or major increased by a semitone.

    diminished. Perfect or minor decreased by a semitone.

    major. Spans of 2, 4, 9, or 11 semitones (second, third, sixth, or seventh).

    minor. Spans of 1, 3, 8, or 10 semitones (second, third, sixth, or seventh).

    parallel. Span separating two melodies which are identical but in different registers.

    perfect. Spans of 5, 7, or 12 semitones (fourth, fifth, or octave).

introvert. Person preoccupied with his own attitudes and mental processes. Cf. *extravert.*

iso principle. Notion that a patient's mood and "mental tempo" should match the mood and tempo of the music.

key. Family of tones held together by their relation to a tonic from which the key is named.

key-note. Lowest and principal note of a scale; the tonic.

leading tone. Major seventh or subtonic, so-called because it leads up to the tonic.

leger lines. Additional short lines added above or below the staff for notes that cannot be accommodated on the staff.

major

    chord. Three simultaneously or successively played notes comprising intervals of a major third plus a minor third. Cf. *minor chord.*

    interval. Cf. *interval.*

    mode. Cf. *mode.*

    second. Span of 2 semitones.

    seventh. Span of 11 semitones.

    sixth. Span of 9 semitones.

    third. Span of 4 semitones.

massed practice. Concentration of time devoted to learning with little interval between successive practice sessions.

melody. Series of successively sounded tones felt to possess internal organization.

microtone. Scale step smaller than a semitone.

minor

    chord. Three simultaneously or successively played notes comprising intervals of a minor third plus a major third. Cf. *major chord.*

    interval. Cf. *interval.*

    mode. Cf. *mode.*

    second. Span of 1 semitone.

    seventh. Span of 10 semitones.

    sixth. Span of 8 semitones.

    third. Span of 3 semitones.

mode. Forerunner of the key; differs in that the mode has several possible arrangements of scale steps, e.g. 2,2,1,2,2,2,1 semitone steps, or 2,1,2,2,2,1,2 steps, etc.; now only two: major and minor.

modulation. Transition of a melody from one key up or down to another key.

monotone. Person so weak in pitch sensitivity that he cannot recognize or carry a tune.

noise. Complex of sounds in which no definite pitch can be detected.

octave. Span of 12 semitones.

organum. Theme with other voices a fourth below or a fifth above moving parallel to it.

overlearning. Continuing practice beyond the trial where the material can for the first time be reproduced correctly.

overtone. Tone elicited by the vibration of some fraction of the major vibrating body, e.g. $\frac{1}{2}$, $\frac{1}{3}$, $\frac{1}{4}$, etc.

partial. Cf. *overtone.*

phon. Unit of loudness in which the value is equal to the number of decibels a tone of 1,000 d.v. is above the reference intensity when judged equal in loudness to the tone in question. Cf. *decibel.*

polyphony. Applied to music in which several melodies are played simultaneously.

polytonality. Presence of several simultaneous keys in a musical composition.

portamento. The carrying on of the tone from note to note without gaps (voice and bowed instruments); half-staccato (piano).

Prägnanz, law of. Persons tend to perceive objects in the simplest arrangement possible.

register. Pitch level.

reliability. Degree of self-consistency; extent to which the measure is uninfluenced by factors intrinsic to or associated with it.

retroactive inhibition. Impairment of learning by the later learning of something very similar.

rho. Type of correlation coefficient obtained through the handling of rank differences.

rhythm

  objective. Periodicity with one element regularly emphasized.

  polyrhythm. Complex of several simultaneously played rhythms; also called crossrhythm.

  subjective. Rhythm read into sheer periodicity or into weak objective rhythm.

scale. Series of tones arranged in order of pitch and employed as the accepted notes of some system.

  chromatic. The twelve-semitone scale of white and black notes.

  diatonic. Seven-note scale in the major or minor mode.

  equally tempered. Where half steps are all equal in ratio and are exactly half of whole steps.

  just-intoned. Where the ratios use only the primes 1, 3, and 5.

  mean-tone. Compromise scale with some tempering which allows for a degree of modulation.

  Pythagorean. Where the ratios use only the primes 1 and 3.

  whole-tone. Where each step is a whole tone from its nearest neighbor.

score

  mean. Sum of all the scores divided by the number of cases.

  median. Middle score.

  modal. Most frequently occurring score.

sensations

  kinesthetic. Those arising from the stimulation of receptors in muscles, tendons, and joints.

  organic. Those arising from the stimulation of receptors in the internal organs.

sensitivity. Degree to which one can distinguish stimuli which differ very slightly.

sonance. Qualitative effects due to progressive ("horizontal") changes and fusions, e.g. vibrato.

sostenuto pedal. Pedal found mainly on American and Canadian pianos which maintains raised dampers.

stroboscope. Instrument for observing the successive phases of a periodic motion by means of a light periodically interrupted. Cf. *tonoscope.*

syncopation. Placing an accent where there would normally be no accent.

synesthesia. Image of hallucinatory intensity in one sensory area aroused by a stimulus from some other sense modality. Cf. *chromesthesia.*

takt. Cf. *true beat.*

talent. Usually taken to mean high capability; heredity is emphasized.

tempo. Rate of speed at which a musical passage moves.

allegro. Lively tempo.

andante. Slow tempo.

presto. Quick tempo.

tests

achievement. Tests taken to measure what has been learned.

aptitude. Tests used to forecast whether or not training in a particular area will be profitable.

threshold. Inverse of sensitivity (as used in this book).

timbre. Effect due to the constellation of partial tones present; "vertical" quality.

tone clusters. Tones elicited by depressing the piano keys with the fist, flat of the hand, or forearm.

tone symbol. Tonal ratio with powers of 2 extracted.

tonic. Cf. *key-note.*

tonoscope. Stroboscope which gives a visual picture of a vocal or instrumental tone.

tremolo. Vibrato with abnormally wide pitch span; also used to describe a rhythmic unit with three unaccented elements.

trill. Rapid oscillation of two tones which are perceived as two tones.

tritone. Span of six semitones.

true beat. Pulsations which underlie phrase rhythms irrespective of time signatures or number of notes in the phrase.

validity. Extent to which a test is measuring what it claims to be measuring.

vibrato. Periodic oscillations of the vocal or instrumental tone in pitch, intensity, and sometimes in quality; rate is approximately 6.5 per second.

whole learning. Material to be learned is gone through from beginning to end, i.e. is not broken down into parts which are to be learned separately.

NOTES AND REFERENCES ✕

CHAPTER ONE

1. C. K. Aldrich, "The Effect of a Synthetic Marihuana-like Compound on Musical Talent as Measured by the Seashore Test," *Publ. Hlth. Rep.*, Washington, 1944, *59*, 431–33; M. Mezzrow and B. Wolfe, *Really the Blues*, New York, Random House, 1946.
2. One of the most extensive of the studies which compared blacks and whites was that by G. B. Johnson reported in "Musical Talent of the Negro," *Music Superv. J.*, 1928, *15*, 81, 83, 96. After testing 3,350 blacks of fifth grade, eighth grade, and college level on the Seashore Measures of Musical Talent, he states: "It becomes evident that the only fair conclusion to be drawn from the data is that there are no significant differences between whites and Negroes on those basic musical sensibilities measured by the Seashore tests."
3. K. M. Ramm, "Personality Maladjustment Among Monotones," *Smith Coll. Stud. Soc. Wk.*, 1947, *17*, 264–84. That the incidence of monotones in the first six grades has remained for 25 years unchanged at 18 per cent is shown in a study by W. B. Romaine, "Developing Singers From Nonsingers," Ed.D. thesis, Teachers Coll., Columbia U., 1961.
4. M. F. Meyer, *The Psychology of the Other-one*, Columbia, Mo., Missouri Book, 1922.
5. W. T. Bartholomew, "Baton Movements," *Peabody Bull.*, 1933, *29*(2), 37–39. Using a similar technique, F. Giese found that when 35 persons were asked to conduct the same composition there were huge individual differences in the style of conducting. Giese's data show some similarity in the pattern of conducting (a) the different works of the same conductor and (b) compositions of the same musical school ("Individuum und Epoch in Taktierbewegungen bei verschiedenen Komponisten," *Arch. Ges. Psychol.*, 1934, *90*, 380–426).
6. By true beat or takt is meant the pulsations which underlie phrase rhythms irrespective of time signatures or number of notes in the phrase.
7. M. W. Lund, "An Analysis of the 'True-beat' in Music," Doctoral thesis, Stanford U., 1939. In a somewhat similar analysis of the true beat of phonograph recordings, Hodgson found that slightly less than half of the measures fell between 60 and 70 per minute. Although he had undertaken his researches in the belief that true beat may be causally related to heartbeat, Hodgson now admits the impossibility of proving a causal relationship (Walter Hodgson, "Absolute Tempo," *Music Teach. Nat. Assoc. Proc. 1949*, 1951, 43 Ser., 158–69).

8. P. R. Farnsworth, "Aesthetic Behavior and Astrology," *Charact. & Pers.*, 1938, *6*, 335–40. For a report which favors astrology see P. Field, *50 Thousand Birthdays*, La Selva Beach, Calif., Saratoga Publ. Co., 1962. This "research" furnishes a fine example of what the scientist does *not* do. Field sees composition similarities whenever and wherever his theory needs them and where a musicologist would find only differences.

9. The most extensive of the earlier works on the vibrato was done at the Seashore laboratories of the University of Iowa. See the *U. of Iowa Stud. Psychol. Music*, 1932, *1*, which contains articles by E. Easeley, M. Hattwick, M. T. Hollinshead, F. E. Linder, J. Tiffin, M. Metfessel, R. S. Miller, S. N. Reger, D. A. Rothschild, H. G. Seashore, and A. H. Wagner. An earlier research from this same laboratory was that of M. Schoen, "An Experimental Study of the Pitch Factor in Artistic Singing," *Psychol. Monog.*, 1922, *31*, 230–59. Excellent work has also been done by L. Cheslock, "Introductory Study on Violin Vibrato," *Peabody Cons. Music Res. Stud.*, 1931, (1). See also W. E. Kock, "On the Principle of Uncertainty in Sound," *J. Acoust. Soc. Amer.*, 1935, *7*, 56–58; "Certain Subjective Phenomena Accompanying a Frequency Vibrato," *J. Acoust. Soc. Amer.*, 1936, *8*, 23–25; A. M. Small, "An Objective Analysis of Artistic Violin Performance," *U. of Iowa Stud. Psychol. Music*, 1936, *4*, 172–231; J. R. Tolmie, "An Analysis of the Vibrato From the Viewpoint of Frequency and Amplitude Modulation," *J. Acoust. Soc. Amer.*, 1935, *7*, 29–36; L. Sjöström, "Experimentellphonetische Untersuchungen des Vibratophänomens der Singstimme," *Acta Oto-Laryngol.* (Stockholm), Suppl., 1948, *47*, 123–30; H. Fletcher and L. C. Sanders, "Quality of Violin Vibrato Tones," *J. Acoust. Soc. Amer.*, 1967, *41*(6), 1534–44; A. Doschek, "Some Physical Aspects of the Vibrato," *Amer. String Teach.*, 1968, *18*(3), 19–20.

10. J. F. Corso and D. Lewis, "Preferred Rate and Extent of Frequency Vibrato," *J. Appl. Psychol.*, 1950, *34*, 206–12. For proof that vibrato pitch is perceived to be at the midpoint of the vibrato's pitch range, see C. Shackford, "Pitch Range and the Actual Pitch of Vibrato Tones," *Amer. String Teach.*, 1960, *10*(2), 25, 28.

11. A. Bjørklund, "Analyses of Soprano Voices," *J. Acoust. Soc. Amer.*, 1961, *33*(5), 575–82.

12. J. A. Deutsch and J. K. Clarkson, "Nature of the Vibrato and the Control Loop in Singing," *Nature*, 1959, *183*, 167–68.

13. "Explanation" as used in this book is in a sense merely an extension of the concept "description." A phenomenon to be explained is described in the context of the other variables to which it is related. Where these latter are antecedent in time they are popularly referred to as its "causes."

14. J. P. Foley, Jr., "The Occupational Conditioning of Preferential Auditory Tempo," *J. Soc. Psychol.*, 1940, *12*, 121–29.

15. F. A. Saunders, "Violins Old and New—An Experimental Study," *Sound*, 1962, *1*(4), 7–15; "The Mechanical Action of Violins," *J. Acoust. Soc. Amer.*, 1937, *9*, 81–98. A. Small has shown that the timbre of the "better" stringed instruments differs from that of the "poorer" largely in an emphasis on frequency bands below 2,500 cycles ("The Tone-color [Timbre] of Stringed Instruments," *Music Teach. Nat. Assoc. Proc. 1940*, 1941, 354–60). See also E. G. Richardson, "Orchestral Acoustics," *Sci. Monthly*, 1955, *80*, 211–24; C. M. Hutchins, "The Physics of Violins," *Sci. Amer.*, 1962, *207*(5), 78–93.

16. Even the "lost art" of making old Italian violin varnish is lost no longer. See J. Michelman, "Lost Art of Strad Varnish," *Sci. Monthly*, 1955, *81*, 221–23.

17. P. A. Scholes, Ed., *The Oxford Companion to Music*, London, Oxford U. Press, 1943, p. 988.

18. M. G. Rigg, "Favorable Versus Unfavorable Propaganda in the Enjoyment of Music," *J. Exp. Psychol.*, 1948, *38*, 78–81.

19. During the Hitler period in Germany, Wagner's name became associated with the

Nazi movement. As a result, interest in Wagnerian music fell precipitously among some Americans.

20. T. Geiger, "A Radio Test of Musical Taste," *Publ. Opin. Quart.*, 1950, *14*, 453–60.

21. The organist-composer Buxtehude, although largely unknown to the present-day lay public, was well known in the late seventeenth and early eighteenth centuries. Now it is the name of J. S. Bach that is familiar to all Occidental laymen who have had any appreciable degree of formal music education.

22. H. M. Stanton, "Measurement of Musical Talent," *U. of Iowa Stud. Psychol. Music.*, 1935, *2*, 1–140.

23. Even in the short period that scientists have been observing musical behavior, a number of changes in basic activity have been noted. Thus the manner of breath control of the great Schumann-Heink was quite acceptable in her day but causes much distress or even amusement to those of us who listen on recordings to what appear to be her periodic gasps.

24. J. Tiffin, "The Role of Pitch and Intensity in the Vocal Vibrato of Students and Artists," *U. of Iowa Stud. Psychol. Music,* 1932, *1,* 134–65.

25. In a series of books with such eye-catching titles as *Precious Rubbish, Critical Quackery, War on Critics,* and *Hypocrisy About Art* (Stuart Publications, Boston), T. L. Shaws wages war against critics and others who "know" what is absolutely good in the arts.

26. P. E. Vernon, "Method in Musical Psychology," *Amer. J. Psychol.,* 1930, *42*, 127–34.

CHAPTER TWO

1. M. A. Wallach, "Art, Science, and Representation: Toward an Experimental Psychology of Aesthetics," *J. Aesth.*, 1959, *18*, 159–73. For an interesting discussion of some of the difficulties one meets in attempting to define music, see Van Meter Ames, "What Is Music?" *J. Aesth.*, 1967, *26*(2), 241–47.

2. A closely allied aesthetic experience, also sometimes termed "musical," exists in the totally deaf who often enjoy placing their hands on the piano to receive the kinesthetic stimulation the piano performance yields.

3. For an authoritative consideration of tonal characteristics see R. S. Woodworth and H. Schlosberg, *Experimental Psychology,* Rev. Ed., New York, Holt, Rinehart & Winston, 1965.

4. The expression 435 cycles indicates that some sound-giving object—tuning fork, string, air column in a horn or tube, etc.—is vibrating back and forth 435 times a second.

5. C. Stumpf, a psychologist who was a pioneer in the area of musical aesthetics, was perhaps the first to show that naive subjects confuse the two tones of an octave more than any other two tones. When the octave's two tones are simultaneously struck, the musically ignorant tend to think they are hearing but a single tone (*Tonpsychologie,* Leipzig, Hirzel, 1883, 1890).

6. For the sake of convenience, the names given the scale intervals of Western music will be employed here even though the terms may mislead the careless reader. The octave, so called because it makes use of eight successive white notes on the piano, is better described as a span of 12 semitones; the fifth, which involves five successive white notes, as a span of seven semitones; the fourth, named for the four successive white notes used, as five semitones; etc.

7. The notes of the seven-tone diatonic scale of Western music, irrespective of their major key or the pitch placement they are given, are commonly designated as *do, re, mi, fa, sol, la, ti, do.*

8. Although tradition would have the Pythagoreans deriving the diatonic scale by a

succession of musical fifths, some contemporary theorists are more inclined to view the Pythagorean scale as developed by projecting the tone (8:9) inside the musical fourth. For our purposes this controversy is not important, the essential point being that only the prime numbers 1 and 3 were used in this scale. See R. L. Crocker, "Pythagorean Mathematics and Music," *J. Aesth.*, 1963, *22*, 189–98.

9. In "Pythagoras and Aristoxenos Reconciled" N. Cazden (*J. Amer. Musicol. Soc.*, 1958, *11*, 97–105) states: "Thus we may say that the Pythagorean norms for intonation describe correctly objective standards for the measurement and psychoacoustic identification of the terms of musical relations, in precisely the same way as they define tuning standards, whereas the Aristoxenian principle correctly describes the treatment or transformation of these elementary natural materials for the purposes of art, operating on the much higher level of organized musical systems."

10. A scale developed by H. W. Poole, an American organ builder, made use of the prime number 7. See M. F. Meyer, *The Musician's Arithmetic*, Boston, Ditson, 1929 (Long out of print but now available as a paperback).

11. That the listener will adjust to mistunings can be demonstrated. Several travelers have reported that their pitch discrimination is temporarily impaired after repeated contact with uncertain tuning, and one such claim has been verified. It has also been noted that samples of Asiatics from the Chinese hinterland made poorer scores on pitch discrimination tests than did other samples of coastal and American-born Chinese. Coming from similar stock the two samples must have had similar inherent capacities. Hence the poorer scores of the inland Chinese must reflect an adjustment to uncertain intonation. Living largely in villages with meager intercommunication, they were slow to develop pitch standards and so became essentially inattentive to pitch exactitudes. See P. R. Farnsworth, "An Historical, Critical, and Experimental Study of the Seashore-Kwalwasser Test Battery," *Genet. Psychol. Monog.*, 1931, *9*, 291–393.

12. H. H. Dräger, "Zur mitteltönigen und gleichschwebenden Temperatur," *Bericht über die Wissenschaftliche Bachtagung der Gesellschaft für Musikforschung*, Leipzig, 23. bis 26, July 1950, 389–404.

13. O. I. Jacobsen, in "Harmonic Blending in the Natural Versus the Tempered Scale," *J. Musicol.*, 1941, *2*, 126–32, has defended the idea that the tempered and the "natural" scale each has its place for contemporary performance. See also D. W. Martin, "Musical Scales Since Pythagoras," *Sound*, 1962, *1*(3), 22–24; J. W. Link, Jr., "Understanding the Two Great Temperaments: Equal and Meantone," *J. Res. Music Educ.*, 1965, *13*(3), 136–46.

14. J. Yasser, *A Theory of Evolving Tonality*, New York, American Library of Musicology, 1932.

15. Another unit of ratio measurement which has enjoyed some use is the *savart* with a span of approximately four cents. Units like the cent or the savart should not be confused with the mel which is used in scaling pitch. A 1,000-cycle tone is arbitrarily set at 1,000 mels. Mel steps are measured by fractionation, and the number of mels to a given musical interval increases as the pitch increases. See A. G. Pikler, "Mels and Musical Intervals," *J. Music Theory*, 1966, *10*(2), 288–99.

16. C. C. Pratt, "Quarter-Tone Music," *J. Genet. Psychol.*, 1928, *35*, 286–93. Thresholds for intervals made from pure tones are slightly different from those obtained from musical, i.e. impure, tones. Pratt's stimuli were fairly pure and his data were elicited from psychologically trained observers. Hence it is reasonable to suppose that the more typical listener in a more musical setting would have a threshold somewhat above 20 cents. The reader should not confuse "threshold" and "sensitivity," terms which are negatively related. Where the listener's threshold is *low*, i.e., where he perceives the interval quality as changed after very little expansion or contraction of the pitch span, he is said to be *highly* sensitive. See also the

excellent research review by A. G. Pikler, "History of Experiments on the Musical Interval Sense," *J. Music Theory*, 1966, *10*(1), 54–95; and Ch. 22, "Gestalt Hearing of Intervals" by M. Kolinski in G. Reese and Rose Brandel, *The Commonwealth of Music*, New York, The Free Press, 1964.

17. W. D. Ward and D. W. Martin, "Psychophysical Comparison of Just Tuning and Equal Temperament in Sequences of Individual Tones," *J. Acoust. Soc. Amer.*, 1961, *33*(5), 586–88.

18. Theory Series A, Numbers 2 and 3, Musurgia Records, Box 242, Jackson Heights, N.Y. Note also the accompanying manuals issued in 1958 by J. Murray Barbour and Fritz A. Kuttner.

19. H. L. F. Helmholtz, *On the Sensations of Tone*, New York, Longmans, Green, 1912, p. 486. See also M. F. Meyer, "Helmholtz's Aversion to Tempered Tuning Experimentally Shown To Be a Neurological Problem," *J. Acoust. Soc. Amer.*, 1962, *34*, 127–28.

20. P. C. Greene, "Violin Intonation," *J. Acoust. Soc. Amer.*, 1937, *9*, 43–44; W. Lottermoser and F. J. Meyer, "Frequenzmessungen an gesungenen Akkorden," *Acustica*, 1960, *10*, 181–84; J. F. Nickerson, "Intonation of Solo and Ensemble Performance of the Same Melody," *J. Acoust. Soc. Amer.*, 1949, *21*, 593–95; J. A. Mason, "Comparison of Solo and Ensemble Performances With Reference to Pythagorean, Just, and Equi-Tempered Intonation," *J. Res. Music Educ.*, 1960, *8*(1), 31–38; C. Shackford, "Some Aspects of Perception," Part I, *J. Music Theory*, 1961, *5*, 162–202, Part II, *6*, 66–90, Part III, *6*, 295–303.

21. J. M. Barbour, *Tuning and Temperament*, East Lansing, Michigan State Coll. Press, 1951.

22. M. F. Meyer *(The Musician's Arithmetic, op. cit.)* and others have long advocated the introduction of quarter-tones into our music system and have argued that a new staff which omits key signatures and all sharps and flats is in order. One such staff has been suggested with the staff lines arranged as are the piano's black keys. The only sign needed in this new staff would be for the quarter-tone. See also P. Moon, "A Proposed Musical Notation," *J. Franklin Inst.*, 1952, *253*, 125–43.

23. C. C. Pratt, *op. cit.* The majority of children can accurately discriminate quarter-tones by age seven. See A. Bentley, *Musical Ability in Children and Its Measurement*, London, Harrap, 1966.

24. An organ with a 31-note scale to carry out the harmonic ideas of the seventeenth-century mathematician Christiaan Huygens has been built by the Dutch physicist A. D. Fokker ("Equal Temperament and the Thirty-one-keyed Organ," *Sci. Monthly*, 1955, *81*, 161–66). The basic interval of about 39 cents would appear to be functional only for an audience of very sensitive listeners.

25. P. R. Farnsworth and C. F. Voegelin, "Dyad Preferences at Different Intensities," *J. Appl. Psychol.*, 1928, *12*, 148–51.

26. J. L. Mursell, "Psychology and the Problem of the Scale," *Music Quart.*, 1946, *32*, 564–73.

CHAPTER THREE

1. A number of the phenomena we shall be describing concern chords and melodies as well as intervals and could quite logically have been treated in other chapters. The reader must forgive the rather arbitrary decision to consider them here.

2. For an example of a person's ability to categorize an interval see M. F. Meyer, "New Illusions of Pitch," *Amer. J. Psychol.*, 1962, *75*, 323–24; see also W. D. Ward, "On the Perception of the Frequency Ratio 55:32," *J. Acoust. Soc. Amer.*, 1962, *34*(5), 679.

3. E. M. Edmunds and M. E. Smith, "The Phenomenological Description of Musical Intervals," *Amer. J. Psychol.*, 1923, *34*, 287–91. For another phenomenal description which at least puts the intervals somewhat in musical context, see Ch. 2 of D. Cooke, *The Language of Music*, London, Oxford U. Press, 1959. See also A. Pike, "The Phenomenological Approach to Musical Perception," *Philosophy & Phenomenological Res.*, 1966, *27*(2), 247–54.

4. David Allen, "Octave Discriminability of Musical and Non-musical Subjects," *Psychonomic Sci.*, 1967, *7*(12), 421–22; A. G. Pikler, "History of Experiments on the Musical Interval Sense," *J. Music Theory*, 1966, *10*(1), 54–95.

5. O. Ortmann, "On the Melodic Relativity of Tones," *Psychol. Monog.*, 1926, *35*(1), 1–47.

6. C. v. Maltzew, "Das Erkennen sukzessiv gegebener musikalischer Intervalle in den äussern Tonregionen," *Z. f. Psychol.*, 1913, *64*, 161–257. There is now available an instrument called the "melometer" which indicates how accurately a person can discriminate intervals. See J. R. Trotter, "The Psychophysics of Melodic Interval Definitions, Techniques, Theory and Problems," *Australian J. Psychol.*, 1967, *19*(1), 13–25.

7. Some authorities call an exaggerated and unpleasant vibrato a tremolo. However, since the term has also been attached to other phenomena, it will not be used here.

8. C. E. Seashore, "The Vocal Trill," *Music Educ. J.*, 1943, *29*(3), 40.

9. C. Stumpf, *Tonpsychologie*, Leipzig, Hirzel, 1883, 1890; A. G. Ekdahl and E. G. Boring, "The Pitch of Tone Masses," *Amer. J. Psychol.*, 1934, *46*, 452–55.

10. H. J. Watt, *The Psychology of Sound*, Cambridge, Cambridge U. Press, 1917.

11. C. W. Valentine, "The Aesthetic Appreciation of Musical Intervals Among School Children and Adults," *Brit. J. Psychol.*, 1913, *6*, 190–216.

12. P. R. Farnsworth, "Notes on the Pitch of a Combination of Tones," *Brit. J. Psychol.*, 1924, *15*, 82–85; "The Pitch of a Combination of Tones," *Amer. J. Psychol.*, 1938, *51*(3), 536–39.

13. C. A. Alchin, *Applied Harmony*, Los Angeles, published by the author, 1921.

14. P. R. Farnsworth, "The Effect of Repetition on Ending Preferences in Melodies," *Amer. J. Psychol.*, 1926, *37*, 116–22.

15. A study which demonstrates the finality effects of falling inflection is that by L. Kaiser, "Contribution to the Psychologic and Linguistic Value of Melody," *Acta Psychol.*, 1953, *9*, 288–93.

16. K. E. Zener, "The Perception of Finality in Simple Tonal Sequences as Determined by Pitch," Doctoral thesis, Harvard U., 1926.

17. A good English language account of the T. Lipps views can be found in Vol. 2 of *Psychology Classics*, K. Dunlap, Ed., Baltimore, Williams and Wilkins, 1926.

18. M. F. Meyer, "Elements of a Psychological Theory of Melody," *Psychol. Rev.*, 1900, *7*, 241–73; "Experimental Studies in the Psychology of Music," *Amer. J. Psychol.*, 1903, *14*, 456–78.

19. P. R. Farnsworth, "Atonic Endings in Melodies," *Amer. J. Psychol.*, 1925, *36*, 394–400.

20. P. R. Farnsworth, "Further Data Concerning the Lipps-Meyer Law" in "Studies in the Psychology of Tone and Music," *Genet. Psychol. Monog.*, 1934, *15*(1), 40–44.

21. J. Handschin, in *Der Toncharakter: Eine Einführung in die Tonpsychologie*, Zürich, Atlantis Verlag, 1948, asserts that if the tones of the scale are arranged in an order corresponding to the number of fifths they are removed from F, then the smaller the order number the more masculine will be the character of the tone. Handschin has apparently identified stability and restfulness with masculinity.

22. R. Updegraff, "A Preliminary Study of the Nature of Finality in Melody," *Proc. Iowa Acad. Sci.*, 1926, *23*, 279–82.

23. A gestalt explanation of the power of the symbol 2 comes from J. L. Mursell who suggests the well-known Law of Prägnanz, which holds that persons tend to perceive objects in the simplest arrangement possible. Since the 2 is the smallest symbol to appear among the scale symbols, it furnishes the simplest possible arrangement and so provides the most satisfying of endings. See J. Mursell, "Psychology and the Problem of the Scale," *Music Quart.*, 1946, *32*, 564–73. A biological explanation of tonality, this time keyed to characteristics of the basilar membrane of the inner ear, has been offered by H. Wunderlich in "Theory of Tonality," *J. Gen. Psychol.*, 1947, *37*, 169–76. For the views of a biologically minded musician who believes that the Lipps-Meyer effect is more than a matter of mores, see A. I. Elkus, "Tonal Centers and Central Modalities," *Music Teach. Nat. Assoc. Proc. 1949, 1951, 43 Ser.*, 203–6. E. Franklin has felt that the principles so far suggested to explain finality effects can be subsumed under one rule. His notion is that the Lipps-Meyer law functions only when "applied to melody formation as subordinate to the movement of the bass or the implied bass." (*Tonality as a Basis for the Study of Musical Talent*, Göteborg, Sweden, Gumperts Förlag, 1956, p. 48.)

24. R. C. Pinkerton, "Information Theory and Melody," *Sci. Amer.*, 1956, *194*, 77–86.

25. H. Badings, "Tonaliteit," *Winkler Prins Encyclopaedia*, Amsterdam, 1957, 6th ed., Vol. 17.

26. See Milhaud's *Third Symphony* for an example of six-key polytonality.

27. Most American Indian music, however, shows considerable tonality. See D. P. McAllester, *Enemy Way Music*, Cambridge, Mass., Peabody Museum, 1954.

28. N. Cazden, in "The Principle of Direction in the Motion of Similar Tonal Harmonies," *J. Music Theory*, Nov. 1958, 162–92, has paid particular attention to Hindemith's theory of tonal structure.

29. P. R. Farnsworth and C. F. Voegelin, "Dyad Preferences at Different Intensities," *J. Appl. Psychol.*, 1928, *12*, 148–51.

30. H. L. F. Helmholtz, *On the Sensations of Tone*, Ellis, trans., New York, Longmans, Green, 1912. For an attempt to give at least some small support to the Helmholtz position, see R. Plomp and W. J. M. Levelt, "Tonal Consonance and Critical Bandwidth," *J. Acoust. Soc. Amer.*, 1965, *38*, 548–60.

31. When two tones which are very close to each other in pitch are sounded together, the amplitude of the resulting sound is periodically augmented and decreased, thus eliciting a throbbing or beating effect. For example the sounding of two tones whose frequencies are 1,000 and 1,001 cycles will yield one beat per second. If the number of beats is over 20, the individual beats are not heard; the effect is merely one of roughness. When under certain conditions two tones with, say, frequencies of 8,000 and 8,700 cycles are sounded, a difference tone of 700 cycles may be distinctly heard. Before the development of instruments which give visual pictures of sound waves, piano-tuners made use of beat counts in adjusting piano strings. It had been assumed that musicians too were relying on beat phenomena to help them tune their instruments. But it can be shown that they depend rather on apparent pitch. See J. F. Corso, "Unison Tuning of Musical Instruments," *J. Acoust. Soc. Amer.*, 1954, *26*, 746–50.

32. F. Krueger, "Differenztone und Konsonanz," *Arch. Ges. Psychol.*, 1903, *1*, 205–75.

33. C. Stumpf, *Tonpsychologie, op. cit.*

34. T. Lipps, *Psychological Classics, op. cit.* What might be regarded as another variant of the Lippsian theory is that proposed by D. B. Irvine, "Toward a Theory of Intervals," *J. Acoust. Soc. Amer.*, 1946, *17*, 350–55. Irvine would classify intervals by families on the basis of the length of the composite wave form. By this scheme the fourth (3:4) and the major sixth (3:5) would belong to one family, the major third (4:5) and the ninth (4:9) to another, etc. In other words, all intervals whose ratios are as 3 to something would be grouped into one classification, 4 to something into another, and 5 to something into still another. For an extremely well

considered article on the relation of number to consonance see N. Cazden, "Musical Intervals and Simple Number Ratios," *J. Res. Music Educ.*, 1959, *7*, 197–220.

35. A. Schoenberg, *Harmonielehre*, 3rd ed., Universal Edition, Wien, 1922.
36. J. Peterson and F. W. Smith, "The Range and Modifiability of Consonance in Certain Musical Intervals," *Amer. J. Psychol.*, 1930, *42*, 561–72; J. Peterson, "A Functional View of Consonance," *Psychol. Rev.*, 1925, *32*, 17–33; N. Cazden, "Sensory Theories of Musical Consonance," *J. Aesth.*, 1962, *20*, 301–19.
37. R. M. Ogden, *Hearing*, New York, Harcourt, Brace, 1924.
38. H. T. Moore, "The Genetic Aspect of Consonance and Dissonance," *Psychol. Monog.*, 1914, *17*(2), 1–68.
39. For an excellent refutation of genetic theories of consonance see E. G. Bugg and A. S. Thompson, "An Experimental Test of the Genetic Theory of Consonance," *J. Gen. Psychol.*, 1952, *47*, 71–90.
40. E. G. Bugg, "An Experimental Study of Factors Influencing Consonance Judgments," *Psychol. Monog.*, 1933, *45*(2); C. P. Heinlein, "An Experimental Study of the Seashore Consonance Test," *J. Exp. Psychol.*, 1925, *8*, 408–33; C. P. Heinlein, "Critique of the Seashore Consonance Test," *Psychol. Rev.*, 1929, *36*, 524–43.
41. C. E. Seashore, *Manual of Instructions and Interpretations for Measures of Musical Talent*, New York, Columbia Graphophone, 1919.
42. J. P. van de Geer, W. J. M. Levelt, and R. Plomp, "The Connotation of Musical Consonance," *Acta Psychol.*, Amsterdam, 1962, *20*(4), 303–19.
43. N. Cazden, "Musical Consonance and Dissonance: A Cultural Criterion," *J. Aesth.*, 1945, *4*, 3–11.
44. R. W. Lundin, "Toward a Cultural Theory of Consonance," *J. Psychol.*, 1947, *28*, 45–49.
45. C. C. Pratt, known through his earliest publications as a formalist who has played down the role of learning in the arts, later espoused what might be called contextual relativism. Although Pratt has backed away from cultural relativism and has approached his problems with a reductionistic (physical science) rather than a social science bias, his theoretical position would not appear to be in complete opposition to that taken in this book (see his "The Stability of Aesthetic Judgments," *J. Aesth.*, 1956, *15*, 1–11).

CHAPTER FOUR

1. G. D. Birkhoff's *(Aesthetic Measure,* Cambridge, Mass., Harvard U. Press, 1933) mathematical formula for assessing unity and variety is $M = \dfrac{O}{C}$ where O represents orderliness, C complexity, and M the aesthetic measure. His treatment of music relates to diatonic chords, diatonic harmony, and melody.

2. Cyril Burt, "The Psychology of Art" chapter of *How the Mind Works*, London, Allen and Unwin, 1933. Sir Cyril's *aesthetic index* is $\left(\exp \dfrac{D+I}{S} \right)^{-1}$, where D is the number of items into which the work is differentiated, I is the number of relations integrating the items, and S is the scope of apprehension under the usual conditions.

3. J. G. Beebe-Center and C. C. Pratt, "A Test of Birkhoff's Aesthetic Measure," *J. Gen. Psychol.*, 1937, *17*, 339–53.
4. L. L. Thurstone, "The Problem of Melody," *Music Quart.*, 1920, *6*, 426–29.
5. L. E. Emerson, "The Feeling-Value of Unmusical Tone-Intervals," *Harvard Psychol. Stud.*, 1906, *2*, 269–74. The work of Emerson and the studies by Max Meyer, "Ele-

ments of a Psychological Theory of Melody," *Psychol. Rev.*, 1900, *7*, 241–73, and by W. V. D. Bingham, "Studies in Melody," *Psychol. Monog.*, 1910, *12*, 1–88, are examples of the excellent early American researches on melody.

6. H. Werner, "Musical 'Micro-scales' and 'Micro-melodies,'" *J. Psychol.*, 1940, *10*, 149–56.

7. B. W. White, "Recognition of Distorted Melodies," *Amer. J. Psychol.*, 1960, *73*, 100–107.

8. O. Ortmann, "On the Melodic Relativity of Tones," *Psychol. Monog.*, 1926, *35*(1), 1–47. See also J. P. Guilford and R. A. Hilton, "Some Configurational Properties of Short Musical Melodies," *J. Exp. Psychol.*, 1933, *16*, 32–54; J. P. Guilford and H. M. Nelson, "Changes in the Pitch of Tones When Melodies Are Repeated," *J. Exp. Psychol.*, 1936, *19*, 193–202; "The Pitch of Tones in Melodies as Compared With Single Tones," *J. Exp. Psychol.*, 1937, *20*, 309–35.

9. C. E. Seashore, D. Lewis, and J. G. Saetveit, *Manual, Seashore Measures of Musical Talents*, New York, Psychological Corp., 1956, 1960.

10. With an arrangement similar to that found in the Seashore Tonal Memory Test, H. Wunderlich ("The Recognition Value of the Steps of the Diatonic Scale," *Amer. J. Psychol.*, 1940, *53*, 579–82) studied the ease of identifying the scale steps. The *fa* and *ti* were quite difficult to identify as having been altered while the *do*, *re*, and *la* were readily identified. See also C. P. Heinlein, "A Brief Discussion of the Nature and Function of Melodic Configuration in Tonal Memory With Critical Reference to the Seashore Tonal Memory Test," *J. Genet. Psychol.*, 1928, *35*, 45–61; and R. Francès, "Recherches expérimentales sur la perception de la mélodie," *J. Psychol. Norm. Path.*, 1954, *47–51*, 439–57.

11. For reviews of the literature on absolute pitch see D. M. Neu, "A Critical Review of the Literature on 'Absolute Pitch,'" *Psychol. Bull.*, 1947, *44*, 249–66; and W. D. Ward, "Absolute Pitch," *Sound*, 1963, *2*(3), 14–21; (4), 33–41.

12. B. L. Riker, "The Ability to Judge Pitch," *J. Exp. Psychol.*, 1946, *36*, 331–46.

13. L. A. Petran, "An Experimental Study of Pitch Recognition," *Psychol. Monog.*, 1932, *42*, No. 193.

14. Building on the early work of Max Meyer ("Is the Memory of Absolute Pitch Capable of Development by Training?" *Psychol. Rev.*, 1899, *6*, 514–16), others have found as he did that, by dint of careful training, errors can be reduced to at least as small a figure as 33 cents. See Helen K. Mull, "The Acquisition of Absolute Pitch," *Amer. J. Psychol.*, 1925, *36*, 469–93; and C. H. Wedell, "A Study of Absolute Pitch," *Psychol. Bull.*, 1941, *38*, 547–48. Descriptions of training with more elaborate equipment can be seen in R. W. Lundin and J. D. Allen, "A Technique for Training Perfect Pitch," *Psychol. Rec.*, 1962, *12*, 139–46; and L. L. Cuddy, "Practice Effects on the Absolute Judgment of Pitch," *J. Acoust. Soc. Amer.*, 1968, *43*(5), 1069–76.

15. A. Bachem is one of the research men of this area who is still convinced that absolute pitch is an inherent type of behavior ("The Genesis of Absolute Pitch," *J. Acoust. Soc. Amer.*, 1940, *11*, 434–39; "Time Factors in Relative and Absolute Pitch Determination," *J. Acoust. Soc. Amer.*, 1954, *26*, 751–53). Max Meyer has strongly opposed Bachem's view in "On Memorizing Absolute Pitch," *J. Acoust. Soc. Amer.*, 1956, *28*, 718–19.

16. W. F. Oakes, "An Experimental Study of Pitch Naming and Pitch Discrimination Reactions," *J. Genet. Psychol.*, 1955, *86*, 237–59.

17. M. Aizawa, "An Investigation of the Judgement of Absolute Pitch by the Group Test," *Tohoku Psychol. Folia*, 1961, *20*, 1–12.

18. L. A. Jeffress, "Absolute Pitch," *J. Acoust. Soc. Amer.*, 1962, *34*(7), 987.

19. Even when the cues do not directly benefit the performance their presence may give the person confidence. Thus L. M. Brammer found that the pitch-level scores of several violinists were no better when they were given the opportunity to tune

their own violins than when the experimenter tuned the instruments for them under their orders. Yet the added kinesthetic cues the manipulation of their own fiddles gave them increased their confidence in their scores ("Sensory Cues in Pitch Judgment," *J. Exp. Psychol.*, 1951, *41*, 336–40).

20. Karl Eitz, *Das Tonwort*, Leipzig, Breitkopf u. Haertel, 1928.
21. C. E. Seashore, "Acquired or Absolute Pitch," *Music Educ. J.*, 1940, *26*, 18.
22. A. Bachem, *op. cit.*
23. For an attempt to develop "types" of absolute pitch ability see A. Wellek, "Das absolute Gehor und seine Typen," *Beith. Z. f. angew. Psychol.*, 1938, (83).
24. A. Silbermann, *The Sociology of Music*, London, Routledge and Kegan Paul, 1963.
25. E. E. Gordon, "An Approach to the Quantitative Study of Dynamics," *J. Res. Music Educ.*, 1960, *8*, 23–30.
26. The tonal intervals were played on a Duo-Art reproducing piano. When the intensity levers were set at "soft" the intervals termed "soft" were elicited. Other combinations of the levers yielded the "medium" and "loud" intensities. See P. R. Farnsworth and C. F. Voegelin, "Dyad Preferences at Different Intensities," *J. Appl. Psychol.*, 1928, *12*, 148–51.
27. H. Fletcher, *Newer Concepts of the Pitch, Loudness and Timbre of Musical Tones*, New York, Bell Telephone, 1935. See also W. Kohler, "Tonpsychologie," *Handbuch der Neurologie des Ohres*, Berlin, Alexander u. Marburg, 1923, pp. 419–64.
28. J. S. Hurley, "A Study of Pitch Tendencies in Certain Phases of Singing as Measured by the Conn Chromatic Stroboscope," Thesis, Syracuse U., 1940. The picture with bowed tones is somewhat different. Here professionals tend to flat with increases in bow pressure but to sharp with each rise in bow velocity. See R. J. Harrington, "The Influence of Pressure and Velocity of the Bow on Violin Intonation: A Stroboscopic Study," Master's thesis, Syracuse U., 1952.
29. O. Ortmann, *The Physical Basis of Piano Touch and Tone*, New York, Dutton, 1925, reprinted in 1962; H. C. Hart, M. W. Fuller, and W. S. Lusby, "Precision Study of Piano Touch and Tone," *J. Acoust. Soc. Amer.*, 1934, *6*, 80–94.
30. C. P. Heinlein, "The Functional Role of Finger Touch and Damper-Pedalling in the Appreciation of Pianoforte Music," *J. Gen. Psychol.*, 1929, *2*, 462–69; "A Discussion of the Nature of Pianoforte Damper-Pedalling Together With an Experimental Study of Some Individual Differences in Pedal Performance," *J. Gen. Psychol.*, 1929, *2*, 489–508; "Pianoforte Damper-Pedalling Under Ten Different Experimental Conditions," *J. Gen. Psychol.*, 1930, *3*, 511–28.
31. As sopranos improve in skill the tones they produce are more likely to contain inharmonic components. See A. Bjørklund, "Analyses of Soprano Voices," *J. Acoust. Soc. Amer.*, 1961, *33*(5), 575–82.
32. One researcher believes he has demonstrated the existence of undertones, which he conceives as the inverse of overtones, but so far few others accept their reality. See C. Révész, *Introduction to the Psychology of Music*, Norman, U. of Oklahoma Press, 1954, pp. 13–14.
33. For an excellent account of the timbre of band and orchestral instruments see Ch. 17 of C. E. Seashore, *Psychology of Music*, New York, McGraw-Hill, 1938.
34. The mounting of the mute on the bridge of a violin dampens certain of the higher overtones and makes the "shade" of the tone "darker." A "dark" vocal tone can be produced by holding the mouth "long," and a "light" tone by a "short" mouth. See D. Preston, "Pitch Variations in the Singing of Specific Vowels on Specific Frequencies Using Bright and Dark Tones," Master's thesis, Syracuse U., 1945.
35. J. K. Van Stone, "The Effects of Instrumental Tone Quality Upon Mood Response to Music," in *Music Therapy, 1959*, E. H. Schneider, Ed., Lawrence, Kan., Allen Press, 1960, pp. 196–202.
36. Variability, a general fact of life, is well illustrated in the area of auditory sensitivity. Many men deafen early while others keep their sensitivity relatively intact

until quite late in life. The average changes in hearing ability are as described above.

37. C. C. Bunch, "Age Variations in Auditory Acuity," *Arch. Otolaryngol., Chicago,* 1929, *9,* 625–36; H. C. Montgomery, "Do Our Ears Grow Old?" *Bell Lab. Rec.,* 1932, *10,* 311–13; N. H. Kelley, "A Study in Presbycusis: Auditory Loss With Increasing Age and Its Effect Upon the Perception of Music and Speech," *Arch. Otolaryngol., Chicago,* 1939, *29,* 506–13. Montgomery pictures the hearing losses of the aging as being somewhat slighter than does Bunch. Kelley presents them as still slighter, particularly for the frequencies below 1,024 cycles.

38. P. R. Farnsworth, "Notes on 'Coldness' in Violin Playing," *J. Psychol.,* 1952, *33,* 41–45.

39. H. Fletcher, E. D. Blackham, and R. Stratton, "Quality of Piano Tones," *Science,* 1961, *134*(3488), 1428; E. D. Blackham, "The Physics of the Piano," *Sci. Amer.,* 1965, *213*(6), 88–99. For a study of the tone quality of a woodwind instrument see T. S. Small, "The Evaluation of Clarinet Tone Quality Through the Use of Oscilloscope Transparencies," *J. Res. Music Educ.,* 1967, *15*(1), 11–22. See also M. D. Freedman, "Analysis of Musical Instrument Tones," *J. Acoust. Soc. Amer.,* 1967, *41*(4), 793–806.

40. M. Metfessel, "Sonance as a Form of Tonal Fusion," *Psychol. Rev.,* 1926, *33,* 459–66. See also O. Ortmann's "The Psychology of Tone Quality," *1939 Intern. Congr. Musicol.,* 1944, pp. 227–32.

41. Research men of the Seashore laboratories at the University of Iowa have made excellent studies of certain of these phenomena. The interested student can refer to C. E. Seashore, *Psychology of Music, op. cit.,* Ch. 9, or to the following monographs by Seashore's student associates for detailed pictures of the portamento and of typical attacks and releases of vocal tones: D. Lewis, M. Cowan, and G. Fairbanks, "Pitch Variations Arising From Certain Types of Frequency Modulation," *J. Acoust. Soc. Amer.,* 1937, *9,* 79; R. E. Miller, "The Pitch of the Attack in Singing," *U. of Iowa Stud. Psychol. Music,* 1936, *4,* 158–71; H. G. Seashore, "An Objective Analysis of Artistic Singing," *U. of Iowa Stud. Psychol. Music,* 1936, *4,* 12–157; A. Small, "An Objective Analysis of Artistic Violin Performance," *U. of Iowa Stud. Psychol. Music,* 1936, *4,* 172–231.

42. W. T. Bartholomew, *Acoustics of Music,* New York, Prentice-Hall, 1942, p. 159.

43. W. G. Hill, "Noise in Piano Tone, a Qualitative Element," *Music Quart.,* 1940, *26,* 244–59.

44. O. Ortmann, "Physiopsychology and Musicology," *Music,* 1946, *4*(6), 23, 26, 54–56.

45. P. R. Farnsworth, H. A. Block, and W. C. Waterman, "Absolute Tempo," *J. Gen. Psychol.,* 1934, *10,* 230–33.

46. M. Lund, "An Analysis of the 'True Beat' in Music," Doctoral thesis, Stanford U., 1939.

47. For a definition of takt and true beat see Glossary.

48. G. Brelet, *Le temps musical,* Paris, Press. U. de France, 1949.

49. M. T. Henderson, "Rhythmic Organization in Artistic Piano Performance," *U. of Iowa Stud. Psychol. Music,* 1936, *4,* 281–305. The work of Henderson and the other Iowa psychologists who have studied piano performance was made possible by a specially designed camera. For more detail on its use see L. Skinner and C. E. Seashore, "A Musical Pattern Score of the First Movement of the Beethoven *Sonata, Opus 27, No. 2,*" *U. of Iowa Stud. Psychol. Music,* 1936, *4,* 263–80.

50. H. E. Weaver, "Syncopation: A Study of Musical Rhythms," *J. Gen. Psychol.,* 1939, *20,* 409–29. It should be noted that the jazz musician syncopates not only with rhythmic beats but with melodic contours as well. See also P. Fraisse and S. Ehrlich, "Note sur la possibilité de syncoper en fonction du tempo d'une cadence," *Année Psychol.,* 1955, *55,* 61–65.

51. J. B. Eggen, "A Behavioristic Interpretation of Jazz," *Psychol. Rev.,* 1926, *33,* 407–9.

P. Fraisse, G. Oléron, and J. Paillard ("Les effets dynamogéniques de la musique. Étude expérimentale," *Année Psychol.*, 1953, *53*, 1–34) have made the not very surprising finding that the simpler rhythms of marches and waltzes elicit more overt movements in listeners than do the more varied rhythms to be found in Debussy and Stravinsky.

52. Kate Gordon, *Esthetics*, New York, Holt, 1913.
53. J. L. Mursell, *The Psychology of Music*, New York, W. W. Norton, 1937, p. 177. Mursell's table is reproduced here with the permission of W. W. Norton Co. For an excellent book on musical rhythms, see G. W. Cooper and L. B. Meyer, *The Rhythmic Structure of Music*, Chicago, U. of Chicago Press, 1960.
54. R. W. Lundin, *An Objective Psychology of Music*, New York, Ronald Press, 1953, p. 95.
55. K. Dunlap, *A System of Psychology*, New York, Scribner, 1912, pp. 309–13.
56. See *Kitten on the Keys* or *I Can't Give You Anything but Love, Baby*.
57. P. R. Farnsworth, "Concerning Cross-Rhythms," *School Music*, 1933, *33*, 11–12.
58. E. Jaques-Dalcroze, *Rhythm, Music and Education*, New York, Putnam, 1921.
59. This is not to imply that expectancy is the only basic principle of learning. Those who wish more acquaintance with learning principles would do well to devote the time necessary to reading the learning sections of one of the elementary textbooks in psychology.

CHAPTER FIVE

1. For an excellent general account of music in a language context see L. B. Meyer, *Emotion and Meaning in Music*, Chicago, U. of Chicago Press, 1956; see also Meyer, "Some Remarks on Value and Greatness in Music," *J. Aesth.*, 1959, *17*(4), 486–500. Somewhat different views on musical meanings can be seen in Glen Haydon, *On the Meaning of Music*, Washington, Library of Congress, 1948, and in Roger Sessions, *The Musical Experience*, Princeton, Princeton U. Press, 1950. Charles Seeger, in an interesting but highly technical musicological article ("On the Moods of a Music-Logic," *J. Amer. Musicol. Soc.*, 1960, *13*, 224–61), considers the messages words and music can send and decides that there are points of identity, of similarity, and of difference. See also J. Margolis, *The Language of Art and Art Criticism*, Detroit, Wayne State U. Press, 1965.
2. A. D. DeGroot, "Het "Ick-en-weet-niet-wat' in de Kunst," *Ned. Tijdschr. v. Psych.*, 1954, *6*, 4.
3. This first criterion of language is in one sense missing in some so-called "experimental music" composed on a digital computer from the rules of older composers. Yet attention may be paid the desires to communicate of those composers whose rules of composition have been so abstracted in whole or in part and fed into the machine. See L. A. Hiller and L. M. Isaacson, *Experimental Music*, New York, McGraw-Hill, 1959.
4. A. Pike, "Perception and Meaning in Serial Music," *J. Aesth.*, 1963, *22*(1), 55–61.
5. N. Cazden, "Towards a Theory of Realism in Music," *J. Aesth.*, 1951, *10*(2), 135–51; "Realism in Abstract Music," *Music & Letters*, 1955, *36*(1), 17–38.
6. L. B. Meyer, "Meaning in Music and Information Theory," *J. Aesth.*, 1957, *15*(4), 412–24; E. Coons and D. Kraehenbuehl, "Information as a Measure of Structure in Music," *J. Music Theory*, 1958, *2*, 127–61; R. C. Pinkerton, "Information Theory and Melody," *Sci. Amer.*, 1956, *194*(2), 77–86; J. E. Youngblood, "Style as Information," *J. Music Theory*, 1958, *2*, 24–35; R. Arnheim, "Information Theory: An Introductory Note," *J. Aesth.*, 1959, *17*(4), 501–3; D. Kraehenbuehl and E. Coons, "Information as a Measure of the Experience of Music," *J. Aesth.*, 1959, *17*(4), 510–22;

J. E. Cohen, "Information Theory and Music," *Beh. Sci.*, 1962, *7*(2), 137–63; J. E. Youngblood, "Music and Language: Some Related Analytical Techniques," Thesis, Indiana U., 1960; G. Rochberg, "Indeterminacy in the New Music," *Score*, Jan., 1960; F. Attneave, *Application of Information Theory to Psychology*, New York, Holt, 1959; G. Roller, "Development of a Method for Analysis of Musical Compositions Using an Electronic Digital Computer," *J. Res. Music Educ.*, 1965, *13*(4), 249–52; L. Hiller and C. Bean, "Information Theory Analyses of Four Sonata Expositions," *J. Music Theory*, 1966, *10*(1), 96–137; J. G. Brawley, Jr., "Application of Information Theory to Musical Rhythm," Thesis, Indiana U., 1959; B. Reimer, "Information Theory and the Analysis of Musical Meaning," *Counc. Res. Music Educ.*, 1964, *2*, 14–22; A. Moles, *Théorie de l'information et perception esthétique*, Paris, Flammarion, 1958. The Moles book has now been translated by J. E. Cohen (*Information Theory and Aesthetic Perception*, Urbana, Ill., and London, U. of Illinois Press, 1966). Thoughtful criticisms of the book can be seen in C. Burt, "Information Theory and Aesthetic Education," *J. Aesth. Educ.*, 1966, *1*(2), 55–69, and in R. Arnheim's review in *J. Aesth.*, 1968, *26*(4), 552–54.

7. L. A. Hiller and L. M. Isaacson, *Experimental Music*, New York, McGraw-Hill, 1959. An interesting recording, Microgroove 122227B, was put on sale in 1960 by the Bell Telephone Laboratories under the caption "Music From Mathematics." In 1961 a booklet by B. E. Strasser was issued to accompany the recording. See also H. F. Olson and H. Belar, "Aid to Music Composition Employing a Random Probability System," *J. Acoust. Soc. Amer.*, 1961, *33*(9), 1163–70, and J. A. Sowa, *A Machine To Compose Music*, New York, Oliver Garfield, 1956.

8. I. Stravinsky, *An Autobiography*, New York, Simon and Shuster, 1936, p. 53.

9. A. Copland, *What To Listen for in Music*, New York, McGraw-Hill, 1939, p. 12.

10. F. Mendelssohn, Letter to M. A. Souchay, Berlin, Oct. 5, 1842.

11. One is reminded of the legislative threats against rock 'n' roll during the summer of 1956.

12. For an exception to this statement, see the next section of this chapter.

13. M. F. Meyer, *The Musician's Arithmetic*, Boston, Ditson, 1929.

14. C. W. Valentine, "The Aesthetic Appreciation of Musical Intervals Among School Children and Adults," *Brit. J. Psychol.*, 1913, *6*, 190–216.

15. C. P. Heinlein, "The Affective Characters of the Major and Minor Modes in Music," *J. Comp. Psychol.*, 1928, *8*, 101–42. See also J. F. Corso, "Absolute Judgments of Musical Tonality," *J. Acoust. Soc. Amer.*, 1957, *29*(1), 138–44.

16. K. Hevner, "The Affective Character of Major and Minor Modes in Music," *Amer. J. Psychol.*, 1935, *47*, 103–18.

17. P. R. Farnsworth, "The Discrimination of Major, Minor, and Certain Mistuned Chords," *J. Gen. Psychol.*, 1928, *1*, 377–79.

18. C. P. Heinlein, *op. cit.*

19. L. Kaiser, "Contribution to the Psychologic and Linguistic Value of Melody," *Acta Psychol.*, 1953, *9*, 288–93.

20. Note that it is not the blues third per se which yields a minor effect but rather the overall melody in which the third is embedded. Intervals, it will be recalled, have no modal characteristics.

21. For detailed material on the effect of tempo see M. G. Rigg, "Speed as a Determiner of Musical Mood," *J. Exp. Psychol.*, 1940, *27*, 566–71. Rigg has verified Heinlein's work on the effect of pitch in "The Effect of Register and Tonality Upon Musical Mood," *J. Musicol.*, 1940, *2*, 49–61. See also K. B. Watson's extensive work on "happy" and "sad" music in "The Nature and Measurement of Musical Meanings," *Psychol. Monog.*, 1942, *54*(2).

22. A. L. Sopchak, "Individual Differences in Responses to Music," *Psychol. Monog.*, 1955, *69*(11), 1–20.

23. Y. Murzin, "Color Music in the Soviet Union," *Music J.*, 1968, *26*(1), 27.

24. Taken from P. A. Scholes, *The Oxford Companion to Music*, 2nd Ed., London, Oxford U. Press, 1943 (reproduced by permission of the publisher). Two Americans, amateur pianists of some skill, have reported key-hue associations which in some degree resemble those of Scriabin. See J. B. Carroll and J. H. Greenberg, "Two Cases of Synethesia for Color and Musical Tonality Associated With Absolute Pitch Ability," *Percept. Mot. Skills*, 1961, *13*, 48.

25. L. Omwake, "Visual Responses to Auditory Stimuli," *J. Appl. Psychol.*, 1940, *24*, 468–81. It has also been demonstrated that there is a slight tendency for persons who are more interested in color than in form to prefer tone to form. See W. A. McElroy, "Colour Form Attitudes, an Analogue From Music," *Austral. J. Psychol.*, 1953, *5*, 10–16. For some reason not easily discernible, sixth-graders who preferred major and slow music to minor and fast music were found in one experiment to prefer Scottish tartans which were preponderantly blue-green. See M. J. White, "Comparisons in Visual and Auditory Aesthetic Preferences Among Elementary School Children," Thesis, Wesleyan U., 1957. See also M. Aizawa, "Auditory Near-synaesthetic Impressions and Music (1), (2)," *Memoirs of the Faculty of Educ.* (Niigata U.), 1959, *1*, 32–40; 1960, *2*, 70–78.

26. C. E. Seashore, "Color Music," *Music Educ. J.*, 1938, *25*(2), 26.

27. J. Delay *et al.*, "Les synesthésies dans l'intoxication mescalinique," *Encéphale*, 1951, *40*, 1–10.

28. The fact that synesthesias and other color-tone linkages are not entirely chance associations between two sense modalities is emphasized by D. I. Masson in "Synesthesia and Sound Spectra," *Word*, 1952, *8*, 39–41. See also R. H. Simpson, M. Quinn, and D. P. Ausubel, "Synesthesia in Children: Association of Colors With Pure Tone Frequencies," *J. Genet. Psychol.*, 1956, *89*, 95–103; P. F. Ostwald, "Color Hearing," *Arch. Gen. Psychiat.*, 1964, *11*(1), 40–47.

29. E. Uhlich, "Synästhesie und Geschlecht," *Z. f. Angew. Psychol.*, 1957, *4*, 31–57.

30. P. F. Ostwald, "Color Hearing," *Arch. Gen. Psychiat.*, 1964, *11*(1), 40–47.

31. E. L. Kelly, "An Experimental Attempt To Produce Artificial Chromesthesia by the Technique of the Conditioned Response," *J. Exp. Psychol.*, 1934, *17*, 315–41.

32. T. H. Howells, "The Experimental Development of Color-Tone Synesthesia," *J. Exp. Psychol.*, 1944, *34*, 87–103.

33. O. Ortmann, "Theories of Synesthesia in the Light of a Case of Color Hearing," *Human Biol.*, 1933, *5*, 155–211; L. A. Riggs and T. Karwoski, "Synaesthesia," *Brit. J. Psychol.*, 1934, *25*, 29–41; M. J. Zigler, "Tone Shapes: A Novel Type of Synaesthesia," *J. Gen. Psychol.*, 1930, *3*, 277–87; P. E. Vernon, "Synaesthesia in Music," *Psyche*, 1930, *40*, 22–40.

34. C. C. Pratt, *The Meaning of Music*, New York, McGraw-Hill, 1931; "The Design of Music," *J. Aesth.*, 1954, *12*(3), 289–300. Essentially the same position is taken by O. K. Bouwsma in Ch. 5 of *Aesthetics and Language*, W. Elton, Ed., New York, Philosophical Library, 1954.

35. Sidney Zink, "Is the Music Really Sad?" *J. Aesth.*, 1960, *19*(2), 197–207.

36. W. V. Bingham, *Mood Music*, Orange, N.J., Thomas A. Edison, 1921. See also J. Dryer, "The Moods of Music," *Inst. Appl. Psychol. Rev.*, 1965, *5*(3), 105–11. That listeners typically have great difficulty seeing a necessary relationship between the characteristics of compositions and what the composers have entitled them was shown as early as 1929 by F. L. Wells in "Musical Symbolism," *J. Abn. Soc. Psychol.*, 1929, *24*, 74–76. This finding was later confirmed in a study by M. G. Rigg in "An Experiment To Determine How Accurately College Students Can Interpret the Intended Meanings of Musical Compositions," *J. Exp. Psychol.*, 1937, *21*, 223–29. For an amusing but devastating attack on a celebrated critic's claim that he understands what Mozart's *Figaro* means, see N. Cazden, "Mozart in Current Esthetics," *Science & Study*, 1953, *17*(1), 65–71.

37. A somewhat more recent study along the Edison lines is that of A. Capurso *et al.*, *Music and Your Emotions*, New York, Liveright, 1952, pp. 56–86. Sixty-one pieces

were found which provided listener agreement (1,075 nonmusical students were the listeners) of 50 per cent or more when the task was to sort the compositions into six categories. But a 50 per cent agreement leaves much to be desired.

38. A. L. Sopchak, *op. cit.* See also S. and R. L. Fisher, "The Effects of Personal Security on Reactions to Unfamiliar Music," *J. Soc. Psychol.*, 1951, *34*, 265–73, who report that a large percentage of those who react to "dramatic" music with unusually extreme favorableness or unfavorableness seem to possess marked personal insecurity.

39. M. Schoen and E. L. Gatewood, Ch. 7 in *The Effects of Music*, M. Shoen, Ed., New York, Harcourt, Brace, 1927; H. K. Mull, "A Study of Humor in Music," *Amer. J. Psychol.*, 1949, *62*, 560–66.

40. R. E. Dreher, "The Relationship Between Verbal Reports and Galvanic Skin Responses to Music," Doctoral thesis, Indiana U., 1947.

41. P. J. Hampton, "The Emotional Element in Music," *J. Gen. Psychol.*, 1945, *33*, 237–50.

42. I. G. Campbell, "Basal Emotional Patterns Expressible in Music," *Amer. J. Psychol.*, 1942, *55*, 1–17; B. Shimp, "Reliability of Associations of Known and Unknown Melodic Phrases With Words Denoting States of Feeling," *J. Musicol.*, 1940, *1*(4), 22–35.

43. K. Hevner, "Expression in Music: A Discussion of Experimental Studies and Theories," *Psychol. Rev.*, 1935, *47*, 186–204; Experimental Studies of the Elements of Expression in Music," *Amer. J. Psychol.*, 1936, *48*, 246–68. (The Hevner Adjective Checklist is reproduced by permission of the *Psychological Review* and the American Psychological Association.) That there is at least moderate stability over time in the classification of moods is shown by A. L. Sopchak, "Retest Reliability of the Number of Responses to Music," *J. Psychol.*, 1957, *44*, 223–26, who queried 553 college students about preferred modal names for 15 compositions on two occasions approximately six weeks apart. The two sets of responses correlated .76.

44. C. A. Winold, "The Effects of Changes in Harmonic Tension Upon Listener Response," Thesis, Indiana U., 1963.

45. P. R. Farnsworth, "A Study of the Hevner Adjective List," *J. Aesth.*, 1954, *13*, 97–103. What might be considered as a variant of the Hevner descriptive-word methodology is the "semantic differential." In using it, musical material is assessed in terms of a long series of words arranged in polar opposites. There are "potency" dyads like relaxed-tense and sentimental-hardboiled, "evaluative" pairs such as valuable-worthless and meaningful-meaningless, and ones more heterogeneous and thus difficult to classify of the order fresh-stale and sensitive-insensitive. The assessor must decide which of each pair of words is more descriptive of his material and in what degree. See P. H. Gray and G. E. Wheeler, "The Semantic Differential as an Instrument To Examine the Recent Folksong Movement, *J. Soc. Psychol.*, 1967, *72*, 241–47. K. Nordenstreng, "A Comparison Between the Semantic Differential and Similarity Analysis in the Measurement of Musical Experience," *Scandinavian J. Psychol.*, 1968, *9*(2), 89–96.

46. The mood expressed by the adjectives of cluster A resembles most closely the mood of clusters B and I, and resembles least the mood of clusters E and F. The adjective "frustrated" describes a mood which only cluster F reflects, but even here the affect is expressed with little precision.

47. K. Hevner, "Studies in Expressiveness of Music," *Music Teach. Nat. Assoc. Proc. 1938,* 1939, pp. 199–217. See also Hevner, "Experimental Studies of the Elements of Expression in Music," *op. cit.;* "The Affective Value of Pitch and Tempo in Music," *Amer. J. Psychol.*, 1937, *49*, 621–30; "Expression in Music," *op. cit.*

48. Factor analysis is a method for resolving a set of interrelated variables or tests into a few "factors" which are regarded as being the fundamental variables underlying the original complex of variables.

49. The tables that follow, reproduced by permission of *The American Journal of*

Psychology, are from R. Gundlach, "Factors Determining the Characterization of Musical Phrases," *Amer. J. Pychol.*, 1935, *47*, 624–43; "A Quantitative Analysis of Indian Music," *Amer. J. Psychol.*, 1932, *44*, 133–45. See also S. DeGrazia's attempted analysis of a Shostakovich composition in "Shostakovich's *Seventh Symphony:* Reactivity-Speed and Adaptiveness in Musical Symbols," *Psychiat.*, 1943, *6*, 117–22. His descriptive categories are intra-opus repetition, short and symmetrical themes, figurative background, simplicity of fugal form, regular chord progressions, rhythmic background, and correlative description.

50. R. W. Brown, R. A. Leiter, and D. C. Hildum, "Metaphors From Music Criticism," *J. Abn. Soc. Psychol.*, 1957, *54*, 347–52. The three descriptive categories these authors found are the same three usually seen whenever the semantic differential is employed.

51. R. I. Henkin, "A Factorial Study of the Components of Music," *J. Psychol.*, 1955, *39*, 161–81; "A Reevaluation of a Factorial Study of the Components of Music," *J. Psychol.*, 1957, *43*, 301–6.

52. R. V. Fay, "Tension and Development as Principles in Musical Composition," *J. Musicol.*, 1947, *5*, 1–12.

53. Actually only a portion of the Hevner list was presented.

54. G. O. Rogge, "Music as Communication, With Special Reference to Its Role as Content," Doctoral thesis, U.C.L.A., 1952, pp. 66–67.

55. *Ibid.*, p. 76.

56. A. Pepinsky, "The Contribution of the Frequency Factor to the Psychological State of Tension," *Music Teach. Nat. Assoc. Proc. 1939*, 1940, pp. 134–43.

57. M. J. Tyrrel, "Affective Reactions to Musical Variables," Thesis, U. of Utah, 1958.

58. D. N. Ferguson, *Music as Metaphor*, Minneapolis, U. of Minnesota Press, 1960.

59. Using an intuitional rather than a more typically scientific approach, the German psychologist Albert Wellek offers his views on the conditions under which titles, mottoes, and programs are appropriate to music. See his "The Relation Between Music and Poetry," *J. Aesth.*, 1962, *21*, 149–56.

60. R. H. Knapp and H. Ehlinger, "Stylistic Consistency Among Aesthetic Preferences," *J. Proj. Tech.*, 1962, *26*(1), 61–65.

61. R. Morey, "Upset in Emotions," *J. Soc. Psychol.*, 1940, *12*, 333–56.

62. T. F. Karwoski, H. S. Odbert, and C. E. Osgood, "Studies in Synesthetic Thinking: II. The Role of Form in Visual Responses to Music," *J. Gen. Psychol.*, 1942, *26*, 199–222; L. Omwake, "Visual Responses to Auditory Stimuli," *op. cit.*; H. S. Odbert, T. Karwoski, and A. B. Eckerson, "I. Musical and Verbal Associations of Color and Mood," *J. Gen. Psychol.*, 1942, *26*, 153–73.

63. J. T. Cowles, "Experimental Study of Pairing Certain Auditory and Visual Stimuli," *J. Exp. Psychol.*, 1935, *18*, 461–69; W. L. Wehner, "The Relation Between Six Paintings by Paul Klee and Selected Musical Compositions," *J. Res. Music Educ.*, 1966, *14*(3), 220–24. See also D. Offer and D. Stine, "Function of Music in Spontaneous Art Productions," *Arch. Gen. Psychiat.*, Nov. 1960, *3*(5), 490–503.

64. R. R. Willmann, "An Experimental Investigation of the Creative Process in Music," *Psychol. Monog.*, 1944, *57*(1).

65. A. Montani, "Psychoanalysis of Music," *Psychoanal. Rev.*, 1945, *32*, 225–27. See also S. S. Friedman, "One Aspect of the Structure of Music," *J. Amer. Psychoanal. Assoc.*, 1960, *8*, 427–49.

66. D. Mosonyi, "Die irrationalen Grundlagen der Musik," *Imago*, 1935, *21*, 207–26.

67. J. Schnier, "Restitution Aspects of the Creative Process," *Amer. Imago*, 1957, *14*, 211–23.

68. F. Hannett, "The Haunting Lyric," *Psychoanal. Quart.*, 1964, *33*(2), 226–69.

69. D. C. Beardslee and R. Fogelson, "Sex Differences in Sexual Imagery Aroused by Musical Stimulation," pp. 132–42 in J. W. Atkinson, Ed., *Motives in Fantasy, Action, and Society*, New York, Van Nostrand, 1958.

70. M. A. Wallach and C. Greenberg, "Personality Functions of Symbolic Sexual Arousal to Music," *Psychol. Monog.*, 1960, *74*(7), 1–18.
71. M. A. Wallach, "Two Correlates of Symbolic Sexual Arousal: Level of Anxiety and Liking for Esthetic Material," *J. Abn. Soc. Psychol.*, 1960, *61*, 396–401.
72. A. L. Sopchak, "Individual Differences in Responses to Music," *op. cit.*
73. I. M. Altshuler, "The Case of Horace F.," *Music Teach. Nat. Assoc. Proc. 1946*, 1946, pp. 368–81.
74. M. Tilly, "The Psychoanalytic Approach to the Masculine and Feminine Principles in Music," *Amer. J. Psychiat.*, 1947, *103*, 477–83.
75. P. R. Farnsworth, J. C. Trembley, and C. E. Dutton, "Masculinity and Femininity of Musical Phenomena," *J. Aesth.*, 1951, *9*, 257–62; C. H. Rittenhouse, "Masculinity and Femininity in Relation to Preferences in Music," Thesis, Stanford U., 1952; P. R. Farnsworth, "The Musical Taste of an American Musical Elite," *Hinrichsen Musical Year Book*, 1952, *7*, 112–16.
76. A cleverly written article on art and Freudianism is that by R. Arnheim, "Artistic Symbols—Freudian and Otherwise," *J. Aesth.*, 1953, *12*(1), 93–97. Other articles on the same general topic can be found in this same issue of the *Journal of Aesthetics and Art Criticism*. See also P. Noy, "The Psychodynamic Meaning of Music: IV. A Critical Review of the Psychoanalytic and Related Literature," *J. Music Therapy*, 1967, *4*(3), 81–94.
77. I. A. Berg, "Observations Concerning Obsessive Tunes in Normal Persons Under Stress," *J. Clin. Psychol.*, 1953, *9*, 300–302.
78. H. F. Olson and H. Belar, "Aid to Music Composition With a Random-Probability System," *Science*, 1961, *133*, 1368.
79. A good digest of some of the more important studies of the "emotional" character of music can be found in M. G. Rigg, "The Mood Effects of Music: A Comparison of Data From Four Investigators," *J. Psychol.*, 1964, *58*, 427–38.
80. A. R. Chandler, *Beauty and Human Nature*, New York, Appleton-Century, 1934, p. 213, by permission of the publisher.
81. M. G. Rigg, "The Autonomy of Music," *Music J.*, 1964, *22*(5), 84, 100.
82. Thus persons who possess tonal-visual associations which differ markedly from those of Walt Disney and his staff may have found his *Fantasia* extremely distasteful. See H. B. English, "*Fantasia* and the Psychology of Music," *J. Aesth.*, 1943, *7*, 27–31.
83. For musical analyses which purport to demonstrate that the meaning of music is not due entirely to associations, see D. Cooke, *The Language of Music*, London, Oxford U. Press, 1959.
84. The calling up of imagery is certainly not essential to the musical enjoyment of adults. Evidence is at hand that this generalization also holds true for children 10 to 14 years of age. See J. H. Higginson, "The Associational Aspect of Musical Response in School Children," *J. Educ. Psychol.*, 1936, *27*, 572–80.
85. See also F. Howes, *Music and Its Meanings*, London, Athlone Press, U. of London, 1958; and G. Epperson, *The Musical Symbol*, Ames, Iowa State U. Press, 1967. The latter gives a chronological account of theories in the area.

CHAPTER SIX

1. D. D. Runes, Ed., *The Dictionary of Philosophy*, New York, Philosophical Library, 1942.
2. A portion of the material in this and the following chapter is reprinted from the author's *Musical Taste: Its Measurement and Cultural Nature* with the permis-

sion of the publishers, Stanford University Press. Copyright 1950 by the Board of Trustees of Leland Stanford Junior University.

3. Mary M. (Mrs. Timothy) Richard, *Chinese Music*, Shanghai, Presbyterian Mission Press, 1923.

4. M. F. Meyer, *The Musician's Arithmetic*, Boston, Ditson, 1929, p. 109.

5. *Ibid.*, p. 81.

6. P. R. Farnsworth, "Aesthetic Behavior and Astrology," *Charact. & Pers.*, 1938, *6*, 335–40. For a report which attempts to uphold astrology see P. Field, *50 Thousand Birthdays*, La Selva Beach, Calif., Saratoga Publ. Co., 1962. The author of this little book sees similarities between composers and compositions which musicologists fail to see. Field's "research" is intuitional and lacks scholarship.

7. The reader who enjoys speculations based on physics and neurology is referred to the interesting articles by N. Rashevsky: "Suggestions for a Mathematical Biophysics of Auditory Perception With Special Reference to the Theory of Aesthetic Ratings of Combinations of Musical Tones," *Bull. Math. Biophys.*, 1942, *4*, 27–32, and "An Alternate Approach to the Mathematical Biophysics of Perception of Combinations of Musical Tones," *ibid.*, pp. 89–90.

8. See Ch. 4 of A. Einstein, *Greatness in Music*, New York, Oxford U. Press, 1941.

9. P. R. Farnsworth, "Musicologists Look to the Future," *Music J.*, 1965, *23*(7), 44, 46. For data on a 1951 study of musicological attitudes see the author's "The Musical Taste of an American Musical Elite," *Hinrichsen's Musical Year Book*, 1952, *7*, 112–16.

10. P. R. Farnsworth, "Stereotypes in the Field of Musical Eminence," *Genet. Psychol. Monog.*, 1941, *24*, 347–81; "Musical Eminence," *School and Society*, 1939, *50*, 158–60; "Musicological Attitudes on Eminence," *J. Res. Music Educ.*, 1966, *14*(1), 41–44.

11. Unless otherwise stated, it is to be assumed that wherever coefficients of correlation are mentioned the rank method was employed, and that the 92 names mentioned in the 1938 survey formed the list of items to be correlated.

12. H. de Jager, "Listening to the Audience," *J. Res. Music Educ.*, 1967, *15*(4), 293–99. The table reproduced in the text appears by courtesy of the author and the *J. Res. Music Educ.* Of interest to those with a reading knowledge of Dutch will be de Jager's *Cultuuroverdracht en Concertbezoek* (Leiden, Netherlands, Stenfert Kroese N.V., 1967) which has a 4½-page English summary.

13. J. H. Mueller, "The Aesthetic Gap Between Consumer and Composer," *J. Res. Music Educ.*, 1967, *15*(2), 151–58.

14. P. R. Farnsworth, "Musical Eminence and Year of Birth," *J. Aesth.*, 1945, *4*, 107–9.

15. When the birth years of a group of composers are arranged in order from most remote to most recent, the middle birth year is the *median*. That year which more than any other contains birth dates of composers is the *mode*.

16. Alfred Frankenstein, "What People Think They Should Think," *San Francisco Chronicle*, Feb. 2, 1941. During the spring of 1947 A. F. Michaelis, program manager of the (California) Standard Oil Company's "The Standard Hour," conducted a survey among the listeners to this regular NBC Sunday evening broadcast. The 8,000 who returned their questionnaires voted Beethoven the most popular composer. The next few in descending order of popular regard were Tchaikovsky, Gershwin, Chopin, Wagner, and Johann Strauss. The most frequently requested of all compositions was Gershwin's *Rhapsody in Blue*. Beethoven's *Fifth Symphony* came a close second, followed by Tchaikovsky's *Nutcracker Suite* and Chopin's *Polonaise Militaire*.

17. E. E. E. Folgmann, "An Experimental Study of Composer-Preference of Four Outstanding Symphony Orchestras," *J. Exp. Psychol.*, 1933, *16*, 709–24.

18. H. K. Mull, "Peferred Regions in Music Compositions and the Effect of Repetition Upon Them," *Amer. J. Psychol.*, 1940, *53*, 583–86; G. Märill and H. K. Mull, "A

Further Study of Preferred Regions in Musical Compositions and the Effect of Repetition Upon Them," *Amer. J. Psychol.*, 1942, *55*, 110–11.

19. W. S. Foster and M. A. Tinker, *Experiments in Psychology*, Rev. Ed., New York, Holt, 1929, p. 316.

20. C. W. Valentine, *The Experimental Psychology of Beauty*, London, Methuen, 1962, p. 210. This book is now available as a paperback (New York, Barnes & Noble, 1968).

21. P. R. Farnsworth, "Studies in the Psychology of Tone and Music," *Genet. Psychol. Monog.*, 1934, *15*(1), 24–30. See also O. W. Eagleson and L. E. Taylor, "A Study of Chord Preference in a Group of Negro Women," *J. Exp. Psychol.*, 1940, *26*, 619–21; and "The Preference of Twenty-five Negro College Women for Major and Minor Chords," *J. Exp. Psychol.*, 1941, *28*, 439–42.

22. P. R. Farnsworth, "An Historical, Critical, and Experimental Study of the Seashore-Kwalwasser Test Battery," *Genet. Psychol. Monog.*, 1931, *9*(5), 291–393.

23. P. R. Farnsworth, "Studies in the Psychology of Tone and Music," *Genet. Psychol. Monog.*, 1934, *15*(1), 50–84.

24. The subjects were asked to check all names they were certain they recognized. The scoring was the simple procedure of tabulating the number of votes each name received.

25. H. E. Johnson, *Symphony Hall, Boston*, Boston, Little, Brown & Co., 1950.

26. J. H. Mueller and Kate Hevner, "Trends in Musical Taste," *Indiana U. Publ.*, Humanities Ser., 1942, No. 8, p. 59. Reproduced by permission of the Indiana U. Press. See also J. H. Mueller, *The American Symphony Orchestra, a Social History of Musical Taste*, Bloomington, Indiana U. Press, 1951; and D. Nash, "The Construction of the Repertoire of a Symphony Orchestra," Thesis, U. of Washington, 1950.

27. These broadcast programs were obtained through the courtesy of R. R. Gros, an official of the company.

28. J. H. Mueller and Kate Hevner, *op. cit.*

29. J. H. Mueller, "Methods of Measurement of Aesthetic Folkways," *Amer. J. Sociol.*, 1946, *51*(4), 276–82. See also the more recent orchestral data in Ch. 4 of Mueller's *The American Symphony Orchestra, op. cit.* For data on social roles within the orchestra see M. Kaplan, "Telopractice: A Symphony Orchestra as It Prepares for a Concert," *Soc. Forces*, 1955, *33*, 352–55.

30. In the case of certain of the histories where the space technique could not be followed, the score was based on the relative number of page mentions the composer received.

31. J. H. Mueller and Kate Hevner, *op. cit.* Further data can be obtained in Mueller's article, "Methods of Measurement of Aesthetic Folkways," *op. cit.*

32. C. E. Seashore, *Psychology of Music*, New York, McGraw-Hill, 1938, p. 267. According to L. Vernon, pianists play at least half of their chords asynchronously ("Synchronization of Chords in Artistic Piano Music," *U. of Iowa Stud. Psychol. Music*, 1936, *4*, 306–45). See also W. H. Lichte, "One Man's Preferred Fifth," *Amer. J. Psychol.*, 1955, *68*, 312–15.

33. F. Howes, *The Borderland of Music and Psychology*, London, Kegan Paul, 1926.

34. E. H. Staffelbach, "The Psychology of Music Appreciation," *School Musician*, 1928, *29*, 9–13.

35. C. E. Seashore, *Why We Love Music*, Philadelphia, Ditson, 1941, p. 9.

36. M. A. Wallach, "Two Correlates of Symbolic Sexual Arousal: Level of Anxiety and Liking for Esthetic Material," *J. Abn. Soc. Psychol.*, 1960, *61*, 396–401.

37. M. J. Keston and I. M. Pinto, "Possible Factors Influencing Musical Preference," *J. Genet. Psychol.*, 1955, *86*, 101–13.

38. B. Mikol, "The Enjoyment of New Musical Systems," pp. 270–84 in *The Open and*

Closed Mind, M. Rokeach, Ed., New York, Basic Books, 1960. See also S. V. Zagona and M. A. Kelly, "The Resistance of the Closed Mind to a Novel and Complex Audio-Visual Experience," *J. Soc. Psychol.*, 1966. *70*(1), 123–31. This latter research also found the more dogmatic to be more hostile to unorthodox music, this time to a far-out jazz-film presentation.

39. R. R. Hornyak, "An Analysis of Student Attitudes Towards Contemporary American Music," *Counc. Res. Music Educ.*, 1966, *8*, 1–14.

40. C. W. Valentine, "The Aesthetic Appreciation of Musical Intervals Among Children and Adults," *Brit. J. Psychol.*, 1913, *6*, 190–216.

41. J. F. Dashiell, "Children's Sense of Harmonies in Colors and Tones," *J. Exp. Psychol.*, 1917, *2*, 466–75.

42. M. Aizawa, "The Musical Taste of School Children," *Tohoku Psychol. Folia*, 1938, *6*, 111–26.

43. T. W. Harrell, Factors Influencing Preference and Memory for Auditory Rhythm," *J. Gen. Psychol.*, 1937, *17*, 63–104.

44. I. Frischeisen-Kohler, "The Personal Tempo and Its Inheritance," *Charact. & Pers.*, 1933, *1*, 301–13.

45. J. P. Foley, Jr., "The Occupational Conditioning of Preferential Auditory Tempo," *J. Soc. Psychol.*, 1940, *12*, 121–29.

46. K. F. Schuessler, "Social Background and Musical Taste," *Amer. Sociol. Rev.*, 1948, *13*, 330–35. For a study of age, sex, regional, educational, and urban-rural differences in the preference for popular music during 1942, see J. G. Peatman, "Radio and Popular Music," in *Radio Research 1942–43*, P. F. Lazarsfeld and F. Stanton, Eds., New York, Duell, Sloan and Pearce, 1944.

47. K. M. Miller and M. A. Nicol, "Occupational Status, Sex and Age as Factors in Radio Programme Choice," *U. Tasmania Dept. Psychol.*, 1958, Publ. No. 1.

48. J. Johnstone and E. Katz, "Youth and Popular Music: A Study of the Sociology of Taste," *Amer. J. Sociol.*, 1957, *62*, 563–68. An interesting review of studies on cultural (school) transmission of musical taste, written by the Dutch sociologist H. de Jager, appears in "Musical Socialization and the Schools," *Music Educators J.*, 1967, *53*(6), 1–8.

49. V. R. Rogers, "Children's Musical Preferences," *El. Sch. J.*, 1957, *57*, 433–35.

50. V. H. Baumann, "Teen-age Music Preferences," *J. Res. Music Educ.*, 1960, *8*(2), 75–84. See also D. T. Kelly, "A Study of the Musical Preferences of a Select Group of Adolescents," *J. Res. Music Educ.*, 1961, *9*(2), 118–24; B. Reimer, "Effects of Music Education: Implications From a Review of Research," *J. Res. Music Educ.*, 1965, *13*(3), 147–58; G. L. Duerksen, "A Study of the Relationship Between the Perception of Musical Processes and the Enjoyment of Music," *Counc. Res. Music Educ.*, 1968, *12*, 1–8.

51. N. L. Gerren, "A Study of the Relationship Between Intelligence, Musicality, and Attitude Toward Music," Dissertation, U. of Kansas, 1953.

52. N. Erneston, "A Study To Determine the Effect of Musical Experience and Mental Ability on the Formulation of Musical Taste," Dissertation, Florida State U., 1961.

53. R. H. Wheeler, "Climate and Human Behavior," in P. L. Harriman, Ed., *The Encyclopedia of Psychology*, New York, Philosophical Library, 1946, pp. 78–86; R. H. Wheeler and T. Gaston, "The History of Music in Relation to Climatic and Cultural Fluctuations," in *Music Teach. Nat. Assoc. Proc. 1940*, 1941, pp. 432–38.

54. An example of a governmental determination of taste can be seen in the official "advice" given a number of the leading composers of the USSR, Feb. 10, 1948. Translations of the governmental pronouncement and the composers' answering statements appear in the American Russian Institute's pamphlet, *On Soviet Music*, published in May 1948 in Hollywood.

55. The task of an officially constituted committee on musical standards is made easier by the tendency of the masses to accept what the "experts" claim is "good music."

For an experiment on the effect of expert opinion on musical taste see H. T. Moore, "The Comparative Influence of Majority and Expert Opinion," *Amer. J. Psychol.*, 1921, *32*, 16-20.

56. M. J. Keston and I. M. Pinto, "Possible Factors Influencing Musical Preferences," *J. Genet. Psychol.*, 1955, *86*, 101-13.

57. L. E. Tyler, "An Exploratory Study of Discrimination of Composer Style," *J. Gen. Psychol.*, 1946, *34*, 153-63.

58. C. L. Stone, "Identification of Nationality in Music," *Psychol. Bull.*, 1937, *35*, 756.

59. J. Stone, "War Music and War Psychology in the Civil War," *J. Abn. Soc. Psychol.*, 1941, *36*, 543-60.

60. W. Robinson, "War Songs of America," in *Writers Congress, Proceedings*, Berkeley, U. of Calif. Press, 1944, pp. 284-304.

61. P. A. Gardner and R. W. Pickford, "Relation Between Dissonance and Context," *Nature* (London), 1944, *154*, 274-75. For a study of the effects on appreciation of playing Bach and jazz in the same program, see G. D. Williams, "The Effect of Order of Appearance on the Appreciation of Musical Selections," *J. Gen. Psychol.*, 1942, *27*, 295-310.

62. L. Wynn-Jones, paper in *8th Intern. Congr. of Psychol.*, Groningen, Neth., 1926. See also S. D. Koh, "Time-error in Comparisons of Preferences for Musical Excerpts," *Amer. J. Psychol.*, 1967, *80*(2), 171-85.

63. G. Wiebe, "The Effect of Radio Plugging on Students' Opinions of Popular Songs," *J. Appl. Psychol.*, 1940, *24*, 721-27.

64. E. A. Suchman, "Invitation to Music: A Study of the Creation of New Music Listeners by the Radio," in *Radio Research 1941*, P. F. Lazarsfeld and F. Stanton, Eds., New York, Duell, Sloan and Pearce, 1941.

65. For an experiment on the effectiveness of program notes see G. D. Williams, "The Effect of Program Notes on the Enjoyment of Musical Selections," *J. Gen. Psychol.*, 1943, *29*, 261-79.

66. R. W. Yingling, "Classification of Reaction Patterns in Listening to Music," *J. Res. Music Educ.*, 1962, *10*, 105-20.

67. H. T. Moore, "The Genetic Aspect of Consonance and Dissonance," *Psychol. Monog.*, 1914, *17*, 1-68; M. F. Washburn *et al.*, "The Effects of Immediate Repetition on the Pleasantness or Unpleasantness of Music, in *The Effects of Music*, New York, Harcourt, Brace, 1927, Ch. 10; A. R. Gilliland and H. T. Moore, "The Immediate and Long-time Effects of Classical and Popular Phonograph Selections," *J. Appl. Psychol.*, 1924, *8*, 309-23; H. E. Krugman, "Affective Response to Music as a Function of Familiarity," *J. Abn. Soc. Psychol.*, 1943, *38*, 388-92; J. E. Downey and G. E. Knapp, "The Effect on a Musical Programme of Familiarity and of Sequence of Selections," in *"The Effects of Music, op. cit.*, Ch. 12; H. K. Mull, "The Effect of Repetition Upon the Enjoyment of Modern Music," *J. Psychol.*, 1957, *43*, 155-62; R. P. Getz, "The Effects of Repetition on Listening Response," *J. Res. Music Educ.*, 1966, *14*(3), 178-92; L. R. Lieberman and W. M. Walters, Jr., "Effects of Repeated Listening on Connotative Meaning of Serious Music," *Percept. Mot. Skills*, 1968, *26*(3, Pt. 1), 891-95.

68. E. M. Verveer *et al.*, "Change in Affectivity With Repetition," *Amer. J. Psychol.*, 1933, *45*, 130-34.

69. H. K. Mull, "Preferred Regions in Musical Compositions and the Effect of Repetition Upon Them," *op. cit.*, pp. 583-86. For further data on the gradient conception as it applies to music, see G. H. S. Razran, "Studies in Configurational Conditioning. VII: Ratios and Elements in Salivary Conditioning to Various Musical Intervals," *Psychol. Rec.*, 1938, *2*, 370-76.

70. L. B. Meyer, "On Rehearing Music," *J. Amer. Musicol. Soc.*, 1960, *14*(2), 257-67.

71. G. A. Marco, "Communication to Editor," *J. Amer. Musicol. Soc.*, 1962, *15*, 115-16.

72. R. W. Haber, "Discrepancy From Adaptation Level as a Source of Affect," *J. Exp.*

Psychol., 1958, *56*, 370–75; H. Helson, *Adaptation Level Theory*, New York, Harper & Row, 1964. See also C. R. Simon and J. F. Wohlwill, "An Experimental Study of the Role of Expectation and Variation in Music," *J. Res. Music Educ.*, 1968, *16*(3), 227–38.

73. This suggestion is supported by a study by H. F. Olson, "Frequency Range Preference for Speech and Music," *J. Acoust. Soc. Amer.*, 1947, *19*, 549–55, who found that when an all-acoustic filter was placed between sound and audience the preference was for a full frequency range.

74. H. A. Chinn and P. Eisenberg, "Tonal Range and Sound-Intensity Preferences of Broadcast Listeners," *Inst. Radio Eng., Proc.*, 1945, *33*, 571–81.

75. "The New Sound," *Time*, 1955, *66*(26), 40. For research on the relation of spatial capabilities and the perception of music, see E. A. Lippman, "Spatial Perception and Physical Location as Factors in Music," *Acta Musicol.*, Basel, 1963, *35*(1), 24–34.

76. M. Schoen, "The Aesthetic Attitude in Music," *Psychol. Monog.*, 1928, *39*, 162–84. See also P. E. Vernon, "The Phenomena of Attention and Visualization in the Psychology of Musical Appreciation," *Brit. J. Psychol.*, 1930, *21*, 50–63.

77. C. S. Myers, "Individual Differences in Listening to Music," *Brit. J. Psychol.*, 1922, *13*, 52–71.

78. O. Ortmann, "The Sensorial Basis of Music Appreciation," *J. Comp. Psychol.*, 1922, *2*, 227–56.

79. For a criticism of aesthetic response typologies see R. A. M. Gregson, "Aspects of the Theoretical Status of Aesthetic Response Typologies," *Psychol. Rept.*, 1964, *13*(1), 3–10. Gregson prefers a learning model for aesthetic choices. For a discussion of the idea that satisfaction may be secured from music in a variety of ways—from melody, rhythm, and harmony, as well as from ideas and imagery—see J. P. Jensen, "Different Modes of Music-Aesthetic Experiences," *Nord. Psykol.*, 1965, *17* (7), 455–63.

80. J. B. Eggen, "A Behavioristic Interpretation of Jazz,' *Psychol. Rev.*, 1926, *33*, 571–81.

81. G. Rubin-Rabson, "The Influence of Age, Intelligence, and Training on Reactions to Classic and Modern Music," *J. Gen. Psychol.*, 1940, *22*, 413–29; E. G. Plotkin, "An Experimental Study of the Factors Involved in the Appreciation of Standard Music," Thesis, Columbia U., 1931; M. J. Keston, "An Experimental Evaluation of the Efficiency of Two Methods of Teaching Music Appreciation," *J. Exp. Educ.*, 1954, *22*, 215–26. For an experiment on increasing tolerance with age see P. R. Farnsworth, "Changes in Musical Taste," *J. Musicol.*, 1939, *1*, 1–4.

82. R. L. Fisher, "Preferences of Different Age and Socio-economic Groups in Unstructured Musical Situations," *J. Soc. Psychol.*, 1951, *33*, 147–52.

83. At the time this book went to press one could find in the daily press occasional statements from users of hallucinatory drugs to the effect that their "trips" had markedly improved their musical taste. But just what are these persons implying? Are they saying that after the ingestion of the drug they thrill more to music? Do they believe that the drug somehow engenders new ideas that tell them what music is best? It could be of course that the claim of improvement in taste is but a cover, a rationalization for a desire to use the drug. The only recent research the author has come upon would suggest that those in psilocybin-induced states are in no condition to judge music. They appear rather to suffer losses in ability to grasp music as it is; e.g., tones may seem lengthened, tempos may appear reduced. See K. Weber, "Veränderungen des Musikerlebens in der experimentellen Psychose (psilocybin)," *Confinia Psychiatrica*, 1967, *10*(3–4), 139–76.

CHAPTER SEVEN

1. Hungerland has reviewed the problem of aesthetic standards in the field of painting and has offered a relativistic view which is consonant with that expressed throughout this book. See Helmut Hungerland, "Suggestions for Procedure in Art Criticism," *J. Aesth.*, 1947, *5*(3), 189–95. A slightly more recent rejection of the absolutistic position can be seen in T. Munro, "The Concept of Beauty in the Philosophy of Naturalism," *Rev. Intern. Phil.*, 1955, *31*, 1–43.

2. The page-mention method can be considered as a variety of the measure of space allocations.

3. C. E. Seashore, *Manual of Instructions and Interpretations for Measures of Musical Talent*, New York, Columbia Graphophone, 1919.

4. The reliability of a test is its degree of self-consistency, the extent to which it is uninfluenced by factors intrinsic to or associated with it. For most purposes a reasonable reliability is one in the high .80's or low .90's. As a test is lengthened (but not so much as to induce boredom or fatigue) it tends to become more reliable.

5. J. Kwalwasser, *Tests and Measurements in Music*, Boston, Birchard, 1927, p. 26.

6. J. Kwalwasser and P. W. Dykema, *Manual of Directions, K-D Tests*, New York, Fischer, 1930, p. 18.

7. The authors realize that a 10-item test tends to have poor reliability and suggest a repetition under conditions such that the subjects are deceived into believing they are hearing a 20-item test. But even with 20 items the test is quite unreliable. J. A. Holmes has improved the reliability a bit by changing the answer choices to read "*A* better," "*B* better," and "equally good." See J. A. Holmes, "Increased Reliabilities, New Keys, and Norms for a Modified Kwalwasser-Dykema Test of Musical Aptitudes," *J. Genet. Psychol.*, 1954, *85*, 65–73.

8. Holmes has also raised the reliability of this test by changing the answer choices to "up," "down," and "same as last note actually heard."

9. S. A. Courtis, *Courtis Standard Research Tests, Series M, Music*, Detroit, S. A. Courtis, 1922, p. 5. Before the days of formal psychological tests an even earlier attempt to study music moods was that by B. J. Gilman, "Report on an Experimental Test of Musical Expressiveness," *Amer. J. Psychol.*, 1892, *4*, 42–83; 1893, *5*, 558–87.

10. E. J. Schultz, "Testing Listening Power in Music," *Music Supervisors Nat. Conf. Yearbook*, 1933, pp. 306–12.

11. S. K. Gernet, *Musical Discrimination at Various Age and Grade Levels*, College Place, Wash., College Press, 1940.

12. L. B. Bower, "A Factor Analysis of Music Tests," Thesis, Catholic U., 1945.

13. M. J. Keston and I. M. Pinto, "Possible Factors Influencing Musical Preference," *J. Genet. Psychol.*, 1955, *86*, 101–13.

14. W. M. Lifton, *A Pilot Study of the Relationship of Empathy to Aesthetic Sensitivity*, Urbana, Bureau of Educational Research, U. of Illinois, 1956.

15. N. Erneston, "A Study To Determine the Effect of Musical Experience and Mental Ability on the Formulation of Musical Taste," Dissertation, Florida State U., 1961.

16. G. H. Kyme, "Are Musical Tastes Indicative of Musical Capacity?" *J. Res. Music Educ.* 1956, *4*(1), 44–51.

17. M. J. Adler, "Music Appreciation: An Experimental Approach to Its Measurement," *Arch. Psychol.*, 1929, *17*(110), 1–102. In a far more recent study it has been shown that deforming a tune completely destroys it for some young children while others simply fail to notice the deformations (M. Pflederer and L. Sechrest. "Conservation-type Responses of Children to Musical Stimuli," *Counc. Res. Music Educ.*, 1968, *13*, 19–36.

18. M. R. Trabue, "Scales for Measuring Judgment of Orchestral Music," *J. Educ. Psychol.*, 1923, *14*, 545–61.

19. B. Semeonoff, "A New Approach to the Testing of Musical Ability," *Brit. J. Psychol.*, 1940, *30*, 326–40; "Further Developments in a New Approach to the Testing of Musical Ability, With Special Reference to Groups of Secondary School Children," *Brit. J. Psychol.*, 1940, *31*, 145–61.

20. R. B. Cattell and D. R. Saunders, "Music Preferences and Personality Diagnosis," *J. Soc. Psychol.*, 1954, *39*, 3–24; R. B. Cattell and J. C. Anderson, "The Measurement of Personality and Behavior Disorders by the I.P.A.T. Music Preference Test," *J. Appl. Psychol.*, 1953, *37*, 446–54; C. Butsch and H. Fischer, "Der 'Music Preference Test' im entwicklungs-psychologischen Verlauf," *Schweiz. Z. Psych. Anwend.*, 1961, *20*, 317–28.

21. C. Schultz, "The Reliability of Music Preference Under Varying Mood Conditions," Thesis, Fairleigh-Dickinson U., 1962.

22. John H. Mueller *et al.*, "Studies in Appreciation of Art," *U. Oregon Publ.*, 1934, *4*(6), 115–30; N. H. Long, "A Revision of the U. of Oregon Music Discrimination Test," Thesis, Indiana U., 1965.

23. John H. Mueller *et al.*, *op. cit.*, pp. 131–37. A preliminary form of a new *Battery of Musical Concept Measures*, intended for the 4th grade, is now available. One finding of considerable interest is the fact that subjects who can report stimulus changes orally may or may not be able to demonstrate the changes by overt movement, and vice versa (F. M. Andrews and N. C. Deihl, "Development of a Technique for Identifying Elementary School Children's Musical Concepts," *Counc. Res. Music Educ.*, 1968, *13*, 1–7).

24. J. Hoffren, "The Construction and Validation of a Test of Expressive Phrasing in Music," *J. Res. Music Educ.*, 1964, *12*(2), 159–64.

25. H. Wing, "Tests of Musical Ability and Appreciation," *Brit. J. Psychol., Monog. Suppl.*, 1948, No. 27; "A Revision of the Wing Musical Aptitude Test," *J. Res. Music Educ.*, 1962, *10*, 39–46.

26. M. Schoen, "Tests of Musical Feeling and Musical Understanding," *J. Comp. Psychol.*, 1925, *5*, 31–52.

27. H. Lowery, "Cadence and Phrase Tests in Music," *Brit. J. Psychol.*, 1926, *17*, 117–18.

28. R. M. Drake, "Four New Tests of Musical Talent," *J. Appl. Psychol.*, 1933, *17*, 136–47; *Drake Musical Aptitude Tests*, Chicago, Science Research Associates, 1954.

29. The difference between a test of taste and one of musical "capacity" is sometimes slight. See Ch. 9 for a discussion of the latter type of measure.

30. J. Kwalwasser, *Tests and Measurements in Music, op. cit.*, pp. 90–98.

31. M. Young, "A Study of the Kwalwasser Test of Music Information and Appreciation, and the Construction for This Field of a More Reliable and Advanced Test," Master's thesis, Stanford U., 1932.

32. B. Semeonoff, *op. cit.*

33. P. E. Vernon, "A Method for Measuring Musical Taste," *J. Appl. Psychol.*, 1930, *14*, 355–62.

34. John H. Mueller *et al.*, *op. cit.*, pp. 138–42.

35. P. R. Farnsworth, "Has the Status of Music Changed in 30 Years?" *J. Psychol.*, 1963, *56*, 269–72.

36. P. R. Farnsworth, "New Weights for the Seashore-Hevner 'Tests for Attitude Toward Music,'" *Rev. Psychol. Music*, 1964, Issue No. 3, pp. 1–6.

37. P. R. Farnsworth, "Rating Scales for Musical Interests," *J. Psychol.*, 1949, *28*, 245–53. Even simpler rating scales have been developed for interest in music, happiness with music, relaxation while listening to music, desire to remain quiet while listening to music, confusion with music, and arousal of mental pictures by music. See

L. Crickmore, "An Approach to the Measurement of Music Appreciation (I)," *J. Res. Music Educ.*, 1968, *16*(3), 239–53.

38. P. R. Farnsworth, "Agreement With the Judgments of Musicologists as a Measure of Musical Taste," *J. Psychol.*, 1949, *28*, 421–25.

39. Q. McNemar, "Opinion-Attitude Methodolgy," *Psychol. Bull.*, 1946, *43*, 289–374.

40. For extremely interesting program analyses which are too technical (in a mathematical sense) for review here, see G. K. Zipf, "On the Dynamic Structure of Concert-programs," *J. Abn. Soc. Psychol.*, 1946, *41*, 25–36.

41. Because of the peculiar arrangement of the Haggin book, it proved necessary to employ the page-mention technique.

42. J. McKeen Cattell, "A Statistical Study of Eminent Men," *Pop. Sci. Monthly*, 1903, *62*, 359–77. Apparently Cattell's data were gathered many years before they were published.

43. Under the direction of R. S. Tangeman of the University of Indiana, space measurements have been taken from five sets of general-interest encyclopedias, each written in a different language. It is worth noting that Rossini was given the second largest amount of space in *Enciclopedia Italiana*. He achieved eighth place in *Enciclopedia Universal* (Spanish), a rank of 8.5 in *Larousse du XX*ᵉ *Siècle*, a rank of 18 in the *Encyclopaedia Britannica*, and one of 22.5 in *Meyers Lexikon*. G. H. Stempel, who has reported these studies, has found that in the *Encyclopedia Americana* Rossini was seventh in space allocation. (Note that this allocation is completely out of line with what Rossini is given in other English-language encyclopedias.) When Stempel combined his data with those of Tangeman, Rossini's placement was seventh. From these data comes the hint that Rossini may be regarded far more favorably in Italy and Spain than in Germany and the Anglo-Saxon countries (G. H. Stempel, "C Sharp Minor," *Bloomington [Ind.] Star*, Aug. 6, 1943).

44. P. R. Farnsworth, "Elite Attitudes in Music as Measured by the Cattell Space Method," *J. Res. Music Educ.*, 1962, *10*, 65–67; "Attitudes Toward Composers as Reflected in Three General Encyclopedias of the Early 1960's," *J. Res. Music Educ.*, 1963, *11*, 142–43; "The Limitations of Cattell's Space Method of Studying Eminence," *J. Psychol.*, 1957, *44*, 169–73.

45. It can be taken as axiomatic that the greater the variability in the lengths of the encyclopedia articles, the more exact will be the differences in eminence that can be expressed. If it is found that the largest encyclopedias possess articles with the greatest range in length, it would seem to follow that these massive treatises can supply the most adequate material for work on eminence. Support for this possibility can be seen in the *rho* of .54 which obtains between the sizes of the encyclopedias and the spread in the length of the articles.

46. From most to least boring these compositions were said to be: Rimsky-Korsakov's *Scheherezade*, César Franck's *Symphony in D Minor*, Ravel's *Bolero*, Wagner's *Parsifal*, Beethoven's *Missa Solemnis*, Brahms's *German Requiem*, Dvořák's *New World Symphony*, Beethoven's *Ninth Symphony*, Wagner's *Tristan und Isolde*, Tchaikovsky's *Fifth Symphony*.

47. *San Francisco Chronicle*, Apr. 4, 1954.

48. In numerous public addresses the contemporary German composer Stockhausen has maintained that boredom has an important place in music. It would seem difficult to disagree with him on this point, for surely under skillful hands the introduction of occasional periods of boredom may well enhance interest. Where there is disagreement it will likely concern the size and placement of the boring passages.

49. See the Broadcast Music Inc.'s annual program analyses of 417 U.S. and Canadian orchestras.

CHAPTER EIGHT

1. R. M. Drake, "Factorial Analysis of Music Tests by the Spearman Tetrad-difference Technique," *J. Musicol.*, 1939, *1*, 6–16. Over the years Drake has convinced himself that his early conclusions were in error. He now feels that there are two important facets to musical ability—music memory and rhythmic ability. See *Drake Music Aptitude Tests*, Chicago, Science Research Associates, 1954.

2. H. D. Wing, "A Factorial Study of Musical Tests," *Brit. J. Psychol.*, 1941, *31*, 341–55.

3. J. McLeish in *The Fourth Mental Measurements Yearbook*, New Brunswick, N.J., Rutgers U. Press, 1953.

4. P. Vernon, *The Structure of Human Abilities*, New York, Wiley, 1950, p. 93.

5. C. W. Manzer and S. Marowitz, "The Performance of a Group of College Students on the Kwalwasser-Dykema Music Tests," *J. Appl. Psychol.*, 1935, *19*, 331–46.

6. E. Franklin, *Tonality as a Basis for the Study of Musical Talent*, Göteborg, Sweden, Gumperts Förlag, 1956.

7. G. E. R. Burroughs and J. N. Morris, "Factors Involved in Learning a Simple Musical Theme," *Brit. J. Educ. Psychol.*, 1962, *32*, 18–28.

8. J. E. Karlin, "A Factorial Study of Auditory Function," *Psychometrika*, 1942, *7*, 251–79; "Factor Analysis in the Field of Music," *J. Musicol.*, 1941, *3*, 41–52.

9. L. B. Bower, "A Factor Analysis of Music Tests," Thesis, Catholic U., 1945.

10. R. S. Morrow, "An Analysis of the Relations Among Tests of Musical, Artistic, and Mechanical Abilities," *J. Psychol.*, 1938, *5*, 253–63.

11. E. K. Strong, Jr., *Manual for Vocational Interest Blanks for Men and Women*, Palo Alto, Calif., Consulting Psychologists Press, 1969. Now available is a "basic music interest" scale.

12. R. K. White, "The Versatility of Genius," *J. Soc. Psychol.*, 1931, *2*, 460–89.

13. E. D. Williams, L. Winter, and J. M. Woods, "Tests of Literary Appreciation, *Brit. J. Educ. Psychol.*, 1938, *8*, 265–84; E. D. Williams, "The General Aesthetic Factor II (Reply)," *Brit. J. Stat. Psychol.*, 1960, *13*, 88–90; C. Burt, "The General Aesthetic Factor III," *Brit. J. Stat. Psychol.*, 1960, *13*, 90–92; E. D. Williams and C. Burt, "The General Aesthetic Factor (Reply)," *Brit. J. Stat. Psychol.*, 1961, *14*, 75–77.

14. C. R. Paterson, "The General Aesthetic Factor I," *Brit. J. Stat. Psychol.*, 1960, *13*, 87–88; R. A. M. Gregson, "The General Aesthetic Factor I," *Brit. J. Stat. Psychol.*, 1961, *14*, 72–74.

15. C. Alexander, "The Longevity of Scientists," *J. Soc. Psychol.*, 1954, *39*, 299–302.

16. M. Schoen, *The Psychology of Music*, New York, Ronald Press, 1940.

17. C. Cox, *Genetic Studies of Genius*, Vol. 2, Stanford, Calif., Stanford U. Press, 1926.

18. C. F. Lehman, "A Study of Musically Superior and Inferior Subjects as Selected by the Kwalwasser-Dykema Music Tests," *J. Educ. Res.*, 1952, *45*, 517–22; R. Colwell, "An Investigation of Musical Achievement Among Vocal Students, Vocal-Instrumental Students, and Instrumental Students," *J. Res. Music Educ.*, 1963, *11*, 123–30.

19. R. W. Lundin, "The Development and Validation of a Set of Musical Ability Tests," *Psychol. Monog.*, 1949, *63*(10). For a resume of the studies in this area see J. L. Mursell, "Intelligence and Musicality," *Education*, 1939, *59*, 559–62. A more recent study using the Seashore battery, a series of intelligence tests, and a factor analysis technique claims to show a "close relationship" between musical aptitude and general intelligence. Unfortunately for the authors' theory, the subjects ranged in age from 10 to 15 years, a fact that would in itself elicit a sizable correlation between almost any two tests (H. Fischer and C. Butsch, "Musikalische Begabung und Intelligenz," *Z. f. exp. Angew. Psychol.*, 1961, *8*, 508–18).

20. L. S. Hollingworth, "The Musical Sensitivity of Children Who Test Above 135 I.Q.," *J. Educ. Psychol.*, 1926, *17*, 95–109.

21. E. Ehrsam, "Über den Fall einer einseitigen musikalischen Begabung eines blinden Kindes bei hochgradigen Leistungsrückstand," *Psychiat. Neurol. Med. Psychol.*, *Leipzig*, 1955, *7*, 149–54.

22. D. C. Rife and L. H. Snyder, "Studies in Human Inheritance," *Human Biol.*, 1931, *3*, 547–59. See also W. A. Owens and W. Grimm, "A Note Regarding Exceptional Musical Ability in a Low-grade Imbecile," *J. Educ. Psychol.*, 1941, *32*, 636–37.

23. A. Anastasi and R. F. Levee, "Intellectual Defect and Musical Talent: A Case Report," *Amer. J. Ment. Defic.*, 1960, *64*(4), 695–703.

24. IQ data from high schools sometimes show music students to be brighter than average. Of course this finding could conceivably mean that music students per se have higher than average IQs. More plausible is the hypothesis that the surveys were selective and that this superiority is not the rule (D. K. Antrim, "Do Musical Talents Have Higher Intelligence?" *Etude*, 1945, *63*, 127–28).

25. R. Moore, "The Relationship of Intelligence to Creativity," *J. Res. Music Educ.*, 1966, *14*(4), 243–53. Attention should also be called to the claim that it is not academic intelligence per se to which musical ability is related but rather mathematical ability. To check on this persistent belief, G. Révész has surveyed both mathematicians and musicians and has found no unduly large number of musical mathematicians or mathematically minded musicians *(Introduction to the Psychology of Music*, Norman, U. of Oklahoma Press, 1954; "Beziehung zwischen mathematischer und musikalischer Begabung," *Schweiz. Z. Psychol. Anwend.*, 1946, *5*, 269–81).

26. G. Révész, *The Psychology of a Musical Prodigy*, New York, Harcourt Brace, 1925. See also C. Stumpf, "Akustische Versuche mit Pepito Areola," *Z. f. Angew. Psychol.*, 1909, *2*, 1–11; F. Baumgarten, "Der Werdegang eines Wunderkindes," *Z. f. Angew. Psychol.*, 1932, *41*, 473–98. It is of interest that there have been virtually no child prodigies in 'cello, clarinet, flute, or voice, and but few in composition. A fairly recent style is for prodigy conductors. In the past the most fertile areas for prodigies were violin and piano. See N. Slonimsky, "Musical Children, Prodigies or Monsters?" *Etude*, 1948, *66*, 591–92.

27. R. Updegraff, L. Heiliger, and J. Learned, "The Effect of Training Upon the Singing Ability and Musical Interest of Three-, Four-, and Five-year-old Children," *U. of Iowa Stud. Child Welf.*, 1938, *14*, 83–131; A. T. Jersild and S. Bienstock, "A Study of the Development of Children's Ability To Sing," *J. Educ. Psychol.*, 1934, *25*, 481–503; M. S. Hattwick and H. M. Williams, "The Measurement of Musical Development, II," *U. of Iowa Stud. Child Welf.*, 1935, *11*, 1–100; G. E. Moorhead and D. Pond, "Music of Young Children," *Pillsbury Found. Stud.*, 1941, 1942; E. N. Drexler, "A Study of the Development of the Ability To Carry a Melody at the Preschool Level," *Child Develpm.*, 1938, *9*, 319–32.

28. H. Christianson, *Bodily Rhythmic Movements of Young Children in Relation to Rhythm in Music*, Teach. Coll. Contrib. Educ., No. 736, New York, Teachers Coll., Columbia U., 1938; A. T. Jersild and S. Bienstock, "Development of Rhythm in Young Children," *Child Develpm. Monog.*, 1935, *22*.

29. R. F. Wyatt, "Improvability of Pitch Discrimination," *Psychol. Monog.*, 1945, *58* (2); A. A. Capurso, "The Effect of an Associative Technique in Teaching Pitch and Interval Discrimination," *J. Appl. Psychol.*, 1934, *18*, 811–18; E. Connette, "The Effect of Practice With Knowledge of Results," *J. Educ. Psychol.*, 1941, *32*, 523–32; M. Wolner and W. H. Pyle, "An Experiment in Individual Training in Pitch-Deficient Children," *J. Educ. Psychol.*, 1933, *24*, 602–8; G. M. Whipple, "Studies in Pitch Discrimination," *Amer. J. Psychol.*, 1903, *14*, 289–309; R. H. Seashore, "Improvability of Pitch Discrimination," *Psychol. Bull.*, 1935, *32*, 546. For

training data on other music abilities see G. M. Gilbert, "Sex Differences in Musical Aptitude and Training," *J. Gen. Psychol.*, 1942, *26*, 19–33.

30. C. E. Seashore, *Psychology of Music*, New York, McGraw-Hill, 1938, p. 57.

31. See L. S. Hollingworth, *op. cit.*

32. H. Koch and F. Mjön, "Die Erblichkeit der Musikalität," *Z. f. Psychol.*, 1931, *121*, 104–36; H. Stanton, "The Inheritance of Specific Musical Capacities," *Psychol. Monog.*, 1922, *31*, 157–204; V. Haecker and T. Ziehen, "Beitrag zur Lehre von der Vererbung u.s.w.," *Z. f. Psychol.*, 1931, *121*, 1–103; R. S. Friend, "Influences of Heredity and Musical Environment on the Scores of Kindergarten Children on the Seashore Measures of Musical Ability," *J. Appl. Psychol.*, 1939, *23*, 347–57; A. Scheinfeld, *You and Heredity*, New York, Stokes, 1939.

33. J. Mjön, "Zur Erbanalyse der musikalischen Begabung," *Hereditas*, 1926, *7*, 109–28; G. Voss, "Die Familie G.," *Deut. Z. f. Nervenhk.*, 1925, *83*, 249–63. The fact that identical twins score more similarly on music tests than fraternal twins can be interpreted as favoring either the nature or nurture hypothesis. See the nature side espoused by R. P. G. Shuter, "An Investigation of Hereditary and Environmental Factors in Musical Ability," Thesis, U. of London, 1964.

34. C. Terry, *The Origin of the Family of Bach Musicians*, London, Oxford U. Press, 1929; K. Geiringer, *The Bach Family*, New York, Oxford U. Press, 1954.

35. In the category of folktales is the belief that music ability arises through being born at an astrologically propitious time. There is one folktale which says that musicians do not enjoy normal longevity and another which states that they live beyond their "proper" span. These notions, however, have been disproved by the insurance statisticians who find the lives of musicians to be of normal length. See W. Schweisheimer, "Do Musicians Live Longer Than Others?" *Etude*, 1949, *67*, 54–55; A. H. Whittaker, "Occupational Diseases of Musicians," in *Music and Medicine*, D. M. Schullian and M. Schoen, Eds., New York, Schuman, 1948. Note, however, that musicians enjoy less longevity than educators, whose life-span is above average. One study showed the blood pressure of musicians to be slightly lower than that of nonmusicians but the difference was not statistically significant (L. F. Sunderman, "A Study of Some Physiological Differences Between Musicians and Non-Musicians: I. Blood-pressure," *J. Soc. Psychol.*, 1946, *23*, 205–15).

36. C. J. Lamp and N. Keys, "Can Aptitude for Specific Musical Instruments Be Predicted?" *J. Educ. Psychol.*, 1935, *26*, 587–96.

37. J. H. Taylor, "The Relation Between Finger Length, Hand Width and Musical Ability," *J. Appl. Psychol.*, 1936, *20*, 347–52.

38. S. Graf, "Measurements of Hand Length, Muscular Control, and Motility Related to Handedness," Master's thesis, Syracuse U., 1952.

39. E. Bauer, E. Fischer, and F. Lenz, *Human Heredity*, New York, Macmillan, 1931; R. Breithaupt, "Pianistic Talent and Race," *Etude*, 1924, *42*, 455–56; E. Kretschmer, *The Psychology of Men of Genius*, New York, Harcourt, Brace, 1931. A typical racist generalization is that of S. Günther. Western music, says he, is better integrated than that of the Dinaric people but lacks the empathic or emotional potential of the latter ("Rassenseelenkundliche Beiträge zur musikalischen Stilforschung," *Arch. Musikforsch.*, 1938, *3*, 385–427). E. Rittershaus maintains that most creative musicians of the nineteenth century had Nordic features ("Die Vererbung musikalischer Eigenschaften," *Arch. Rass.- u. Ges.-Biol.*, 1935, *29*, 132–52).

40. R. Braine, "The Making of a Virtuoso Violinist," *Etude*, 1925, *43*, 157–58. Keith Sward ("A Jewish Musicality in America," *J. Appl. Psychol.*, 1933, *17*, 675–712) points out that in 1932 half of the American violin virtuosos, maestros, and first violinists of symphony orchestras were of Jewish descent. Ten per cent of American composers were also Jewish. Yet ten- and eleven-year-old Jewish and gentile youngsters score similarly on tests of pitch, time, and intensity discrimination, tonal movement, and tonal memory. It would appear then that the presence of

so many Jews in American musical life must be due to economic and social factors rather than genetic causes.

41. G. B. Johnson, "Musical Talent of the American Negro," *Music Supervisors J.*, 1928, *15*, 81, 83, 96.

42. The study of D. Van Alstyne and E. Osborne, "Rhythm Responses of Negro and White Children Two to Six," *Monog. Soc. Res. Child Develpm.*, 1937, *2*, 4, is almost the only research where black superiority has seemingly been found. Black children appeared to be markedly better in motor rhythm, the superiority being greatest for the simplest rhythms and the youngest subjects. But whether these data are to be explained on genetic grounds, are due to errors of selection, or may be attributed to the blacks being less inhibited or receiving more musical encouragement is not clear. Other studies, e.g. that of R. L. Streep, "A Comparison of White and Negro Children in Rhythm and Consonance," *J. Appl. Psychol.*, 1931, *15*, 53–71, have found slight black superiorities but never differences of impressive magnitude.

43. F. Goodenough and D. B. Morris, "Studies in the Psychology of Children's Drawings," *Psychol. Bull.*, 1950, *47*, 369–433.

44. G. M. Gilbert, "Sex Differences in Musical Aptitude and Training," *J. Gen. Psychol.*, 1942, *26*, 19–33.

45. M. Vaerting, "Die musikalische Veranlagung des Weibes," *Z. f. Psychother. Med. Psychol.*, 1917, *7*, 120–27.

46. H. D. Schwarz, "Die Kunst als seelische Kraftquelle für die Frau," *Psychol. Rundschau*, 1931, *3*, 52–53. See also Phyllis Greenacre, "Woman as Artist," *Psychoanal. Quart.*, 1960, *29*, 208–27.

47. C. E. Seashore, *In Search of Beauty in Music*, New York, Ronald Press, 1947, p. 367.

48. P. R. Farnsworth, "The Effects of Role-taking on Artistic Achievement," *J. Aesth.*, 1960, *18*(3), 345–49.

49. C. Quinan, "A Study of Sinistrality and Muscle Coordination in Musicians, Ironworkers and Others," *Arch. Neurol. and Psychiat.*, 1922, *7*, 352; "The Principal Sinistral Types," *Arch. Neurol. and Psychiat.*, 1930, *24*, 35–47.

50. M. L. Sikes, "Musical Talent and the Left Hand," *Pedagogical Seminary*, 1923, *30*, 156–61.

51. P. R. Farnsworth, "Musical Talent and the Left Hand," *School Music*, 1932, *32*, 11.

52. For data which picture the ambidextrous as better than average in tongue-agility, see J. Kwalwasser, *Exploring the Musical Mind*, New York, Coleman-Ross, 1955, p. 132.

53. E. M. East, "Insanity and Genius," *J. Hered.*, 1938, *29*, 275–79; A. Anastasi and J. P. Foley, Jr., "A Survey of the Literature on Artistic Behavior in the Abnormal, I," *J. Gen. Psychol.*, 1941, *25*, 111–42; "II," *Ann., N.Y. Acad. Sci.*, 1941, *42*, 1–112; "III," *Psychol. Monog.*, 1940, *52*, 1–71; "IV," *J. Gen. Psychol.*, 1941, *25*, 187–237; P. R. Farnsworth, "Musicality and Abnormality," *Confinia Psychiatrica*, 1961, *4*, 158–64. P. E. Vernon believes that composers of the romantic school tend to have been more neurotic than those of the classical school ("The Personality of the Composer," *Music & Letters*, 1930, *11*, 38–48); and E. Payne ("Musical Taste and Personality," *Brit. J. Psychol.*, 1967, *58*, 133–38) has discovered a very slight tendency (*rho*, .36) for the more neurotic to prefer romantic to classical music.

54. P. R. Farnsworth, "Ratings in Music, Art, and Abnormality in the First Four Grades," *J. Psychol.*, 1938, *6*, 89–94.

55. C. C. Miles and L. S. Wolfe, "Childhood Physical and Mental Health Records of Historical Geniuses," *Psychol. Monog.*, 1936, *47*, 390–400. See also J. W. Krutch, "Genius and Neuroticism," pp. 116–20 in W. D. Nunokawa, Ed., *Readings in Abnormal Psychology*, Chicago, Scott Foresman, 1965. A study by R. V. Burton ("Are Musicians Normal?" *Overture*, 1955, *35*(5), 10) on approximately one-third of all musicians employed in the motion picture studios of the Los Angeles area

in 1954 revealed no unusual amount of emotional abnormality. The testing device was the Guilford-Zimmerman Temperament Survey.

56. M. J. Keston, "An Experimental Investigation of the Relationship Between the Factors of the Minnesota Multiphasic Personality Inventory and Musical Sophistication," *Amer. Psychol.*, 1956, *11*, 434. See also J. C. Cooley, "A Study of the Relation Between Certain Mental and Personality Traits and Ratings of Musical Abilities," *J. Res. Music Educ.*, 1961, *9*(2), 108–16, who found that among students in college music classes Bernreuter Personality Inventory scores were not related to Seashore Aptitude scores, sight-reading aptitude, musical performance, or applied music grades.

57. A. Adler, "Character and Talent," *Harpers*, 1927, *155*, 64–72.

58. H. Rosenthal, "Die Musikalität der Juden," *Intern. Z. f. Indiv.-psychol.*, 1931, *9*, 122–31.

59. P. C. Squires, "The Problem of Beethoven's Deafness," *J. Abn. Soc. Psychol.*, 1937, *32*, 11–62.

60. P. R. Farnsworth, "Auditory Acuity and Musical Ability in the First Four Grades," *J. Psychol.*, 1938, *6*, 95–98.

61. In a parallel study S. Atwell looked for evidence of color weakness among artistic and inartistic children. Her findings were contrary to what might have been expected from the Adlerian doctrine in that it was the artistic youngster who tended to possess slightly better color vision ("Color Vision in Relation to Artistic Ability," *J. Psychol.*, 1939, *8*, 53–56).

62. P. R. Farnsworth, "Further Data on the Adlerian Theory of Artistry," *J. Gen. Psychol.*, 1941, *24*, 447–50.

63. L. B. Bower, "A Factor Analysis of Music Tests," Thesis, Catholic U., 1945.

64. M. Bodkin, "Archetypal Patterns in Tragic Poetry," *Brit. J. Psychol.*, 1930, *21*, 183–202; M. Philipson, *Outline of a Jungian Aesthetics*, Evanston, Ill., Northwestern U. Press, 1963.

65. G. Szucharewa and S. Ossipowa, "Materialen zur Erforschung der Korrelationen zwischen den Typen der Begabung u. d. Konstitution," *Z. Ges. Neurol. u. Psychiat.* 1926, *100*, 489–526.

66. B. Gross and R. H. Seashore, "Psychological Characteristics of Student and Professional Musical Composers," *J. Appl. Psychol.*, 1941, *25*, 159–70.

67. M. J. Keston and I. M. Pinto, "Possible Factors Influencing Musical Preference," *J. Genet. Psychol.*, 1955, *86*, 101–13. See also E. Payne, "Musical Taste and Personality," *Music Rev.*, 1965, *26*(2), 129–45.

68. M. A. Wallach and C. Greenberg, "Personality Functions of Symbolic Sexual Arousal to Music," *Psychol. Monog.*, 1960, *74*(7), 1–18.

69. M. A. Wallach, "Two Correlates of Symbolic Sexual Arousal: Level of Anxiety and Liking for Esthetic Material," *J. Abn. Soc. Psychol.*, 1960, *61*, 396–401.

70. M. J. Keston and I. M. Pinto, *op. cit.*

71. R. J. Rankin, "Auditory Discrimination and Anxiety," *Psychol. Rept.*, 1962, *11*, 391–94.

72. A number of researchers have attempted to study personality variables through the construction of a tonal equivalent of the famous Rorschach Ink-Blot Test. Music is used to elicit imagery and attitudinal sets which are interpreted more or less in the fashion of the Rorschach. For studies in this area see J. O. Grimmett, "Personality Diagnosis Through Music," Master's thesis, Stanford U., 1950, and L. Van den Daele, "A Music Projective Technique," *J. Proj. Tech.*, 1967, *31*(5), 47–57. Personality has also been studied by the aid of musical preference tests. See also R. B. Cattell and D. R. Saunders, "Music Preferences and Personality Diagnosis," *J. Soc. Psychol.*, 1954, *39*, 3–24; R. B. Cattell and Jean C. Anderson, "The Measurement of Personality and Behavior Disorders by the I.P.A.T. Music Preference Test," *J. Appl. Psychol.*, 1953, *37*, 446–54.

73. S. Freud, *A General Introduction to Psychoanalysis*, New York, Liveright, 1935. See also H. Racker, "Contributions to Psychoanalysis of Music," *Amer. Imago*, 1951, *8*, 129–63; "Psychoanalytic Considerations on Music and the Musicians," *Psychoanal. Rev.*, 1965, *52*(3), 75–94. For a discussion of the Rankian adaptation of Freudianism see A. Michel, *Psychoanalyse de la musique*, Paris, U. de Paris, 1951, and *L'ecole Freudienne devant la musique*, Paris, Editions du Scorpion, 1965. Michel connects the oral stage of sex development with the use of the piano, the anal with the trumpet, and the phallic with the flute. H. Kohut ("Observations on the Psychological Functions of Music," *J. Amer. Psychoanal. Assoc.*, 1957, *5*, 389–407) sees music as contributing to the relief of primitive, preverbal tensions and to enjoyable submission to rules. For T. Reik's views on music and psychoanalysis see his *Psychoanalytic Experiences in Life and Music*, New York, Grove Press, 1960. See also A. Ehrenzweig, *The Psychoanalysis of Artistic Vision and Hearing*, New York, Braziller, 1966.

74. For an attempt to link Mozart's creativity with sublimation see A. H. Esman, "Mozart, A Study of Genius," *Psychoanal. Quart.*, 1951, *20*, 603–12. See also R. Still, "Gustav Mahler and Psychoanlysis," *Amer. Imago*, 1960, *17*, 217–40.

75. A. Hartmann, "Untersuchungen über metrisches Verhalten in musikalischen Interpretationsvarianten," *Arch. Ges. Psychol.*, 1932, *84*, 103–93; K. L. Bean, "The Use of Visual, Auditory, and Kinesthetic Imagery in the Transfer of Musical Notation to the Piano Keyboard," *J. Educ. Psychol.*, 1939, *30*, 533–41; J. Mainwaring, "Kinaesthetic Factors in the Recall of Musical Experience," *Brit. J. Psychol.*, 1932, *23*, 284–307.

76. P. C. Squires, "The Creative Psychology of Carl Maria von Weber," *Charact. & Pers.*, 1938, *6*, 203–17.

77. M. Agnew, "A Comparison of Auditory Images of Musicians, Psychologists, and Children," *Psychol. Monog.*, 1922, *31*, 268–78.

78. M. Agnew, "The Auditory Images of Great Composers," *Psychol. Monog.*, 1922, *31*, 279–87.

79. R. Kochmann, "Über musikalische Gedächtnisbilder," *Z. f. Angew. Psychol.*, 1924, *23*, 329–51; T. Zaworski, "Akustyczne wyobrazenia ejdetyczne," *Kwart. Psychol.*, 1947, *13*, 156–203.

80. H. Cowell, "The Process of Musical Creation," *Amer. J. Psychol.*, 1926, *37*, 233–36.

81. H. S. Forbes and H. B. Forbes, "Fetal Sense Reaction: Hearing," *J. Comp. Psychol.*, 1927, *7*, 353–55; K. Fleischer, "Untersuchungen zur Entwicklung der Innerohrfunktion," *Z. Laryngol.*, 1955, *34*, 733–40; J. Bernard and L. W. Sontag, "Fetal Reactivity to Tonal Stimulation," *J. Genet. Psychol.*, 1947, *70*, 205–10.

82. M. W. Haller, "The Reactions of Infants to Changes in the Intensity and Pitch of Pure Tones," *J. Genet. Psychol.*, 1932, *40*, 162–80.

83. G. M. Simons, "Comparisons of Incipient Music Responses Among Very Young Twins and Singletons," *J. Res. Music Educ.*, 1964, *12*(3), 212–26.

84. W. Platt, "Temperament and Disposition Revealed in Young Children," *Charact. & Pers.*, 1934, *2*, 246–51.

85. H. Werner, "Die melodische Erfindung im frühen Kindesalter," *Phil.-Hist. Klasse Sitzungsberichte*, 1917, *182;* T. F. Vance and M. Grandprey, "The Evaluation of the Musical Capacity of Nursery School Children," *Proc. Iowa Acad. Sci.*, 1929, *36*, 321–28. For further data on the music of preschool children see M. G. Colby, "Instrumental Reproduction of Melody by Preschool Children," *J. Genet. Psychol.*, 1935, *47*, 413–30.

86. A. Wells, "A Comparison of Chord Figures and Scale Progressions in Early School Music Learning," *Peabody Bull.*, 1933, *30*, 21–23; D. Doig, "Creative Music: Music Composed for a Given Test," *J. Educ. Res.*, 1941, *35*, 263–75; 1942, *35*, 344–55.

87. M. S. Hattwick, "The Role of Pitch Level and Pitch Range in the Singing of Pre-

school, First-grade, and Second-grade Children," *Child Develpm.*, 1933, *4*, 281–91. See also H. M. Williams, "Immediate and Delayed Memory of Preschool Children for Pitch in Tonal Sequences," *U. of Iowa Stud. Child Welf.*, 1935, *11*, 85–94.

88. E. Fröschels, "Untersuchungen über die Kinderstimme," *Zentr. f. Physiol.*, 1920, *34*, 477–84.

89. A. T. Jersild and S. F. Bienstock, "A Study of the Development of Children's Ability To Sing," *J. Educ. Psychol.*, 1934, *25*, 481–503.

90. A. T. Jersild and S. F. Bienstock, "The Influence of Training on the Vocal Ability of Three-year-old Children," *Child Develpm.*, 1931, *2*, 272–90. See also E. A. Mal'tseva's chapter in E. I. Ignat'ev's *Psikgologiya Mladshego Shkol'nika*, RSFSR Acad. Ped. Sc., Moscow, 1960; C. Christozov, "Quelques problèmes musicaux vus à la luminière des conceptions physiologiques," *Annales Médico-Psychologiques*, 1967, *2*(4), 519–39; R. B. Smith, "The Effect of Vocal Training on the Singing Ability of Nursery School Children," *J. Res. Music Educ.*, 1963, *11*, 137–41. For an approach to the music training of mental defectives see M. H. Richards, *Threshold to Music*, San Francisco, Fearon Publ., 1964.

91. K. C. Garrison, "Psychology of Special Abilities," *Peabody Reflector*, 1939, *12*, 11–13.

92. M. Cochran, "Kinesthesis and the Piano," *Austral. J. Psychol.*, 1930, *8*, 205–9.

93. R. W. Brown, "The Relation Between Age (Chronological and Mental) and Rate of Piano Learning," *J. Appl. Psychol.*, 1936, *20*, 511–16. See also R. Leibold, "Kind und Metronom," *Z. Pädag. Psychol.*, 1936, *37*, 317–22; M. Varro, "The Musical Receptivity of the Child and the Adolescent," *Music Teach. Nat. Assoc. Proc.*, 1942, 1943, pp. 77–88.

94. K. Sarch, "The Pied Piper of Japan," *Julliard News Bull.*, 1964, *2*(6), 1–3, and C. Lekberg, "Pied Piper of Fiddledom," *Music J.*, 1968, *26*(5), 20–21, 38, 46–47. See also A. Denk, "Report on Suzuki Experiment," *Amer. String Teach.*, 1967, *17*(4), 35–37.

95. R. G. Petzold, "The Development of Auditory Perception of Musical Sounds by Children in the First Six Grades," *J. Res. Music Educ.*, 1963, *11*(1), 21–43.

96. C. W. Valentine, "The Aesthetic Appreciation of Musical Intervals Among School Children and Adults," *Brit. J. Psychol.*, 1913, *6*, 190–216.

97. E. Walker, *Das musikalische Erlebnis und seine Entwicklung*, Göttingen, Vanderhoeck u. Ruprecht, 1927.

98. C. E. Seashore, *Manual of Instructions and Interpretations of Measures of Musical Talent*, New York, Columbia Graphophone, 1919. M. Aizawa ("The Development of Pitch-Discrimination," *The Memoirs of Takada Branch, Niigata U.*, 1959, *4*, 24–37) has found that Japanese schoolchildren do not improve their pitch scores much after age 12 unless they have special training.

99. C. E. Seashore, D. Lewis, and J. G. Saetveit, *Manual, Seashore Measures of Musical Talents*, New York, Psychological Corp., 1960.

100. For a genetic study of the voices of 44 choir boys see F. J. Hell, "Physiologische und musikalische Untersuchungen über die Singstimme der Kinder," *Arch. Ges. Phonel.*, 1938, *2*, 65–102. Another study which compares the musical productions of children from preschool to adolescence is that by A. Nestele, "Die musikalische Produktion im Kindesalter," *Beih. z. Z. f. Angew. Psychol.*, 1930, *15*(52). For still another study of the musical abilities of the adolescent see M. Van Briessen, *Die Entwicklung der Musikalität in den Reifejahren*, Langensalza, Beyer, 1929.

101. The music educators are gradually becoming interested in the experimental design of their studies. See R. Colwell, "The importance of Design in Research Studies," *Counc. Res. Music Educ.*, 1964, *3*, 20–33; J. M. Watson, "Patterning of Research Problems," *Counc. Res. Music Educ.*, 1964, *3*, 1–11; D. J. Shelter, "Some Problems in the Evaluation of New Teaching Media," *Counc. Res. Music Educ.*, 1964, *2*, 23–28. See also W. S. Larson, "Bibliography of Re-

search Studies in Music Education 1949–1956," *J. Res. Music Educ.*, 1957, *5*, 64–225; G. W. Barth, "Music Education," *Rev. Educ. Res.*, 1964, *34*(2), 222–35; J. Mainwaring, "Psychological Factors in the Teaching of Music, Part I," *Brit. J. Educ. Psychol.*, 1951, *21*, 105–21, "Part II, Applied Musicianship," 199–213; J. L. Mursell, *Music and the Classroom Teacher*, Boston, Silver Burdett, 1951; M. E. Wilson, *How To Help Your Child With Music*, New York, Schuman, 1951; Mary Tolbert, "Music Education Materials: A Selected Bibliography," *J. Res. Music Educ.*, 1959, *7*(1), 9–144; R. A. Choate, "Research in Music Education," *J. Res. Music Educ.*, 1965, *13*(2), 67–86; W. G. Fullard, Jr., "Operant Training of Aural Musical Discriminations With Preschool Children," *J. Res. Music Educ.*, 1967, *15*(3), 201–9; T. B. Jeffries, "The Effects of Order of Presentation and Knowledge of Results on the Aural Recognition of Melodic Intervals," *J. Res. Music Educ.*, 1967, *15*(3), 179–90. The researches of the period from 1930 to 1962 are examined by E. H. Schneider and H. L. Cady in *Evaluation and Synthesis of Research Studies Relating to Music Education*, Cleveland, Bell and Howell, 1965.

102. R. W. Lundin, "Musical Learning and Reinforcement Theory," *Music Educ. J.*, 1960, *46*, 46–49; C. Hoffer, *Teaching Music in the Secondary School*, Belmont, Calif., Wadsworth, 1964.

103. C. C. O'Brien, "Part and Whole Methods in the Memorization of Music," *J. Educ. Psychol.*, 1943, *34*, 552–60.

104. R. W. Brown, "A Comparison of the 'Whole,' 'Part,' and 'Combination' Methods of Learning Piano Music," *J. Exp. Psychol.*, 1928, *11*, 235–47; G. Rubin-Rabson, "Studies in the Psychology of Memorizing Piano Music, III: A Comparison of the Whole and the Part Approach," *J. Educ. Psychol.*, 1940, *31*, 460–76; L. E. Eberly, "Part Versus Whole Method in Memorizing Piano Music," Thesis, Columbia U., 1921.

105. G. Rubin-Rabson, "Studies in the Psychology of Memorizing Piano Music, IV: The Effect of Incentive," *J. Educ. Psychol.*, 1941, *32*, 45–54.

106. G. Rubin-Rabson, "Studies in the Psychology of Memorizing Piano Music, VI: A Comparison of Two Forms of Mental Rehearsal and Keyboard Overlearning," *J. Educ. Psychol.*, 1941, *32*, 593–602; "VII: A Comparison of Three Degrees of Overlearning," *J. Educ. Psychol.*, 1941, *32*, 688–96.

107. G. Rubin-Rabson, "Mental and Keyboard Overlearning in Memorizing Piano Music," *J. Musicol.*, 1941, *3*, 33–40.

108. S. Kovacs, "Untersuchungen über das musikalische Gedächtnis," *Z. f. Angew. Psychol.*, 1916, *11*, 113–35.

109. G. Rubin-Rabson, "The Influence of Analytic Prestudy in Memorizing Piano Music," *Arch. Psychol.*, 1937, *31*(220), 1–53; "Studies in the Psychology of Memorizing Piano Music, V: A Comparison of Prestudy Periods of Varied Lengths," *J. Educ. Psychol.*, 1941, *32*, 101–12.

110. L. E. Woelflin, "Teaching Clarinet Fingerings With Teaching Machines," *J. Res. Music Educ.*, 1964, *12*(4), 287–94.

111. G. Rubin-Rabson, "Studies in the Psychology of Memorizing Piano Music, II: A Comparison of Massed and Distributed Practice," *J. Educ. Psychol.*, 1940, *31*, 270–84.

112. K. Dunlap, *Habits: Their Making and Unmaking*, New York, Liveright, 1932.

113. J. A. McGeoch and A. L. Irion, *The Psychology of Human Learning*, New York, Longmans Green, 1952.

114. G. Wakeham, "Query on 'A Revision of the Fundamental Law of Habit Formation,'" *Science*, 1928, *68*, 135–36.

115. J. R. Bergan, "Factors Affecting Pitch Discrimination," *Counc. Res. Music Educ.*, 1966, *8*, 15–21.

116. G. Rubin-Rabson, "Studies in the Psychology of Memorizing Piano Music, VIII:

The Inhibitory Influence of the Same and of Different Degrees of Learning,"
J. Musicol., 1947, *5*, 25.

117. R. W. Brown, "The Relation Between Two Methods of Learning Piano Music,"
J. Exp. Psychol., 1933, *16*, 435–41; G. Rubin-Rabson, "Studies in the Psychology
of Memorizing Piano Music, I: A Comparison of the Unilateral and Coordinated
Approaches," *J. Educ. Psychol.*, 1939, *30*, 321–45.

118. D. G. Él'kin, "Rol'parnosti bol'shikh polusharii v vospriiatii vremeni," *Dokl.
Akad. Pedag. Nauk RSFSR*, 1962, *4*, 81–84.

119. C. E. Noble, *The Psychology of Cornet and Trumpet Playing*, Missouli, Mont.,
The Mountain Press, 1964. See also R. M. Diamond and T. C. Collins, "The
Use of 8 mm Loop Films To Teach the Identification of Clarinet Fingering, Em-
bouchure, and Hand Position Errors," *J. Res. Music Educ.*, 1967, *15*(3), 224–28.

120. W. T. Bartholomew, "Imagery in Voice Pedagogy," *Peabody Bull.*, 1934, *31*,
20–28; "The Paradox of Voice Teaching," *J. Acoust. Soc. Amer.*, 1940, *11*, 446–50.

121. P. R. Farnsworth, "Psychology and Double Stops," *School Music*, 1926, 27, 21.

122. R. W. Brown, "A Preliminary Study of the Touch Method of Learning Piano
Music," *J. Appl. Psychol.*, 1934, *18*, 516–27.

123. G. S. Rigina, "Razvitie zvykovýsotnogo slukha v protsessa obucheniya igre na
skripe," *Vopr. Psikhologii*, 1963, *4*, 116–24.

124. To tie imagery to action rather than to tones, F. Fredrich (*Playing by Seeing*,
Medina, Ohio, Lynne, 1950) suggests the use of note pictures where sketches
of the piano keyboard are placed over the staff and lines are drawn from the
piano keys to their staff notes.

125. D. E. Andrews, "Comparative Study of Two Methods of Developing Music
Listening Ability in Elementary School Children," *J. Res. Music Educ.*, 1962, *10*,
59–64.

126. Leo Horacek, "Programmed Instruction in Music," *Rev. Psychol. Music*, 1963,
1(2), 1–6; C. L. Spohn, "Programming the Basic Materials of Music for Self-in-
structional Development of Aural Skills," *J. Res. Music Educ.*, 1963, *11*, 91–98;
J. C. Carlsen, "Programmed Learning in Melodic Dictation," *J. Res. Music Educ.*,
1964, *12*(2), 139–48; W. R. Ihrke, "Automated Music Training," *Counc. Res.
Music Educ.*, 1964, *2*, 6–8; "Trends in Music Education Research," *ibid.*, pp. 29–
31; R. A. Barnes, "Programmed Instruction in Music Fundamentals for Future
Elementary Teachers," *J. Res. Music Educ.*, 1964, *12*(3), 187–98; P. LaBach, "A
Device To Facilitate Learning of Basic Music Skills," *Counc. Res. Music Educ.*,
1965, *4*, 7–10; T. B. Jeffries, "The Effects of Order of Presentation and Knowledge of Results on the Aural Recognition of Melodic Intervals," Ph.D. thesis,
U.C.L.A., 1965; T. H. A. Ashford, "The Use of Programmed Instruction To
Teach Fundamental Concepts in Music Theory," *J. Res. Music Educ.*, 1966,
14(3), 171–77; R. R. Fink, "Programmed Part Writing," *J. Res. Music Educ.*, 1967,
15(2), 159–64; E. A. Tarratus, Jr., and C. L. Spohn, "Cooperative Research in Programmed Learning," *J. Res. Music Educ.*, 1967, *15*(3), 210–14; W. E. Kuhn and
R. L. Allvin, "Computer-Assisted Teaching," *J. Res. Music Educ.*, 1967, *15*(4),
305–15; R. J. Hutcheson, Jr., "Programmed Instruction in Music Education,"
Missouri J. Res. Music Educ., 1967, *2*(1), 9–52.

127. K. L. Bean, "An Experimental Approach to the Reading of Music," *Psychol.
Monog.*, 1938, *50*(6); "Reading Music Instead of Spelling It," *J. Musicol.*, 1939, *1*,
1–5; "The Use of Visual, Auditory, and Kinesthetic Imagery in the Transfer of
Musical Notation to the Piano Keyoard," *J. Educ. Psychol.*, 1939, *30*, 533–41.

128. O. Ortmann, "Span of Vision in Note Reading," *Music Educ. Nat. Conf. Yearbook*, 1937, pp. 88–93.

129. G. Hargiss, "The Acquisition of Sight-Singing Ability in Piano Classes for Students Preparing To Be Elementary Teachers," *J. Res. Music Educ.*, 1962, *10*, 69–
75.

130. V. Lannert and M. Ullman, "Factors in the Reading of Piano Music," *Amer. J. Psychol.*, 1945, *58*, 91–99.

131. H. Lowery, "On Reading Music," *Dioptric Rev. and Brit. J. Physiol. Optics*, 1940, *1*, 78–88.

132. L. F. Wheelwright, *An Experimental Study of the Perceptibility and Spacing of Music Symbols*, Teach. Coll. Contr. Educ., No. 775, New York, Teachers Coll., Columbia U., 1939.

133. H. E. Weaver, "A Survey of Visual Processes in Reading Differently Constructed Musical Selections," *Psychol. Monog.*, 1943, *55*(1), 1–30.

134. K. Van Nuys and H. E. Weaver, "Memory Span and Visual Pauses in Reading Rhythms and Melodies," *Psychol. Monog.*, 1943, *55*(1), 33–50.

135. O. I. Jacobsen, "An Analytic Study of Eye-movements in Reading Vocal and In-strumental Music," *J. Musicol.*, 1941, *3*, 1–32, 69–100, 133–64; 1942, *3*, 197–226.

136. H. Hammer, "An Experimental Study of the Use of the Tachistoscope in the Teaching of Melodic Sight Singing," *J. Res. Music Educ.*, 1963, *11*, 44–54.

137. G. Hargiss, *op. cit.* See also L. A. Hansen, "A Study of Score-Reading Ability of Musicians," *J. Res. Music Educ.*, 1961, *9*(2), 147–56, whose study comes to the not very surprising conclusion that a 2-year period of theory training is significantly superior to a 1-year period in effecting improved score-reading.

138. E. Ross, "Improving Facility in Music Memorization," *J. Res. Music Educ.*, 1964, *12*(4), 269–78.

139. H. Cowell, "The Process of Musical Creation," *Amer. J. Psychol.*, 1926, *37*, 233–36.

140. W. R. Reitman, *Cognition and Thought: An Information-Processing Approach*, New York, Wiley, 1965, Ch. 6.

141. E. Benham, "The Creative Activity," *Brit. J. Psychol. (Gen. Sec.)*, 1929, *20*, 59–65. For somewhat similar research on children eight to eleven, see the series of arti-cles entitled "Creative Music" by D. Doig. Of special interest is number 2 which is to be found in *J. Educ. Res.*, 1942, *36*, 241–53. For a survey of the more recent work on teaching creativity to schoolchildren see *Experiments in Musical Crea-tivity*, Washington, Music Educ. Nat. Conf., 1966, edited by Contemporary Music Project for Creativity in Music Education.

142. J. Bahle, *Der musikalische Schaffensprozess*, Leipzig, Hirzel, 1936. A cogent crit-icism of the Bahle and other somewhat similar studies on creativity can be seen in C. Jacobs, "Psychology of Music: Some European Studies," *Acta Psychol.*, 1960, *17*, 273–97.

143. C. G. Cambor, G. M. Lisowitz, and M. F. Miller, "Creative Jazz Musicians: A Clinical Study," *Psychiat.*, 1962, *25*(1), 1–15.

144. F. Rudáš, "K Problému Špecifickosti Umeleckého Vnímania," *Psychologica* (Bratis-lava), 1962, *13*(2), 155–69.

145. B. Gross and R. H. Seashore, "Psychological Characteristics of Student and Pro-fessional Musical Composers," *J. Appl. Psychol.*, 1941, *25*, 159–70.

146. W. G. Whittaker, W. O. Hutchison, and R. W. Pickford, "Symposium on the Psychology of Music and Painting," *Brit. J. Psychol.*, 1942, *33*, 40–57.

147. C. L. Lastrucci, "The Professional Dance Musician," Thesis, Stanford U., 1941.

148. H. S. Becker, "The Professional Dance Musician and His Audience," *Amer. J. Sociol.*, 1951, *57*, 136–44. A somewhat similar study was made of contemporary American composers of "serious" music by D. Nash ("Challenge and Response in the American Composer's Career," *J. Aesth.*, 1955, *14*(1), 116–22).

149. A. Hutchings, *The Invention and Composition of Music*, London, Novello, 1958.

150. D. Nash, "The Socialization of an Artist: The American Composer," *Soc. Forces*, 1957, *35*, 307–13; "The Alienated Composer," in *The Arts in Society*, R. Wilson, Ed., Englewood Heights, N.J., Prentice Hall, 1964.

151. Max Graf, *From Beethoven to Shostakovich; The Psychology of the Composing Process*, New York, Philosophical Library, 1947.

152. J. Jancke, "Das Spezifisch-Musikalische und die Frage nach dem Sinngehalt der Musik," *Arch. Ges. Psychol.*, 1930, *78*, 103–84.

153. L. Loar, "An Adventure in Musical Psychoanalysis," *J. Musicol.*, 1940, *2*(1), 15–23.

154. Anton Ehrenzweig, *The Psycho-analysis of Artistic Vision and Hearing*, London, Routledge and Kegan Paul, 1953; New York, Braziller, 1966.

155. M. I. Stein, "Creativity and Culture," *J. Psychol.*, 1953, *36*, 311–22. See also H. H. Anderson, Ed., *Creativity and Its Cultivation*, New York, Harper & Row, 1959. For a psychoanalytic approach see L. Bellak, "Creativity: Some Random Notes to a Systematic Consideration," *J. Proj. Tech.*, 1958, *22*, 363–80.

156. While an IQ of 120 seems essential if one is to be highly creative, the research data so far gathered suggest that still higher IQs yield no further bonus for creativity (R. Moore, "The Relationship of Intelligence to Creativity," *J. Res. Music Educ.*, 1966, *14*(4), 243–53).

157. G. Révész, in his *Introduction to the Psychology of Music*, Norman, U. of Oklahoma Press, 1954, maintains that there is a single homogeneous talent for composing which manifests itself in very young children much less often than does the reproductive-interpretative talent.

158. A. H. Maslow, "The Creative Attitude," *Structuralist*, 1963, *3*, 4–10.

159. Biographical studies by psychologists and psychiatrists are the following: J. Bahle, *Eingebung und Tat im musikalischen Schaffen*, Leipzig, Hirzel, 1939; H. Jancke, "Beiträge zur Psychologie der musikalischen Komposition," *Arch. Ges. Psychol.*, 1928, *66*, 437–92; R. Schramek, "Franz Liszt," *Arch. Ges. Psychol.*, 1934, *92*, 45–84; P. C. Squires, "The Creative Psychology of César Franck," *Charact. & Pers.*, 1938, *7*, 41–49; P. C. Squires, "The Creative Psychology of Chopin," *J. Musicol.*, 1940, *2*(1), 27–37; P. C. Squires, "Peter Ilich Tschaikowsky (a Psychological Sketch)," *Psychoanal. Rev.*, 1941, *28*, 445–65; P. C. Squires, "The Creative Psychology of Carl Maria von Weber," *Charact. & Pers.*, 1938, *6*, 203–17; P. E. Vernon, "The Personality of the Composer," *Music & Letters*, 1930, *11*, 38–48; J. A. Brussel, "The Tschaikowsky Troika," *Psychiat. Quart. Suppl.*, 1962, *36*(2), 304–22; "The Brobdingnag of Bayreuth," *ibid.*, 1963, *37*(2), 212–29; W. F. Mooney, "Gustav Mahler: A Note on Life and Death in Music," *Psychoanal. Quart.*, 1968, *37*(1), 80–102.

160. H. C. Lehman, "Intellectual vs. 'Physical Peak' Performance," *Sci. Monthly*, 1945, *61*, 127–37.

161. J. Bjorksten, "The Limitation of Creative Years," *Sci. Monthly*, 1946, *62*, 94.

162. W. Dennis, "Predicting Scientific Productivity in Later Maturity From Records of Earlier Decades," *J. Gerontol.*, 1954, *9*, 465–67.

163. H. C. Lehman and D. W. Ingerham, "Man's Creative Years in Music," *Sci. Monthly*, 1939, *48*, 431–43; H. C. Lehman, *Age and Achievement*, Princeton, N.J., Princeton U. Press, 1953.

164. W. Dennis, "Variations in Productivity Among Creative Workers," *Sci. Monthly*, 1955, *80*, 1–2.

165. T. Munro, "What Causes Creative Epochs in the Arts?" *J. Aesth.*, 1962, *21*(1), 35–48.

166. J. Szigeti, "Composer, Performer, and Audience," pp. 303–14 in *Conflict and Creativity*, S. M. Farber and R. H. Wilson, Eds., New York, McGraw-Hill, 1963.

167. Most authorities find no evidence for a unitary creative ability in the arts. See J. P. Guilford, "Creative Abilities in the Arts," *Psychol. Rev.*, 1957, *64*, 110–18.

168. For a Marxist discussion of creativity, see F. Rudáš, "Psychologicky, Rozbor Zaciatocnej Fázy Umeleckého Tvorivého Procesu," *Psychologica* (Bratislava), 1961, *12*(1), 129–44. For a consideration of the creativity of Hindu musicians see M. Raychaudhuri, *Studies in Artistic Creativity: Personality Structure of the Musician*, Calcutta, India, Rabindra Bharati, 1966.

CHAPTER NINE

1. A number of paper-and-pencil tests in music give no publication dates. Hence, in the interest of uniformity, no dates will be given here even when available.
2. F. A. Beach and H. E. Schrammel, *Beach Standardized Music Tests,* Emporia, Bureau Educ. Meas., Kansas State Normal School.
3. G. Gildersleeve and W. Soper, *Music Achievement Tests,* New York, Bureau of Publications, Teachers Coll., Columbia U.
4. T. L. Torgerson and E. Fahnestock, *Torgerson-Fahnestock Music Test,* Indianapolis, Ind., Bobbs-Merrill.
5. J. Kwalwasser and G. Ruch, *Kwalwasser-Ruch Test of Musical Accomplishment,* Iowa City, Bureau of Educ. Res. and Serv., U. of Iowa.
6. C. E. Strouse and H. E. Schrammel, *Strouse Music Test,* Emporia, Bureau Educ. Meas., Kansas State Teach. Coll.
7. H. E. Hutchinson, *Hutchinson Music Tests,* Indianapolis, Ind., Bobbs-Merrill.
8. W. E. Knuth, *Knuth Achievement Tests in Music,* Philadelphia, Educ. Test Bureau.
9. C. J. McCauley, *McCauley Experiment in Public School Music,* Knoxville, Tenn., J. E. Avent.
10. R. D. Allen, W. H. Butterfield, and M. Tully, *Providence Inventory Test in Music,* Yonkers, N.Y., World Book.
11. L. C. Pressey, *The Special Vocabularies of the Public School Subjects,* Indianapolis, Ind., Bobbs-Merrill.
12. C. P. Wood, *Ear Tests in Harmony,* New York, American Book.
13. M. L. Kotick and T. L. Torgerson, *Diagnostic Tests of Achievement in Music,* Los Angeles Test Bureau.
14. S. E. Farnum, *Farnum Music Notation Test,* New York, Psychological Corp.
15. A. A. Swinchoski, "A Standardized Music Achievement Test Battery for the Intermediate Grades," *J. Res. Music Educ.,* 1965, *13*(3), 159–68.
16. A. N. Jones, *Jones Music Recognition Test,* New York, Carl Fischer.
17. H. D. Wing, "Review of 'Jones Music Recognition Test,'" pp. 622–23 in *The 6th Mental Measurements Yearbook,* Highland Park, N.J., Gryphon Press, 1965.
18. B. E. Bailey, "The Development and Validation of a Test of Listening Skill," *J. Res. Music Educ.,* 1968, *16*(1), 59–63.
19. J. Aliferis and J. E. Stecklein, *Aliferis-Stecklein Music Achievement Tests,* Minneapolis, U. of Minnesota Press. See also "The Development of a College Entrance Test in Music Achievement," *J. Res. Music Educ.,* 1953, *1*(2), 83–96; "Measurement of Music Achievement at College Entrance," *J. Appl. Psychol.,* 1955, *39*(4), 263–72.
20. Educational Testing Service, *Music Education: National Teacher Examinations,* Princeton, N.J., Educ. Test. Serv.
21. *Graduate Record Examinations,* Advanced Music Test, Princeton, N.J., Educ. Test. Serv.
22. E. K. Hillbrand, *Hillbrand Sight-Singing Test,* Yonkers, N.Y., World Book.
23. R. M. Mosher, *Mosher Test of Individual Singing,* Teach. Coll. Contrib. Educ., No. 194, New York, Bureau of Publications, Teachers Coll., Columbia U.
24. A. W. Otterstein and R. M. Mosher, *O-M Sight-Singing Test,* Stanford, Calif., Stanford U. Press.
25. M. S. Thostenson, "The Study and Evaluation of Certain Problems in Ear-Training Related to Achievement in Sight-Singing and Music Dictation," *Counc. Res. Music Educ.,* 1967, *11*, 14–35.
26. K. U. Gutsch, "One Approach Toward the Development of an Indivdual Test for

Assessing One Aspect of Instrumental Music Achievement," *Counc. Res. Music Educ.*, 1964, *2*, 1–5.

27. J. G. Watkins, *Objective Measurement of Instrumental Performance*, Teach. Coll. Contrib. Educ., No. 860, New York, Bureau of Publications, Teachers Coll., Columbia U.

28. J. G. Watkins and S. E. Farnum, *The Watkins-Farnum Performance Scale*, Winona, Minn., Leonard Music.

29. E. A. Alluisi, "Rater-Rater Reliabilities in Judging Musical Performances," *Percept. Mot. Skills*, 1962, *14*(1), 145–46.

30. See for example *Plymouth Educational Tests*, Chicago, Plymouth Press; *Music Achievement Test*, Baltimore, Dept. Educ.; *Krone Recognition, Tonal and Rhythmic Dictation Tests*, Indianapolis, M. T. Krone, Butler U.; *Mosher Group Tests*, Teach. Coll. Contrib. Educ. No. 194, New York, Columbia U. See also A. Roe, "A Study of the Accuracy of Perception of Visual Musical Stimuli," *Arch. Psychol.*, 1933, *158;* F. S. Salisbury and H. B. Smith, "Prognosis of Sight-Singing Ability of Normal School Students," *J. Appl. Psychol.*, 1929, *13*, 425–39; T. G. Stelzer, "Construction, Interpretation, and Use of Sight-Reading Scale in Organ Music, With an Analysis of Organ Playing Into Fundamental Abilities," *J. Exp. Educ.*, 1938, *7*, 35–43; S. T. Burns, "The Value of Prognostic Tests for Instrumental Pupils," *School Music*, 1931, *31*, 6–9; J. H. Fluke and J. N. Sparks, "The Construction, Validation, and Standardization of a Test of Music Perception for High School Performance Groups," *J. Res. Music Educ.*, 1965, *13*(4), 220–26.

31. With Russian ideology what it is, the Soviets have had a difficult time with the concept of talent. Yet from time to time, what Americans would call fairly formal tests have appeared. More should be expected now that the ban on genetics has been lifted. See B. M. Teplov, *Problemy Individnal'nykh Razlichii,* Moscow, RSFSR Acad. Ped. Sci., 1961.

32. C. Stumpf, "Akustische Versuche mit Pepito Areola," *Z. f. Angew. Psychol.*, 1909, *21*, 1–11.

33. T. H. Pear, "The Classification of Observers as 'Musical' and 'Unmusical,' " *Brit. J. Psychol.*, 1911, *4*, 89–94.

34. M. F. Meyer, "Special Ability Tests as Used in Missouri; Including a Demonstration of a Typical Test," *Psychol. Bull.*, 1924, *21*, 114–16.

35. G. Révész, *The Psychology of a Musical Prodigy*, New York, Harcourt, Brace, 1925.

36. G. Révész, *Introduction to the Psychology of Music*, Norman, U. of Oklahoma Press, 1954.

37. H. Rupp, "Über die Prüfung musikalischer Fähigkeiten," *Z. f. Angew. Psychol.*, 1919, *9*, 1–76.

38. T. Billroth, *Wer ist musikalisch?* Gebrüder Paetel, 1898.

39. J. von Kries, *Wer ist musikalisch?* Berlin, Springer, 1926.

40. J. A. Mjön, "Zur psychologischen Bestimmung der Musikalität," *Z. f. Angew. Psychol.*, 1926, *27*, 217–73.

41. For a somewhat more contemporary European view of music tests see E. Haisch, Über Musikalische Testverfahren," *Arch. Neurol. u. Psychiat.*, 1955, *75*, 67–76.

42. V. Haecker and T. Ziehen, *Zur Vererbung und Entwicklung der musikalischen Begabung*, Leipzig, Barth, 1923.

43. H. Lowery, "Cadence and Phrase Tests in Music," *Brit. J. Psychol.*, 1926–27, *17*, 111–18.

44. O. Ortmann, *Tests of Musical Talent*, Baltimore, Peabody Conservatory of Music, unpublished.

45. M. Schoen, "Tests of Musical Feeling and Musical Understanding," *J. Comp. Psychol,.* 1925, *5*, 13–52.

46. E. Franklin, *Tonality as a Basis for the Study of Musical Talent*, Göteborg, Sweden, Gumperts Förlag, 1956.

47. J. W. Conrad, *Conrad Instrument-Talent Test*, New York, Mills Music, 1941.

48. T. H. Madison, "Interval Discrimination as a Measure of Musical Aptitude," *Arch. Psychol.*, 1942, No. 268.
49. C. J. Lamp and N. Keys, "Can Aptitude for Specific Musical Instruments Be Predicted?" *J. Educ. Psychol.*, 1935, *26*, 587–96.
50. C. E. Seashore, "The Tonoscope and Its Use in the Training of the Voice," *The Musician*, 1906, *11*, 331–32; E. W. Scripture, "Das Strobilion," *Z. f. Psychol.*, 1928, *59*, 166–70; P. R. Farnsworth, "Two Independent Developments of the Strobilion," *J. Gen Psychol.*, 1929, *2*, 556–58.
51. J. Kwalwasser, *Exploring the Musical Mind*, New York, Coleman-Ross, 1955, Ch. 10.
52. O. I. Jacobsen, "Dynamic and Temporal Control in Music," *J. Gen. Psychol.*, 1936, *15*, 171–90.
53. R. H. Seashore, "Studies in Motor Rhythm," *Iowa Stud. Psychol.*, 1926, *9*, 142–99; J. T. Nielsen, "A Study in the Seashore Motor Rhythm Test," *Psychol. Monog.*, 1930, *40*, 74–84; O. W. Smith, "Relationships of Rhythm Discrimination to Motor Rhythm Performance," *J. Appl. Psychol.*, 1957, *41*, 365–69. For a note on the *Sievers Rhythm Test* see H. M. Williams, "A Study in the Prediction of Motor Rhythmic Performance of School Children," *J. Genet. Psychol.*, 1933, *43*, 377–88.
54. C. E. Seashore, *The Psychology of Musical Talent*, Boston, Silver Burdett, 1919, Ch. 11. See also G. H. Smith, "Auditory Imagery in Music Reading," Thesis, Stanford U., 1947.
55. J. R. Bergan, "Pitch Perception, Imagery, and Regression in the Service of the Ego," *J. Res. Music Educ.*, 1965, *13*(1), 15–32.
56. C. E. Seashore, *Manual of Instructions and Interpretations for Measures of Musical Talent*, New York, Columbia Graphophone, 1919.
57. F. W. Pinkerston, "Talent Tests and Their Application to the Public School Instrumental Music Program," *J. Res. Music Educ.*, 1963, *11*(1), 75–80.
58. H. Lowery, "On the Integrative Theory of Musical Talent," *J. Musicol.*, 1940, *2*, 1–14; J. Mainwaring, "The Assessment of Musical Ability," *Brit. J. Educ. Psychol.*, 1947, *17*, 83–96.
59. The leader of this group was J. L. Mursell. See his *The Psychology of Music*, New York, Norton, 1937.
60. R. Wyatt, "A Note on the Use of 'Omnibus' Training To Validate Seashore's Capacity Hypothesis," *Amer. J. Psychol.*, 1939, *52*, 638–40.
61. C. E. Seashore, *The Psychology of Musical Talent*, *op. cit.* For a survey through 1930 of the research articles on this first set of Seashore measures see P. R. Farnsworth, "An Historical, Critical and Experimental Study of the Seashore-Kwalwasser Test Battery," *Genet. Psychol. Monog.*, 1931, *9*, 291–393.
62. E. M. McGinnis, "Seashore's Measures of Musical Ability Applied to Children of the Pre-School Age," *Amer. J. Psychol.*, 1928, *40*, 620–23.
63. F. S. Salisbury and H. B. Smith, "Prognosis of Sight-Singing Ability," *J. Appl. Psychol.*, 1929, *13*, 425–39.
64. M. S. Hattwick, "Manual of Instructions and Interpretations for a Pitch Discrimination Test for Young Children," *U. of Iowa Stud. Child. Welf.*, 1935, *11*, 69–74.
65. E. A. Gaw, "Five Studies of the Music Tests," *Psychol. Monog.*, 1928, *39*, 145–56.
66. P. R. Farnsworth, "Studies in the Psychology of Tone and Music," *Genet. Psychol. Monog.*, 1934, *15*, 45–49; "Further Notes on the Seashore Music Tests," *J. Gen. Psychol.* 1938, *18*, 429–31.
67. M. E. Brown, "A Note Concerning the Seashore Measures of Musical Talent," *School and Society*, 1929, *30*, 274–75. That Hindu norms are not identical with those obtained by Seashore is shown in a study by K. Parthasarathy, "Musical Aptitude and Appreciation Among High School Students," *J. Psychol. Res., Mysore*, 1957, *1*(2), 49–59.

68. J. O'Connor, "Steps Toward the Isolation of Tonal Memory as a Mental Element," *Human Engng. Lab. Tech. Rept.*, 1938, *21.*

69. L. M. Tilson, *The Tilson-Gretsch Musical Aptitude Test,* Chicago, Publ. Sch. Music Dept., Fred Gretsch Mfg., 1941.

70. P. R. Farnsworth, "Data on the Tilson-Gretsch Test for Musical Aptitude," *J. Musicol.,* 1945, *4,* 99–102.

71. C. E. Seashore, D. Lewis, and J. G. Saetveit, *Manual, Seashore Measures of Musical Talents,* New York, Psychological Corp., 1960.

72. J. G. Saetveit, D. Lewis, and C. E. Seashore, *Revision of the Seashore Measures of Musical Talent,* Iowa City, U. of Iowa, 1940. For a review of the literature on this battery up to 1957, see R. W. Lundin, "What Next in the Psychology of Musical Measurement?" *Psychol. Rec.,* 1958, *8,* 1–6. Several researchers have adapted portions of the Seashore battery for their own nonmusical purposes. See A. Ford, "The UCDWR Pitch-Memory Selection Test," *OSRD Report,* Mar. 1944; J. D. Harris and D. Charney, "A Revision of the Navy Pitch-Memory Test," *Med. Res. Lab.,* U.S. Naval Submarine Base, New London, Conn., 1950, *9,* 1–10.

73. For a relatively unstandardized version of the tonal memory test, modified to make it more challenging to music majors, see R. Ottman, "A Statistical Investigation of the Influence of Selected Factors on the Skill of Sight-Singing," Ph.D. thesis, North Texas State College, 1956.

74. F. S. Salisbury and H. B. Smith, "Prognosis of Sight-Singing Ability of Normal School Students," *J. Appl. Psychol.,* 1929, *13,* 425–39.

75. F. A. Wright, "The Correlation Between Achievement and Capacity in Music," *J. Educ. Res.,* 1928, *17,* 50–56.

76. H. C. Manor, "A Study in Prognosis," *J. Educ. Psychol.,* 1950, *41,* 31–50. Unpublished work of Professor Paul Green of Memphis State University appears to show that the Seashore measures are too easy for college music majors and do not separate the good from the poorer students.

77. P. R. Farnsworth, "Are Music Capacity Tests More Important Than Intelligence Tests in the Prediction of Several Types of Music Grades?" *J. Appl. Psychol.,* 1935, *19,* 347–50.

78. A. R. Roby, "A Study in the Correlation of Music Theory Grades With the Seashore Measures of Musical Talents and the Aliferis Music Achievement Test," *J. Res. Music Educ.,* 1962, *10*(2), 137–42.

79. C. H. Lawshe, Jr., and W. F. Wood, "Membership in Musical Organizations as a Criterion of Talent," *Amer. J. Psychol.,* 1947, *60,* 250–53.

80. P. J. Fay and W. C. Middleton, "Relationship Between Musical Talent and Preferences for Different Types of Music," *J. Educ. Psychol.,* 1941, *32,* 573–83.

81. E. C. Dunlevy, "Musical Training and Measured Musical Aptitude," *J. Musicol.,* 1944, *4,* 1–5.

82. P. R. Farnsworth, "The Relation of the Auditory Capacities to the Feeling of Being Musical," *J. Musicol.,* 1941, *2,* 119–22.

83. H. M. Stanton, "Measurement of Musical Talent: The Eastman Experiment," *U. of Iowa Stud. Psychol. Music,* 1935, *2,* 1–140.

84. W. S. Larson, "Practical Experience With Music Tests," *Music Educ. J.,* 1938, *24,* 31. See also R. C. Larson, "Finding and Guiding Musical Talent," *Music Educ. J.,* 1955, *42,* 22–25.

85. E. M. Taylor, "A Study in the Prognosis of Musical Talent," *J. Exp. Educ.,* 1941, *10,* 1–28.

86. J. McLeish, "The Validation of Seashore's Measures of Musical Talent by Factorial Methods," *Brit. J. Psychol., Stat. Sect.,* 1950, *3,* 129–40.

87. J. Kwalwasser and P. W. Dykema, *Kwalwasser-Dykema Music Tests,* New York, Fischer, 1930.

88. P. R. Farnsworth, "Studies in the Psychology of Tone and Music," *Genet. Psychol. Monog.,* 1934, *15,* Sect. 9.

89. For descriptions of the K-D measures of melodic taste and tonal movement see Ch. 7.

90. G. M. Gilbert, " 'Aptitude' and Training: A Suggested Restandardization of the K-D Music Test Norms," *J. Appl. Psychol.*, 1941, *25*, 326–30; P. R. Farnsworth, "Studies in the Psychology of Tone and Music," *op. cit.*

91. J. A. Holmes, "Increased Reliabilities, New Keys, and Norms for a Modified Kwalwasser-Dykema Test of Musical Aptitudes," *J. Genet. Psychol.*, 1954, *85*, 65–73.

92. M. T. Whitley, "A Comparison of the Seashore and Kwalwasser-Dykema Music Tests," *Teachers Coll. Rec.*, 1932, *33*, 731–51.

93. J. Kwalwasser, *Kwalwasser Music Talent Test*, New York, Mills Music, 1953.

94. C. A. Storey (Monticello Junior High School), unpublished test.

95. R. M. Drake, "Four New Tests of Musical Talent," *J. Appl. Psychol.*, 1933, *17*, 136–47.

96. R. M. Drake, *Drake Musical Aptitude Tests*, Chicago, Science Research Associates, 1954. For a review of this battery up to 1957 see R. W. Lundin, *op. cit.* See also J. Ferrel, "A Validity Investigation of the Drake Musical Aptitude Tests," Ph.D. thesis, U. of Iowa, 1961, and J. R. Bergan, "The Relationships Among Pitch Identification, Imagery for Musical Sounds, and Musical Memory," *J. Res. Music Educ.*, 1967, *15*(2), 139–50. Some unpublished research by Professor Paul Green of Memphis State University would seem to indicate that Drake's tests are more effective diagnostic devices than are Seashore's.

97. E. Gordon, "A Study To Determine the Effects of Training and Practice on Drake Musical Aptitude Test Scores," *J. Res. Music Educ.*, 1961, *9*, 63–74.

98. R. W. Wheeler, Jr., "A Study of the Measurement of Musical Aptitude," Ph.D. thesis, U. of Oklahoma, 1959.

99. H. S. Whistler and L. P. Thorpe, *Whistler-Thorpe Musical Aptitude Test*, Los Angeles Test Bureau, 1950.

100. R. W. Lundin, "The Development and Validation of a Set of Musical Ability Tests," *Psychol. Monog.*, 1949, *63*, No. 10.

101. E. T. Gaston, *A Test of Musicality*, Lawrence, Kan., Odell's Instrumental Service, 1957.

102. H. D. Wing, *Tests of Musical Ability and Appreciation*, New York, Cambridge U. Press, 1968; "Some Applications of Test Results to Education in Music," *Brit. J. Educ. Psychol.*, 1954, *24*, 161–70; "The Measurement of Musical Aptitude," *Occup. Psychol.*, 1957, *31*, 31–37. See also J. Heller, "The Effects of Formal Training on Wing Musical Intelligence Scores," Ph.D. thesis, U. of Iowa, 1962; D. J. Pitman, "The Musical Ability of Blind Children," *Rev. Psychol. Music*, 1965, *2*(2), 19–28; L. G. Holmstrom, *Musicality and Prognosis*, Uppsala, Sweden, Almquist & Wiksells, 1963.

103. H. D. Wing, "A Revision of the Wing Musical Aptitude Test," *J. Res. Music Educ.*, 1962, *10*, 39–46.

104. R. L. Raim, "A Comparison of the Musical Aptitude Profile and the Seashore Measures of Musical Talents," M.A. thesis, U. of Iowa, 1965. See also V. V. Tarrell, "An Investigation of the Validity of the Musical Aptitude Profile," *J. Res. Music Educ.*, 1965, *13*(4), 195–206.

105. Edwin Gordon, *Musical Aptitude Profile*, Boston, Houghton Mifflin, 1965; "The Musical Aptitude Profile: A New and Unique Musical Aptitude Test Battery," *Counc. Res. Music Educ.*, 1965, *6*, 12–16; "Implications for the Use of the Musical Aptitude Profile With College and University Freshman Music Students," *J. Res. Music Educ.*, 1967, *15*(1), 32–40; *A Three-Year Study of the Musical Aptitude Profile*, Iowa City, U. of Iowa, 1967; "The Contribution of Each Musical Aptitude Profile Subtest to the Overall Validity of the Battery: A Note From the Author," *Counc. Res. Music Educ.*, 1968, *12*, 32–36; R. E. Lee, "An Investigation of the Use of the Musical Aptitude Profile With College and University Freshman Music Students," *J. Res. Music Educ.*, 1967, *15*(4), 278–88.

M. Pflederer ("Conservation Laws Applied to the Development of Musical Intelligence," *J. Res. Music Educ.,* 1967, *15*(3), 215–23), following the principles of
the Swiss educator Piaget, feels that Gordon's test is one of the few really musical
ones. The others are either wholly atomistic like Seashore's or partially atomistic.
Gordon himself feels that the *MAP* predicts music achievement well but that IQ
tests are of little help in this regard. He rationalizes his own finding that measures of intelligence correlate higher with teachers' ratings than does the *MAP*
by suggesting that the ratings tend to be polluted by "halo effects" (E. Gordon,
"A Study of the Efficacy of General Intelligence and Musical Aptitude Tests in
Predicting Achievement in Music," *Counc. Res. Music Educ.,* 1968, *13*, 40–45).

106. C. H. Taylor, "Techniques for the Evaluation of Musical Status," *J. Res. Music
Educ.,* 1963, *11*(1), 55–62.

107. A. Bentley, *Musical Ability in Children and Its Measurement,* London, Harrap,
1966; J. McLeish, "The Validity and Reliability of Bentley's Measures of Musical
Abilities," *Brit. J. Educ. Psychol.,* 1968, *38*(2), 201.

108. E. K. Strong, Jr., *Vocational Interest Blanks for Men and Women,* Palo Alto,
Calif., Consulting Psychologists Press, 1969.

109. For an example of the multiplicity of meanings attached to the term rhythm see
J. Tanner and M. Loess, "Intercorrelations Among Rhythm Subtests of Three
Tests of Musical Aptitude," *Percept. Mot. Skills,* 1967, *25*(3), 721–26, who found
Form B of the Drake Rhythm Test correlating at only .08 with Wing's Rhythmic
Accent Test.

110. E. L. Rainbow, "A Pilot Study To Investigate the Constructs of Musical Aptitude," *J. Res. Music Educ.,* 1965, *13*(1), 3–14.

111. For a survey and critique of music testing see W. E. Whybrew, *Measurement and
Evaluation in Music,* Dubuque, Iowa, W. C. Brown, 1962; H. L. Cady, "Tests
and Measures in Higher Education: School Music Teachers," *J. Res. Music Educ.,*
1967, *15*(2), 139–50; and particularly the excellent book by R. Shuter, *The Psychology of Musical Ability,* London, Methuen, 1968 (distributed by Barnes &
Noble, New York). For criticisms of specific tests see the several members of the
series entitled *Mental Measurements Yearbook* edited by O. K. Buros, Highland
Park, N.J., Gryphon Press.

CHAPTER TEN

1. I. A. Taylor and F. Paperte, "Current Theory and Research in the Effects of
Music on Behavior," *J. Aesth.,* 1958, *17*(2), 251–58.

2. D. M. Johnson and M. Trawick, "Influence of Rhythmic Sensory Stimuli Upon
the Heart-Rate," *J. Psychol.,* 1938, *6*, 303–10.

3. C. M. Diserens and H. Fine, *A Psychology of Music,* Cincinnati, published by the
authors, 1939, p. 253.

4. I. D. London, "Research on Sensory Interaction in the Soviet Union," *Psychol.
Bull.,* 1954, *51*, 531–68.

5. A. Dannenbaum, "The Effect of Music on Visual Acuity," *Sarah Lawrence Stud.,*
1945, *4*, 18–26.

6. O. Lowenstein, *Der Psychische Restitutionseffekt,* Basel, Schwabe, 1937. See also
M. Grunewald in *Music Therapy,* E. Podolsky, Ed., New York, Philosophical Library, 1954, pp. 241–51. K. Maruyama also studied the effect of tones on brightness
sensitivity and concluded that brightness was not affected retroactively by the inter-
polated tone but rather proactively ("The Effect of Tone on the Successive Comparison of Brightness," *Tohoku Psychol. Folia,* 1957, *15*, 56–69).

7. R. E. Dreher, "The Relationship Between Verbal Reports and Galvanic Skin Responses to Music," Thesis, Indiana U., 1947.

8. The galvanic skin response refers to the fact that the electrical resistance of the skin is measurably decreased whenever, during emotional states, perspiration is produced on the skin surfaces; see R. I. Henkin, "The Prediction of Behavior Response Patterns to Music," *J. Psychol.*, 1957, *44*, 111–27.

9. S. Vincent and J. H. Thompson, "The Effects of Music Upon Human Blood Pressure," *Lancet*, 1929, *I*, 534–37.

10. S. Vincent, A. T. Cameron, and H. P. Armes, "The Effects of Music Upon the Blood Pressure," *Trans. Roy. Soc. Can.*, 1914, *IV, VIII*, 255–60.

11. G. H. Zimny and E. W. Weidenfeller, "Effects of Music Upon GSR of Children," *Child Develpm.*, 1962, *33*, 891–96.

12. E. W. Weidenfeller and G. H. Zimny, "Effects of Music Upon GSR of Depressives and Schizophrenics," *J. Abn. Soc. Psychol.*, 1962, *64*(4), 307–12.

13. G. H. Zimny and E. W. Weidenfeller, "Effects of Music Upon GSR and Heart-Rate," *Amer. J. Psychol.*, 1963, *76*(2), 311–14.

14. C. A. Winold, "The Effect of Changes in Harmonic Tension Upon Listener Response," Thesis, Indiana U., 1963.

15. W. W. Sears, "The Effect of Music on Muscle Tonus," pp. 199–205 in *Music Therapy 1957*, E. G. Thayer, Ed., Lawrence, Kan., Nat. Assoc. Music Therapy, 1958.

16. D. S. Ellis and G. Brighouse, "Effects of Music on Respiration and Heart-Rate," *Amer. J. Psychol.*, 1952, *65*, 39–47; also published in *Music Therapy, op. cit.*, pp. 158–69.

17. C. G. Skelly and G. M. Haslerud, "Music and the General Activity of Apathetic Schizophrenics," *J. Abn. Soc. Psychol.*, 1952, *47*(2), 188–92.

18. M. Critchley, "Two Cases of Musicogenic Epilepsy," *J. Roy. Naval Med. Serv.*, 1942, *28*, 182–84; S. Taylor, "Musicogenic Epilepsy: Case," *J. Roy. Naval Med. Serv.*, 1942, *28*, 394–95; D. D. Daly and M. J. Barry, Jr., "Musicogenic Epilepsy: Report of Three Cases," *Psychosomat. Med.*, 1957, *19*, 399–408; M. Yvonneau and M. de Barros Ferreira, "L'epilepsie musicogénique," *Evolut. Psychiat.* 1963, *28*(1), 147–69.

19. J. R. Miles and C. R. Tilly, "Some Physiological Reactions to Music," *Guy's Hospital Gazette*, 1935, *49*, 319–22.

20. R. W. Husband, "The Effects of Musical Rhythms and Pure Rhythms on Bodily Sway," *J. Gen. Psychol.*, 1934, *11*, 328–36.

21. That music can stimulate compensatory movements which can aid one's sense of balance has been demonstrated by W. Lavere in "The Influence of Musical Training and Musical Accompaniment on the Sense of Equilibrium," Master's thesis, Syracuse U., 1950.

22. E. J. Martin and R. O. Hamilton, "Observations on Hypnotic Effects of Rhythmic Sounds at Respiratory Rates," pp. 177–87 in *Music Therapy 1958*, E. H. Schneider, Ed., Lawrence, Kan., Nat. Assoc. Music Therapy, 1959.

23. C. M. Diserens and H. Fine, *op. cit.*, pp. 273–74. See also M. Rieber, "The Effect of Music on the Activity Level of Children," *Psychonomic Science*, 1965, *3*(8), 325–26.

24. M. B. Jensen, "The Influence of Jazz and Dirge Music Upon Speed and Accuracy of Typing," *J. Educ. Psychol.*, 1931, *22*, 458–62.

25. P. L. Whitely, "The Influence of Music on Memory," *J. Gen. Psychol.*, 1934, *10*, 137–51.

26. P. R. Farnsworth, "Continued Training With the Omission of Certain Nebenreize," *J. Genet. Psychol.*, 1937, *50*, 277–82.

27. P. Fendrick, "The Influence of Music Distraction Upon Reading Efficiency," *J. Educ. Res.*, 1937, *31*, 264–71.

28. M. T. Henderson, A. Crews, and J. Barlow, "A Study of the Effect of Music Distraction on Reading Efficiency," *J. Appl. Psychol.*, 1945, *29*, 313–17.

29. R. H. Knapp and H. B. Green, "The Judgment of Music-Filled Intervals and *n* Achievement," *J. Soc. Psychol.*, 1961, *54*, 263–67.

30. C. M. Freeburne and M. Fleischer, "The Effect of Music Distraction Upon Reading Rate and Comprehension," *J. Educ. Psychol.*, 1952, *43*, 101–9.

31. J. C. Hall, "The Effect of Background Music on the Reading Comprehension of 278 8th and 9th Grade Students," *J. Educ. Res.*, 1952, *45*, 451–58.

32. B. Mikol and M. R. Denny, "The Effect of Music and Rhythm on Rotary Pursuit Performance," *Percep. Mot. Skills*, 1955, *5*, 3–6.

33. B. Isern, "The Influence of Music Upon the Memory of Mentally Retarded Children," pp. 162–65 in *Music Therapy 1958, op. cit.*; "Summary, Conclusions, and Implications: The Influence of Music Upon the Memory of Mentally Retarded Children," pp. 149–53 in *Music Therapy 1960*, E. H. Schneider, Ed., Lawrence, Kan., Nat. Assoc. Music Therapy, 1961. For the use of music therapy with the mentally retarded see also H. Joseph and E. P. Heimlich, "The Therapeutic Use of Music With 'Treatment Resistant' Children," *Amer. J. Ment. Defic.*, 1959, *64*, 41–49.

34. J. C. Baugh and J. R. Baugh, "The Effects of Four Types of Music on the Learning of Nonsense Syllables," *J. Music Therapy*, 1965, *2*(2), 69–71.

35. J. A. Carlson and B. R. Hergenhahn, "Effects of Rock-n-Roll and Classical Music on the Learning of Nonsense Syllables," *Psychol. Rept.*, 1967, *20*(3, Pt. 1), 1021–22.

36. According to E. Podolsky as reported in *Music for Your Health*, New York, Ackerman, 1945, almost any musical rhythm can be employed in factories since the rhythm of the worker's task is little affected by the rhythm of the music he hears. This is an astonishing claim and one with which many "experts" do not agree. See also "Soap Wrappers' Jig," *J. Amer. Med. Assoc.*, 1955, *157*, 1329–30.

37. R. I. Newman, Jr., D. L. Hunt, and F. Rhodes, "Effects of Music on Employee Attitude and Productivity in a Skateboard Factory," *J. Appl. Psychol.*, 1966, *50*(6), 493–96. For another well-designed experiment which could find no beneficial effects of background music on monotonous tasks, see G. K. Poock and E. L. Wiener, "Music and Other Auditory Backgrounds During Visual Monitoring," *J. Ind. Engineer.*, 1966, *17*(6), 318–23. See also W. McGehee and J. E. Gardner, "Music in a Complex Industrial Job," *Personnel Psychol.*, 1949, *2*, 405–17; W. A. S. Smith, "Effects of Industrial Music in a Work Situation Requiring Complex Mental Activity," *Psychol. Rept.*, 1961, *8*, 159–62; W. A. Kerr, "Experiments on the Effects of Music on Factory Production," *Appl. Psychol. Monog.*, 1945, No. 5.

38. A. Wisner and C. Tarriere, "Les effets des bruits sur la vigilance en fonction de leurs caractéristiques physiques et psychophysiologiques," *Acustica*, 1964, *14*, 216–26.

39. W. Adorno, "The Radio Symphony," in *Radio Research 1941*, P. F. Lazarsfeld and F. N. Stanton, Eds., New York, Duell, Sloan and Pearce, 1941.

40. H. C. Smith, "Music in Relation to Employee Attitudes, Piecework Production, and Industrial Accidents," *Appl. Psychol. Monog.*, 1947, No. 14.

41. For a most optimistic report of British industrial music see L. Kaplan and R. Nettel, "Music in Industry," *Biol. Human Affairs, London*, 1948, *13*, 129–35. For discussions of the part played by Muzak in getting music to industry see E. M. Werner, *Work Music by Muzak*, New York, Muzak Corp., 1948; Muzak Corporation's *Effects of Muzak on Office Personnel* (C-1 [4] 28), and *How Muzak Affects Profits* (C-1 [4] 28a), New York, 1958. A popular account of Muzak procedures can be found in *Time*, Aug. 30, 1963, pp. 34, 36. See also R. L. Cardinell, "Music in Industry," in *Music and Medicine*, D. M. Schullian and M. Schoen, Eds., New York, Schuman, 1948, pp. 352–66. For an excellent critique of the subject of industrial music see R. S. Uhrbrock's "Music on the Job: Its influence on Worker Morale and Production," *Personnel Psychol.*, 1961, *14*(1), 9–38. See also R. Paul and V. M. Staudt, "Music Therapy for the Mentally Ill: I. A Historical Sketch and Brief Review of the Literature on the Physiological Effects and on Analysis of the Elements of Music," *J. Gen. Psychol.*, 1958, *59*, 167–76.

42. The reader will not be surprised to learn that music rated as extremely loud tends to inhibit time spent in supermarkets. See P. C. Smith and R. Curnow, "Arousal

Hypothesis and the Effects of Music on Purchasing Behavior," *J. Appl. Psychol.*, 1966, *50*, 255–56.

43. The caption music therapy now denotes a young but vigorous and growing profession. For some years the house organ of the music therapists was the *Proceedings of the National Association for Music Therapy (Music Therapy 1951* through *1962)*, but since 1964 the profession has had a special medium of publication, the *Journal of Music Therapy*. There is now available a rating scale which purportedly differentiates between "good" and "poor" musical therapists (L. Shatin, G. Douglas-Longmore, and W. K. Kotter, "Qualified Criterion for Evaluating the Music Therapist," *J. Rehabilit.*, 1963, *29*(1), 18–19). Another study shows successful musical therapists to have less strong musical interests than have professional musicians (L. Shatin, W. K. Kotter, and G. Douglas-Longmore, "A Psychological Study of the Musical Therapist in Rehabilitation," *J. Gen. Psychol.*, 1964, *71*(2), 193–205). Although a course on "musicotherapy" was offered at Columbia University as early as 1919, the first four-year course designed to create specialists in the field was not introduced until 1944. The institution which started the curriculum was Michigan State College (now Michigan State University). For a history of the profession see R. Boxberger. "A Historical Study of the National Association for Music Therapy," pp. 133–97 in *Music Therapy 1962*, E. H. Schneider, Ed., Lawrence, Kan., Allen Press, 1963. See also the several "Abstracts From Medical Literature Concerning the Use of Music," published by the Hospitalized Veterans Service of the Musicians Emergency Fund, Inc. of New York City; and R. Dreikurs, "Music Therapy With Psychotic Children," *Psychiat. Quart.*, 1960, *34*, 722–34.

44. F. Densmore, "Importance of Rhythm in Songs for the Treatment of the Sick by American Indians," *Sci. Monthly*, 1954, *79*, 109–12.

45. J. Colbert, "On the Musical Effect," *Psychiat. Quart.*, 1963, *37*(3), 429–36.

46. See for example E. May, "Music for Children With Cerebral Palsy," *Amer. J. Physic. Med.*, 1956, *35*, 320–23; P. Nordoff, C. Robbins, and H. Geuter, "Curative Music," *Cerebral Palsy Revue*, 1963, *24*(3), 2–8; B. Fields, "Music as an Adjunct in the Treatment of Brain-Damaged Patients," *Amer. J. Physic. Med.*, 1954, *33*, 273; M. Josepha (O.S.F.), "Therapeutic Values of Instrumental Performance for Severely Handicapped Children," *J. Music Therapy*, 1964, *1*(3), 73–79; A. Juliette, *Music for the Handicapped Child*, New York, Oxford U. Press, 1965; P. Nordoff and C. Robbins, *Music Therapy for Handicapped Children*, New York, Rudolf Steiner Publ., 1965; D. E. Michel, "Music Therapy in Cleft Palate Disorders," pp. 126–31 in *Music Therapy 1960, op. cit.*

47. L. Cholden, "Panel: Psychiatric Concepts of Music Therapy," pp. 27–36 in *Music Therapy 1952*, E. G. Gilliland, Ed., Lawrence, Kan., Nat. Assoc. Music Therapy, 1953; T. Ishiyama, "Music as a Psychotherapeutic Tool in the Treatment of Catatonics," *Psychiat. Quart.*, 1963, *37*(3), 437–61.

48. I. M. Altshuler, "Rational Music-Therapy of the Mentally Ill," *Music Teach. Nat. Assoc. Proc. 1939*, 1940, pp. 153–57.

49. A. Gillis, C. Lascelles, and N. Crone, "A Comparison of Rhythmic and Non-rhythmic Music in Chronic Schizophrenics," *Proc. 2nd Intern. Congr. Psychiat.*, Zurich, Sept., 1957.

50. A. Zanker and M. Glatt, "Individual Reactions of Alcoholics and Neurotic Patients to Music," *J. Nerv. Ment. Dis.*, 1956, *234*(4), 395–402.

51. M. G. Ruegnitz, "Applied Music on Disturbed Wards," *Occup. Ther. and Rehabilit.*, 1946, *25*, 203–6.

52. S. D. Mitchell and A. Zanker, "The Use of Music in Group Therapy," *J. Ment. Sci.*, 1948, *94*, 737–48.

53. A. Van Krevelen, "The Influence of Music on Reactions to Frustration," *J. Gen. Psychol.*, 1963, *68*(1), 107–10.

54. W. C. Middleton *et al.*, "The Effect of Music on Feelings of Restfulness-Tiredness, and Pleasantness-Unpleasantness," *J. Psychol.*, 1944, *17*, 299–318.

55. H. R. Brickman, "Psychiatric Implications of Functional Music for Education," *Music Educ. J.*, 1950, *36*, 29–30; M. Chace, "Dance Therapy for the Mentally Ill," *Dance Mag.*, 1956, *30*, 37–39, 58; I. G. Weintraub, "Emotional Responses of Schizophrenics to Selected Musical Compositions," *Delaware Med. J.*, 1961, *33*(6), 186; C. Boenheim, "Music and Group Therapy," *J. Music Therapy*, 1966, *3*(2), 49–52; B. Butler, "Music Group Psychotherapy," *J. Music Therapy*, 1966, *3*(2), 53–56; W. F. White and W. R. Allen, "Psychodramatic Effects of Music as a Psychotherapeutic Agent," *J. Music Therapy*, 1966, *3*(2), 69–71; R. P. Wortis, "Music Therapy for the Mentally Ill: II. The Effect of Music on Emotional Activity and the Value of Music as a Resocializing Agent," *J. Gen. Psychol.*, 1960, *62*, 311–18; C. Christman, "Family Group Therapy: Implications for Music Therapy," *J. Music Therapy*, 1967, *4*(3), 100–105.

56. H. L. Bonny, M. Cistrunk, R. Makuch, E. Stevens, and J. Tally, "Some Effects of Music on Verbal Interaction in Groups," *J. Music Therapy*, 1965, 2(2), 61–63.

57. R. V. Heckel, S. L. Wiggins, and H. C. Salzberg, "The Effect of Musical Tempo in Varying Operant Speech Levels in Group Therapy," *J. Clin. Psychol.*, 1963, *19*(1), 129.

58. L. Shatin and C. Zimet, "Influence of Music Upon Verbal Participation in Group Psychotherapy," *Diseases of the Nervous System*, Feb., 1958, *19*(2).

59. When 120 psychiatrists were polled about the functions of music therapy, the items most mentioned were improving the interpersonal relationship between patient and therapist and the enhancing of self-expression. Next most often mentioned was socialization, next came providing ego strength, and fifth, helping to contact the patient (D. E. Michel, "Concluding Report: A Survey of Three Hundred Seventy-Five Cases in Music Therapy," pp. 137–52 in *Music Therapy 1959*, E. H. Schneider, Ed., Lawrence, Kan., Nat. Assoc. Music Therapy, 1960).

60. V. Goertzel, P. R. May, J. Salkin, and T. Schoop, "Body-ego Technique: An Approach to the Schizophrenic Patient." *J. Nerv. Ment. Dis.*, 1965, *141*(1), 53–60.

61. H. E. Browne, "The Use of Music as a Therapy," *Ment. Hyg.*, N.Y., 1952, *36*, 90–103; F. Knoblich, M. Postolka, and J. Srnec, "Musical Experience as Interpersonal Process," *Psychiat.*, 1964, *27*(3), 259–65.

62. H. S. Whiting, in "Effect of Music on Hospital Accident Rate," *Amer. J. Ment. Defic.*, 1947, *51*, 397–400, maintains that music played over the radio in a hospital for mental defectives can produce a drastic reduction in the number of accidents on the wards. For further material on music in hospitals for mental defectives see A. Wendelin and T. L. Engle, "A Survey of Musical Activities in Institutions for the Mentally Deficient," *Amer. J. Ment. Defic.*, 1954, *59*, 206–9; M. Murphy, "Rhythmic Responses of Low Grade and Middle Grade Mental Defectives to Music Therapy," *J. Clin. Psychol.*, 1957, *13*(4), 361–64.

63. H. Klingler and D. Peter, "Techniques in Group Singing for Aphasics," pp. 108–12 in *Music Therapy 1962, op. cit.;* H. Goodglass, "Musical Capacity After Brain Injury," *ibid.*, pp. 101–7.

64. B. Kaplan, "Music With Nitrous Oxide-Oxygen," *Anaesthesia (London)*, 1956, *11*(2), 160–63; R. Schermer, "Distraction Analgesia Using the 'Stereogesic Portable,'" *Military Med.*, Dec., 1960, *125*, 843; "Music and 'White Sound,'" *ibid.*, June, 1961, *126*, 440; W. Gardner, J. Licklider, and A. Weisz, "Suppression of Pain by Sound," *Science*, 1960, *132*, 32–33.

65. For some insight into the patient's own view of music therapy see D. T. Sommer, "Music in the Autobiographies of Mental Patients," *Ment. Hyg.*, N.Y., 1961, *45*(3), 402–7.

66. B. Simon *et al.*, "The Recognition and Acceptance of Mood in Music by Psychotic Patients," *J. Nerv. Ment. Dis.*, 1951, *114*, 66–78.

67. A. Zanker and M. M. Glatt, "The Influence of Music on Groups of Alcoholic and Neurotic Patients in a Mental Hospital," *J. Nerv. Ment. Dis.*, 1956, *123*, 403–5.

68. G. W. Ainlay, "The Place of Music in Military Hospitals," *Etude*, 1945, *63*, 433, 468, 480.
69. L. M. Brown in *Music Therapy, op. cit.*, pp. 135–38.
70. G. E. Arrington, Jr., in *Music Therapy, op. cit.*, pp. 252–87. See also the longer lists from the chapter by H. G. Price *et al.* in the same book, pp. 95–100.
71. P. Sugarman in *Music Therapy, op. cit.*, pp. 151–54.
72. B. Hillard in *Music Therapy, op. cit.*, pp. 121–29.
73. J. Girard in *Music Therapy, op. cit.*, pp. 101–6.
74. For further references on music therapy see L. Gilman and F. Paperte, *Music and Your Emotions*, New York, Liveright, 1952, pp. 24–55; S. H. Licht, *Music in Medicine*, Boston, New England Conservatory of Music, 1946; D. M. Schullian and M. Schoen, Eds., *Music and Medicine, op. cit.*; D. Soibelman, *Therapeutic and Industrial Uses of Music*, New York, Columbia U. Press, 1948; W. Van de Wall, "Funtional Use of Music in Industry and Therapy," *Music Teach. Nat. Assoc. Proc. 1944*, 1944, pp. 147–53; E. T. Gaston, *Music in Therapy*, New York, Macmillan, 1968. See also H. A. Dinklage, "Music Therapy, A Selected Bibliography," pp. 249–93 in *Music Therapy 1958, op. cit.*; "Addendum: Music Therapy Bibliography," pp. 183–85 in *Music Therapy 1960, op. cit.*; H. R. Teirich, Ed., *Musik in der Medizin: Beitrage zur Musiktherapie*, Stuttgart, Germany, Fischer, 1958; G. R. Heyer, "Zur Musiktherapie," *Prax. Psychother.*, 1960, *5*, 187–90; A. G. Pikler, "Music as an Aid in Psychotherapy," *Acta Psychol., Amsterdam*, 1961, *18*(5), 317–31; E. G. Gilliland, "Progress in Music Therapy," *Rehabilit. Lit.*, 1962, *23*(10), 298–306, 316. Note the *Abstracts From Medical Literature Concerning the Use of Music*, published by Hospitalized Veterans Service of the Musicians Emergency Fund, Inc., 745 5th Ave., New York City.
75. D. Blair and M. Brooking, "Music as a Therapeutic Agent," *Ment. Hyg., N.Y.*, 1957, *41*, 228–37.
76. P. Wenger, "The Value of Music in the Successful Psychotherapy of a Schizophrenic Patient," *Psychiat. Quart. Suppl.*, 1952, *26*, 202–9.
77. See M. L. Sears and W. W. Sears, "Abstracts of Research in Music Therapy," *J. Music Therapy*, 1964, *1*(2), 33–60.

SUBJECT INDEX ✠
(See also entries in Glossary and Notes sections)

abilities, musical, 16
  Adlerian views on, 162, 163
  contrasted with aptitudes, capacities, and talents, 151
  critical levels in, 13
  and family lines, 158, 159
  Freudian views on, 164, 165, 178
  generality of, 152–54
  heritability of, 156–59
  how they develop, 166–75
  imagery as a source of, 165, 166
  Jungian views on, 163, 164
  measurement of; *see* tests of musical aptitudes, tests of musical achievement
  nature of, 151–83
  and physical and mental structure, 159–62
  "race" differences in, 4, 159, 160, 162, 163
  related to academic intelligence, 155, 156, 179
  related to other art abilities, 154, 155
  sex differences in, 160, 161, 168
  training methods for developing, 168–75
  use of factor analysis to study, 152–54
abnormality, and musicality, 161, 162
absolute pitch, 50–53, 73
  defined, 53
absolute tempo, 60, 61
achievement, in music
  forecasting, 13
  tests of; *see* tests of musical achievement
adaptation level, and musical taste, 131
Adler Music Appreciation Tests, 138
Adlerian views, on musical abilities, 162, 163

Aeolian Corporation; *see* player pianos
aesthetic index, 242
aesthetic measure, 242
African music, 5, 17, 24, 63, 64, 75, 90, 91, 100
Aliferis-Stecklein Music Achievement Tests, 188
alternative hypotheses, consideration of, 6–8
American Indian music, 85
American Musicological Society, 101–4, 106–9, 125, 142, 143, 147, 148, 227, 228
American in Paris (Gershwin), 223
art abilities, as related to musical aptitudes, 154, 155
Asiatic music, 28, 39, 56, 63, 75, 90, 93, 99, 100; *see also* scales, musical
astrology, and music, 7, 8, 98, 99
atonal music, 27, 70
Ave Maria (Schubert), 80, 224
Aviation Suite (Grofé), 224

Bach family, 158
Bailey Test of Listening Skill, 188
baton movements, 6; *see also* Takt
Beach Standardized Music Tests, 185
Beale Street Mamma (Turk & Robinson), 75
beauty; *see also* taste, musical
  defined, 122
Bentley Measures of Musical Abilities, 206, 207
beta learning, in music, 170, 171
biographies, musical, 175–80
Blue Danube Waltz (J. Strauss), 216
Blue Interval (Hall), 212
"blues" effects, 75

Bolero (Ravel), 259
boredom, in music, 148, 149
Boston Evening Transcript, 114
Boston Symphony Orchestra, 53, 95, 111,
    113, 114, 116, 121, 143–45, 148
Bower Musical Moods Test, 137

Cadence Test (Lowery), 141
Cantata, No. 2 (Bach), 224; *No. 21,* 224
Caprice Viennois (Kreisler), 75
Cavalleria Rusticana (Mascagni), 223
cent, in scale measurement, 24–26, 28, 30,
    31, 34, 59
child prodigies, 156, 157, 168, 191
Children's Corner Suite (Debussy), 224
chromesthesia, 77, 78
Clair de Lune (Debussy), 81, 224
climatic cycles, and musical taste, 127, 128
Clock Symphony (Haydn), 224
color-tone linkage, 76–78
    chromesthesia, 77, 78
common sense, invalidity of, 4, 5
composer space allocations, 117–19, 144–
    48
concert programs, 113–16, 143–45
Concerto in A (Bach), 223
Concerto in D Minor (Bach), 12, 13, 224
Concerto in G Minor (Prokofiev), 138
Concerto, No. 2 in A (Liszt), 224
concertometer, 191
Conrad Instrument-Talent Test, 193
consonance
    adjectives to describe, 81, 87
    and beat roughness, 42
    children's reactions to, 166, 167
    and cultural and individual adaptation,
        43
    and dissonance, 42–44
    and fusion, 42
    "general stylistic consonance," 90
    and learning, 44
    and simplicity of interval ratio, 43
    test of, 112, 135, 136
cornet and tuba techniques, 172, 173
Courtis Test, 137
creativity, 159–61, 175–81
    causes of epochs in, 181
    General Problem Solver, 176
    items allegedly necessary for, 179
    and madness, 179
    peak year for, 180
CSS76 Criterion Sightsinging Test (Thos-
    tenson), 189, 190

Daphnis and Chloe (Ravel), 87, 89
designative meaning, in music, 71, 72
Diagnostic Tests of Achievement in Mu-
    sic (Kotick & Torgerson), 187
Dictionary of Philosophy, 97
dissonance; *see* consonance

Don Giovanni (Mozart), 223
Doppelgänger (Schubert), 91
Drake Musical Aptitude Tests, 201, 202
drone bass, 37, 66

Ear Tests in Harmony (Wood), 187
Eddie Duchin Album (Berlin), 223
Egmont Overture (Beethoven), 223
eidetic imagery, 165, 166, 175
Elijah (Mendelssohn), 223
embodied meaning, in music, 70, 71
eminence; *see* taste, musical
Encyclopaedia Britannica, 147, 148
enjoyment of music; *see also* taste, mu-
    sical
    relation to taste, 110–12
equal temperament, scales of, 20, 23–27,
    30, 38, 40, 72, 99
Erneston Preference Record, 138
Eroica Symphony (Beethoven), 61

Farnsworth's taste scales, 142
Farnum Music Notation Test, 187
Fidelio (Beethoven), 223
Fifth Symphony (Beethoven), 116, 129,
    252
Fifth Symphony (Dvořák), 74
Fifth Symphony (Tchaikovsky), 259
finality effects, 37–41, 45, 74, 87, 97
    alleged gestaltish effects, 38, 39, 99
    alleged neurological effects, 38, 39, 99
    described by Lipps-Meyer Law, 38–40,
        74
    effect of emphasis and familiarity, 37–
        39
    effect of falling inflection, 37
    effect of size of interval, 37
    effect of slowing the tempo, 37
    and tonality, 41
Finlandia (Sibelius), 224
First Piano Concerto (Chopin), 223
formalism, 47, 48, 50
Freudian views on music abilities; *see*
    psychoanalysis and music

Gaieté Parisienne (Offenbach), 223
galvanic skin response, 86, 212
German Requiem (Brahms), 259
Gernet Music Preference Test, 137
Graduate Record Examinations, Advanced
    Tests, 189
*Gramophone Shop Encyclopedia of Re-
    corded Music, The,* 146
Grand Larousse, 147
*Groves Dictionary of Music and Musi-
    cians,* 147
Guide to Recorded Music, A, 146

handedness, and musicality, 161
harmony; *see also* melody
  and meaning, 83, 84, 86
  as perceived by baby, 166
hereditarianism (nativism), 3, 4, 50, 51,
  156–61
High Fidelity, 117
Hillbrand Sight-Singing Test, 189
history lag, 5, 6
Home, Sweet Home (Bishop), 80
Hungarian Rhapsody No. 1 (Liszt), 223
Hungarian Rhapsody No. 2 (Liszt), 212,
  223
Hutchinson Music Tests, 186
hymnometer, 191

idiot-savant, 155, 156
imagery, in music learning, 173
Individual Test for Assessing One Aspect
  of Instrumental Music Achievement
  (Gutsch), 190
industrial music, 217–19
intelligence, and music abilities, 155, 156,
  179
  in great composers, 155
Intermezzo in E Flat (Brahms), 223
*International Cyclopedia of Music and
  Musicians,* 108, 109
intervals, musical, 18–46, 53, 125
  apparent pitch of, 35, 36, 45
  augmented, 42
  "blues" thirds and sevenths, 27, 75
  diminished, 42
  discrimination of, 24–26
  distinctive quality, 33, 34, 43, 44
  fifth, 18, 19, 21, 23–26, 29, 33, 37, 40,
    42, 43, 56, 66, 112, 129
  finality effects of, 37
  fourth, 19, 24, 26, 33, 37, 39, 42, 66,
    112, 166
  major-minor, naming of, 36, 45
  major second, 19–21, 24, 27, 28, 33, 39,
    40, 42, 54, 73, 84, 86, 112
  major seventh, 21, 25, 29, 33, 34, 39,
    42, 43, 112
  major sixth, 21, 26, 29, 33, 36, 39, 42,
    66, 112
  major third, 21, 26, 29, 33, 34, 40, 42,
    44, 66, 83, 112, 166
  minor second (semitone, semit), 18–20,
    23, 24, 27, 28, 38–40, 42, 51, 54, 84,
    86, 112
  minor seventh, 34, 42, 112
  minor sixth, 34, 36, 42, 66, 112
  minor third, 29, 34, 42, 66, 86, 112, 166
  octave, 18–21, 23, 24, 27–30, 33–35, 42,
    43, 65, 66, 99, 112, 129, 166
  quarter-tone, 28, 29
  resolutions of, 39, 40
  trill, 34, 35
  tritone, 34, 112

I.P.A.T. Music Preference Test (Cattell &
  Saunders), 139
Isle of the Dead (Rachmaninov), 224
"iso" principle, 221
Italian Concerto (Bach), 224
Italian Symphony (Mendelssohn), 223

jazz, 27, 60, 62–64, 75, 97, 98, 106, 110,
  126, 216
  and creativity, 177
  Negro "soul music," 123
  and "plugging," 129
  and temperament, 124, 164
Jones Music Recognition Test, 188
Jungian views on music abilities, 163, 164
just intonation, scales of, 20–22, 25–27, 29,
  30, 40, 74, 99

Keston Music Preference Test, 137
Keston Music Recognition Test, 138
key, 37, 39, 40, 58, 97
  and color association, 77
  Lavignac Table, 73
  and mode effects, 72, 73
keynote; *see* finality effects
knowledge of composers; *see also* taste,
  musical
  relation to taste, 112, 113
Knuth Achievement Tests in Music, 186
Kwalwasser-Dykema Music Tests, 112,
  125, 136, 137, 198, 200
Kwalwasser Music Talent Test, 200
Kwalwasser-Ruch Test of Musical Accomplishment, 186
Kyme Test of Esthetic Judgment of Music, 138

language aspects of music, 28, 33, 34, 36–
  42, 56, 57, 60, 63, 66–96
  adjective lists for classifying music, 80–
    83
  color-tone linkage, 76–78
  designative meaning, 71, 72
  desire for communication, 69, 70
  embodied meaning, 70–71
  and emotions, 78–80
  and expression of tensions, 87–90
  major and minor modes, 73–76
  mode and key effects, 72, 73
  universality of, 90, 91
  variables which give meaning to mu-
    sic, 83–87
Larousse de la Musique, 147
La Valse (Rand), 224
Lavignac Table, 73
learning, in music
  beta, 170, 171
  coordinated vs. unilateral technique,
    172

cornet and tuba techniques, 172, 173
feedback, 171
individual vs. group techniques, 173
mass vs. distributed, 170
mental prestudy and rehearsal, 170
motivated vs. unmotivated, 169
overlearning, 169
programmed instruction, 173, 174
retroactive inhibition, 171, 172
role of imagery in, 173
sight-reading, 174, 175
whole vs. part, 168
L'Histoire du Soldat (Stravinsky), 87, 89, 129
Lincoln Portrait (Copland), 223
Lipps-Meyer Law, 38–40, 74
listener "types," 131, 132
loudness; *see also* tonal attributes
factor in major-minor discriminations, 75
losses with age, 56, 57
and meaning, 84, 87, 91, 93, 94
Lullaby (Brahms), 224
Lundin Tests, 203, 204

major chords, 36, 37, 40, 73, 74, 90
distinguished from minor chords, 75
major music, 60, 62, 63, 73–76, 90
marijuana, and music ability, 4
Masquerade Suite (Khachaturian), 223
Mass in E Minor (Bruckner), 224
massed vs. distributed learning, in music, 170
McCauley Experiment in Public School Music, 186, 187
mean-tone temperaments, scales of, 22, 23, 25, 26, 30
Melodic and Harmonic Sensitivity Tests (Kwalwasser), 112, 125, 136
Melodic Taste Test (Kwalwasser-Dykema), 136
melody, 47–68
and attention and learning, 48–52
in children, 166,
defined, 47
and harmony, 65–67
and loudness, 53–55
and meaning, 83, 84, 86
and noise, 59, 60
and pitch level, 50–53
and rhythm, 61–65
and sonance, 58
and tempo, 60, 61
and timbre, 56–58
Melody in F (Rubinstein), 224
mental prestudy and rehearsal, in music, 170
mescaline (peyote), and musical behavior, 77, 78
metaphysical rationalizations, in music, 20, 21, 29, 30

minor chords, 36, 37, 40, 56, 74, 167
confused with Siamese, whole-tone, 75
distinguished from major chords, 75
minor music, 60, 62, 63, 73–76, 90, 92, 167
Miserere (Allegri), 166
Missa Solemnis (Beethoven), 259
Mississippi Suite (Grofé), 223
mode, 27, 28, 41, 72–76, 83, 84, 97
Grecian, 72
and key effects, 72, 73
major, 28, 41, 73–76
and meaning, 83, 84
minor, 28, 41, 73–76
polymodality, 41
modulation, 21, 23, 30, 53, 72
Mohler Scales for Measuring Judgment of Orchestral Music, 138, 139
monotones, 4, 5
mood adjectives, 80–83
mood music, 79–96
Moonlight Sonata (Beethoven), 223, 224
Mosher Test of Individual Singing, 189
Musical Achievement Test (Gildersleeve & Soper), 185, 186
Musical Aptitude Profile (Gordon), 205, 206
Music Education: National Teacher Examinations, 188, 189
music effects
as employed for industry, 218, 219
as employed in therapy, 219–24
on general activity, 214–17
on nonrepetitive work, 217, 218
on physiological processes, 210–14
on repetitive work, 217
theories concerning, 209, 210
Music Reaction Test (Lifton), 138
Music on Records, 146
music study
and art study described and defined, 17
biological approach to, 3, 4
sociopsychological approach to, 4
music therapy, 219–24
Muzak Corporation, 219

Narcissus (Nevin), 224
New World Symphony (Dvořák), 259
New York Herald Tribune, 148, 149
New York Philharmonic Symphony Orchestra, 18, 121
New York Symphony Orchestra, 121
Ninth Symphony (Beethoven), 116, 259
Nocturne in D Flat (Chopin), 64, 224
Nocturne in G Minor (Chopin), 224
noise, in music, 59, 60
Nutcracker Suite (Tchaikovsky), 252

obe-imeter, 191
O-M Sight-Singing Test (Otterstein & Mosher), 189
opera, musical taste in, 122

Opus 53 (Chopin), 62
Oregon Music Discrimination Tests (Hevner & Landsbury), 139
overlearning, in music, 169
Oxford Companion to Music, 108, 109

Pacific Gas & Electric Co., 115, 144, 145, 148
Parsifal (Wagner), 259
Peer Gynt Suite (Grieg), 74
pentatonic scales, 27, 30, 75, 98
perception, unconscious, 22, 26, 43
Performance Test for the Cornet or Trumpet (Watkins), 190
Perpetual Motion (Victor 74581), 137
personality, of listener; *see* temperament, of listener
Philadelphia Orchestra, 111, 122
phon, a measure of loudness, 55
phrasing, 90
Piano Sonata No. 4 (Anthiel), 224
pitch; *see also* tonal attributes
    absolute, 50–53, 73
    factor in major-minor discriminations, 75
    and meaning, 84, 85
    and melody, 50–53
    range in children, 166, 167
    training in, 4, 5, 157, 158, 167
player pianos, 6, 60, 65
Polonaise Militaire (Chopin), 252
Polynesian music, 90
polyrhythms, 64, 65
polytonal music, 41
positive pitch; *see* absolute pitch
preferences; *see also* taste, musical
    effects of suggestion on, 12, 13
    for intervals, 29, 42, 54
    and pitch range, 53
    and symbolic sexual arousal, 93
    for tempos, 11
Prelude (Rachmaninov), 149
Prelude, Opus 28 (Chopin), 223
Prelude to the Afternoon of a Fawn (Debussy), 212
Prelude and Fugue in E Minor (Bach), 223
Prince Igor (Borodin), 223
PRM 78 Dictation Test (Thostenson), 190
programmed instruction, in music study, 173, 174
Providence Inventory Test in Music, 187
psychoanalysis and music, 91–94, 164, 165, 178
psychomusical investigations, limitations of, 8, 9
Pythagorean scale, 19–21, 23, 25, 29

quarter-tone music, 28, 29, 31
Quartet in B Flat Minor (Schubert), 224

Quartet in F (Ravel), 224
Quartet No. 5 (Bartók), 224

"race" differences, in music ability, 159, 160, 162, 163
ratio measurement; *see* cent
Record Book, The, 146
recordings on discs, and musical taste, 117, 145, 146, 148
Records in Review, 117
register, 75, 77, 84, 85, 90, 94
research possibilities, in experimental aesthetics, 9–13
    absence of absolutes, 13, 14
    causal function, 10–12
    descriptive function, 9, 10
    forecasting function, 12, 13
    resolutions; *see* finality effects
Rhapsody in Blue (Gershwin), 252
rhythm, 5, 61–65, 99, 125
    in children, 166, 167
    and meaning, 83, 84, 86, 87, 90, 92
    polyrhythms (crossrhythms), 64, 65
    subjective, 63
rhythmometer, 191
Ring Cycle (Wagner), 90

Saul (Handel), 62
scales, musical, 17–31
    Chien Lohtze's, 28
    chromatic, 19
    diatonic defined, 19
    of equal temperament, 20, 23–27, 30, 38, 40, 72, 99
    in Ganda culture, 24
    Hindu 22-note, 28
    of the Javanese, 23–27, 30, 99
    of just intonation, 20–22, 25–27, 29, 30, 40, 74, 99
    with mean-tone temperaments, 22, 23, 25, 26, 30
    pentatonic, 27, 30, 75, 98
    Pythagorean, 19–21, 23, 25, 29
    quarter-tone, 28, 29, 31
    Scriabin's, 28
    of the Siamese, 23–27, 29, 30, 75, 99
    12-tone, 27, 30
    using the prime number 7, 20
    whole-tone, 27, 28, 30, 44, 75
Scheherezade (Rimsky-Korsakov), 259
Schelomo (Bloch), 87–89
Schwann Long-Playing Record Catalogue, 146
Seashore Measures of Musical Talents, 13, 44, 99, 112, 135, 153, 157, 163, 164, 167, 168, 194–98, 201, 202, 205, 207, 208
Second Concerto (Rachmaninov), 223
Semeonoff's music tests, 139
Sense of Consonance Test (Seashore), 44,

112, 135, 136
Sérénade Mélancolique (Victor 74711), 137
Seventh Symphony (Beethoven), 95
sex differences, in music ability, 160, 161, 168
sight reading, in music, 174, 175
Sixth Symphony (Beethoven), 224
Sixth Symphony (Tchaikovsky), 140, 223
sonance, 58
Sonata in D (Prokofiev), 224
Sonata No. 2 for Violin and Piano (Ives), 224
Sonata for Piano (Bartók), 224
Sonata for Violin (Bartók), 224
Special Vocabularies of the Public School Subjects, The (Pressey), 187
Standardized Music Achievement Test Battery for the Intermediate Grades (Swinchoski), 187
Storey Test, 200, 201
String Quartet No. 1 (Debussy), 138
Strong Vocational Interest Test, 154, 162, 207
Strouse Music Test, 186
student ballots, 104–7, 110–13, 125, 126, 128, 144, 145
Study of the Measurement of Musical Aptitude, A (Wheeler), 202
suggestions and preferences, 12, 13
Suite Française (Milhaud), 224
Suite No. 1 in D Minor (Bach), 138
Suor Angelica (Puccini), 138
Suzuki method, in violin instruction, 167
Swan, The (Saint Saëns), 224
Swan Lake Ballet Suite (Tchaikovsky), 224
Symphony in D Minor (Franck), 81, 224, 259
Symphony No. 3 (Ives), 224
syncopation, 62

Takt (true beat), 6, 7, 60, 61, 99; *see also* tempo
Tales of Hoffman (Offenbach), 223
Tannhauser Overture (Wagner), 61
taste, musical, 97–149, 227, 228
    and adaptation level, 131
    auditory tests of, 135–41
    and climatic cycles, 127, 128
    as created by the state, 128
    criteria and conditioners of, 122–32
    defined, 97
    individual and group differences, 119–22
    as measured by boredom, 148, 149
    paper-and-pencil tests of, 141–43
    relation to eminence, 100–10, 227, 228
    relation to enjoyment, 110–12
    relation to knowledge of composers, 112, 113

relation to programs, 113–16, 143–45
relation to recordings, 117, 145, 146, 148
relation to space allocations, 117–19, 144–48
reverence for the past, 108–10
studied through polling, 100–113, 143
and training, 128–32
and "types" of listeners, 131, 132
whimsical or lawful? 97–100
Taylor Tests, 206
temperament, of listener, 75, 76, 80
    introversion and extraversion, 92, 93, 124, 164
tempo, 94; *see also* Takt
    factor in major-minor discrimination, 75
    and meaning, 83–85, 91, 93
    and melody, 60, 61
    preferences, 10, 11, 125, 126
    rubato, 90
terpometer, 191
Test of Attitude Toward Music (R. Seashore & K. Hevner), 141, 142
Test of Expressive Phrasing in Music (Hoffren), 140
Test of Intuition (Drake), 141
Test of Listening Power in Music (Schultz), 137
Test for Musical Concepts (Hevner), 139, 140
Test of Musicality (Gaston), 204
Test of Musical Taste (Vernon), 141
Test of Music Information and Appreciation (Kwalwasser), 141
tests of music taste
    Adler, 138
    Bower, 137
    Cattel & Saunders, 139
    Courtis, 137
    Drake, 140, 141
    Erneston, 138
    Farnsworth, 142
    Gernet, 137
    Hevner-Landsbury, 139, 140, 153
    Hoffren, 140
    Keston, 137, 138
    Kwalwasser, 136, 141
    Kwalwasser-Dykema, 112, 125, 136, 137
    Kyme, 138
    Lifton, 138
    Lowery, 140, 141
    Mohler, 138, 139
    Schoen, 140, 141
    Schultz, 137
    Seashore, 44, 112, 135, 136
    Seashore & Hevner, 142
    Semeonoff, 139, 141
    Vernon, 141
    Wing, 140
    Young, 141
tests of musical achievement
    Aliferis-Stecklein, 188

Bailey, 188
Beach, 185
Farnum, 187
Gildersleeve & Soper, 185
Graduate Record Examinations, 188
Gutsch, 190
Hillbrand, 189
Hutchinson, 186
Jones, 188
Knuth, 186
Kotick & Torgerson, 187
Kwalwasser-Ruch, 186
McCauley, 186
Mosher, 189
Music Education: National Teacher Examinations, 188
Otterstein & Mosher, 189
Pressey, 187
Providence, 187
Strouse, 186
Swinchoski, 187
Thostenson, 189, 190
Torgerson-Fahnestock, 186
Watkins, 190
Watkins-Farnum, 190
Wood, 187
tests of musical aptitude
Bentley, 206, 207
Drake, 201, 202
Gaston, 204
Gordon, 205, 206
Kwalwasser, 200
Kwalwasser-Dykema, 198–200
Lundin, 203, 204
Meyer, 191
Seashore, 13, 44, 49, 112, 135, 153, 157, 163, 164, 167, 168, 194–98, 205, 207, 208
Storey, 200, 201
Strong, 154, 162, 207
Taylor, 206
Tilson-Gretsch, 195, 196
unstandardized, 191–94
Wheeler, 202
Whistler-Thorpe, 202, 203
Wing, 140, 153, 204, 205
Tilson-Gretsch Musical Aptitude Test, 195, 196
timbre; *see also* tonal attributes
and age, 56, 57
and meaning, 84–87, 90, 93
of violins, *see* violin quality

Time on My Hands (Adamson), 223
time signatures, instinctive or acquired bases for, 5
tonal attributes
density, 17
duration, 17
loudness, 17, 53–55
pitch, 17, 18, 25, 50–53
sonance, 6
timbre (purity, quality), 6, 10, 11, 50, 51, 54, 56–58
Tonal Movement Test (Kwalwasser-Dykema), 136, 137
Tonal Sequence Test (Schoen), 140, 141
tonality
atonality, 41
defined, 40
"modern," 42
polytonality, 41
tonic; *see* finality effects
tonoscope, 193
Toreador's Song (Bizet), 223
Torgerson-Fahnestock Music Test, 186
Tragic Sonata (MacDowell), 64
training methods; *see* learning, in music
transposition, 18, 20–23, 30
trill, 34, 45
Tristan und Isolde (Wagner), 259
true beat; *see* Takt

Utrecht Symphony Orchestra subscribers, 104, 105

vibrato, 6, 9, 10, 13, 14, 25, 34, 45, 58, 90, 168
violin quality, 11, 12, 56, 57

Waltzes in A and C (Chopin), 223
Watkins-Farnum Performance Scale, 190
Way You Look Tonight, The (Fields), 223
Whistler-Thorpe Musical Aptitude Test, 202, 203
whole vs. part learning, in music, 168
whole-tone scale, 27, 28, 30, 44, 75
Wing Musical Aptitude Test, 140, 153, 204, 205

Xerxes (Handel), 74